THE HILLIER BOOK OF
GARDEN PLANNING & PLANTING

THE HILLIER BOOK OF
GARDEN PLANNING & PLANTING

KEITH RUSHFORTH

RODERICK GRIFFIN

DENNIS WOODLAND

David & Charles
Newton Abbot   London   North Pomfret (Vt)

ACKNOWLEDGEMENTS

We gratefully acknowledge the excellent
line drawings by Sue Oldfield,
assistance with the preparation of the garden
plans by Suzanne Oldrey and Paul Collins,
with manuscript typing by Judith Dawkins
and Wendy Kemish and preparation of index
and botanical corrections by Hatton
Gardener.

The authors also wish to extend grateful
thanks to the owners of many gardens large
and small who have generously allowed them
to take the photographs featured in this book.

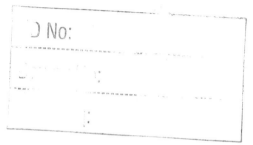

British Library Cataloguing in Publication Data

Rushforth, Keith D.
　The Hillier book of garden planning and planting.
　1. Gardens——Design　2. Gardening
　I. Title　II. Griffin, Roderick
　III. Woodland, Dennis
　712'.6　　SB473

ISBN 0–7153–9097–X

Typeset by Typesetters (Birmingham) Limited
Smethwick, West Midlands
and printed in West Germany
by Mohndruck GmbH
for David & Charles Publishers plc
Brunel House　Newton Abbot　Devon

Published in the United States of America
by David & Charles Inc
North Pomfret　Vermont 05053　USA

CONTENTS

1 GARDEN AND HOME 6

2 WHAT DO YOU WANT FROM YOUR GARDEN? 10
Possible features for inclusion 12 – Surveying the Garden 30

3 GROUNDWORK 40
Soil 40 – Nutrients 42 – Climate 46 – How Plants Grow 52 – Weeds 56 – Pests 57

4 DESIGNING YOUR GARDEN 58
Basic Design Work 60 – Drawing the Plan 69 – Detailing the Design 76
The Inherited Garden 113 – The Smaller Garden 137

5 PLANTING AND ESTABLISHMENT 144

6 MANAGEMENT AND MAINTENANCE 162
Weed Control 162 – Feeding 172 – Watering 174 – Pest and Disease Control 175
Trees 177 – Shrubs 182 – Hedges 186 – Grass 188 – Herbaceous Borders 190
Groundcover 192 – Ponds 193 – Paths 194 – Waste Disposal 194

7 CHOOSING PLANTS FOR THE DESIGN 196
Soil Type 196 – Height and Size 199 – Climate 200 – Plants for Solving Problems 201
Shrubaceous Borders and Island Beds 212 – Groundcover 216
Plants for Special Features 229 – Dry Gardening 241 – Wall Shrubs and Climbers 248
Rock Gardens 252 – Water Gardens 253 – Plant Grouping for Effect 257

8 PLANT PROFILES FOR THE PLANT-LOVER 270
Berberis and Mahonia 272 – Betula (Birches) 274 – Ceanothus 278 – Clematis 281
Conifers 288 – Cornus 301 – Cotoneasters 304 – Daphnes 308 – Hardy Ferns 311
Hardy Ornamental Grasses and Bamboos 313 – Hydrangeas 318 – Ilex (Holly) 325
Japanese Maples 326 – Ligustrum (Privet) 333 – Magnolias 334
Rhododendrons and Azaleas 341 – Roses 352 – Salix (Willow) 362
Sorbus (Rowan and Whitebeam) 366 – Viburnums 373

FURTHER READING 375

LIST OF SUPPLIERS AND USEFUL ADDRESSES 376

INDEXES 377

1
GARDEN AND HOME

A garden gives space, love, character and beauty to a home's surroundings; it provides scope for outdoor living in summer and interest and colour all the year round. It adds a dimension that is always changing – with the seasons, with each day's weather and as the plants mature. It provides a breath of fresh air for mind and body. In this book we aim to give ideas and information to help you plan, plant and look after a garden that is right for you, your lifestyle and your home.

The garden should be an intrinsic part of the home. It can be enjoyed from inside the house – the views can be enhanced by well-placed lighting. As your outdoor room, it gives you sheltered spots to sit and read, write, sunbathe or do nothing. It gives the children a place for active play or games of imagination in 'private' castles or tree-houses: no child should be deprived of a garden! It gives you mental stimulation as it changes from day to day: gradually the new foliage and colour of spring give way to the flowers, warmth and perfume of summer, to the brilliance of autumn leaves and fruits, to the subtle colours and tracery of trees in winter. Your everyday outlook alters hourly with the light – a view is quite different under a cloudless summer sun, in a misty early morning, in low evening sunlight or in a storm. Your view can be framed to give a more dramatic focus; unsightly objects or activities can be masked.

You have the chance to develop a hobby or specialist interest, whether growing dahlias for exhibition, growing food for the family, conserving rare plants or creating a patch of the Himalayas or some other plant-rich part of the world. The work involved in garden creation, planting and maintenance gives useful exercise – achieving something at the same time.

It also has educational value, for both adults and children. It will offer a home or feeding-place for wildlife – birds, small mammals, butterflies. If you put up nesting-boxes and in winter stock your bird-table, you encourage a healthy bird population, particularly if you provide evergreen trees and shrubs for winter shelter, and berrying plants such as rowans, cotoneasters and barberries. A rich and colourful butterfly population will follow the planting of suitable food-plants for the caterpillar stages and nectar-producing plants such as buddleia or

A satisfying blend of foliage and flower

sedums for the adults. A garden pond becomes a world in itself, holds your fish and attracts magnificent dragonflies. As a microcosm of the world's plant life, the garden gives an understanding of the world's richness – how plants grow, flower and fruit, how leaves are broken down in autumn, feeding fungi and small invertebrates – of how the cycle of life goes on year by year.

There is even considerable monetary value in a well planned and well kept garden, when you eventually come to sell. A house standing in an open field or an overgrown wilderness deters potential purchasers; a pleasantly laid-out garden, whether large, medium or small, makes it far more appealing. The purchaser's estimation of the attractions of the neighbourhood includes the setting and appearance of the house.

FIRST CONSIDERATIONS

For everyone there are some constraints to be considered before designing or re-designing a garden, such as our available time and money and the size and location of the plot. Also there may be some good features you do not wish to change in an existing garden, a view that should not be blocked or an eyesore that must be hidden.

Probably the first consideration is the time you will have available. If this is short, there is no point in planning an intricate rock garden or ornate herbaceous border, however much you like these, as the end result will be only mediocre at best. You can design the garden around low-maintenance features, such as trees and shrubs, areas of rough grass and groundcover. Good design and practice do however help you use your time more efficiently: you may be able to keep the border or rock garden small so that its maintenance takes less time.

You may have time at certain seasons but not others: there is little point in designing a good sitting-out area if no one is free to use it until December! Other hobbies, such as sailing, may leave little time in summer for either maintenance or enjoyment, but leave you

time for both at other seasons. This must affect how you plan the garden. You cannot have an ornamental lawn of high standard if you are away for six weeks or more in the summer; meadow lawns rich in bulbs such as snakeshead fritillary and daffodils, and meadow flowers such as speedwells and ox-eye daisies, may be an attractive alternative, giving joy in spring and autumn when you are there, and needing to be cut only once or twice, say in July and September.

The timescale over which you want the garden to take shape may be critical. If your principal concern is to enhance the value of your house and you are likely to move within five years, the design needs to show strongly within that period; whereas if you expect to stay there for upwards of twenty years, longer-term planning and planting makes sense.

The size and shape of the plot must influence how you plan. A small garden needs a more intricate layout, partly to give an illusion of space, partly to have sufficient plants to give colour and interest at all seasons. The small rock garden you might include here, however, would look totally lost in a large garden, unless carefully sited in an intimate area.

Look carefully at the existing situation. You may be able to improve it with relatively little effort, perhaps by removing a flowerbed here and planting a shrub bed there, or adding an area of paving. Usually it is better to develop existing features than to start too much from scratch and wait several years for it to come to fruition. Identify the good points there that should be retained: mature trees will give an attractive framework to a new design; there may be a pond already rich in wildlife; the soil may be suitable for a specialist plant collection that interests you, such as rhododendrons or rock-roses.

Then consider the amount of money you can spend on the garden, both as capital in plants, paving and other features, and as recurrent expenditure. A patio, or the use of weed-smothering groundcover plants may be expensive initially but will need little maintenance; a lawn is cheap to establish from seed, but needs cutting and feeding regularly thereafter. Trees and shrubs work out relatively cheap because they cover large areas and are long-lasting; summer bedding or alpine plants are more expensive as far more plants are needed per unit of area, and they need frequent replacement. You can buy plants in larger sizes for quicker effect, at a cost. For example, trees can be planted at sizes ranging from 30–60cm (1–2ft) to 10–12m (33–40ft), at prices from a few pounds to £2,000 or more. The limits on time, effort and expertise can be eased if some competent garden help can be employed.

The costs of a garden are the time required to maintain it, and the effort and the money expended in doing this. The amount of each of these required can be tightly controlled by attention to the design, creation and management. This book will help you to achieve the best result for your own circumstances.

2

WHAT DO YOU WANT FROM YOUR GARDEN?

Before attempting to design a garden, or re-design part of one, you need to establish its possibilities and decide what you personally require. Also, consider its existing features. Even the small, flat rectangular garden of a newly built estate house will have features that cannot be ignored and that dictate the nature of the design.

The first question to ask is 'Who will be using the garden?' Its design revolves around the answer. Here are three examples of how the owners' requirements affect garden design.

FOR THE YOUNG WORKING COUPLE
Due to lack of time for spending in the garden and for working in it, they will probably want a low-maintenance garden. Shrubs and groundcover plants will be chosen rather than herbaceous material, and a simple layout omitting work-intensive features such as rockeries or pools. Entertaining in the garden area near the house and detailed planting around this area will be required.

Seasonal variety must be provided by the shrub and groundcover planting rather than bulbs, annuals and herbaceous perennials. Garden lighting may also be of particular interest.

FOR A FAMILY
There is inevitably a conflict between keeping the garden beautiful and the active habits – or destructive moods – of most children at some stages. There has to be some compromising. However by planning for children's needs and accepting that the whole family should enjoy and use the garden, much can be achieved.

A good-sized lawn area for play near, but not too close to, the house will be desirable and this should be away from vulnerable planting. An area for a climbing frame and sand pit may be allocated, preferably within sight of the kitchen or workroom. In a large garden, any out-of-sight, neglected and over-grown area will be of great interest: young children love to have their own private areas where dens can be constructed and demolished at will. Encouraging this type of activity will help keep them out of your own special-interest areas.

As children grow up and the family changes, so must the garden. Think ahead for the time when the sand pit and the den-

The charm of natural York stone with creeping thyme, Thymus serpyllum

10

making era has gone. The sand pit might become an ornamental pool, the neglected area could be tidied and developed as part of the ornamental garden, or else extended and managed as a wild garden area, encouraging native flora and fauna.

FOR AN ELDERLY COUPLE
Time available for appreciation of the garden may be greater after retiring from working life, but physical strength and agility will inevitably limit the type of garden that can be maintained. A low-maintenance garden similar to that required by a young couple with restricted time would again be suitable, although the aesthetic requirements may be different. There will also be a difference in the type of maintenance that can be tackled. For the elderly, garden work should be easy to do though not necessarily quick. Shrub borders should not be too wide, making some plants difficult or impossible to reach.

Lawn mowing and the handling of garden machinery generally becomes more of an effort, so they should consider whether to have a very small lawn or alternatively devote a large part of the garden to grass so that the entire area can be cut by a 'ride-on' mower.

Paved sitting areas will be important and the provision of permanent seating and low walls will be much appreciated. Obtaining a sun tan may be lower on the list of essentials, whereas having some shade on a hot day is more important. Incorporating trees and shrubs that flower throughout the year and possibly winter-flowering varieties visible from the house will be of enormous value.

After looking at a mere three categories of garden user, without even considering the enthusiastic gardener with special interests, the significance can be seen of considering carefully just what is important to you, the garden owner. These are the general guiding requirements which form the type of garden.

POSSIBLE FEATURES FOR INCLUSION

Before making a list of the most important features you want in the new garden, the options available need some consideration.

The Paved Sitting Area

Almost certainly you will want this, and it will probably be the garden's most-used area. Most people, including the enthusiastic gardener, sometimes want to sit outside – rather than staying in or working non-stop on a fine day. So making a level paved area not far from the house is of prime importance. It may act as the transition between house and garden.

In our experience people tend to underestimate the area of paving that they require, whether from financial caution or from being unsure about how it will look. Certainly paving and walling is expensive, but the aftercare costs are minimal. The paved area should be of a reasonable size – it will look better and serve you better. As a general guide, a small paved area for entertaining one's family and a few friends might be 30–40 sq m (36–48 sq yd), a medium area for entertaining say up to 30 people say 60–80 sq m (72–96 sq yd).

Even a moderate-sized area of paving should include adequate spaces for planting, to avoid looking too harsh. To have plants spilling over walls and spreading over the paved area can also be a delightful way of displaying different types of foliage in particular. Some of the more delicate foliage plants are so easily lost in a mixed planting and are enhanced by a plain background.

There are numerous materials that can be used for the paved surface. Natural stone or secondhand weathered materials such as Old York or traditional brick paviors are ideal, but may be prohibitively expensive, so that artificial equivalents have to be found. Although there are many good products now available on the market, if old materials can be afforded they do blend better with garden planting. For example, the grey-brown colour with hints of purple of York stone, looks particularly well with purple/red creeping thyme (*Thymus drucei* 'Coccineus'). Where artificial stone has to be used, its effect can be softened by combining it with others, such as brick or pebbles. This will tone down the brightness of the new material, and even artificial stone does weather eventually. We have had many suggestions for the weathering of new materials, but perhaps the best and most bizarre is to wet the stones with water from boiled rice! Apparently this assists rapid growth of algae and lichen; well worth a try, but perhaps not practical for a large area.

Low Walls

To add some low walling around the paved area has the particular advantage of providing useful additional seats: Between 380mm (1ft 3in) and 450mm (1ft 6in) is the most comfortable height for this. In the British climate a pleasant sunny spell may be both unexpected and brief, and by the time the deckchairs have been brought out, the clouds have all too often rolled up again. To be able to perch on the terrace wall for a cup of coffee in those few minutes is a valuable pleasure. A wider wall 33cm (13in) or 1½ bricks is more comfortable as a seat.

When designing the layout of the paved area remember to include good-sized planting pockets for climbers against the house walls. Even if the roof eaves overhang the planting pocket, most climbers will find enough soil water, if given a little extra encouragement during the first season.

Lawns

Most gardens in this country, except for the very small, have lawns. Our climate is ideal for the cultivation of a fine green lawn, and people are often proud to own one. However, it must be considered how much of the garden should be allocated to it. It is easy to becomes slaves to our lawn, whilst other important areas of the garden become neglected. Vast sums of money are spent on lawns in this country, yet for all the effort we are only getting a green carpet and an open space. The space is an important one for recreational use (particularly for a young family) but do we need it to be large?

Consider alternatives, such as bold shrub beds to provide interest, colour and structure. Shrubs and groundcover, although more expensive initially, require very little upkeep once established compared with all the mowing, weedkilling and fertilising that are required for grass cover. Getting the balance right between planting and lawn will save time and money and also look well. The lawn should be considered as a part of the whole garden picture, and not simply as an independent requirement which everything else must fit round: nor should it be simply the 'bit that's left over'.

Shrub Borders

Shrub borders can form the structure of the garden and give colour and interest throughout the year – especially valuable in winter, when other planting, such as a herbaceous border, will have died down. Many shrubs are evergreen and they can be planned to show variation in height, shape and foliage. The choice of shrubs is enormous – see Chapters 7 and 8. Obviously when the shrub border is first planted a lot of ground is not covered for three to five years, and you therefore look for some short-term items to fill in, as well as the longer-term planting. You can use either annual plants or some of the cheaper quick-growing groundcover plants. These can be left as a permanent feature and will gradually die out as the larger shrubs grow over them. Groundcover plants have the added advantage of reducing the weeding required in the early establishment period, and add variety of colour and shape.

One other alternative would be to use a ground mulch of coarse bark. This both helps to reduce weed growth and gives a neat, attractive finish to the shrub borders. It is especially useful in a very stony soil – the type of soil where however many stones you remove there always seem to be more!

Play and Recreation Areas

If the growing family is to use the garden, and space permits, a level or near-level area of reasonable lawn will be well used. Obviously there is no point in struggling to establish and maintain a 'perfect' lawn for a games area. How large this area will be is dictated by the requirements of the family and your site. Put the games lawn where the least possible damage will be done from stray footballs and other missiles. It is also worth considering how easily these can be retrieved from any adjacent impenetrable thicket, river or pond, or even the neighbour's dogs! To have a definite area for children to play does reduce damage to other parts of the garden.

Tennis Court

If you have the space available, deciding whether to include a tennis court (dimensions 33.5×16m [110ft×53ft]) is simply a matter of how committed the family are to playing and the cost. A large piece of potentially ornamental or productive garden area will be needed and the boundary netting required is unsightly and will need to be screened from the rest of the garden. Temporary netting may be provided for grass courts, but grass itself needs a lot of work.

Croquet Lawn

Although a croquet lawn in theory should be 32m×25.6m (105ft×84ft), the game can be played on any reasonably level area of lawn. Its advantage is that no permanent features need be left on the lawn when you have finished playing; so a croquet lawn can be considered for most medium-sized gardens.

Sand Pit

One of the most attractive items to be included if you have young children is a sand pit. These are messy, but will keep children happily absorbed for long periods. You do have to cope with the clearing-up involved. Providing that the sand pit can be adequately covered against animals – especially cats – many of the problems will be resolved. To

Evergreen shrubs planted at the base of a wall make a permanent and interesting planting: mahonia, Viburnum davidii *and* Sarcococca

A formal pond in the context of a walled garden

An informal pool with a wealth of associating aquatic plants

avoid the sand becoming waterlogged, it is a good idea to have it raised and also provide a free-draining base, as well as covering it. It need not be large, but if possible have a fair-sized paved surround, so that sand can easily be brushed up and returned to the pit. To avoid getting more sand than necessary into the house, a nearby cupboard or shed for buckets, spades and related play equipment would be helpful.

Paddling Pools

Water is the other big attraction to children; ways to minimise danger to them from ornamental pools are discussed below. If you would like to give them a paddling pool, buy a temporary one you can set out on the lawn on suitable occasions. This also ensures it is filled with clean water every time. Children grow out of paddling pools very quickly and it is a waste of time and money to construct a permanent feature.

Climbing Frames

In our opinion the climbing frame tends to be overrated – all too often bought at great expense, used only occasionally and then left to remain as a permanent and non-beautiful feature in the garden, taking space that could be used more attractively. Obviously if you have no large healthy trees then a climbing frame has some value, but there are other more versatile and temporary play features available.

Ornamental Pools

Some say that every good garden should have water in it. Certainly water has a fascination; even the mere sound of a stream trickling over boulders on a warm sunny day gives an enormous sense of tranquillity. Pools, even if quite shallow, seem to have infinite depth and coolness. Sky, sunshine and foliage reflect into the surface adding another dimension to the garden.

Apart from the immediate aesthetic benefit, a pond or stream attracts a wealth of wildlife and provides a completely different planting environment. There are beautiful marginal aquatic plants that can be grown without the slightest difficulty; water lilies and other submersible and floating plants also add much to the garden. Water can be included in almost any part of the garden, whether in a formal or informal situation.

Water gardening is an enthusiast's subject and does require regular work. Small pools need periodic draining and clearing out (a messy business); in larger pools the main work is the removal of submerged water weeds and marginal plants which have become over-invasive. Aquatic plants can grow at an alarming rate and often one species will become dominant and need reducing to encourage others.

The safety of young children is an important consideration where water is present. We all know that even the shallowest water may be fatal to a young child, and consequently having a pool is a real responsibility. A smaller pool, particularly a formal one, may be made safer, if not entirely safe, without unduly spoiling its charm; put a well supported heavy-duty mesh just below the water surface, which will not look too unsightly.

A water garden can be enormous fun and waterfalls can be easily made with pumps that circulate the water. Make sure that the water garden is part of the whole garden landscape, though: it is all too easy to design a water feature that does not belong to the rest of the garden. If possible have the pool near to the main paved sitting area, or at least provide an area for sitting near it. From a wildlife point of view the further away from the house the better, but try to make the pool visible from the house; even during winter there is always activity around it.

Swimming Pools

To have a swimming pool on a hot summer day attracts the envy of everyone who hasn't got one. Unfortunately, the climate does not produce very many hot days and swimming pools are expensive to install. There are other disadvantages too. From an aesthetic point of view they are difficult to blend into the garden landscape, the colour being a major stumbling-block. Most pools are painted pale blue for the very good reason that a pale blue pool is far more inviting to enter than the brown of a natural lake, particularly if the water isn't very warm! However, it would be worth considering using a pale grey or green colour, which helps blend the pool into a formal garden setting.

Space and money permitting, to have a separate walled garden for the swimming pool is the ideal, and also provides a good environment for growing climbers and other sun-loving plants. Unfortunately the design of swimming pools is generally rather traditional, but there is no reason why yours should not be a different shape, although this may be more expensive. When deciding whether you can afford the space, allow – for an average small garden swimming pool – an area of approx 11m×5.5m (36ft×18ft), plus adequate paving surround.

Greenhouses

Deciding whether or not to include a greenhouse in your garden is a difficult problem. To decide, as a matter of principle, that you *must* have one is certainly a grave mistake. If a greenhouse is not going to be enthusiastically and systematically used, it will tend to be a waste of money and more than likely unsightly. There are a whole range of shapes and sizes to choose from, but generally the free-standing greenhouse is not an elegant feature. A greenhouse needs to have a reasonably bright position and hence cannot be completely screened. It need not be in the sunniest place as one of the major problems in summer is trying to keep the greenhouse cool. As it is most used in winter and early spring it will be necessary to provide an efficient heating system. We think the main benefit of a greenhouse is for the over-wintering of semi-hardy subjects and particularly for starting flower and vegetable seeds, and cuttings, early in the year. Its use can extend the gardening year and give enormous pleasure, but the degree of dedication to the greenhouse and the cost of the heating must be considered. However, in many ways the conservatory offers greater benefits than the traditional greenhouse.

Conservatories and Lean-to Greenhouses

These have a number of advantages over the functional greenhouse. They require less heating as they retain and absorb heat from the house itself. (The heating system can run from the house central heating). The proximity of the house means that it is far more likely to be used and hence kept neater and tidier. It is a delight to be able to sit out in a conservatory on a day when it is fairly warm but not quite warm enough to be outside. As less heating is required than in an ordinary greenhouse you can more easily afford to maintain a higher temperature; this enables you to keep a large range of unusual plants, climbers and other flowering and fruiting subjects. Also a conservatory does, of course, make a very good link between the inside of the house and the garden itself.

There are a wide range of conservatories available now in quite elegant designs. They may also be purpose built to suit the house. In order to make full use of the conservatory or lean-to greenhouse it will be necessary to make an area within it, slightly more out of sight from the rest of the ornamental conservatory planting, for the over wintering plants, potting and material storage.

Summerhouses

A summerhouse can be situated almost anywhere in the garden and may form an interesting focal point. However, the summerhouse is of most use where the orientation of the house is not ideal, and the space that could be paved for a sitting area is north facing. A wide range of prefabricated summerhouses are available, most of them are related to garden sheds but generally of more interesting design, although some can be ugly. It is obviously worth getting a number

*A stream flowing through a moist area
devoted to Hostas*

*Swimming pools need not be rectangular.
This pool is a great deal more interesting
and fun*

*Heavy-duty galvanised mesh supported by
brick columns just beneath the water
surface makes these pools a little safer*

of brochures and having a good look at what is on the market prior to deciding on a purchase. Certainly allow sufficient space for keeping all your garden furniture in the summerhouse as it will be sited, more than likely, some distance away from the house.

Alpine House

The alpine house is only mentioned briefly as it will be slightly different in design and function from the greenhouses and conservatories that we have been discussing. Generally it is a more functional house altogether and a specialist item which should only be considered for inclusion in the garden design if growing alpines is a specialist hobby.

Herbaceous Beds

A traditional English herbaceous border without question is a spectacle. Unfortunately, there is a considerable amount of work involved in creating a successful border. To obtain the traditional effect a good deal of space is required. All other planting types are excluded and the achievement is a riot of colour during the summer period only. The alternative is to use herbaceous material in groups within other shrub planting. The great advantage of this type of herbaceous planting is that a relatively small area is covered with the time-consuming plants, the larger areas can be of shrubs and ground-smothering perennials, specie roses, etc. See Shrubaceous Border planting, p212.

The effects of mixed planting can in fact be more satisfactory than the traditional herbaceous border, particularly as the season will be extended throughout the winter. Even in the small garden the same principles can be applied.

When allocating space for a traditional herbaceous border, it should be noted that in order to achieve diversity of heights it will be necessary to make the border at least 2.5m (8ft) wide, depending on the scale of the garden. A narrow herbaceous border generally does not work satisfactorily.

Rock Gardens

The rockery is very often the ugliest part of a garden, and yet thousands of gardens in Britain have them. One of the problems with a rockery is that unless it is extremely well made it will look out of place. A rock garden should look as if it has always been there. There is nothing worse than the 'pile of stones' or 'bits of concrete' left over from the clearance of building sites.

In general, it is not advisable to include a rockery in the garden. If it *is* to be included, be sure to use large stones and make use of the natural slope of the land. The rocks should ideally look like a possible outcrop of boulders. As large stones are going to be used, it will probably be necessary to employ a contractor with the necessary equipment to position and set your rockery stones correctly.

Screes and Alpine Gardens

These should preferably be associated with rock features and natural slopes. In terms of allocating space, screes and alpine gardens can be as small as you like, even to the point of being an alpine garden in an old stone sink. In contrast you could have a large scree feature, but it should preferably be put into the context of the entire garden rather than treated as a separate entity.

Vegetables and Soft Fruit

The growing of vegetables can be very rewarding, and some would say that a good proportion of the garden should be devoted to vegetable cultivation, which of course is a personal view. Vegetable gardening is, however, a time consuming hobby and may take valuable hours which could otherwise be devoted to the ornamental garden. However, a well tended vegetable garden can look very attractive.

Even the carefully cultivated vegetable plot is only going to look tidy for a short period during the early summer. As crops mature and are harvested gaps are left, and those plants that remain become unsightly as they die down, so vegetables cannot be relied upon to be ornamental for much of the year. It is very much a personal choice as to how large a plot should become. A small area for growing a few unusual vegetables, not commercially available from the shops, is perhaps all that is required. To make access within the vegetable garden easier, small rectangular plots surrounded by paved paths are well worth considering.

Due to the necessity to net soft fruit, there may be difficulties in finding a suitable site in the garden where the cage can be screened. If a suitable area can be found, soft fruit bushes require very little attention for a considerable crop. It is surprising how few plants are required and there is always a danger of overplanting a fruit cage; in July and August, if one is not on holiday anyway, picking and freezing can become a bit of a headache.

Herbs

There is no real reason to segregate herbs into their own garden and although a formal herb garden can be extremely pretty, they are not easy to maintain. Many of the more useful herbs such as mint, fennel, lovage, dill, to name but a few, are vigorous growers and only too quickly the intricate herb garden paths and patterns become completely swamped. Mint obviously needs to have its roots restricted, but many of the other subjects could alternatively be incorporated very successfully into the shrub and ground cover plantings elsewhere in the garden. Some of the smaller plants are ideal used between paving, others such as rosemary and sage make excellent plants for the front of borders and for spreading over paved or gravel areas.

Although fresh herbs are now available to a limited extent in shops, there is no better way of keeping herbs fresh than to grow them; a herb area, in one form or another, is therefore important. It is obviously ideal to position the herbs not too far from the kitchen door. Herbs tend to grow best in a sunny position but this is not essential.

Orchards

There is something rather grand, perhaps even romantic, about having an orchard and there are few prettier sights than a mature orchard in full flower on a spring day. An orchard is also a very convenient way of using up odd areas of land for which there is otherwise no real use, or which would be difficult to maintain as cultivated garden.

A commercial grower might tell you that there is a lot of pruning to be done, pests to be controlled and that the trees have to be well spaced. If heavy cropping is important then this would certainly be the case, but on a domestic scale an established tree will produce more than one family's requirements with only the minimum of attention. To avoid unnecessary picking problems, trees are generally available as bush fruit trees on dwarf rootstocks, these also fruit at an earlier age.

For the convenience of mowing and achieving equal spacing between orchard trees, an orchard is often planted on a grid system. This does of course look rather severe and there is no reason why orchard trees should not be grouped into informal patches or even interspersed with other tree planting in a more arboretum-like arrangement. Planting in this manner, with longer grass and spring bulbs beneath, can give a most harmonious effect, linking the more formal garden to the wild and perhaps native surround to the garden.

Hedges and Screens

Under this heading come some major items which provide a link between your garden, the outside world and the areas within your garden. Let us consider first the perimeter boundary to your property. (This is discussed further later in the chapter when considering what you have inherited in your garden). In most countries, garden boundaries are considered of far less importance than in Britain. As a nation we do seem to value our privacy

The herbaceous border at its best – Jenkyn Place, Bentley, Hampshire

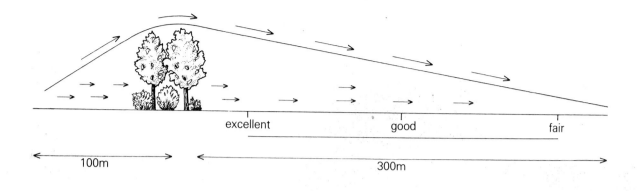

excellent   good   fair

← 100m →   ← 300m →

FIG 1 *Wind speed reductions from a good shelter belt*

very highly: the 1.8m (6ft) overlap fence panels and the Leyland cypress hedge are regretfully our most popular defences. Both are quick to establish and temporarily satisfactory but the former rots and falls down, and the latter grows to become a menace to restrain and a financial burden.

Brick walls are of course permanent and effective, but due to expense may need to be limited to short distances. Near to the house and sitting area walls can form an excellent transition from the house to the garden and also provide space for a variety of climbing plants. A good, solidly made fence (such as a close board fence – for further details refer to chapter 4) will have similar uses to a brick wall. The Leyland hedge does have a place where a tall screen is required and there are few faster growing evergreen trees. However, where height is not of a primary concern there are many types of hedge far more suitable than the Leyland. Some of the traditional hedge plants have been sadly neglected as the result of the popularity of cypress hedges. For example, both beech and yew produce fine hedging which are effective throughout the year and much easier to clip. Given good preparation, including ample farmyard manure dug into the bottom of the planting trench, these will produce an ex-tremely good rate of growth. For example, a beech hedge four years after planting can be 2m (6½ft) tall and will have already been cut back by 90cm (3ft).

There are many other shrubs suitable for hedging, all having merits, the main considerations being hardiness, ease of cutting and, most important, their overall height.

Tall Screens

Fast growing evergreen conifers tend to be the first choice when considering tall screens and these may well be the answer to many requirements. However, depending on the surrounding countryside these can look out of place. As there are few native evergreen trees in Britain, apart from the Scots pine, it encourages the planting of deciduous trees. Although not evergreen, a densely branched group of trees in winter will often quite successfully achieve the screening required. It is not always necessary to have a completely dense block-type screen. Shade tolerant evergreen shrubs planted beneath deciduous trees will achieve the screening at low level. The planting of deciduous trees also has the advantage that large specimens up to 4.5m (15ft) or more may be transplanted instantly. Conifers do not move well as large plants and are generally only planted at less than 1.20m (4ft) in height as anything above this tends to be checked in growth, if they do in fact survive at all when moved. (*See also* chapter 4 for further suggestions on the inherited garden.)

Shelter

Some gardens can be extremely exposed and the use of hedges and screens is particularly important. Walls and fences provide only small local shelter immediately on either side of them, the ideal way to achieve shelter is to reduce the wind – a beech hedge for example will allow the air to go through it rather than funnel over and around it. The extent of the shelter area is largely dependent upon the height of the hedge. The maximum shelter on the leeward side of a hedge is found up to a distance equivalent to ten times its height, with the measurement being made from the base of the hedge. There is some reduction in wind velocity at distances up to thirty times the height of the hedge. See chapter 3.

FIG 2 *The effects of shape and density on shelter*

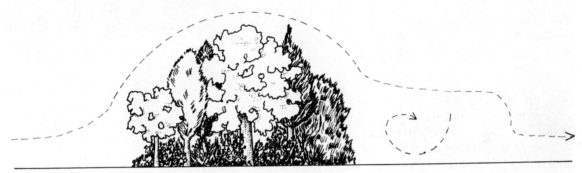

A woodland acts as a solid object
The shelter is less than a narrow belt

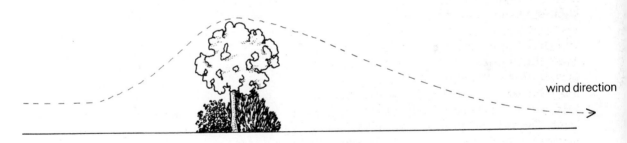

wind direction

The narrow belt increases shelter

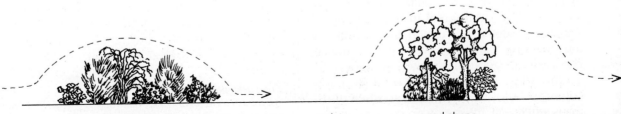

poor shape

good shape

Lighting in the Garden

Outdoor lighting adds another dimension to the garden and when viewed from the house gives the impression of a rather exotically decorated room. Even the simplest of lighting, one solitary spotlight into the garden, will have this effect. A well-laid-out lighting arrangement can produce an even more inviting and intriguing effect. The lighting should be used to shine onto foliage plants and up into trees and not merely as flood-light. (Light sources at different distances from view will give an exaggerated perspective.) In the same way that a photograph tends to highlight the real image, lighting in the garden seems to brighten and strengthen the planting scheme. Even the untidiest garden looks good illuminated at night.

Only white light should be used, avoiding coloured bulbs as these have a rather disastrous effect on most flower colours in the

This former herbaceous border has been re-planted with predominantly shrubby planting and a few herbaceous plants. The effect is similar but substantially less work to maintain

When designing a rock garden, take inspiration from natural rock outcrops such as these in North Wales

garden. All external lighting should be installed by a qualified electrician who will provide adequate coverage for the appropriate fuse and cut-out switches.

Outside lighting is not particularly expensive. However, installation costs may be high since the cables will need to be buried to a good depth to avoid their being disturbed during the course of garden activities. If lights are to be installed, this should be considered at an early stage in order to have the necessary cabling done prior to other construction work.

Irrigation

It is now feasible to consider incorporating an automatic irrigation system for the entire garden. With the advent of plastic plumbing materials this is both cheap and virtually maintenance free. There are a number of specialist firms that will both suggest suitable systems and provide a quotation for the installation.

The English summer does not make an irrigation system a 'must' and although a nice luxury, and a benefit for establishing a new garden, it is by no means necessary. Most trees, shrubs and herbaceous plants can withstand or at least recover from drought periods. The real benefit is perhaps to the lawn in dry weather, but even then one has to be very keen on the grass to justify the expense.

Mundane Considerations

There are a few rather less exciting features for which one must remember to allocate some space. However small a garden you may have there is always garden rubbish to dispose of, and unless you have a convenient space for tipping such material a bonfire and compost area will need to be provided. There are a variety of proprietary-made compost bins which can be really quite compact and require little space. When siting the bonfire area it is vital that this is well away from the garden plants as they are very easily damaged by heat. Remember to provide a site for the washing line and dustbins (especially important with large wheeled bins), a thoughtful bit of planting or walling will suitably screen the area.

Garden Tool Storage

If you have a good sized garage the storage of tools and other large equipment such as mowers may not be a problem, but if this is not the case it will be necessary to provide a garden shed. There are many shapes and sizes, some which can combine storage space and a small area for greenhouse work, likewise the summerhouse may have space allocated for tools.

Water Points

As a minimum requirement an outside water tap on the house wall at a convenient place is essential. If possible provide other points, depending on the size of the garden. Suitable frost protection or a draining facility should be included.

FINANCIAL RESTRAINT AND MAINTENANCE

If money and leisure time were no object, it would not be difficult to include a good proportion of the features we have discussed. Inevitably compromises will have to be made. One should not of course expect to have to undertake the development of the garden all in one go. It may be phased over a number of years; however, to ensure continuity in the design it is highly advantageous to have one overall scheme to work to.

In terms of financial outlay, hard landscape materials — that is paving, walling, pools, greenhouses, etc, are the expensive items. Lawns and plants per square metre are substantially cheaper. For example, a square metre of pre-cast paving costs approximately five times as much as turf and two and a half times as much as the equivalent area of shrub and ground cover. However, in terms of maintenance the paving will require no further work and shrub and ground cover, although initially having quite a high input, reduces quite quickly. The lawn area requires a very high and constant input. It is necessary therefore to try and achieve a happy balance between:

a. capital outlay.
b. further maintenance, your time and possibly someone else's time.
c. the aesthetic balance between hard paved areas, walls, etc and soft materials.
d. the importance of the main features as to how much use and pleasure they will give – will you really use the greenhouse and how often will you use the swimming pool, etc?

Having considered the range of features and options for inclusion in your garden we would suggest making a check list of these and notes on possible sizes, prior to proceeding with your garden design.

We list below those that have been mentioned in this chapter:

Paved sitting areas	Rock Garden
Ornamental and	Screes
recreational lawns	Vegetable garden
Shrub borders	Soft fruit cage
Play areas	Herbs
Tennis Court	Orchard trees
Croquet Lawn	Hedges and screening
Sand Pit	Lighting
Paddling pool	Irrigation
Climbing Frame	Bonfire
Ornamental Pools	Compost area
Swimming pool	Dustbin screen
Greenhouses	Garden Shed
Conservatory	Water point
Summerhouse	Washing line
Herbaceous border	Oil tank screen

THE INHERITED GARDEN

Whatever the shape and size of your garden plot there will be features which give the area a certain character. Even an apparently vacant field or the empty plot left by the builder will have features worth retaining. These may not even be tangible structures, simply the aspect, the fact that part of the proposed garden has an area which gets sun late into the evening, or a view to some distant meadowland.

The land form itself may have a particularly interesting slope or even a variety of changes in it. More often than not you inherit an existing garden with numerous features and it is deciding what should remain and what should go that can be difficult.

Concerning the plants in the garden, if you have in mind to replan the entire garden, you must first establish which trees and shrubs are beyond sensibly digging up and moving. Consider also if the plant in question is in good health and above all is not nearing the end of its mature life.

For example a mature broom (Cytisus) may be an excellent large specimen, but should not be considered as a permanent feature around which to base a planting design. It may only live for a year or two. On the other hand, a mature apple or oak tree although large, will still have many years' growth ahead. Gardens are ever changing as they grow, plants come and go all the time and this is part of the joy of gardening.

The inherited garden will inevitably include shrubs that have overgrown the space provided, unfortunately often the result of an impulse-buy from a garden centre and planted for instant effect. Many of these plants could however be moved and be correctly sited. Deciding whether a plant will move satisfactorily is difficult without some previous experience. As a general rule if you can find out what type of root system is involved this will give some idea. Plants with extensive root growth (such as Cytisus and Cistus) are unlikely to move whereas those plants with dense fibrous roots, like rhododendrons, will probably move well even when quite large. With the exception of conifers, in general, if you feel you could physically dig up the plant in question then it is probably worth a try. Do bear in mind that the check in growth may be high and the planting of a new vigorously growing specimen may be a better bet in the long run. This is certainly true for conifers and many other evergreen subjects.

You may have a garden devoid of mature plants in which case even an old decaying tree may be worth retaining for a period of time until the new planting develops. A very old tree may also provide a sense of time and maturity to complement the new planting. If you have an old tree that is not too well furnished with leaves, it may be sensible to plant a large rambling rose (such as 'Kiftsgate' or a vigorous vine such as *Vitis coignetiae*) to grow up through the tree and extend its benefit for several years.

It may seem sad to cut down plants that are healthy but hard decisions have to be made if one is not to fall into the trap of designing around unimportant features.

When considering hard materials, paving, paths and walls, etc, these too may be movable and reusable. It would be prudent to note down even small quantities of bricks or natural stone which could be included in the planning of a new garden.

For the purposes of planting the garden to its best advantage one should establish the southerly aspect and make a note of where the sun rises and sets. Allow for the difference in the angle of the sun at different times of the year, eg you may plan a sitting area which is fine in the middle of the summer but towards September/October the neighbour's boundary hedge may well shade the area entirely. Try also to establish the prevailing wind direction and make a note of more sheltered areas of the garden.

When a garden is planned it is a good idea to create a merger between house and garden, likewise it is important to consider the surroundings of the garden. The landscape in which your garden is situated can also become an extension of your private garden. Ideally it should be a direct merger from garden to parkland or whatever. Note down the position of adjacent tree groups or abutting woodland as this will influence the design and you may wish to link the garden visually to a distant view, such as a glimpse of

A well conceived rock-and-pool feature under construction

a river or small picturesque hamlet. Noting the position of views and where best they can be seen will be helpful when planning the overall scheme.

It is worth having a good look round the adjacent land as a lot of information can be gained from the type of plants which are most likely to thrive in your garden, eg if there are pines, rhododendrons and bracken, the soil is evidently acid, whereas if there are alders, willows and ash this would suggest a wetter soil and not necessarily acid. Beech, yew and whitebeam usually indicate an alkaline soil. These are just to mention the extremes. All such notes will help when planning the design of your new garden. (*See also* chapter 4.)

SURVEYING THE GARDEN
A certain amount of garden planning can be done on site without the need to prepare a detailed garden plan. However, when you are considering a large area or complete garden, the only way to plan successfully is on paper, in which case it is vital to have accurate information before commencing any planning work. Accuracy at this stage will save enormous problems later, there is nothing more frustrating than having arrived at an entirely satisfactory detailed garden plan and to find on setting it out on the ground that it does not quite fit. Sometimes even the smallest inaccuracy will mean compromise throughout the proposed design or, in the extreme case, necessitate a complete rethink of your plan. The object is therefore to record all the principal features in the garden plot as accurately as possible.

Surveying is a profession in its own right and there are limits to the accuracy required for the average garden. However, if you have

An attractively planted scree garden (see p20)

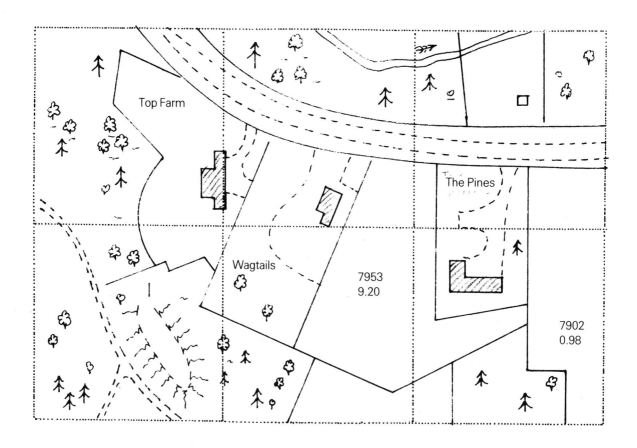

Top Farm

The Pines

Wagtails

7953
9.20

7902
0.98

FIG 3 *A survey map, such as an Ordnance Survey 1:2500, scale would be useful to the rectangular garden plots of The Pines and Wagtails, and particularly to Top Farm with its irregular plot*

a very large garden with a lot of different features to measure, particularly if there are many level changes, it may be worth considering employing a qualified surveyor. The electronic equipment now available to the surveyor does mean that a large survey can be done more quickly and hence work out less expensive than one might expect.

For most gardens there are some basic techniques which can be employed, sufficient to establish the main features such as boundaries and their line. Invariably garden walls

and fences are not square or parallel, even though they may seem so to the naked eye. Looking through the house deeds will often provide an Ordnance Survey of the plot at 1:2500 or larger, or your local library's reference section. This will assist a great deal. You can check the accuracy of the plan and its scale by measuring a few dimensions on site; even if you are unable to use the map as the measurements are not sufficiently accurate, you may well find that the angle of the boundaries will nevertheless be helpful and save some time carrying out a lot of cross measurements.

If you have an architect's drawing of the ground floor plan of the house, this will also provide detailed information and save time. But beware, check some of the measurements as the builder may not have followed every detail on the drawings.

Before making any measurements it is a

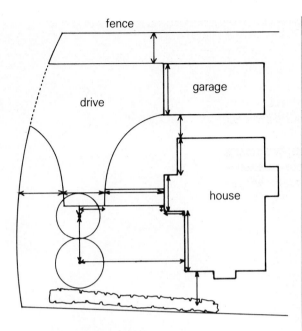

FIG 4 *Arrows indicating measurements required marked on sketch map before measuring*

FIG 5 *Establishing a base line from which to make detailed measurements*

good practice to draw a rough diagram of the main features on paper as you see them, and indicate with arrows the dimensions you require to measure, on to this you can then add the figures when measured. This tends to avoid missing any measurements. The simplest method of undertaking the survey is to base all your measurements from the house walls. House walls, apart from being solid and permanent features, are usually square and can be used as a datum point.

In the event that none of the garden boundaries are straight, a line may be extended from a house wall across the area to be surveyed. This can be achieved by sighting to the line of the house wall and using garden canes (for surveyors' ranging rods) to establish the line. (If it is not possible to sight a line from the end of the house, a line at 90° from the house wall can be made using the 3, 4, 5 triangle method). This is now a base line from which measurements can be made from any point along it. These can either be as offsets at 90° (Fig 6x) or by using triangulation (Fig 6w), in this way you can plot individual features such as trees. Triangulation may

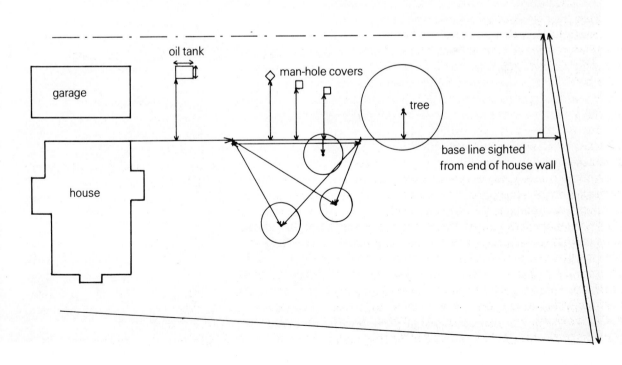

Herbs in a formal arrangement are difficult to control but give a delightful effect (see p21)

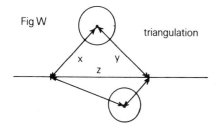

Fig W

triangulation

x   y

z

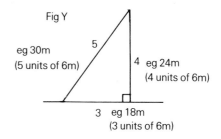

Fig Y

eg 30m
(5 units of 6m)

5

4   eg 24m
(4 units of 6m)

3   eg 18m
(3 units of 6m)

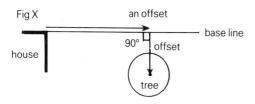

Fig X

an offset

house

90°   offset

base line

tree

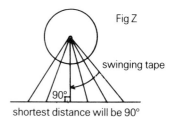

Fig Z

swinging tape

90°

shortest distance will be 90°

FIG 6 *Establishing a 90 degree angle to make an offset as illustrated in X may be achieved by eye, or the 3, 4, 5 triangle method in Y, or the swinging tape method in Z*

also be done from the house corners as these are fixed points, providing of course that a measurement has been made between them.

If you have been able to establish accurately the perimeter of the site, plotting the internal measurements is relatively simple. Deciding what is, and what is not important to measure is perhaps a more difficult task. Major items such as trees, retaining walls and paths should certainly be included. If in doubt at this stage it is better to mark them in as they can always be disregarded at a later stage.

As discussed earlier, now is the moment to record on the rough diagram important notes on prevailing wind direction, sheltered spots, desirable views and the orientation and level changes. Without special equipment accurately establishing the levels of your site will be difficult. In many gardens however, the level changes may not be very great in which case a little guess work (or preferably an experienced eye) and at least an appreciation of where the changes in slope occur should suffice. However, one should bear in mind that it is often very deceptive and usually one tends to underestimate the extent of the changes in height.

Recording the height of existing retaining walls and steps can often give sufficient information. If you only require a few further levels it may be possible to do this using a long plank and spirit level and measuring the height difference.

If your garden does slope appreciably then it will be advisable to hire a level tripod and staff. You would then need to carry out the following procedure:

1 Accurately locate the position of the points where you wish to record the level heights. You may wish to make a grid in order to get a complete cover of the area, but you will still need to know certain specific positions such as the base of a tree which you intend to retain (you should not change the soil level around trees).

2 Decide on a permanent datum point (or bench-mark) such as the top of a manhole or area of paving that you know you are going to retain.

3 Set up the staff in a position that can be seen from all the points you wish to record, preferably centrally between them, and set the tripod level.

4 With your assistant holding the staff at each point, record all the levels you need to know. If not all the positions you wish to record are visible you will need to set up a new position. In this case having moved, refer back to the datum to assess the position of the new location to the previous recordings.

5 By adding or subtracting the figure recorded from the original datum, you will have the height difference from the datum to the desired level point.

Drawing up the Completed Survey

Ideally the drawing up of the plan is best done on a professional drawing board with a parallel motion. The use of a drawing board will be extremely helpful and enable you to work on a larger scale. Using unlined paper and tracing paper, copies can easily be printed off your design. The printing process is known as 'Dye-line' printing and can be undertaken by most large copying shops. However, in the absence of this, it is quite satisfactory to transfer the information on to graph paper. It is important that the survey is drawn to scale. A scale drawing is a drawing which is representative of a unit of measurement on the ground. For example, 1cm on paper representing 50cm on the ground (1:50) or, in imperial, 1in=4ft on the ground (¼in:1ft).

Depending on the area of the garden a suitable scale should be chosen to make the area fit on to a manageable size of paper, say 1m×75cm (3ft 3in×2ft 6in). It may be necessary to divide the garden at a convenient place and make two plans, ie front or back garden, in order to get the survey conveniently on to the paper sizes. Ideally a scale of 1:50 (¼in:1ft) is the best scale to work on as this can be used to do even detailed planting arrangements at a later date without having to enlarge areas from a smaller scale. 1:100 (⅛in:1ft) is quite adequate for designing the layout of the garden, and often the only option for a medium to large garden survey. If you are using graph paper choose squared divisions that suit the scale you have chosen.

The survey should be drawn only in pencil, but not too lightly as the information will need to be visible through an overlay of tracing paper. Pencil is ideal (H, HB or F) because it may be desirable at a later stage to remove some information which you decide you do not require.

Having accurately prepared your survey with all the necessary information you are then in a position to start the artwork of the garden design (see chapter 4).

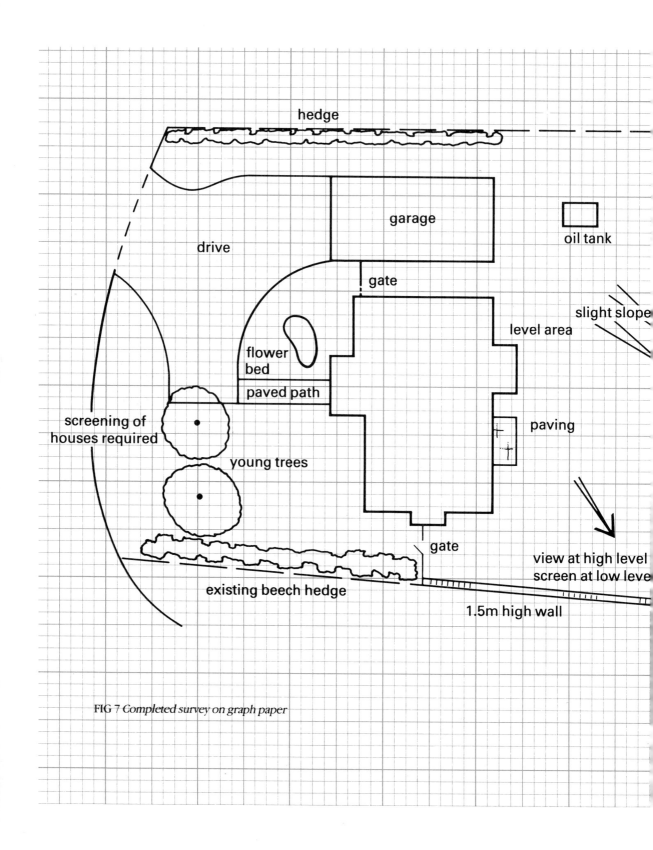

FIG 7 *Completed survey on graph paper*

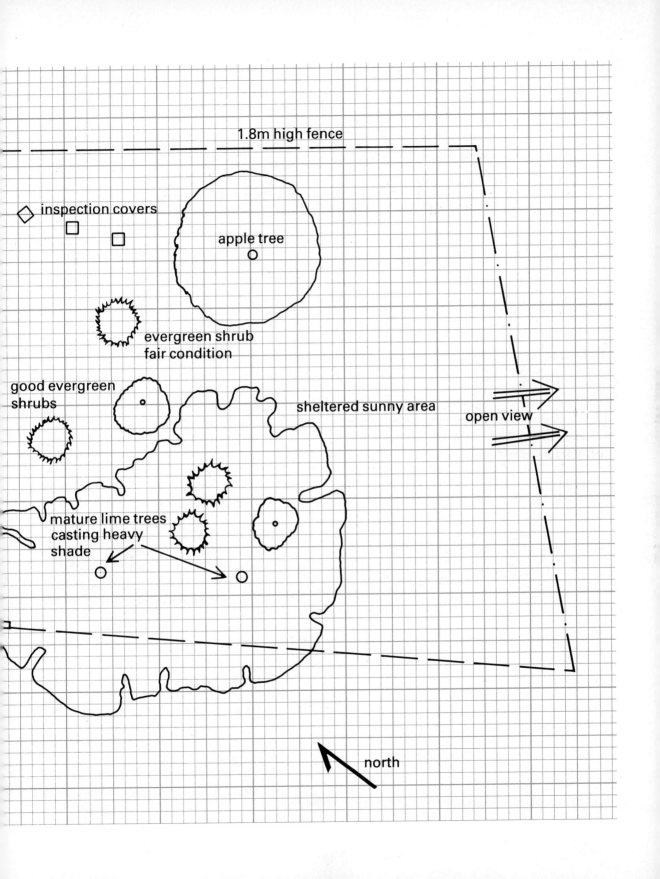

1.8m high fence

inspection covers

apple tree

evergreen shrub
fair condition

good evergreen
shrubs

sheltered sunny area

open view

mature lime trees
casting heavy
shade

north

3
GROUNDWORK

This chapter is designed to give background knowledge necessary to planning and planting and is thus a reference chapter, rather than one full of inspirational ideas. The chapter discusses the soil, how it is formed and how this affects the ease of gardening and which plants can be grown. This is followed by a section on climate, which shows how it affects plants, and how the provision of shelter or other features will modify it and increase the range and quality of plants which can be cultivated. Finally, a brief outline of plant biology is given where this will assist in understanding plants, as this can help both successful planting and satisfactory control of pests or weeds.

SOIL

The soil is the medium into which nearly all plants are rooted, the main natural exceptions being epiphytes, which grow on trees or boulders, and algae and other water plants. An understanding of how soil is formed helps in showing how it should be handled to get the best out of it and also how it affects the plants which can be grown.

The function of the soil is to provide the plants with support, food and water. For support the plant needs to be in contact with a sufficiently large body of soil to withstand the effects of the wind. This is particularly important for trees and the larger shrubs. Food comes in the form of nutrients, which have to be present in the soil in ways in which the plant can absorb them. Most water, which is essential for all life processes, comes from the soil. The soil also has to be the home for the roots and, apart from a few exceptions like swamp cypress (*Taxodium distichum*), all plants need oxygen in the soil for their roots, just as the aerial parts use oxygen for breathing. The soil therefore has to be a fit place in which roots can live. The depth to which plants can root will affect the volume of usable soil on the site, and therefore the size of the reserve of nutrients and water.

Composition and Texture

Soil consists of many different components. It is derived from a mixture of mineral particles and organic matter. It is a living world in its own right, including many animals, fungi and bacteria which live their entire lives there.

The mineral particles in the soil come from the breakdown of rocks. They are graded according to size into stones, sand, silt and clay particles. Stones and larger pieces of rock have a very limited effect upon the soil; they take up space without giving anything in return. Sand is just comfortably visible with the naked eye, whilst silt and clay particles are very much smaller.

Sand particles will fit together badly leaving large empty spaces between the grains. Water can drain through these spaces and air circulates freely through the soil. Even when wet, though, sandy soils hold onto very little water and these soils will dry out very quickly. Sand grains have a small surface area in relation to their size and consequently they have only a limited capability in holding onto nutrients, which are thus easily washed out of the soil. This makes sandy soils essentially ones of low fertility.

Clay particles are minute and fit very closely together; in relation to their size, they have a large surface area onto which nutrients and surface water can be held. Because of the tight fitting of the particles, there is little space for the circulation of either water or oxygen through the soils; drainage is therefore very slow and poor and most plants find rooting in clay soils difficult or impossible. When a clay soil dries out, it can be slow to re-wet. Clay soils generally contain a good supply of nutrients and the problem can be to make these available for plant growth.

Silt particles are smaller than sand and are much more similar in character to clay particles. Soils derived mainly from silt particles are usually very fertile, as they hold onto large quantities of nutrients and water, whilst permitting adequate drainage and exchange of gases.

Organic matter is the fourth main component and is essential for a healthy soil. It improves the structure and water-holding capacity. Organic matter in the soil acts in part like clay particles in being capable of holding onto both nutrients and water, but unlike clay, the organic matter does not form a dense mass. The effect of organic matter incorporated into clay and other heavy soils is to improve the drainage and structure, making them both more fruitful and much easier to manage in the garden; on light soils it increases the water- and nutrient-holding capacity.

The organic matter, though, is of no use in the form in which it falls from the tree as a leaf or as a dead root; first it must be broken down into finer particles. This process is carried out by many different organisms in the soil fauna and flora. Bacteria and fungi tend to be used to break down the coarser material such as wood and hard leaves. Animals such as millipedes and earthworms are involved in incorporating the material into the soil.

Earthworms are the most useful animals in the soil. They ingest raw organic matter, especially from the surface layers where they can prevent the build up of excess dead material, and mix it with calcium carbonate in the gut. The effect of this action is to produce in the wormcast soil an improved water and nutrient holding capacity. As the worms mainly extract organic matter, this soil also contains more nutrients than the normal soil. The other positive benefit of earthworms is that the burrows they make through the soil act as drainage channels. Most of their activity is concentrated in the top 10–15cm (4–6in) but in dry periods they may burrow much deeper; often it is down such burrows that plant roots can reach greater depths in heavy or compacted soils. The most obvious visible signs of worms are the casts made on the surface; in fact only three of Britain's species make worm casts, all the others pass the 'processed' soil out underground.

Apart from earthworms, the soil is home for a whole host of organisms, including many species of small invertebrates, like woodlice, and myriads of bacteria and fungi. Some of these organisms are harmful to garden plants, such as cranefly larvae and cutworms; the overwhelming majority, though, are very positive in their role.

The ideal soil is a loam. Loams are composed of about fifty per cent sand, twenty-five per cent silt, twenty per cent clay particles and five per cent organic matter or humus. This gives a good combination of water and nutrient holding capacity, with drainage and aeration. Naturally these soils are quite fertile, but, more importantly in the garden setting, is that they are able to hold applied nutrients.

Soils with increasing amounts of sand are sandy loams or sandy soils. As the proportion of sand increases, these become progressively less fertile and more freely draining, with a lower capability of holding nutrients and water. One positive aspect of increasing sandiness is that the soils warm up more quickly in the spring, therefore letting plant growth start earlier, but they also cool down more quickly. Sandy soils are light and easily worked, whatever the weather.

Soils with higher proportions of clay or silt particles are clay loams or silty loams. Drainage is much poorer, particularly as the amount of clay in the soil increases. They are also cold soils, taking a long time to warm up in the spring, but holding that warmth for longer in the autumn. They are heavy and difficult to cultivate; digging or rotovating should only be carried out when these soils are on the dry side. Soils with very high proportions of organic matter are peats. These are usually low in nutrients and may be poorly drained.

The depth to which plants can root is determined by the nature of the soil and that of the drainage. Plants cannot root into compacted or, with few exceptions, into airless soil. Rooting into pure clays, therefore, is limited but roots can be very long though sparse in sands.

Plants must have an adequate supply of oxygen available at the roots. Soils with a greater depth suitable for rooting have a much higher volume of water and nutrients available for plant growth, and are inherently more fertile than those with shallower rooting depths. Drainage can improve rooting and is discussed below.

NUTRIENTS

Plants need to absorb nutrients from the soil to be able to make growth by the action of photosynthesis in the leaves. Half a dozen elements are needed in relatively large amounts and are called major or macronutients, whilst some others are required in much smaller quantities and are termed trace elements.

The macro-nutrients are nitrogen (N), phosphorus (P), potassium (K), calcium (Ca), sulphur (S) and magnesium (Mg), as well as carbon (C), oxygen (O) and hydrogen (H). Shortage of any one of these is very damaging to growth, but also an excess can kill. The letter in parentheses after the nutrient is the international chemical letter which will be found on fertiliser packets.

Nitrogen is needed by the plant for the formation of proteins, which are essential for growth. Although nitrogen is the main gas in the air, this is inert and plants have to obtain it from the soil as a nitrate, nitrite or ammonium compound. Nitrogen is usually restricted in the soil to the top few inches.

Phosphorus and potassium are both needed for cell division and for the ripening of fruits. Potassium is very soluble, and therefore easily lost by leaching from many soils. Phosphorus is much less soluble; in fact its very insolubility in some soils can create an artificial shortage as far as the plants are concerned.

Calcium is needed by all plants for the cell walls.

Sulphur is used in root development and as a component of proteins.

Magnesium is an essential constituent of the chlorophyll molecule, which is involved in photosynthesis.

Carbon, hydrogen and oxygen are needed in large quantities to make all organic compounds. Carbon and oxygen come from carbon dioxide in the air and are absorbed by the leaves, and hydrogen comes from water.

Trace elements are required in very small quantities; molybdenum is only needed in the plant tissues at a concentration of one part in one hundred million, and may be fatal if more than ten times this amount is present. Molybdenum is important in the use of nitrate and nitrite forms of nitrogen. Iron is essential for the manufacture of chlorophyll,

boron for the uptake from the soil of calcium, and zinc, manganese and copper in the formation of enzymes and proteins.

Coarse bark mulch use to control weed growth in young shrub planting (see p169)

pH and Nutrient availability

pH is a measure of the alkalinity or acidity of the soil. A neutral soil has a pH of around 6.5 to 7; above pH 7 the soil is alkaline and at pH 6 and below it is acidic. The effect of pH is to alter the way in which nutrients are dissolved in solution, and therefore the way that plants can absorb them.

Some nutrients are only available to plants between certain pH levels. Phosphorus may be plentiful in alkaline soils, but most of it is insoluble; bonemeal will not add usable phosphorus to alkaline soils, although it is a satisfactory way of adding phosphorus to acidic ones.

Certain deficiency symptoms are due to the unavailability of nutrients at certain pH levels. Many plants show a yellowing of the foliage or chlorosis on alkaline sites due to the insolubility of iron on these soils. This form of deficiency cannot be controlled by using rusty nails but is helped by giving iron as iron sequestrine, a compound which makes iron available to plants at higher pH levels. Hydrangeas will tolerate both acidic and alkaline soils, but the aluminium ions which turns the flowers of some hydrangeas blue are not available to the plant on alkaline soils.

Plants differ in their capability to extract nutrients from the soil at different pH levels and therefore some plants can only grow at certain pH levels. Others may naturally be found in areas where a certain nutrient is scarcely available; if planted in a soil where that nutrient is available they may be poisoned by their inability *not* to take it up – rhododendrons and calcium is one such case.

Information on identifying and correcting

nutrient deficiencies from their symptoms is given in *Collins Shorter Guide to the Pests, Diseases and Disorders of Garden Plants* by Stefan Buczacki and Keith Harris (Collins).

Improving soils

There are several ways to improve soils. These include cultivation techniques, using manures and composts, mulches, drainage, and applying fertilisers. In theory the texture can be altered by incorporating clay into sandy soils and vice versa, but the quantities required are so vast as to make this impractical.

The better soils, ie loams, may only need to have their nutrient status increased but other soils will need to have the soil structure improved as well.

Soil structure is the way in which the soil holds together. A sandy soil doesn't, whilst a clay forms a lump as large as the piece of clay. When rubbed in the hand, the ideal soil breaks into small lumps about a quarter inch in diameter, and is said to have a crumb structure. Soil improvement must work towards improving the soil structure, so that on both clay and sandy soils the particles hold together in crumb sized units. Only as this is attained does the addition of chemical fertilisers make sense. Otherwise in sandy soils they will be washed away during the next downpour, whilst on clay ones the added nutrients will be lost either as surface run-off or locked up in the lower part of the soil profile, out of reach of plant roots.

Cultivation can be a good way to improve heavy soils. The act of digging breaks up the soil, incorporating surface organic matter. Even better is the action of frost on the turned clods. Alternate freezing and thawing results in the soil forming into crumb sized particles. Autumn is the best time to cultivate a heavy soil, as it must be carried out when the soil is dryish, as otherwise all that will result will be a mud pie. Avoid walking on the soil in winter and wait for it to dry out in the spring before carrying out any further cultivation.

Ripping or subsoiling is a method of cultivation which does not turn over the soil. A special plough with deep tines is drawn through the subsoil and shatters it, thereby relieving compaction, although it will also introduce temporary drainage along the line of the tines.

On light soils, cultivation will not improve the structure, although it can be used to relieve compaction.

Drainage is mainly of value on the heavier soils. The object of drainage is to improve the aeration of the soil by removing surplus water which is filling all or many of the spaces which could be occupied by air. Improving the aeration of the soil will increase the potential for plant roots to survive at greater depths in the soil, and thus the volume of soil available for plant growth. It will also make it a better environment for soil organisms and will allow them to improve the soil structure at a greater depth. Aeration will also remove toxic compounds caused by anaerobic decomposition of organic material.

Drainage will need to be at closer intervals on the heavier soils. On really heavy ones, it may make little impact as any drainage channels opened may soon close. On light soils, it can be widely spaced, needing only to bypass some impediment.

Drainage can be carried out by placing clay pipes or plastic drainage tubes in a trench, which is filled with coarse gravel. A layer of matting over the top will prevent or slow down the rate at which material falls into the trench and clogs up the gravel or pipeworks. Great care must be taken to ensure that the drains are not expected to run uphill, or they will quickly be blocked by silt. On some soils, drainage can be effected by making slits in the soil and filling these with sand. Provision must always be made for the water drained to be taken off site. Except on a small scale, laying a pattern of drains is best left to a professional drainage contractor. However drainage is carried out, do not expect it to last indefinitely and any scheme will need to be cleaned or relaid at intervals.

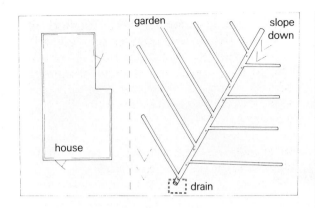

FIG 8 *Herringbone drainage pattern*

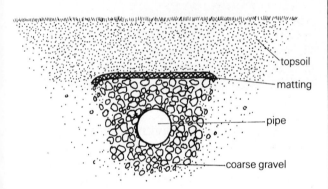

FIG 9 *Cross-section of a drainage pipe in the ground*

Cultivation and drainage are the only two methods to significantly increase the depth of soil available for rooting but the quality of the soil can be improved by incorporating manures and composts into the soil. The organic matter added will benefit the soil structure of both clay and sandy soils, as discussed above. Also the nutrients present in the manure will be added to the stock in the soil. The material can either be left on the surface, relying on earthworms and other soil organisms to take the organic matter into the soil (and for the rain to wash in the nutrients), or dug in by some form of cultivation; the latter will be quicker in effect.

Adding organic matter to poorly drained soils can lead to a decrease in fertility. This is because the organic matter can take what little oxygen there is out of the soil as it breaks down, leaving it anaerobic and make it turn even more sour. On heavy soils, manures should be used in association with other practices.

Raw material like straw can be used; it will take longer to break down into useful humus, and whilst it is doing that it will remove nutrients, primarily nitrogen, from the soil. It is a cheaper option than manures (where there *is* time to wait for the material to be broken down) for plants which are not sensitive to temporary low levels of nitrogen, or where nitrogen is also added as an inorganic fertiliser.

Organic mulches are similar to manures in their effect upon the soil, but are slower. They do not, however, contain any significant quantities of nutrients. Their effect upon soil structure is two-fold: by increasing the level of soil organisms, they lead to an improvement in the organic matter content of the soil, and by covering the surface they prevent compaction and the closing of worm burrows.

Chemicals can be used in three ways to improve soils.

Artificial or inorganic fertilisers can be used to supplement the nutrient supply. Specific deficiencies can be treated this way very quickly. Special formulations of fertilisers are available which can give a slow release of the nutrients. However, these are expensive and the role of fertilisers should be seen as replacing those missing after the soil has been improved, rather than as solving the problem.

Altering the pH of the soil can be of benefit. It is much easier to increase the pH of an acidic soil, such as by the addition of limestone or dolomitic limestone. Reducing the pH can be done by adding flowers of sulphur, and will occur if ammonium sulphate based fertilisers are added over a

Hebe, Helichrysum *and* Elaeagnus *giving a permanent display of flower or foliage in a sunny border*

period of years. The effect will be to alter the availability of several nutrients, as discussed above.

On clays, chemicals can also be used to cause the clay particles to flocculate, or stick together in small clusters. Thus the soil becomes less sticky and more manageable. Lime is often used for this purpose and provided the plants you are planning to use are not affected by increasing the pH, it can be an effective way to improve such soils. Alginates, made from seaweed, can have the same effect.

CLIMATE

The major elements of climate are common to a large region of a country but the local climate can be specific to a very limited area. Plants are dependent upon the climate they experience locally, which is set within the general climate of the country. In this section both the broad and local aspects of climate and how to modify the local climate to improve the range or quality of plants that can be grown are discussed.

Britain's climate is dominated by the proximity of the Atlantic ocean. As an island on the west side of the Continent of Europe, within the latitudes where the earth's rotation causes winds to blow predominantly from the west, Britain receives most of its weather from the Atlantic and has what is called a maritime climate.

The major elements of Britain's weather originate as depressions in the southern Atlantic or Caribbean and are blown north-east across the ocean. Coming from the south the air is relatively mild but never really hot; also passing over water, it becomes moist. The Gulf Stream or North Atlantic Drift is the main current flowing across the Atlantic ocean and follows the same direction. It is a warm current and has a warming influence

on our seas, which makes the country much milder than areas such as Newfoundland at the same latitude but on the western side of the ocean.

When this warm moist air meets the shore, it is forced to rise over the land. This causes it to cool and the moisture condenses into cloud, bringing rain.

As the topography of the British Isles is higher along the western side, most of the rain falls along this western seaboard, with steadily reducing amounts reaching the east. Running from the northwest to the southeast, there is a steady decrease in total rainfall, from over 250cm (100in) per annum to around 50cm (20in). This is remarkably constant for Ireland, Wales, Scotland and England, with the capital cities of each country situated in the driest zones.

Because of this rainfall gradient across the country, generally, there is also less cloud in the sky over the eastern half, giving more sunlight. The wind coming in from the ocean

Rhamnus alaterna 'Argenteovariegata' makes a useful and effective variegated evergreen (see p202)

is slowed down as it crosses land. Sunlight and less wind makes the eastern half of the country warmer during the summer period than the west. Clear skies and still nights, however, give more frost and lower winter temperatures.

The other major influence on our climate is the Continent of Europe to the east. In summer this can bring in hot dry air, but in winter it can cause cold arctic conditions to run across from the east, or down from the north. These conditions are felt most strongly in Kent and along the eastern coast. Kent receives both the strongest impact from continental Europe and the weakest influence of the North Atlantic, giving it the most continental climate found in Britain.

There is relatively little effect of latitude on the climate because the main influences are from the west and the east. Close to the western coast, right up to beyond Ullapool in northwest Scotland, the climate is mild with few frosts. Further east, the temperature can drop to −18°C (0°F) from Kent to Aberdeen.

As two very different climatic influences are involved, it is possible for the temperature to fluctuate widely within very short periods. A mild January day of around 10°C can be succeeded by a night frost of as much or even more below freezing. This switch-back nature to the climate can cause plants from more staid continental ones to start into growth too soon and be caught by frost. Late spring and early autumn frosts are a feature of Britain's climate.

The impact of the lower rainfall and higher temperatures and sunlight in the eastern half is that there is a potential excess of water use by plants over the rainfall received. Part of this deficit is made up from water stored in the soil during the winter, but in dry years, it will cause plants to slow down growth and ripen wood earlier. Plants which come from more continental climates do better in the east, where the extra sunlight and drier summer helps them to ripen the wood.

Where your garden in Britain is situated will affect the type of climate you receive, how much rain falls, the extremes of frosts recorded and the distribution of sunlight.

Local or micro climate

The local climate is dependent upon the national climate but influenced by local features, such as the topography, aspect and planting.

In the above section, the differences between light soils, which warm up quickly and cool down as fast, and heavy soils, which do neither quickly, were discussed. These differences strongly influence the local environment, although they are insignificant on the national scale.

Local topography has a very pronounced impact on the climate. There will be quite marked differences between the south, east, west and north sides of a hill. The south side will receive more sunlight and be sheltered

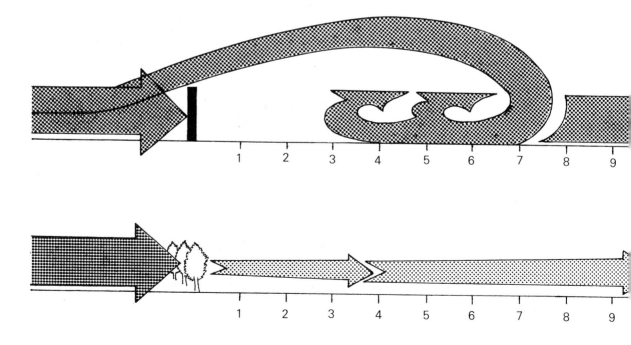

from cold north winds. The east side will get the early sunlight in the morning, with the increased chance of damage by unseasonal frosts; it will be exposed to north and east winds and sheltered from the west wind, so having less rainfall. The west side will receive the full force of the west wind, complete with an extra ration of rain, but will be milder overall than the other sides. The north side will be permanently in the shade, and much colder. It will receive the worst of cold northerly winds; growth will start later in the year but damage from late spring frosts is less likely, although early autumn ones may damage plants if the growth has not ripened in time.

The sides of a hill will tend to be warmer than either the windier top or the bottom. This is because as air cools down, it becomes heavier and will drain down the sides to collect in a frost pocket lower down. Flat land tends to be open and exposed, with no natural air drainage to remove cold air.

The different aspects will receive different amounts of rainfall and sunlight, so that the relative humidity will be different. This can affect the growth of some plants.

The wind will vary with the aspect. The most obvious effect of wind is to cause the abrasion and breakage of plant parts; the main effect, however, is in reducing the rate of growth due to putting the plant under moisture stress. In Britain, this can result in significant losses of yield, and effects ranging up to 20 per cent reduction in yield have been recorded in crops such as potatoes.

Local planting will influence the climate. A screen of trees can reduce the wind speed and also shade the garden, giving a less frosty and more humid environment. If on the east side, they will slow down the rate at which the air warms up in the morning, reducing the damage caused by unseasonal frosts. By drying out the soil, they can cause other plants to slow down their vegetative growth in late summer, leading to better ripening of the wood and possibly a higher set of flowers for next year.

FIG 10 *Effects of solid and permeable shelter on wind speed and turbulence (the numerals indicate multiples of the height of the shelter, in the downwind direction)*

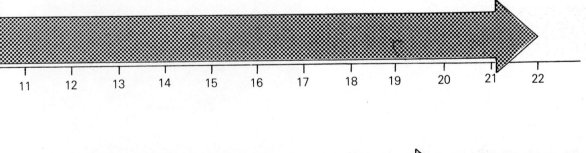

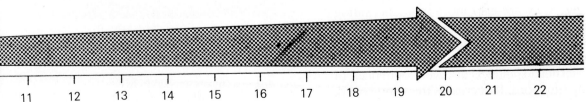

49

How to modify the local environment

The environment can be altered in several ways, although the most effective is to increase the shelter.

Shelter can be provided either by a living screen, such as a line of carefully chosen trees, or by a structure such as a wall. Shelterbelts can also be made from artificial materials, such as pvc webbing.

Walls are very good at creating very local warmer environments. The philosophy of walled gardens is that they provide some shelter and allow many plants to be grown on the walls. The walls of the house are extremely effective locations for slightly tender plants. In each case, the wall reduces the wind speed close to it and will retain heat, releasing it slowly overnight.

Walls, however, do not slow down the speed of wind. They merely deflect it, and can cause it to go faster somewhere else. At a distance of around eight times the height of a solid structure, the wind will start to eddy back and will often reach half way back to the wall; in very windy weather, it can reach the whole way back. Actually to slow down the wind, it is necessary not to have a solid barrier, but to have one which has open spaces occupying about half of the barrier. This prevents turbulence and gives measurable shelter for up to twenty times the height of the belt on the downwind side and half as much upwind.

Shelterbelts can be made either from artificial materials like ICI Paraweb, which is made to have a fifty per cent porosity, or by the use of plants. Artificial materials have the advantage of being immediate in effectiveness, although of limited lifespan and more expensive. Shelters made out of plants take longer to become effective, but will last much longer. They are also more aesthetic, fitting into the garden design. They are more economical, although often requiring some regular maintenance.

Overhead shelter is also very beneficial in many situations. It decreases the wind speed, lowers the temperature during the summer

Ferns and Lamium *provide an ideal setting to show off the impressive bark of* Acer griseum *(Paperbark maple)*

Our native box (Buxus sempervirens) *makes a fine dense evergreen and may be clipped to almost any desired shape*

but raises it in the winter, and increases the humidity. Many rhododendrons, for instance, thrive under the canopy of an oak wood. An overstorey tree must not be too aggressive in its rooting, or cast too much shade.

Another way in which the local climate can be modified is by altering the surface of the soil. With a grass sward covering the soil, the grass insulates the soil, keeping it warmer but causing a more severe frost above. If the soil surface is bare, heat will be radiated from it, preventing the temperature just above the soil going so low, and reducing the danger of frost damage. Mulches over the root spread will also modify the environment, keeping the soil below damp and thereby reducing moisture stress.

Banks will have quite a pronounced effect. Water will drain to the bottom, making that moister and generally cooler, except on an east-west bank where the south side always faces the sun. The top of the bank will be drier, more suited to plants which like hot dry sites or dislike excess damp at the roots.

HOW YOUR PLANTS GROW

If you understand a little about the nature of plants, you can enjoy them more, look after their nutrition, and control pests and weeds, with more confidence. But this section can be skipped if you prefer – or left until later!

Plant nutrition

The essential difference between plants and animals is that plants are able to make their own food from raw materials, whilst animals can only eat either plants or other animals.

In making their food, plants use carbon dioxide, water and sunlight to make sugars, by the process called photosynthesis. Sunlight is trapped by the chlorophyll in the leaves – the substance that makes leaves green – and its energy is used in combining water and carbon dioxide; during that process the oxygen which we ourselves need for breathing is released. The carbon dioxide required is extracted by the leaves from the small quantities always present in the atmo-

sphere. Water is drawn up from the soil by the roots, although small quantities can also enter through the leaves.

The sugars made in the leaves are converted into other organic products using nutrients extracted from the soil (eg into proteins by incorporating nitrogen atoms). The sugars and other products are moved around through the plant to provide food for growth, for storage, or for reproduction. The nutrients and water are carried up to the leaves from the roots in the sap; nearly all of the water extracted from the soil is used not in photosynthesis but to keep the leaves rigid and is lost in transpiration.

For this essential first stage of sugar manufacture to work, several conditions must be satisfied. The leaves must be able to obtain carbon dioxide from the atmosphere, which means that the breathing pores or stomata in them must be open; very windy weather or a shortage of water in the plant will result in them being shut to conserve moisture and thereby prevent photosynthesis. The leaves must be exposed to sunlight, as photosynthesis cannot take place in the dark. Also nutrients must be available, both for the manufacture of the next stage (otherwise the concentration of sugars will prove lethal) and the previous one so that chlorophyll and other enzymes are available.

Flowers The 'perfect' flower consist of sepals, petals, ovaries, stigmas, styles, stamens with anthers and filaments, and nectaries. Its function is to enable the fertilisation of egg cells by the pollen, so leading to the production of seeds to make the next generation. Many flowers are not 'perfect' and one or more of the above parts may be missing.

The sepals are often rather green and leafy and are mainly involved in protecting the flower buds. In a few species they become highly coloured and act like petals, eg in clematis. The petals are usually the attractive parts of the flowers, giving the floral display. The ovaries are where the seeds are developed and the stamens where the pollen is manufactured and shed.

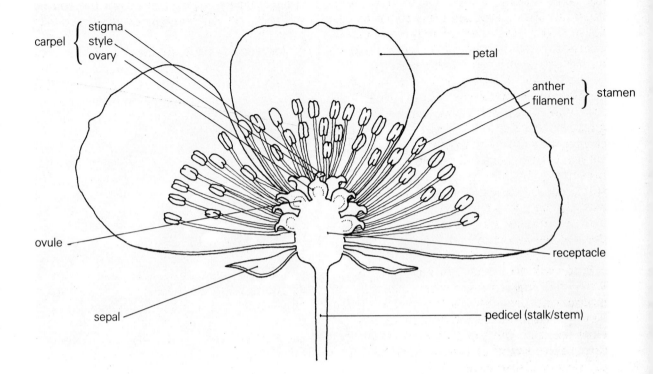

carpel { stigma / style / ovary

petal

anther / filament } stamen

ovule

receptacle

sepal

pedicel (stalk/stem)

FIG 11 *Detail of flower parts (buttercup)*

Most flowers are designed for pollination by various animals, including birds, but some plants are wind pollinated, eg hazel, and these have no need for showy petals. In wind-pollinated plants, the flowers tend to be placed where the wind will catch them, or to open before the leaves. To induce insects to visit, many flowers secrete sugar-rich nectar. Fragrance is also used to attract pollinators.

In many plants, the flowers are imperfect, that is only one sex is present. This is a device to ensure cross-pollination and avoid self-breeding; if these plants are grown for their fruit, both sexes must be present. Hollies are an example.

An alternative strategy for ensuring cross-pollination is for the plant's own pollen to be ineffective at fertilising the flowers. Here the flowers must be fertilised by pollen from a different plant of the same species if fruit and seed are to be formed. Many fruit trees, especially apples, have this mechanism and will only crop if two or more compatible trees are growing nearby.

Many garden plants are selected with abnormal flowers, such as extra petals. Some of these abnormalities occur naturally in certain groups of plants. For instance, a number of clematis have extra petal-like structures which are modified stamens and are called staminoides.

In most plants, flowers are only produced by specimens which are growing satisfactorily. The incitement to produce flowers often follows on a build-up in the amount of sugars in the top of the plant. In fruit trees, this can be artificially stimulated by partially girdling the stem, thereby restricting the passage of sugars down to the roots. Plants will not flower well if grown in more shade than the species likes, although other plants will not tolerate full sun. A severe pruning will cause the plant to concentrate on vegetative growth at the expense of flower production.

Flowers are produced in several different

ways and this has an important impact on pruning. Some species produce flowers on the current season's growth, such as many buddleia or garden roses. In these hard pruning in the spring encourages a period of vigorous growth, leading to larger clusters of flowers. Other plants only produce them on growth made in the previous year. Many shrub and species roses produce them in this way; if they are cut back severely in the spring, there will be no crop of flowers that year (see chapter 6).

Fruits are only made if the flowers were successful and will not be found on male-only plants. The purpose of the fruit is to grow and distribute the seeds. Some, like rowan berries, are carried in large showy clusters to attract birds to feed on them and inadvertently carry the seeds away with them. Many plants which have fleshy fruits have seeds which benefit from passing through the gut, as this helps germination. It also ensures

The glistening white berries of rowan Sorbus glabrescens *persist into winter (see p369)*

Massed flowers of Cornus kousa *var* chinensis *in June (see p302)*

that each seed is planted with its own capsule of nutrients; many bramble plants start life beneath the favoured perches of songbirds. Others, such as sycamore or dandelion, have the seeds modified so that the wind carries them to new territory. A few are designed to stick to passing animals and to drop off later.

For good fruit effect, the plants need to flower well, including having plants of both sexes present for some species, and have sufficient food and nutrients available to develop the fruits. Potassium fertiliser will assist in the ripening of fruits. Early flowering plants, such as some fruit trees, benefit from shelter so that flowers (and thus fruits) are not lost due to frost or bad weather.

Seeds The seed is the blueprint for the next generation. It has to be able to support the

new plant until it can carry out its own photosynthesis. It also needs to be able to germinate at the right time. Many plants will germinate immediately the conditions are suitable but most have some form of dormancy to prevent them germinating at the wrong time. This is of special relevance in the context of weed seeds.

Stems and branches The purpose of the stem is twofold. It acts as the conduction tissue, between the roots and the aerial parts, for the transport of water and nutrients to the foliage and for the return passage of sugars and proteins to the roots. It also has the function of keeping the aerial parts up in the air. Young trees determine the amount of wood to make for structural needs by the way in which the stem bends in the wind; incorrect and over-staking can stop this feedback and lead to too little stem growth.

Roots The functions of roots are to anchor the plant in the soil and to extract nutrients and water. Roots do the former by being in contact with a large volume of soil.

Roots can only grow in soil conditions which suit them; few species will root in waterlogged or compacted soil; neither can roots grow through dry soil, although they will not die if part of the soil around them becomes very dry.

In some plants, a bacterium associated with the roots is able to 'fix' nitrogen from the air to make it into a form usable as a nutrient. Clover and many other legumes, as well as alders and elaeagnus, are able to do this. The bacterium receives sugars from the plant, in return for nitrogen in a form in which the plant can use it.

Another association found on roots is with several species of fungi. The fungus invades the root but does not damage it. Instead, the extensive system of fungal hyphae or strands in the soil extract nutrients and water which are exchanged for sugars and proteins. These roots are called *mycorrhizae*, literally fungus roots. The association assists plants especially on very barren sites but is often destroyed by the generous use of fertiliser. The fungi frequently fruit around the base of the plant and may be mistaken for decay fungi. The strongly coloured fly agaric toadstool (*Amanita muscaria*) is the fruit body of a mycorrhizal fungus beneficial to birch.

WEEDS

An understanding of weed biology is useful as a prerequisite of control on the 'know your enemy' principle.

Although 'any plant out of place' is the best definition of a weed, in practice the main ones are those which spring up in no time on bare ground and seem to take ages to remove. These are mainly weeds of agricultural ground.

These weeds require disturbed ground for germination. In the absence of disturbance the seeds will remain dormant in the soil, in some cases for more than a hundred years. Often they will only germinate if brought sufficiently close to the surface and many have a requirement for light to germinate. One way to reduce the number germinating is not to disturb the soil unnecessarily. This can be achieved by avoiding cultivation and relying upon either herbicides properly used or mulches for weed control; as the plants cover the ground, they too will act to discourage weed seed germination. Hoeing can be used to produce a shallow dry surface tilth, but not for long in the average British summer and can be damaging to the surface root systems of plants if carried out too deeply. Only hoe if you find it therapeutic!

Many weeds produce masses of small seeds. Even if in the right conditions, these will not all germinate immediately; some will do so, others will come up after one year and some after several years. If a crop of groundsel (*Senecio vulgaris*) is allowed to seed, sufficient seeds will be made to make more than enough groundsel plants for the next ten or so years, even if no further ones set seeds. This also means that you can't blame the neighbours for all the weeds which germinate, as they were already present in your garden soil.

Many weeds complete their lifecycle in a very short time. Groundsel takes less than ten weeks, and if cut off from its roots after flowering, it can still set viable seed, even if buried in the soil.

Finally, because weeds have very short lifecycles, strains resistant to particular herbicides can be selected within a short number of years. In some parts of the country, groundsel is resistant to simazine, making this herbicide ineffective for control.

Why control weeds?

The two main reasons for controlling weeds are that they can be unsightly and mar the effect of the garden, and because they compete for nutrients and water to the detriment of the intended plants.

Controlling weed growth can have a very pronounced impact on the growth of plants, especially newly planted ones. Weeds by their nature are fast growing plants, often annuals, and have short lifespans. They grow much faster than newly planted trees and shrubs and most other garden plants – after all, if they didn't they wouldn't be a problem! Their effect on plant growth is threefold. Most serious is their use of water, thus drying the soil. Less significant effects are using the available nutrients and, where growth is rampant, swamping the plants and shading them out. Experiments with newly planted trees where weeds are not controlled have found that applying extra fertiliser will usually reduce the growth made by the trees. This is because the weeds make a quicker response to the extra fertiliser and therefore compete more effectively against the trees for the available water.

Methods of weed control are fully discussed in Chapter 6 (p162).

PATHENOGENIC FUNGI

Most fungi are beneficial in their effect and only exist off dead plant or animal material. A few are pathogens and cause considerable loss.

Fungi are members of the plant kingdom which cannot carry out photosynthesis. They have to rely on finding an existing source of organic matter and reproduce by means of masses of minute spores, the vast majority of which never germinate. However, because there are so many, they are always present in the air, although with most species more are present at certain times of the year. The spores have very precise germination requirements.

Some fungi, such as mildews on roses, can be controlled relatively easily by spraying the susceptible foliage at regular intervals. Others, such as honey fungus (*Armillaria*) cannot be contained by this method as most of their growth and spread is carried out underground; for this the only effective control is to remove all possible food material, which is scarcely possible in most situations.

INSECT PESTS

Insect pests include beetles, such as vine weevil which as a grub chews the roots of plants and as an adult eats portions out of leaves, and aphids. Control requires knowledge of the insect to know when and how to disrupt its lifecycle.

Weevils are not usually a problem except in nursery plants. There are a number of insecticides which will kill them, such as gamma HCH.

Aphids are more serious. They feed by sucking the sap from plants but as the sap contains very little protein in relation to sugars, the excess sugars are excreted as 'honey dew'. Aphids are capable of breeding very quickly and one fertile female and her offspring will produce astronomical quantities of aphids, if allowed to get on with it in peace. Aphids have many natural predators, especially species of ladybirds, and the indiscriminate use of insecticides can kill the predators more completely than the aphids; if this happens, the next generation will be bigger than the first and more difficult to deal with. Caution should always be exercised before an insecticide is used on aphids.

4

DESIGNING YOUR GARDEN

INTRODUCTION

The design and contents of the garden are as unique to its owner as the interior decorations are in the house. The object of this chapter is to assist in a creative way the development of an individual's garden, rather than enforce rigid designs. We all know what we like and dislike when we see it. However, when faced with an empty plot or vacant corner of the garden, being able spontaneously to know what to do and what will look entirely satisfactory is unfortunately extremely difficult. The successful professional garden designer is one who can correctly identify the requirements of his client and apply his knowledge, experience, and above all observations to that client. For most of us, even if we are able to recall some garden theme that we admire, it is unlikely to be adaptable to the particular space in question. Even in the event that this desired theme could be achieved, being able to reproduce the effects satisfactorily can be a major problem.

At its simplest therefore, the garden designer's problem is knowing what his client wants to achieve and how to create it. Our first piece of advice, if you are reading this with the idea of finishing the chapter and starting your garden design, is quite simply don't! Observe other gardens, borrow some glossy gardening books with good illustrations, consider all the options. (Chapter 2 should be of some assistance in this respect.) Do not attempt any designing unless you have a very clear overall idea as to how it should look. Delay doing anything for a few days or a few weeks, simply observe. Make notes and get a few basic ideas. You may not end up developing any of them, but without a few basic ideas it will be difficult to make a start at all. If some of the ideas you are intending to develop were directly inspired by books, when you come to start your work it is best to put them away and keep an open mind, allowing your design to develop as the details are added.

Brick around each paving slab in scale with the smaller space (see p64)

58

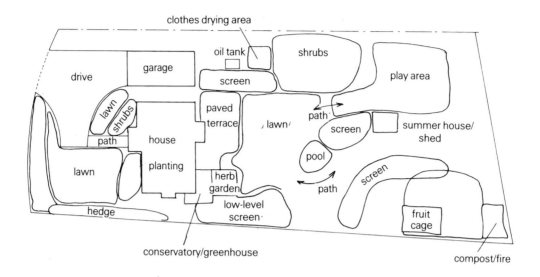

clothes drying area

oil tank

shrubs

garage

drive

screen

play area

lawn

shrubs

paved terrace

path

lawn

path

screen

summer house/ shed

path

house

screen

planting

pool

lawn

herb garden

path

screen

hedge

low-level screen

fruit cage

conservatory/greenhouse

compost/fire

BASIC DESIGN WORK

In chapter 2 the full range of possible garden features were discussed in order to assess the most important ones for inclusion. How to undertake and draw up a detailed survey was also described. Armed with this information decisions can be made on the positions of features on the plot.

Let us assume, in order to cover as many eventualities as possible, that the garden, after careful consideration of what is essential to retain, is basically an empty plot apart from a few trees, slightly sloping ground and a few isolated large shrubs (see p38). Lay a piece of tracing paper over the survey and mark on possible sites for the features you wish to include (as for example Fig 12) showing the different areas, lawns, vegetable garden, and how these can relate to the house and paths; the sizes of these items are very important.

If some idea of the shape instantly strikes you draw in a simple outline developing the idea of the shape. It is at this stage that there will probably be some re-thinking required as to the importance of certain items. For example, can you really afford the space for a tennis court with the loss of orchard area and hence the fruiting potential? It may be that your garden is so small that a lawn, to be

FIG 12 *Initial sketch showing position of features*

FIGS 13, 14, 15, 16 *Corner of a garden shown as a plan and then from three different angles*

effective, would take most of the garden. Would it be better to use planting and paving, or gravel only? By doing this would there be sufficient room for a greenhouse? At this stage the survey information on orientation, prevailing winds, exposure and other points of interest will be important. Consider alternative sites for the features you are planning at this early stage. Good decisions now will save having to discard more detailed work later.

Dividing the garden

Many of the most memorable gardens that one can visit have hedges, walls, trellis or pergolas dividing parts of the garden: for example Hidcote Manor in Gloucestershire and Sissinghurst in Sussex, to mention but two. These are of course good-sized gardens, but the scale of their divisions is very much

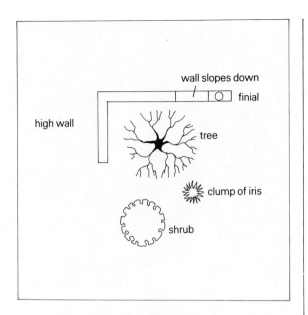

high wall

wall slopes down

finial

tree

clump of iris

shrub

elevated view

within the scope of most gardens.

Apart from the obvious screening uses, divisions encourage the urge to explore and provide the element of surprise. If the whole garden can be seen from one window of the house, do we need to go out? Dividing the garden also enables different design ideas (or even complete gardens) to be isolated and successfully included in the garden as a whole. Bold divisions between differently designed areas of the garden will avoid any unfortunate conflicts if they were simply to merge into one another. Hedges, walls and trellis would provide these divisions in the garden, and also by virtue of their height add to achieving a good sense of scale.

Finding a sense of scale

What is scale, and why is it important? The definition of scale is that something is 'in proportion to its surroundings'. Your sense of scale has to do with the spatial relationship between you and everything that you see around you. In the extreme, if you stood at the top of a mountain looking over a vast valley below, your sense of scale would contrast dramatically with that derived from standing in a narrow alleyway between two buildings.

*A small compartment within a larger
garden*

*An old sundial forms the focal point to a
small garden area*

Getting the relative sizes of the items in your design right and getting the feeling of good 'scale' in your garden is most important and often extremely difficult. Looking at another example, let us consider the paving pattern such as paving slabs and brick panels (which can look very effective). By putting brick around one paving slab, or three paving slabs, or nine paving slabs the scale is affected. In a very large area the size of the paving panels must be large to complement the space. Likewise, a very small area could require brick around only one paving slab (see p59).

The really good gardens have been those where the designer had an eye to achieving a good sense of scale. Good proportion is a three dimensional problem and can be a somewhat abstract consideration. To most of us perhaps it is sufficient simply to ask oneselves, is what I have just planned on paper going to look and feel right amongst its surroundings?

Planning in three dimensions

Unless you already have artistic ability it is only possible to draw a garden plan in two dimensions, a sort of bird's-eye view or map. However, although you may not be indicating the third dimension, you must at least be actively considering it. Think not only of the height of a proposed feature, but what it would look like viewed from different places (Figs 13, 14, 15 and 16).

An occasional rough three-dimensional sketch may often be useful whilst doing your design to check the success or failure of the plan that you are drawing in two dimensions. Considering the three dimensions is particularly important when considering the levels in the garden, getting slopes gentle rather than too steep, retaining walls at convenient heights and, above all, the design of steps from one level to another. There is a limitation to the height each step riser should be, which in turn will dictate the number of steps required, and hence the area on the plan. It is very easy to under-estimate the number of steps necessary. A wonderful design on paper can be spoilt quite significantly by finding out later that having designed for only three steps, you need nine steps, which take you half way across the garden lawn. We shall discuss step building and the correct dimensions under a special heading later.

Making a good pattern

Having decided on the approximate positions of the main items, lawns, terrace and so on, we need to consider the shapes in more detail to arrive at a good pattern which will form the basis of the garden design. It is very easy to fall into the trap of going into a lot of detail in one part of the garden too early and then having to work around this area when designing the adjacent features. There are a few basic design concepts which we will mention briefly at this point as they will help in arriving at a satisfactory overall design. The way that one feature is positioned in relation to another can have a profound effect. To take a very simple example, if we have decided to plant a small shade tree into a rectangular lawn or courtyard area the visual effect could be very different, depending on the position. Similarly, how the various trees, shrubs, or other items in the garden are positioned will have a different result.

For a garden design to work well there needs to be a certain unity to the pattern, even to the point of some repetition, this will add strength to the design.

Points of interest

When one walks round a garden it is pleasing to come across different focal points, points to walk to and from and to view from different angles. You may already have certain pieces of garden furniture, benches, bird bath, or sun dial, perhaps even some sculpture. These need careful siting and will influence the design of the garden considerably. Often there are areas in the garden that apparently have no real functional purpose that could be brought delightfully to life in this manner.

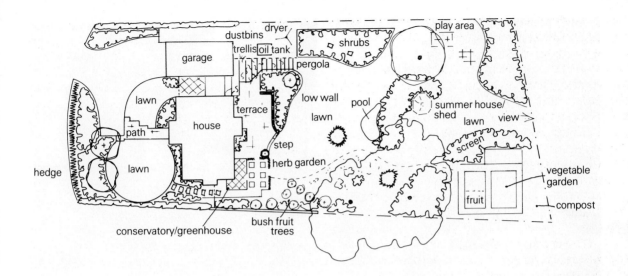

The following labels appear on the plan:

dustbins · dryer · trellis · oil tank · shrubs · play area · garage · pergola · lawn · terrace · low wall · pool · summer house/shed · lawn · view · house · path · lawn · step · herb garden · screen · hedge · lawn · conservatory/greenhouse · bush fruit trees · fruit · vegetable garden · compost

Formal and informal treatments

In garden history the trend for formal and informal gardens has swung from one to the other. In some cases these formal gardens were later ripped out by the suggestions of others, such as Capability Brown, who was more interested in the landscape as a whole.

At the present time, we seem to be in a mixed period with traditional formal layouts being increasingly popular, albeit on a

FIG 17 *Here the rough sketch in Fig 12 has been developed further*

FIG 18 *Positioning a small tree in a rectangular lawn or courtyard*

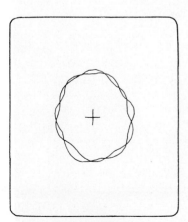

Central
obvious, static and formal

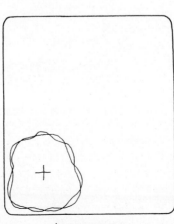

In one corner
crammed and uncomfortable

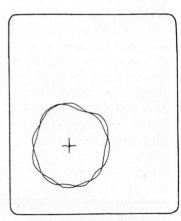

Informal and satisfactory

(above) Formal clipped yew trees and
perennial border planting in the walled
rose garden at Mottisfont, Hampshire

(above, left) A classical and formal garden,
Bowood in Wiltshire

(left) Here the informal landscape is the
garden. Is there any need to cultivate a
garden if the landscape surrounding your
house is like this?

smaller scale. As the formal garden is very
expensive to construct and time consuming
to maintain it is certainly inappropriate to
plan a large area on these lines, but this type
can be most suitable for small areas, such as
the herb garden. Formality is not of course
only grand pattern making, and from the
design point of view represents an important
part of contemporary designs. This formality
is achieved simply by using straight lines,
squares, rectangles and circles, all of which
will be combined to a greater or lesser extent
with the informal treatment.

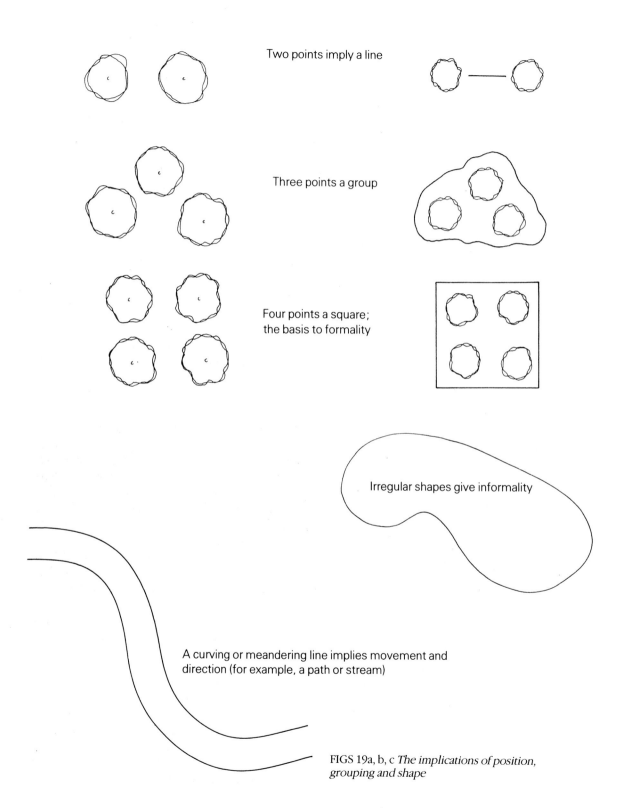

Two points imply a line

Three points a group

Four points a square;
the basis to formality

Irregular shapes give informality

A curving or meandering line implies movement and
direction (for example, a path or stream)

FIGS 19a, b, c *The implications of position,
grouping and shape*

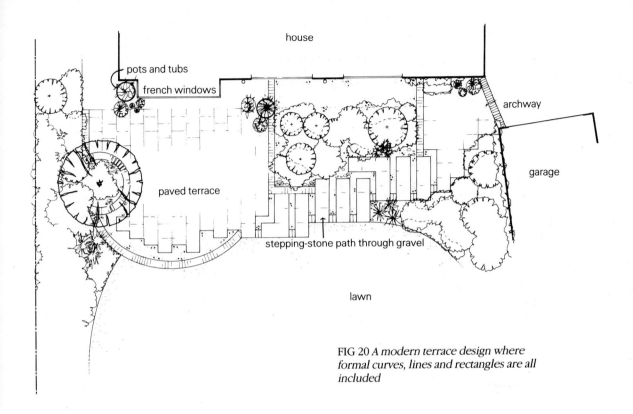

house

pots and tubs

french windows

archway

garage

paved terrace

stepping-stone path through gravel

lawn

FIG 20 *A modern terrace design where formal curves, lines and rectangles are all included*

As most houses are formal in their planned shape we often design the formal garden areas immediately adjacent to the house, gradually becoming more informal towards the surrounding perimeter, forming a merger from garden to the surrounding countryside. Having the formal garden area near the house also has the advantage that it is more likely to get the attention it requires, being seen every day. It cannot be ignored and allowed to become overgrown.

Having arrived at a reasonable garden lay-out plan (Fig 24), before going into the final details it is a good idea to use overlays of tracing paper to consider alternative arrangements. In the improved scheme in Fig 25, the pools and vegetable plots have been moved to give a better view from the living room.

It is often found that although the initial scheme seems satisfactory, a few minutes' thought and further drawing sometimes comes up with alternatives that are substantial improvements on the original.

DRAWING THE PLAN ACCURATELY

Some basic techniques and symbols to make your ideas come to life on paper are suggested here. By using good graphic symbols you will have a clearer picture of the garden you have designed and hence how successful it looks or not, as the case may be. Before actually undertaking this exercise, it is important that you have considered and decided on the exact materials, both hard (paving, walling, etc) and soft (trees, shrubs, grass, etc).

Later in the chapter available materials and their use in design work are discussed in more detail. The dimensions of the materials, particularly hard materials, are very important. For example you could use paving slabs that are 45cm (18in) square or 60cm (2ft) square, likewise bricks may be used on edge, 7.5cm (3in) wide or laid flat 10cm (4in) wide. It is vital to design with the materials in mind. This will save a lot of time, money and effort on construction of the garden.

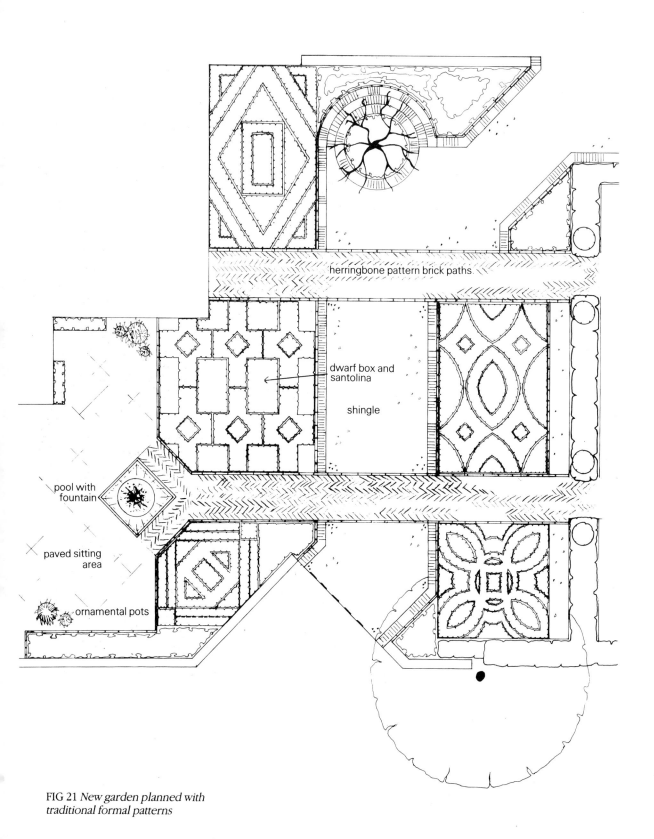

herringbone pattern brick paths

dwarf box and
santolina

shingle

pool with
fountain

paved sitting
area

ornamental pots

FIG 21 *New garden planned with*
traditional formal patterns

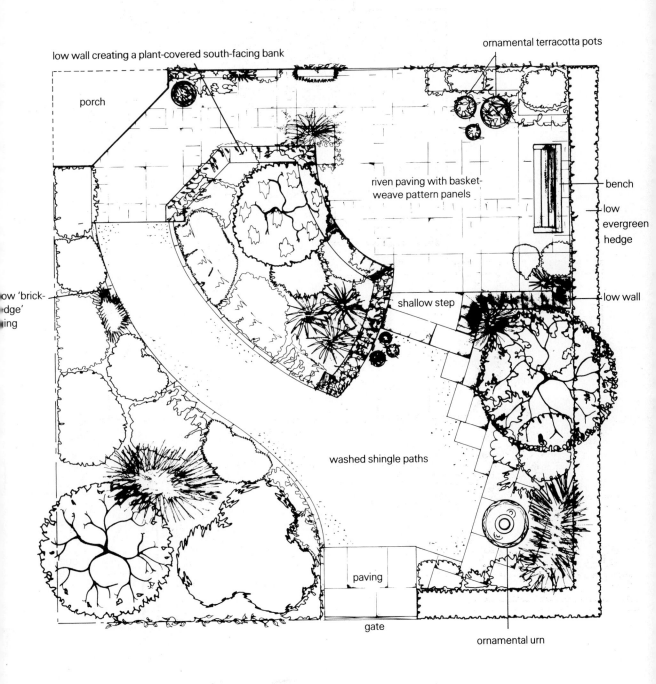

low wall creating a plant-covered south-facing bank

ornamental terracotta pots

porch

riven paving with basket-weave pattern panels

bench

low evergreen hedge

low 'brick-dge' ing

shallow step

low wall

washed shingle paths

paving

gate

ornamental urn

FIG 22 *Small garden with formal and informal features*

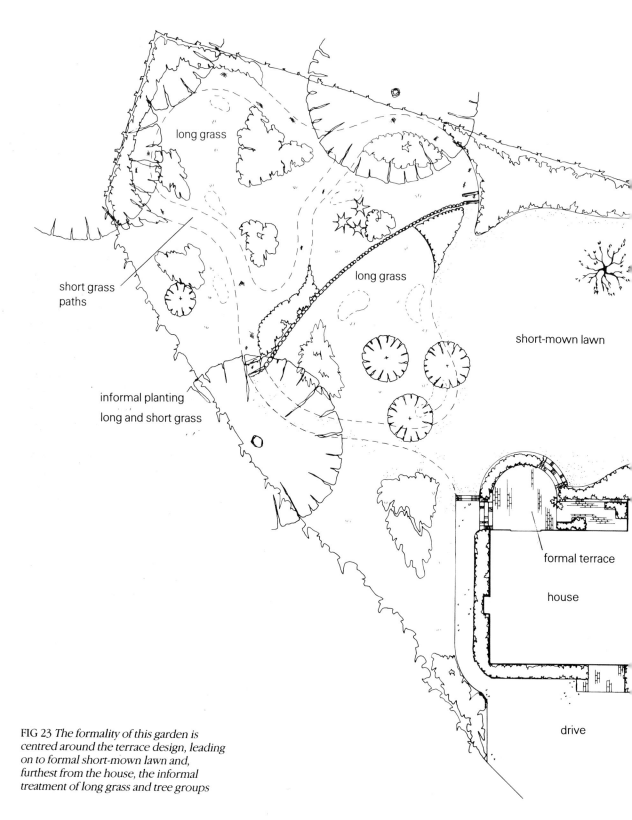

long grass

short grass
paths

long grass

short-mown lawn

informal planting
long and short grass

formal terrace

house

drive

FIG 23 *The formality of this garden is
centred around the terrace design, leading
on to formal short-mown lawn and,
furthest from the house, the informal
treatment of long grass and tree groups*

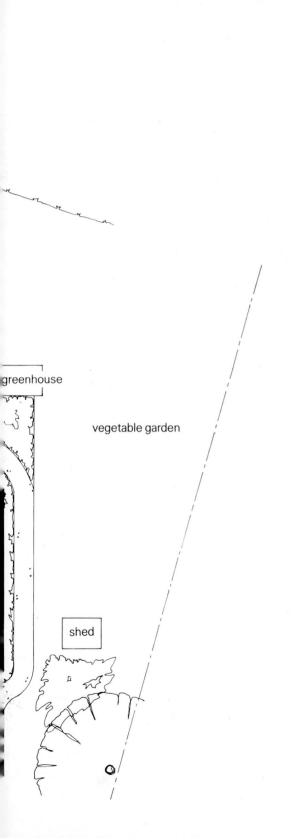

greenhouse

vegetable garden

shed

A selection of standard materials and their dimensions is given (Fig 28) which will be useful when carrying out detailed design work. Working with this type of information you can accurately dimension the features in the design. This still should be in pencil. Having completed the design, even if messy, use a fresh piece of paper to trace over the design to make the final drawing.

A professional would choose a selection of special ink pens (such as Isograph) in a variety of sizes eg 0.2, 0.35, 0.5 and 0.7mm. These are however, relatively expensive and need to be regularly used to prevent them from drying out and would not be worth purchasing for a one-off design. But if you are keen to get a professional finish a lot of people do use these pens in their work and you might well be able to borrow them for your design. There are now a variety of fine-point felt-tip pens which are cheap, effective and easy to use. Ink is not essential though, pencil is quite adequate, but beware of being too gentle of hand as this will make the pencil line too weak to print successfully. The drawing does not have to be pretty, but to bring the design alive and make it clear and realistic you will need to represent each material you have used with a suitable symbol. Let your natural artistic ability prevail and make up your own symbols. Above all, make up a collection of symbols that work well together but are distinct and clear.

You may feel at this point that drawing symbols and making pretty patterns on paper is unnecessary to your garden planning. As only you will see the plan, you may think, 'what does it matter?' However, this part of the garden design process is extremely important for the following reasons. It brings the reality of your design to life, and hence gives you a better insight into what your design will look like; it provides an opportunity to make improvements and, particularly, results in clarifying your design. It introduces another creative opportunity which might result in new ideas that would otherwise have been unexplored.

Drawing on planting details

If space permits, you may wish to put all the planting on your design drawing. For clarity it is wise however to do the detailed planting on a separate tracing overlay (or larger scale plan, see p108/109) and indicate only trees, hedges and certain other specimen shrubs.

Front garden

The design of the front garden is mentioned separately as it does need to be considered in a different way from the rest of the garden. The front garden is your public garden – the garden that you, your visitors, the postman, milkman and dustman all go through regularly. From a plantsman's angle here is the perfect challenge to come up with a planting scheme which provides interest throughout the year, particularly the winter months, when this garden unlike the back garden is used as much as at any other time of the year. At the same time, however, most of us would probably prefer to be doing our gardening out of the public eye. In this respect we need to make this a low-maintenance area, using ground-smother planting of a permanent nature, but nevertheless providing an inviting display all year.

Good access needs to be supplied for fuel supplies and, above all, the car. Whatever the size your garden may be, so small that only one car space is permissible, or large with drives and turning circles, you will need to allow adequate space. Remember also to allow for at least one to two visitors' cars to park out of the turning area/driveway. It may be prudent to remember to install a water-pipe for adequate drainage for car washing. The dustbins will need to be collected and may be permanently located in the front garden, and hence adequate screening and, if possible, a covered walkway to the dustbins is going to be much appreciated (log stores and coal bunkers similarly). Likewise, oil and gas tanks need to be within easy reach of the supply lorry and their routes for pipes allocated in order that the planting does not get damaged. All these items will necessitate a

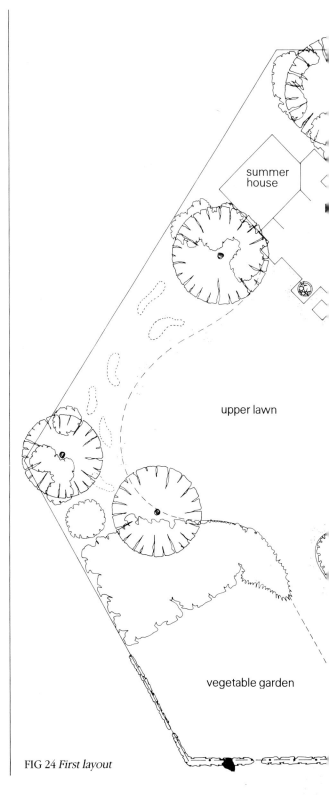

summer house

upper lawn

vegetable garden

FIG 24 *First layout*

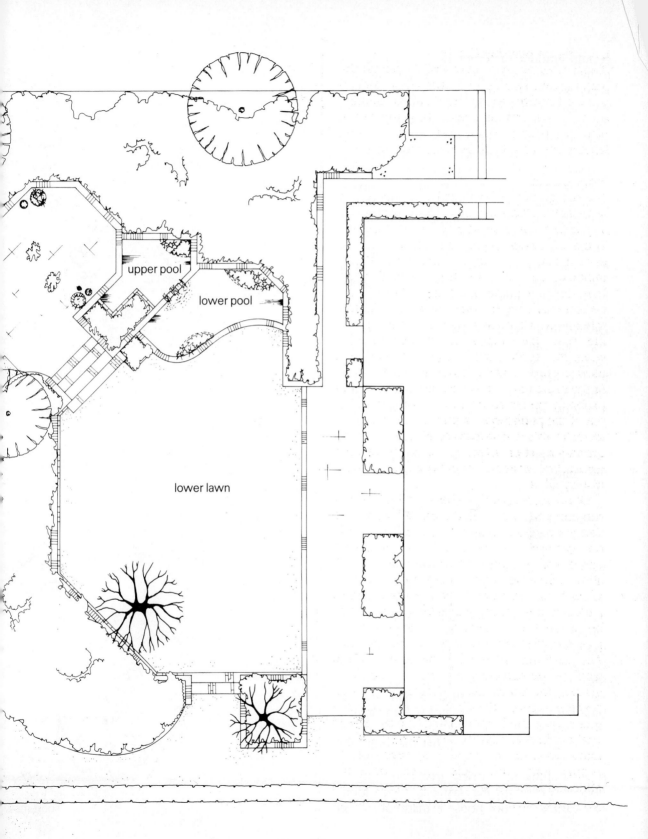

upper pool

lower pool

lower lawn

certain amount of screening by wall, fence, trellis or evergreen shrub planting. Lighting is necessary in the front garden, particularly if you have some distance to walk from parking the car to the front door. There are numerous electrical control systems, light sensors or time delayed switches which may be helpful.

If you live near a busy road, apart from the obvious screening requirements, if space permits, road noise can be reduced by dense planting; consider also the possibility of soil mounding. When choosing your plants a variety of different shrubs with different leaves and branches tend to have the effect of absorbing more noise than a single hedge or belt of one-plant species alone.

DETAILING THE DESIGN

For choosing hard landscape materials (bricks, paving, etc) the materials available for use in the garden are endless. Deciding which to use can be very hard, rather similar to the decisions one makes when decorating a room inside the house when colour matching and design continuity is very important. The big difference in the garden is that of durability. Can your chosen materials stand up to continuous soaking, freezing, bleaching by the sun, not to mention the battering from garden machinery, heavy boots, bicycles, cricket balls and the like?

Walls

Garden walls give a real permanence to a garden. They will store a certain amount of heat and hence offer a better environment for tender climbers and make for a pleasant merging of the house with the garden setting. Generally speaking the local building material offers the best choice for garden walling if you live in an area with natural building stone. In the Cotswolds, for instance, brick walls will certainly be out of place. Likewise, despite the fact that the builders' merchants probably stock stone, introducing stone walling to a brick area needs to be done very carefully if a clash is to be avoided. **Brick walls** If your house is made of a good

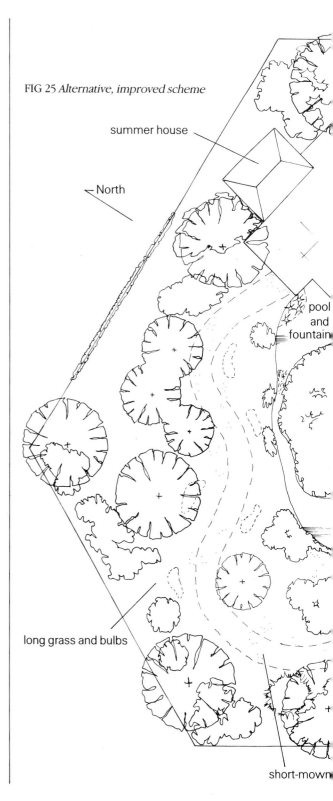

FIG 25 *Alternative, improved scheme*

summer house

← North

pool
and
fountain

long grass and bulbs

short-mown

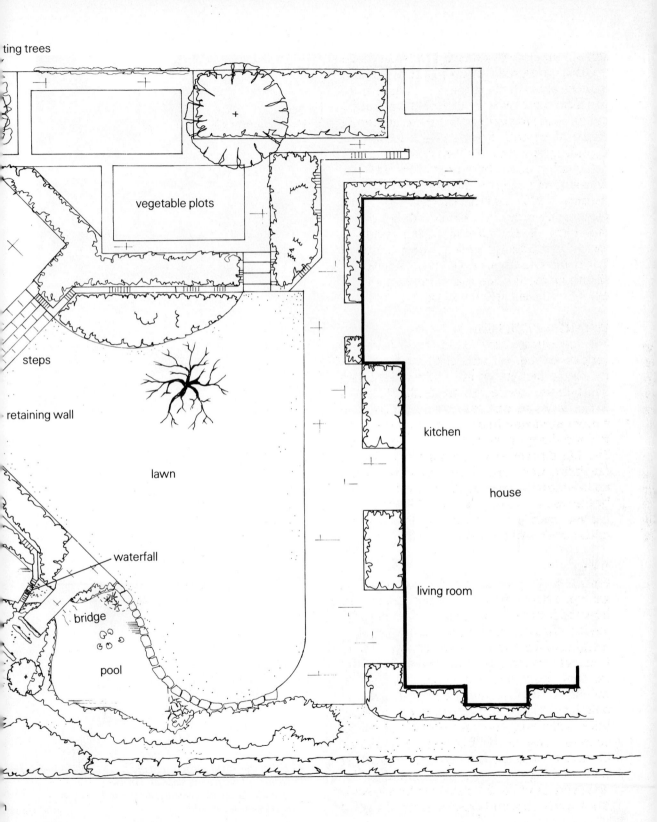

ting trees

vegetable plots

steps

retaining wall

lawn

waterfall

bridge

pool

kitchen

house

living room

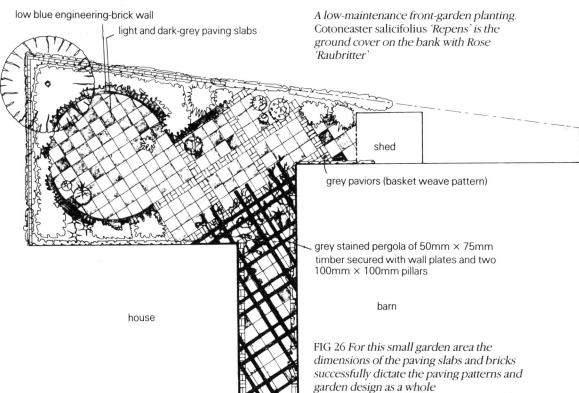

low blue engineering-brick wall

light and dark-grey paving slabs

A low-maintenance front-garden planting. Cotoneaster salicifolius 'Repens' is the ground cover on the bank with Rose 'Raubritter'

shed

grey paviors (basket weave pattern)

grey stained pergola of 50mm × 75mm timber secured with wall plates and two 100mm × 100mm pillars

barn

house

FIG 26 For this small garden area the dimensions of the paving slabs and bricks successfully dictate the paving patterns and garden design as a whole

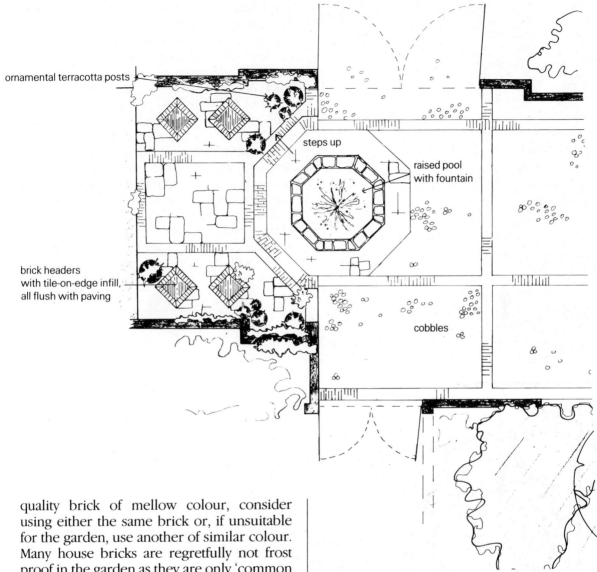

ornamental terracotta posts

steps up

raised pool
with fountain

brick headers
with tile-on-edge infill,
all flush with paving

cobbles

quality brick of mellow colour, consider
using either the same brick or, if unsuitable
for the garden, use another of similar colour.
Many house bricks are regretfully not frost
proof in the garden as they are only 'common
clay' bricks 'faced' with a sand finish which,
although weather proof when used as a
vertical house wall, would absorb water in
the open and crack in the frost. Also these
bricks once chipped in a garden situation will
expose their true unfaced clay colour and
consequently look tatty quickly. Look for
bricks that are not colour faced and are hard
(highly baked) resistant types. 'Stock bricks'
are ideal, they normally have a good multi-
colour and some brickworks (and merchants) will sell you seconds or rough stocks

FIG 27 *In this formal courtyard, accurate
design is vital to maintain the symmetry
and pattern*

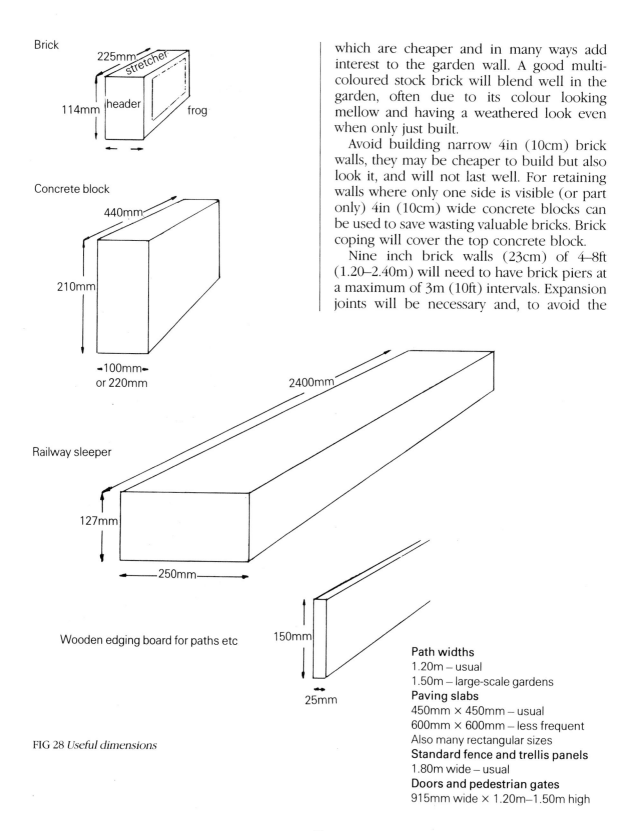

Brick

225mm stretcher

114mm header frog

Concrete block

440mm

210mm

◄100mm►
or 220mm

2400mm

Railway sleeper

127mm

◄250mm►

Wooden edging board for paths etc

150mm

25mm

which are cheaper and in many ways add interest to the garden wall. A good multi-coloured stock brick will blend well in the garden, often due to its colour looking mellow and having a weathered look even when only just built.

Avoid building narrow 4in (10cm) brick walls, they may be cheaper to build but also look it, and will not last well. For retaining walls where only one side is visible (or part only) 4in (10cm) wide concrete blocks can be used to save wasting valuable bricks. Brick coping will cover the top concrete block.

Nine inch brick walls (23cm) of 4–8ft (1.20–2.40m) will need to have brick piers at a maximum of 3m (10ft) intervals. Expansion joints will be necessary and, to avoid the

Path widths
1.20m – usual
1.50m – large-scale gardens
Paving slabs
450mm × 450mm – usual
600mm × 600mm – less frequent
Also many rectangular sizes
Standard fence and trellis panels
1.80m wide – usual
Doors and pedestrian gates
915mm wide × 1.20m–1.50m high

FIG 28 *Useful dimensions*

FIG 29 *Collection of symbols*

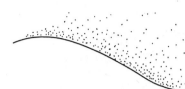

Grass

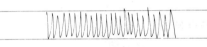

Water

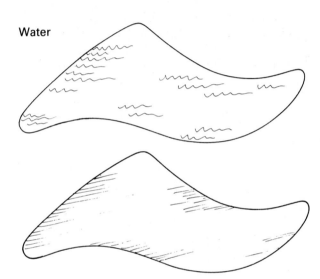

hedges

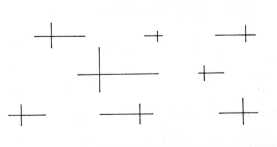

Paving

Cobbles and boulders

Trees

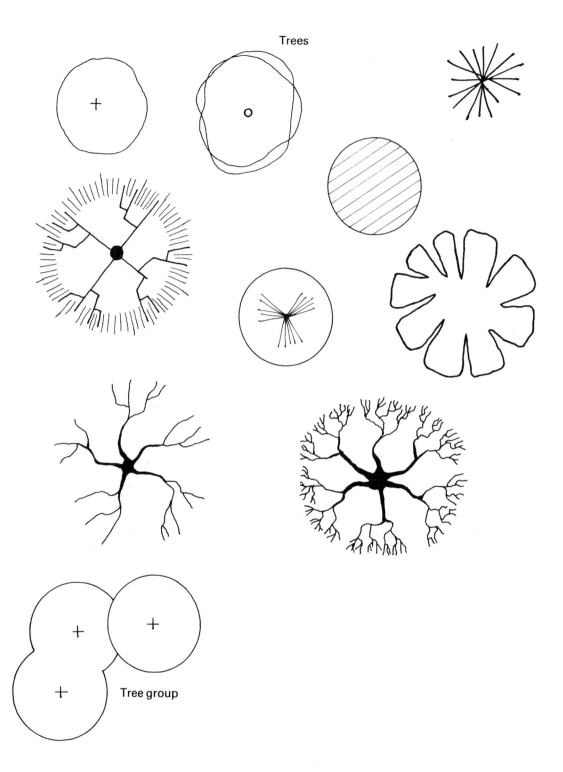

Tree group

Shrubs

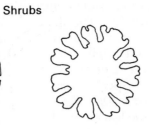

Spiky plants

FIG 30 *The importance of clarity*

Good, clear and precise combination for trees, shrubs and spiky plants

Poor, confused combination for the same planting

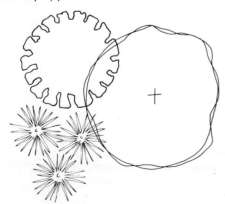

83

possibility of the wall blowing over, damp proof courses should be avoided. The illustration shows a typical brick wall. Note the foundations being continued 45cm (18in) below the soil to avoid frost damage. Most brick manufacturers make special bricks which can add greatly to your walling design, such as 'Cant bricks' (as on the low pool edge shown on p122). But beware! They are very expensive compared with standard bricks, but in certain circumstances for small detailed areas they do add that extra touch.

Bond types The way in which bricks are laid in a wall can be varied to give differing patterns and also to strengthen the wall. The standard types are listed below (see Fig 37).

1 Stretcher Bond – Easy to lay but not a strong bonding wall, only suitable for low walls and metal ties should be included in the brickwork to add additional strength.
2 English Bond – Good strong bond.
3 English Garden Wall Bond – (Old Traditional Bond). This cuts down on the number of header ends of bricks required.
4 Flemish Bond – Not as strong as English Bond.

The cement mortar jointing between the bricks is very important visually. There are five main jointing types. The 'keyed' technique is recommended as this looks softer and is easy to undertake (using a stick or the back of a spoon) (see Fig 38).

If you are going to use a special brick colour, grey engineering bricks for example, bear in mind that dyes can be added to the mortar mix. You may wish to add a little black to make the mortar greyer to avoid a big contrast between the light mortar and the dark brick colour.

One further note is that when constructing a retaining wall, the wall should taper slightly from bottom to top into the bank.

Stone walls As Hilliers is Hampshire-based the firm is entrenched in brick country, and stone walling is envied. The beauty of a stone wall is the fact that plants can survive and be deliberately grown in its crevices.

It is the retaining walls that are so especially interesting as these, being backed by moist soil, can support a wide range of plants from alpines to ferns. A specially designed alpine garden may not seem appropriate to your garden, or simply there is inadequate space, but at least a few favourites can be catered for in a length of retaining wall.

As one visits different areas of the country when on holiday, you will recall the differing styles of walls encountered, the slate stone walls in North Wales and Scotland, stone and earth bank walls in Cornwall, etc all have age old traditions and involve some considerable skill in their building, particularly the free standing walls. However, low retaining walls, that is those not likely to be taking too much weight, can quite easily be constructed. After all you only need to worry about the front face, the back can be packed with any material and a certain amount of soil.

Dry stone walls, that is those without mortar pointing, are the best from a planting point of view, but are of course ideal for the uninvited weed! Regretfully walls are expensive whether in brick or stone, and the labour costs alone can often mean that you have to use wood rather than brick, especially for long garden boundaries.

FIG 31 *This simple front-garden design allows adequate space for car turning. The gates are positioned to allow the car to get properly off the main road before they need to be opened*

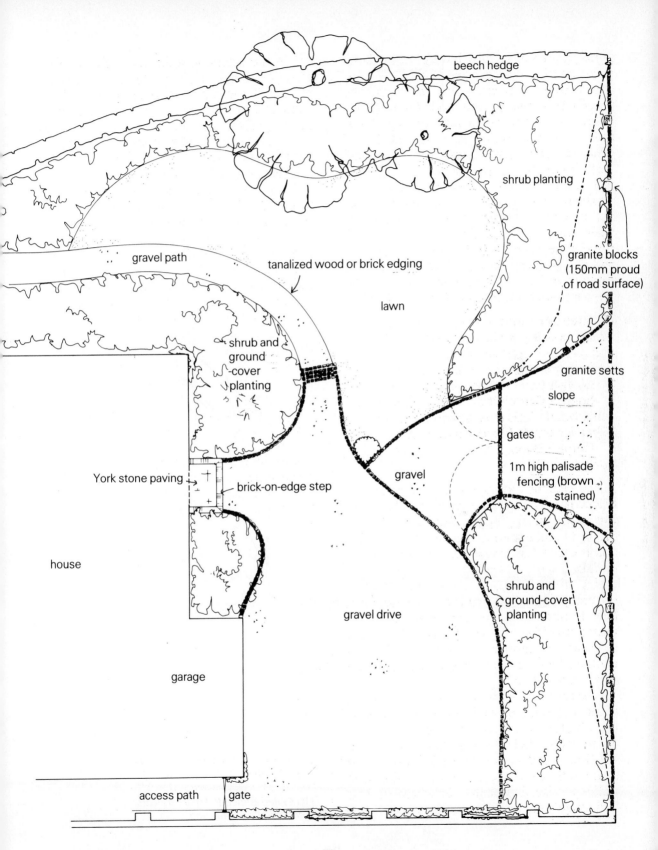

beech hedge

shrub planting

gravel path

tanalized wood or brick edging

granite blocks
(150mm proud
of road surface)

lawn

shrub and
ground
-cover
planting

granite setts

slope

gates

York stone paving

brick-on-edge step

gravel

1m high palisade
fencing (brown
stained)

house

shrub and
ground-cover
planting

garage

gravel drive

access path

gate

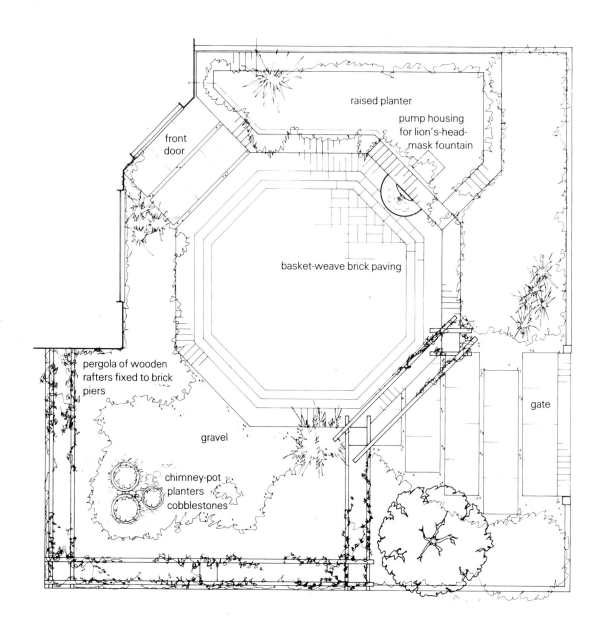

raised planter

front
door

pump housing
for lion's-head-
mask fountain

basket-weave brick paving

pergola of wooden
rafters fixed to brick
piers

gate

gravel

chimney-pot
planters
cobblestones

FIG 32 *Permanent structural interest in a
small front garden*

FIG 33 *Recommended space for cars,
access widths and turning*

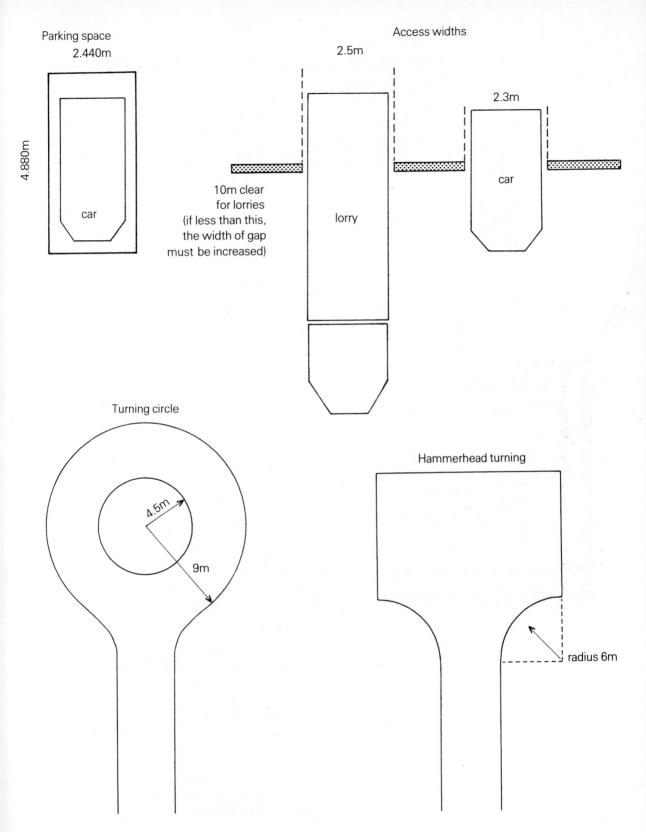

Parking space
2.440m
4.880m
car

Access widths
2.5m
lorry

10m clear
for lorries
(if less than this,
the width of gap
must be increased)

2.3m
car

Turning circle
4.5m
9m

Hammerhead turning
radius 6m

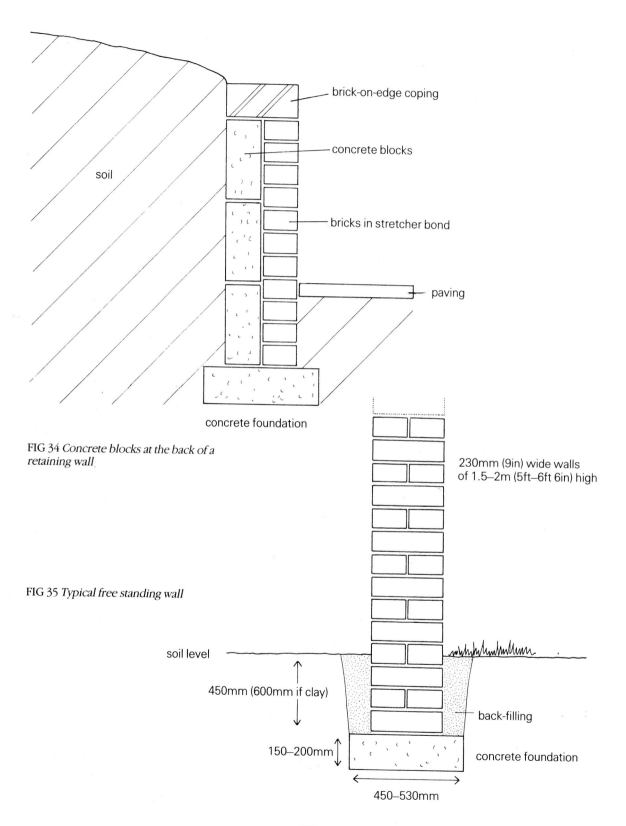

brick-on-edge coping

concrete blocks

bricks in stretcher bond

paving

soil

concrete foundation

FIG 34 *Concrete blocks at the back of a retaining wall*

FIG 35 *Typical free standing wall*

230mm (9in) wide walls
of 1.5–2m (5ft–6ft 6in) high

soil level

450mm (600mm if clay)

150–200mm

back-filling

concrete foundation

450–530mm

FIG 36 *A variety of finishes for tops of walls*

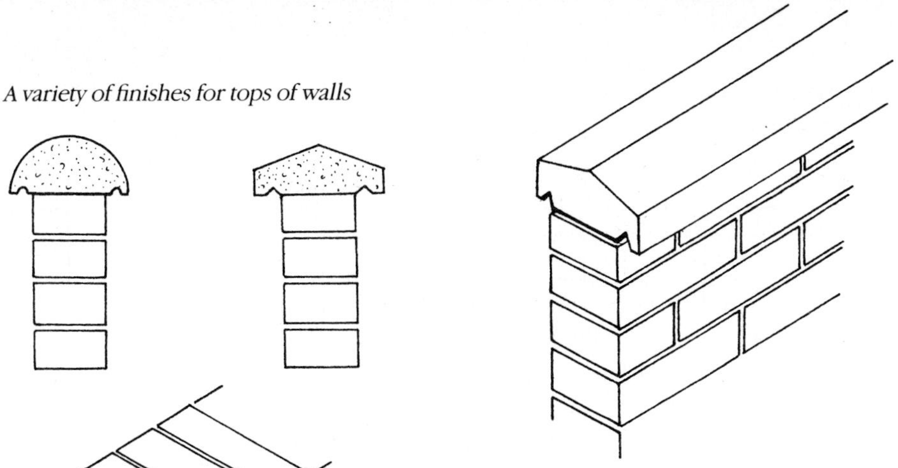

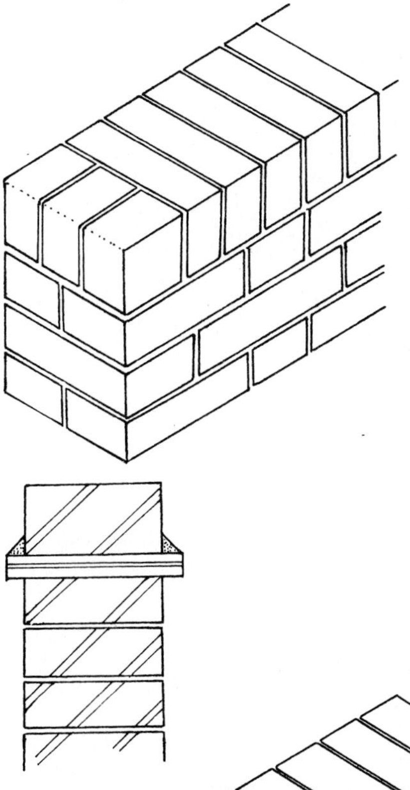

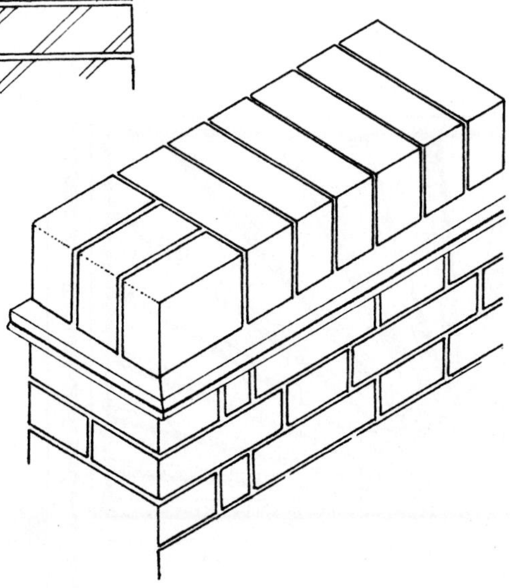

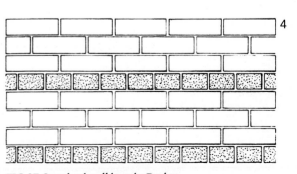

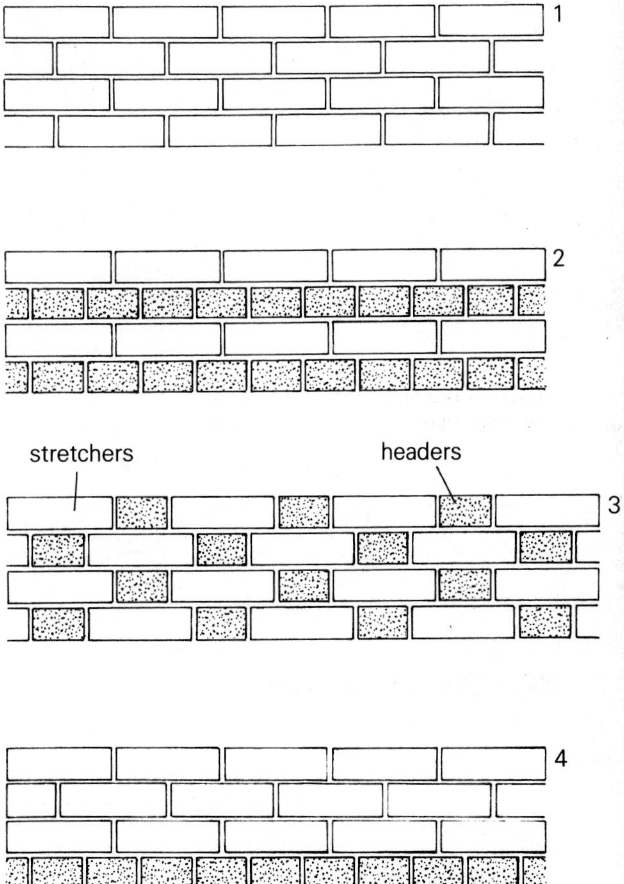

stretchers

headers

1

2

3

4

FIG 37 *Standard wall bonds. Darker
header bricks will accentuate the pattern*

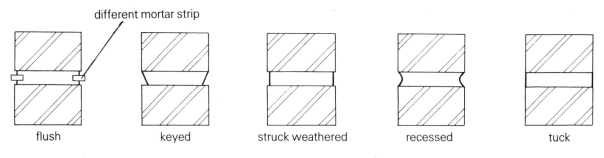

different mortar strip

flush   keyed   struck weathered   recessed   tuck

FIG 38 *Types of mortar jointing*

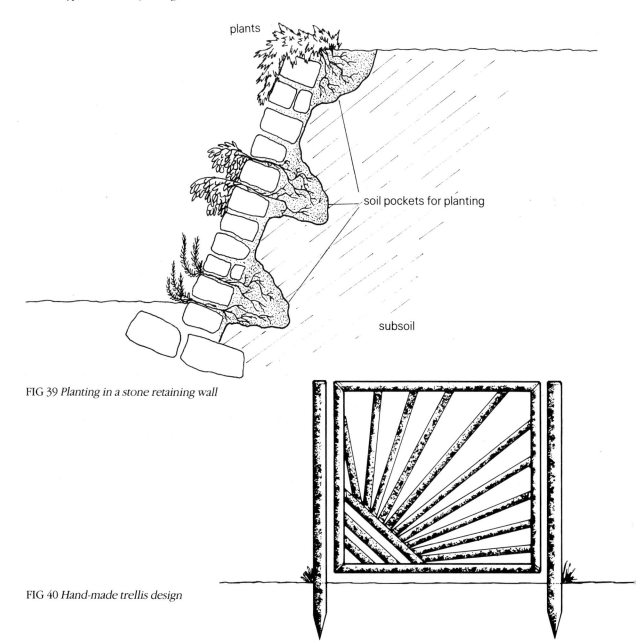

plants

soil pockets for planting

subsoil

FIG 39 *Planting in a stone retaining wall*

FIG 40 *Hand-made trellis design*

Woodwork in the garden

Fences and trellis Wood is a very amenable material and its uses in the garden afford endless possibilities. Let us first consider the solid fence as the alternative to wall or hedge. Most garden centres and builders' merchants stock the standard 2m (6ft 8in) wide panels at between 1.20–2m (4–6ft 8in) high. These are usually made of larch and either overlap or are interwoven, overlap being stronger and a little more expensive. These are, however, cheap and instant but regretfully look it, and tend not to last more than a few years. They are also generally rather unnaturally coloured orange (although they do fade) and one must be prepared to accept this or stain them yourself. Do give the fence an extra coat of preservative, particularly at the junction at the level of the soil surface. The fence posts tend to rot at this point considerably in advance of the general decay of the fence itself.

White palisade fencing, so often out of place, looks well here in a cottage setting

These fences can, and should of course, be screened by covering with climbers. It will be necessary to provide good training wires (plastic coated 8-gauge) fixed with galvanised staples, three to four strands for a 6ft (1.8m) high fence. Unfortunately it is likely that by the time the climbers are fully mature, the fence itself needs replacing. It is for this reason that we would advocate a stronger fence.

A much more substantial and longer lasting fence is the type that is put together on site, called closeboard (or feather board). To have such a fence erected for you will be more expensive (half as much again), but nevertheless worth the money. If you are in a position to undertake the work yourself, the cost of course is much more reasonable. Be sure to have the timber tanalised, a pressure impreg-

91

nating preservative, this will increase the life span to approximately 20 years. The only disadvantage to the closeboard fence is that it is usual to face the fence outward towards your neighbour, ie the less attractive side facing into your garden. This is obviously a matter of goodwill and frequently the fence will be within your garden, abutting another hedge. You will probably be covering the fence with climbers and, in fact, the posts make the securing of climbing wires much easier. If you are putting climbing wires on the outer face, it may be necessary to have 1in (25mm) square battens at intervals along the fence onto which to fix the wires and staples.

Fences as boundaries and stockproofing A complete visual block may not be required. Where the purpose of the fence is merely to keep livestock out and mark the boundary, there is little to compare with the simplicity of the post and rail fence, with the exception perhaps of the ha-ha. If you are creating a cottage garden or have that type of property, there is still a place for the traditional low palisade fencing.

Chestnut paling is used extensively as temporary movable fencing, particularly in the landscape industry, to protect planting in public areas during their establishment period. Chestnut as a wood is a very durable timber and will last 20–30 years. The temporary chestnut paling with its wire fastening is not a particularly tidy fence; however, it is possible to make a more respectable edition by using the palings only, nailed directly onto a fence framework. This gives a rather pleasing informal looking fence and will be long lasting.

A visit to your local woodyard/fencing specialist is recommended rather than settling for the standard products available in garden centres. They will also be prepared to make up fencing to your own requirements. You will find that, surprisingly, it does not inevitably work out more expensive than the standard panels. Similarly, trellis panels can be made up to any size squares or diamonds. The standard panels generally available

tend to be rather thin on the wood and 37mm×20mm (1½×¾in) thickness of timber produces a far more substantial and satisfactory panel.

Trellis is primarily for the support of climbing plants and as light is available on both sides of the trellis panel your climbers will grow better at a lower level than on an equivalent fence panel. Again, the trellis should be good and substantial. Trying to extract a mature climber from decayed trellis is not to be recommended. Even if you manage to get the old one off, the climber will still need to be supported and it will be difficult to reinstate a new panel. Trellis is easy to make yourself if you have the time. It will be well worthwhile as you will be able to experiment with the size of the squares, possibly even fanning the wood into a pattern as shown in Fig 40.

There are, at the top end of the market, now at last a few firms specialising in trellis designs, both traditional and contemporary. With the advent of numerous coloured wood stains there is further scope for the more ambitious trellis designer.

Timber retaining walls

Being a soft material and a natural one, wood is rarely out of place in the garden and it can be considered as an alternative to nearly every 'hard' landscape surface. Logs may be used as retaining walls and either driven hard into the subsoil or set with concrete in a trench. Be sure to purchase reasonably straight timbers that will butt well together for this purpose or you may find your retaining wall leaks soil. Designers have used wood in this way to create the most exciting features particularly suited to children's play areas. The wood of this quality and quantity is however not cheap so do not get too carried away unless you have a good budget. A visit to Norway and Sweden would really be the place to pick up ideas for the use of wood.

Steps

Steps are as important in the garden as a bridge is over a river. We all know how beautiful a bridge can look with its reflection in the water, and our first inclination would be to design an elegant bridge. Similarly, steps should be designed in the same way. The design and the choice of materials used will make a very profound impression on the feel of the garden as a whole. Although they are of course essentially functional, a means of physically getting from one level to another, steps must be:

1 Easy to walk up and down,
2 Elegant and not obtrusive,
3 Sturdy and safe.

The steps should be plenty wide enough, particularly if plants are to spill over the sides. As mentioned earlier in the chapter, it is very easy to underestimate the number of steps required. To illustrate the point, Fig 41 shows what appears to be a totally satisfactory design, but with the knowledge that the retaining wall is 5ft (1.5m) high and therefore requires 12 steps, the effect on the design would be Fig 42. A solution to this problem may be to divide the steps into two flights at 90° with a platform between them. This would also be more pleasant to walk up having a 'break' in the journey (Fig 43). Alternatively, a complete rethink of the levels to create the less steep change by terracing may be the correct procedure. Fig 44 indicates the range of height and distance for the tread (or going) and riser. The tread is usually 13in wide (33cm) but can be more. The riser is usually no greater than 5in (13cm).

The choice of material to use must of course marry in with the adjacent materials. In an informal situation log steps might be ideal in which case chestnut logs or tanalised softwood with the bark having been removed is ideal. In a slightly more formal situation, railway sleepers or other heavy timber rails may be used as retainers in the path. Slices of log or tree trunk sections may also be used, but restricted for 'occasional use' steps only, as these are not for hurrying up and down, and can be slippery.

Brick steps give the greater sense of permanence and unity where brickwork has been used in the paving design. These will need to be laid on edge to prevent their being dislodged. To achieve a height of 5in (13cm) for step risers, a tile insert can form an attractive detail. Where the steps are to be paved, the slab may extend beneath the brick riser and should extend over the front end of the riser below by 1½in (37mm). This has the effect of making a step look shallower and also nicer to walk on. Long flights of steps are best formed of concrete and then faced with brick and/or paving to avoid any possible cracking or sinkage.

Paving and paving patterns

You cannot really afford to make a mistake when choosing what type of paving would look best. Paving materials alone are expensive and the labour of installation equally so. As with choosing walling materials, if you live in a natural stone area, you probably cannot do better than use the natural paving. If in a brick area, incorporate some brick to marry the paving to the surround. This may well be necessary to break up a large expanse. Old York stone flag paving is one of the most universally accepted aristocrats of paving, having the depth and subtle variation in colour. Regretfully, due to its weight and availability, it is extremely expensive. However, you do get what you pay for, and it will last more than a lifetime.

A cheaper way to buy natural stone is in smaller pieces to create a crazy paving effect, but this is rather less impressive. It is however, useful for paving curved paths and border edgings.

There are now a variety of imitation paving slabs. In the early days there was nothing to commend them. Now, however, there are some really extremely realistic slabs on the market, but do shop around, there are still 'cheap and nasty' ones to be avoided. Do also

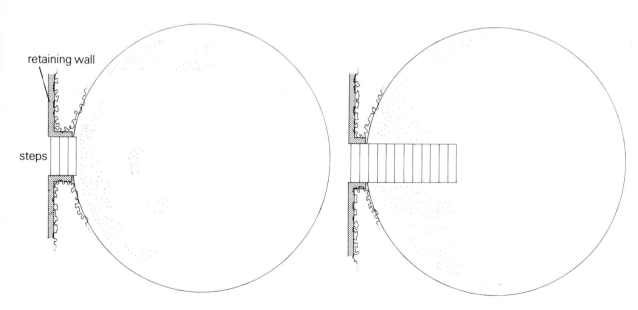

FIG 41 *Steps into a circular lawn: proposed design*

FIG 42 *Actual need, bearing in mind height of wall*

Wood is used here most successfully to form a water feature

(left) Logs used effectively as retaining walls for planting beds

consider slabs that are not pretending to be real stone. There are some good textured finishes. Even the most boring looking grey slab can be enhanced by using other materials, particularly brick, to create a pattern that gives strength and interest to a paved area.

Bricks as paving on their own give a very traditional feel to the garden. Due to their porous nature they also readily support the growth of moss, particularly in the joints between the bricks whether cement mortar pointed or not. Properly done, this will add years to the maturity of the garden. For brick paving you will need to choose brick that will withstand the frost, particularly where the bricks are being laid flat. There are also special brick paviors made for this purpose, if the colour brick you want is not available in a sufficiently hard standard brick. There are some lovely old fashioned brick patterns – herringbone, basket weave etc (see p99). Make up your own pattern to add a little

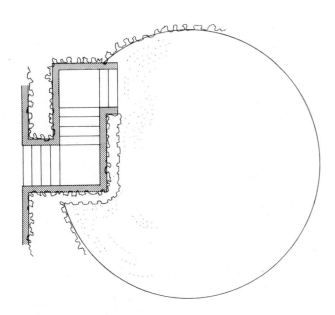

FIG 43 *Proposed solution*

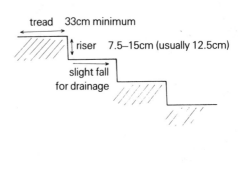

tread   33cm minimum

riser   7.5–15cm (usually 12.5cm)

slight fall
for drainage

FIG 44 *Satisfactory dimensions for steps*

personality and interest. Another good use for brick paving is for curving paths or radiating brick around some garden ornament or even a tree.

There are now a wide range of interlocking paviors which are easy to lay and fairly hardwearing, these are excellent for driveways as an alternative to tarmac and cover a wide range of colours. However, it is hard to beat the traditional materials such as granite sets, cobbles and the grey stableblock paviors. These can be expensive but used with other cheap materials will go a long way and add enormously to the charm of the garden.

Gravel

You may be surprised to find that gravel has a separate heading. Who wants gravel in their garden anyway, you may ask? We try to get rid of stones, not import them! Gravel is, however, both amenable and cheap and has considerable variety in shape and colour. There are many possible uses in the garden. If the correct grade of gravel is used, your garden plants can grow through the gravel but the weed seedlings are unable to germinate on the dry coarse surface – a sort of gravel mulch. This needs to be 20mm (¾in)

washed shingle where the fine gravel and sand dust has been removed.

Gravel is used primarily as a path material, for which it is ideal, and traditionally as dug from the quarry is a mixture of aggregates that compact down to a hard surface. This surface although functional, can look a little untidy and have a tendency to be dirty and muddy in wet weather. Thus, a thin blinding layer of the cleaner and neater looking washed shingle can be spread over this. Pea shingle (10mm or ⅓in) is usually used, but even this has a tendency to be trodden into the house and we would again recommend the 20mm (¾in) shingle. Two important constructional points should be mentioned to ensure success:

1 The shingle finishing layer (blinding) should be a very thin layer, too thickly spread and it will be difficult to walk on and constantly rut and look untidy.

2 If a hardcore or other larger stone base (such as limestone scalpings) has been used, this must have a finer blinding layer over it which has been well consolidated. This will avoid later problems of the layers mixing with constant use and the larger stones working to the surface.

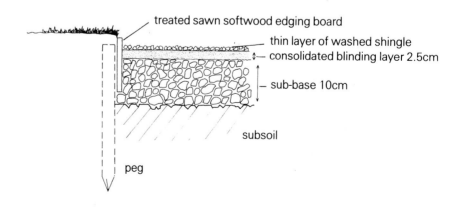

FIG 45 *Gravel path cross-section*

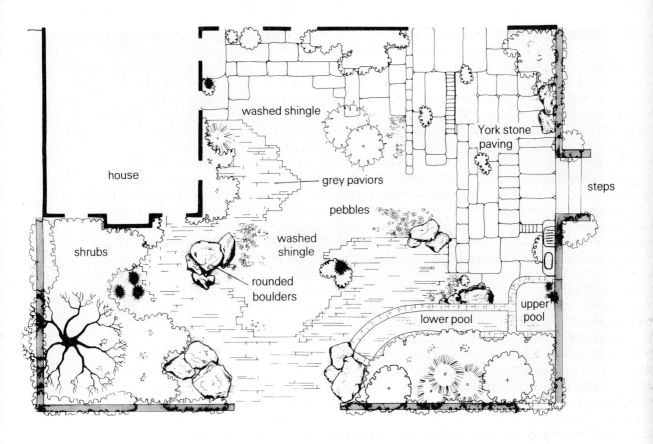

In the plan the following labels appear: washed shingle, house, shrubs, grey paviors, washed shingle, rounded boulders, pebbles, York stone paving, steps, lower pool, upper pool

As gravel is a loose material it will need to be contained adequately by brick or wooden edging. The bricks should be set in concrete and the wood, tanalised planks (25mm× 150mm, pegs 450mm long 50mm square – see illustration).

Gravel (or shingle) is very useful as a linking surface to join other materials of different shapes and rigidity. A gravel path may merge from its formal boundaries to informal planting groups, and the incorporation of large pebbles, natural stone slabs and boulders, associate particularly well and are used very effectively in oriental gardens.

Rocks and boulders

When one thinks of rocks and boulders in a garden situation the real experts in this field are the Japanese; their art is the imitation and

FIG 46 *Plan of garden shown in colour photograph p99*

insight into what is beautiful in the natural landscape. It is therefore quite evident that the stones used should ideally have a weathered appearance, perhaps even water-worn. Unfortunately such stone is difficult to purchase and expensive, as they need to be, as it were, hand selected from the natural landscape itself, usually many miles from your house. Perhaps one could argue, as a conservationist, that this is not to be encouraged – rather like picking wild flowers? The most readily available of this type of rock is Westmorland weathered stone, this is a very pitted rock sometimes to the point of being almost too ornate. The quarried stone is

certainly cheaper and available in all sizes, shapes and colours.

You will need to visit a stone merchant to appreciate fully the range and colours and, as every lorry load varies, select and order your stone at the time. Unfortunately, it is not often possible to select only the best stones from a load and you will have to take the rough with the smooth. However, let us consider the arrangement of the boulders. Some of the most pleasant looking rocks are merely outcrops emerging from the surrounding soil or vegetation, it is therefore only necessary that part of the stone be visible, and thus only one or two good faces are important. If your stone is very angular and blocky or simply on the small side, carefully butting one stone to another, to make the joints appear as a natural fault or crack, will give the illusion of a much larger substantial stone.

It is important when forming the appearance of rock outcrops to imitate the natural rock strata and avoid creating one isolated

(above) Random York stone paving must be the most satisfactory garden paving

(above right) Striking use of herringbone brick pattern paving

(right) Gravel serves here as a useful linking surface between other materials

rock patch. Positioning smaller and larger outcrops throughout a whole area of the garden will give a more harmonious and natural effect. Rocks are hand movable up to about 250kg (5cwt). Generally if you ask for a range from 150–250kg (3–5cwt) this will suffice. However, it is well worth considering employing a specialist firm with the appropriate lifting equipment (or at least a team of suitable strong men) to enable you to use the really large stones to get a sense of permanence to a rock feature. As we mentioned earlier in chapter 2 rockeries as such can go sadly wrong. They require a great deal of skill if they are to succeed.

Garden furniture

There is good money to be made in selling garden furniture, pots, statues and other such garden related hardware, consequently there tends to be an overwhelming choice available. Regrettably, however, you do need to sift through substantial quantities of poorly designed and cheaply made material to find anything that is likely to be suitable. Perhaps the worst area in this respect is sculpture for the garden. For some unknown reason, the suppliers of garden sculpture seem to have the notion that we all have historical gardens and want cherubs or gnomes. Where is the contemporary work that would blend into today's garden? We cannot all have a Henry Moore in our garden, but with the advent of fibreglass resin bond work it is possible to produce good statuary at relatively low prices. Sculptures can be dramatic, particularly when used in silhouette against the skyline. They may be used as focal points in the garden and by virtue of their interest inspire movement from one area to another.

The historical pieces do have their place and can give a strong atmosphere and tranquillity to an area of the garden.

One area that has improved in recent years is that of terracotta, stone and fibreglass pots. There are some extremely elegant often simply designed pots being produced in this country, and being imported from abroad. A nicely grouped selection of pots can transform an area, particularly around the house and on the terrace, or as in France, down flights of steps, all of which give real scope for the annual planting schemes. Unless you are absolutely sure that your pots are frost proof you will need to bring them in during the winter, particularly some of the pots from abroad, such as Italy.

When you are considering tables, chairs and the like for the garden this is very much a matter of personal taste and we will not dwell on this, apart from commenting that as natural wood looks well in the garden, perhaps this should be the first choice. The traditional is again very much to the fore with the suppliers, but the market is certainly widening. Unfortunately, the well designed wooden furniture tends to be expensive but hopefully this will improve, and with a little looking around there should be no problem in finding something suitable.

Ornamental pools

Over the years we have had a great deal of experience in installing pools and as many experiences where the schemes have worked well as where they have not! Experience is most important where pools are concerned and we will try to pass on as much as we can to assist you in achieving success. (See chapter 2 for discussion of formal and informal designs – the informal pool can generally be larger.)

The visual design, technical detailing and choice of materials must all be carefully considered together and cannot be isolated. An intricate small garden design with a high proportion of paving and walling will require a detailed pool design that is appropriate. The pool and cascade features illustrated show successful small scale water features. Whether the design be formal or informal, areas suitable for bog plants and oxygenating plants must be included. Fish are not essential to the wellbeing of a pool, but do add a further interest. Appropriate plants are discussed on p253. Let us at first discuss the

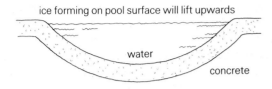

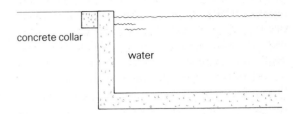

FIG 47 *Concrete pool cross-sections*

three main waterproofing materials and their limitations.

Concrete and brick rendered pools Being rigid materials the greatest problem is that of cracking. Usually this results from the subsoil base having moved and hence stressing the rigid structure. Damage from freezing can also cause cracking. To avoid this problem, either design a dish-shaped section to allow free space for the expansion of ice, or where a vertical profile is being used, an additional strengthening collar. If these cannot be provided, for example where the pool edge is a free standing wall, the only solution is to float wood or some such similar material in the water during the winter period to divert the freezing ice force from the pond sides. The advantages of concrete are limited to difficult formal shapes, compatibility with brickwork, and to a lesser extent, suitability to take cascade pipework and support fountain structures. We would say it was essential to paint the rendered pool with a proprietary waterproofing paint as an additional precaution.

Flexible liners Polythene and other plastic liners are generally unsuitable, they tend not to last long and puncture quite readily unless sandwiched between other protective materials. Butyl rubber liners are undoubtedly the most reliable being very flexible and long lasting. Since their introduction

many years ago, there has been no deterioration of the liner material. The butyl is ideal for informal pools and particularly larger areas where concrete would be too expensive and vulnerable to cracking. They are also ideal for streams linking one pool to another. The lining should be laid on a 5cm (2in) minimum of builder's sand to protect it from the subsoil stones, etc. Adding a little cement to the sand will also add a little strength and help hold the edges of the pool. There are, however, a few disadvantages which should be considered at the design stage; at the edge of the pool, unless the liner abuts a paved edge where the liner can run underneath, the black liner will be visible and need trailing plants such as Vinca, *Cotoneaster dammeri*, Lysimachia, ivy, etc to cover it successfully. The liner will however become green from

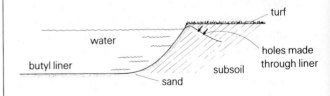

FIG 48 *Section through butyl rubber lined pool*

101

algae growth in a relatively short time. The liner is also difficult to stick to other surfaces such as brick, although there are glue-type tapes which work satisfactorily on completely dry bricks. Bricks in this situation are usually wet or at least slightly damp. Where a lawn area meets a liner edge this will need careful installation to conceal the edge and holes put through the liner where it is tucked beneath the turf to allow soil moisture to reach the grass roots.

There are two potential problems that have the same alarming effect on a pool liner where the liner can be forced up from the pool bottom to the surface. Firstly, this can happen either where the existing water table rises during the winter period and, secondly, if there is organic matter in the subsoil beneath the pool which on rotting gives off methane gas; this will cause air (gas) bubbles. Neither problem arises frequently, but should certainly be considered. Both problems may be overcome by providing pipes as air vents or drains, if there is somewhere to drain the water to. Finally, it is best to avoid having pipes going through the butyl liner. There are, however, specially made bolted flanges to facilitate this, if you wish to avoid the only alternative of having the pipework visibly going over the liner.

Where rocks are to be used as a cascade feature, it is well worth taking a liner underneath the rockwork to retain any water possibly leaking or soaking through the rockwork. All water will then be returned to the system.

Pool design and circulating pumps If you are going to have more than one pool with a cascade there are some important technical design considerations to adhere to. Firstly, the size of the pools; the lower pool will need to be substantially larger than the upper pool in order to hold sufficient water to fill the system when running without appearing empty and exposing the unsightly pool sides. The water in the upper pools and streams will rise by approximately 25mm (½in). We usually make our pools about 45–60cm (18–

(right) Water worn rocks in their natural environment in the Yorkshire Dales

(below) Water worn rocks used in a garden situation

(right) Plants spilling over gravel show up well and give a pleasant informal atmosphere to this path (Stachys olympia left and Helichrysum plicatum right foreground)

102

24in) deep, but this will of course vary according to the pool size.

Pumps, fountains and cascades There are conflicting views on the best type of pumps to use. Generally, submersible pumps are the easiest to install, most readily available and ideal for the small pool. Some would claim they are less reliable than the surface (or dry) pump. This unreliability of the submersible pump is mainly connected with a neglect on the part of the owner to clean the filter (which is in the bottom of the pool) and run the pump periodically through the winter period. The submersible pump should not be positioned directly on the bottom of the pool where the sediment will collect and block the filter. Ideally this pump is best fitted in a separate chamber with easy access for cleaning.

Problems with the surface or dry pump are usually experienced when the pump chamber is located below ground where flooding or simply condensation can damage the motor.

When considering the fountain display, it is well to bear in mind that the finer the jets, the more they will be prone to blocking. The bubble-type fountain displays are the best in this respect. There are numerous types of fountain displays available and the choice is very much a matter of personal taste. The size of the display should be in scale with the pool. Do bear in mind that in an exposed position a fountain jet will easily be blown by the wind if too high or delicate. Finally, the size of the pump is most important. Generally it is better to be over-powered rather than under as it is always possible to turn a pump down. Working out accurately what size you need is far safer than guessing. Be prepared to spent a little money, pumps are fairly expensive. One of the most common mistakes made when designing a circulating water system is making the cascades too wide and having a pump too small, the effect being a dribble over the side of some large rock. Your supplier should be able to do some sums for you given good information. He will need to know:

The number and width of cascades.
Fountain display requirements.
Height from top to bottom pool.
Length of pipe required (distance from pump to outlet).
Personal preference on flow over cascades (ie impressive and noisy or a gentle trickle).

Lighting in the garden

Choosing light units and their positions As we mentioned in chapter 2 there is much to commend providing garden lights. Surprisingly few lights are required and only low power lamps, 100 watt is the maximum that you are likely to need. The cabling should be installed at the earliest possible stage to avoid unnecessary disturbance later and should be put in by a qualified electrician, using armour cable and the necessary safety switches. When deciding the position of the lights in your garden consider the main view points, ie living room window, kitchen, etc and site the lamps at varying distances to highlight certain features. The lights ideally should have extra flex to allow you to move them to different plants as they come into flower or produce autumn colour, etc. The glare from the lights, or the reflected glare from glossy foliage plants, may be a problem and again some consideration must be given to the positioning. If the garden is newly planted the lighting requirement will be less but later requirements must be catered for in terms of location of power points for the developing planting.

Where large-scale lighting is required (large gardens and parks with mature trees) larger light units may be required, in which case there are two alternative non-coloured lights that do produce a different hue. Sodium gives a warm orange light, if a little artificial, and high pressure mercury produces a most effective almost ghostly silver light. Regretfully neither can be produced as a small light unit for use in smaller gardens and ordinary coloured lamps do tend to detract from the garden's natural colouring.

For white light in the small garden 100 watt spotlights are the most commonly used, although there are a variety of other units available. Some free standing lamps, shaded lanterns and clear glass globes, are all available but are a matter of personal choice.

Choosing soft landscape materials

Lawns – turf or seed?   There are advantages and disadvantages to turfing and seeding and it would be wrong to advise dogmatically one preference. To a certain extent price is an important consideration. Seeding is certainly cheaper. Turf is variable in quality and price, the best being a specialist seeded turf such as 'Rolawn' or 'Bravola', which is itself sold in a number of grades. The next is good quality or special meadow turf and at the lower end, standard meadow turf.

If you want a good lawn without coarse grasses you should go for the 'Rolawn' (or similar), but it is twice the price of good meadow turf which for most people is adequate. Standard meadow turf should generally be avoided as it will have a lot of coarse grass and possibly other weeds. The problem generally with non-seeded (or naturally seeded) turves are the presence of coarse grasses which cannot be selectively killed. There is no chemical that will distinguish one grass from another and in this respect 'Rolawn' and similar seeded turves are of great advantage. Turfing has a considerable advantage if you have a poor stony soil. A seeded area can take a while before developing sufficiently to smother the stones.

Quite apart from the saving, sowing a lawn does guarantee that you have a control of the grass species in the lawn. This can be particularly advantageous if you wish to have a lawn in a shaded area or an extremely wet or dry part of the garden. A seed merchant will be able to advise which mixture is the most suitable. You will find, however, that some unwanted broadleaf weeds and coarse grass seedlings will appear in your lawn as there will be dormant seeds in your soil which will germinate at the same time as the sown grass. Most will be annuals or tall perennials which will not survive regular grass mowing. A mild broadleaf weedkiller such as Ioxynil ('Actrilawn' by May and Baker) may be used at an early stage without damage to the young grass seedlings.

Timing   Turf may be laid almost throughout the year, with the exception of periods of drought or frozen ground. If you turf during the summer it will be essential to water regularly and thoroughly the entire area as it is prone to drying out and shrinking in the early period before rooting into the soil. When to sow seed is more critical. For best results the spring period (April/May) will produce very quick germination. Similarly late August/September. At other times of the year when germination is either slow (or when very cold completely delayed) other weed seeds will germinate at these lower temperatures and compete with the grass when it starts its growth in the warmer weather.

Soil mounding/cut and fill   Soil mounding is hardly a soft landscape 'material' but nevertheless it needs discussion in this section of the book. Soil mounding and grading is another one of those areas where subtlety and skill are essential for success. A relatively small rise in soil level will have a surprising effect and often transform an otherwise flat garden. It is all too easy to have a load of soil delivered, rake it over a little and leave it 'as dumped' and expect it not to look like a burial mound!

You need to try and copy nature and re-create it on a smaller scale in a garden. The photograph on p122 shows a gently rolling landscape with the very gradual slopes required to give a soft appearance to the eye. Soil mounding can greatly assist screening exercises and is instant. Mounding can also reduce road noise and is particularly advantageous for establishing planting in areas that would otherwise be flat and poorly drained.

Whilst discussing soil mounding mention

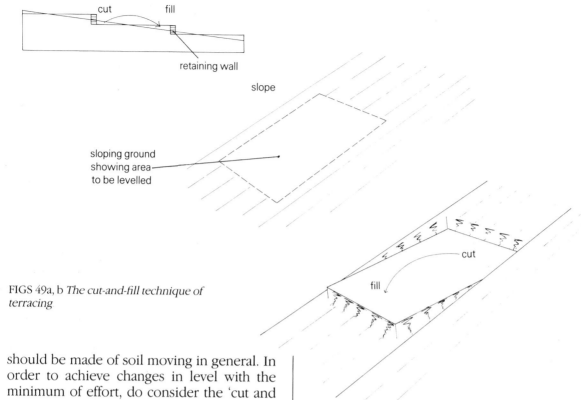

FIGS 49a, b *The cut-and-fill technique of terracing*

should be made of soil moving in general. In order to achieve changes in level with the minimum of effort, do consider the 'cut and fill' technique. Fig 49 shows how this system works. As a result of this, drainage may be necessary

Trees, shrubs and herbaceous plants

More detailed information on plants and specific combinations are discussed in chapter 7. Here the overall design is considered, and for this purpose it is assumed that you are planning a garden which is empty of planting. Deciding which plants to include in your garden and preparing detailed planting plans is one of the most time consuming planning operations. There are after all so many plants to choose from and so many restraints; suitability to the soil, height, flower colours, spread, leaf shape, tolerance of shade, speed of growth, and so on. Faced with a vacant garden one can easily be daunted by this planning and be tempted to go to the garden centre and pick up what happens to be looking good at the time. A grave mistake, and you still have to decide

where to put them and discover that perhaps you haven't chosen the right plant for the right reason. It is helpful to first write out a check list of all your favourite plants that would be *suitable* to include in the garden, or garden area you are considering. Divide the list into trees, shrubs, herbaceous and ground cover plants. This 'suitability' list is often a very encouraging start. You must remember to omit the obvious plants, such as acid lovers if you have chalk, large trees if the garden is too small for them, and add more detailed constraints as you progress. The same exercise is equally valuable if you are planning just one border. This 'basic suitability list' or 'pool' of plants to choose from can then be used to form the framework of your planting design.

A carefully and most successfully sited statue

A formal semi-circular seat surrounded by skilful planting

A traditional statue acts as the focal point in a formal garden, with Geranium sanguineum *var lancastriense* in the foreground

FIG 50 *Planting detail, using plants from 'suitability list'*

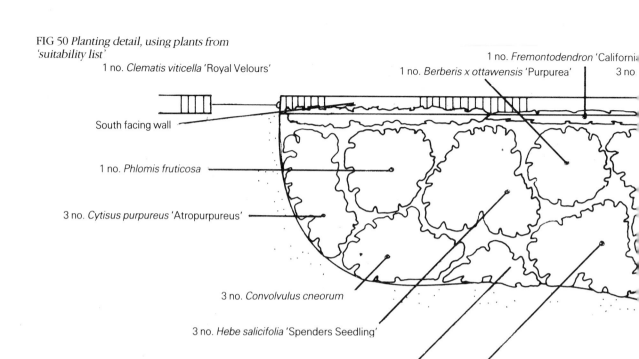

1 no. *Clematis viticella* 'Royal Velours'

1 no. *Fremontodendron* 'Californi.

1 no. *Berberis x ottawensis* 'Purpurea'

3 no

South facing wall

1 no. *Phlomis fruticosa*

3 no. *Cytisus purpureus* 'Atropurpureus'

3 no. *Convolvulus cneorum*

3 no. *Hebe salicifolia* 'Spenders Seedling'

3 no. *Helianthemum* 'Red Dragon'

3 no. *Caryopteris x clandonensis* 'Heavenly Blue'

3 no. *Sedum spectabile* 'Brilliant'

3 no. *Acanthus mollis latifolius*

3 no. *Rosa rubrifoli.*

1 no. *Artemisia* 'Powis Castl

1 no. *Skimmia japo.*

SELECTION OF FAVOURITE PLANTS SUITABLE FOR THE AREA TO BE PLANTED (Fig 50)

*Plants actually used in planting scheme

South-facing wall plants:
Campsis x tagliabuana 'Madame Galen'
*Clematis – in variety
Fremontodendron 'California Glory'
Jasminum officinale
Solanum crispum 'Glasnevin'
Vitis coignetiae
Climbing roses
*Wisteria (white)

Medium and high planting for back of border:
Abelia x grandiflora
x *Stranvinia* 'Redstart'
Deutzia 'Magicien'
Ceanothus 'Delight'
Kolkwitzia amabilis
Phormium cookianum 'Tricolor'
Photinia x fraseri 'Robusta'
Pittosporum 'Garnettii'
*Syringa – in variety
Hibiscus – in variety
Berberis x

Shade loving plants:
*Aucuba
Lonicera peryclymenum 'Serotina'
Mahonia japonica
Choisya ternata
Cotoneaster microphyllus cochleatus
Euonymus fortunei 'Variegata'
Geranium endressii 'A. T. Johnson'
Philadelphus coronarius 'Aurea'
Bergenia
Epimedium rubrum
Euphorbia robbiae
Sarcococca hookerana digyna
Helleborus foetidus
Skimmia 'Fragrans'
Viburnum tinus cultivars
Viburnum davidii
Hemerocallis – in variety
*Hostas – in variety
*Vinca minor – in variety

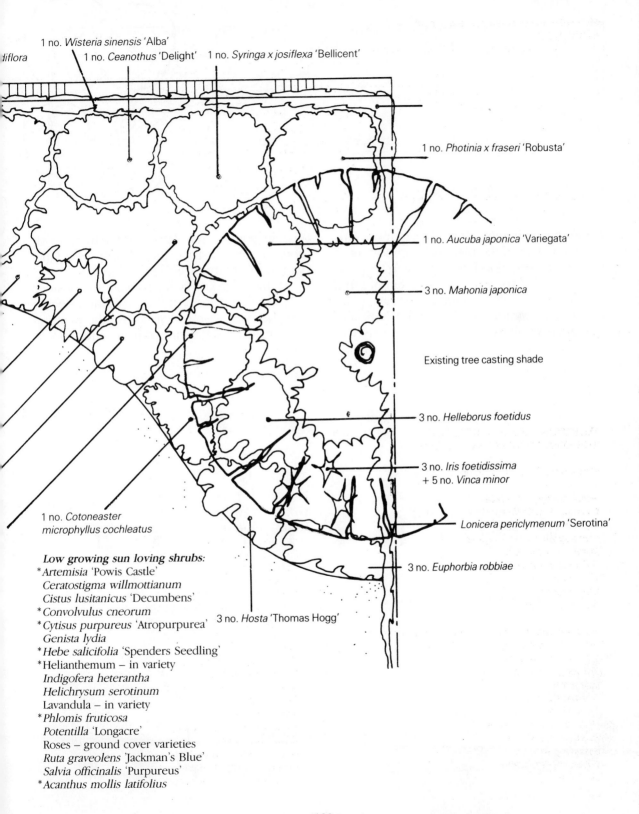

1 no. *Wisteria sinensis* 'Alba'

...iflora

1 no. *Ceanothus* 'Delight'

1 no. *Syringa x josiflexa* 'Bellicent'

1 no. *Photinia x fraseri* 'Robusta'

1 no. *Aucuba japonica* 'Variegata'

3 no. *Mahonia japonica*

Existing tree casting shade

3 no. *Helleborus foetidus*

3 no. *Iris foetidissima*
+ 5 no. *Vinca minor*

Lonicera periclymenum 'Serotina'

1 no. *Cotoneaster
microphyllus cochleatus*

3 no. *Euphorbia robbiae*

Low growing sun loving shrubs:
*Artemisia 'Powis Castle'
Ceratostigma willmottianum
Cistus lusitanicus 'Decumbens'
*Convolvulus cneorum
*Cytisus purpureus 'Atropurpurea'
Genista lydia
*Hebe salicifolia 'Spenders Seedling'
*Helianthemum – in variety
Indigofera heterantha
Helichrysum serotinum
Lavandula – in variety
*Phlomis fruticosa
Potentilla 'Longacre'
Roses – ground cover varieties
Ruta graveolens 'Jackman's Blue'
Salvia officinalis 'Purpureus'
*Acanthus mollis latifolius

3 no. *Hosta* 'Thomas Hogg'

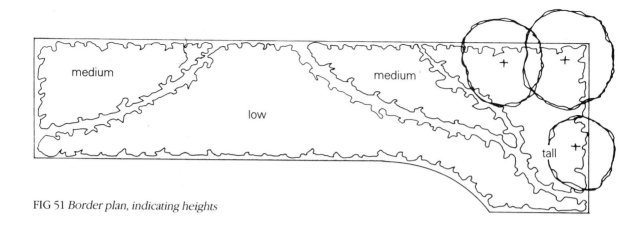

FIG 51 *Border plan, indicating heights*

Designing by height It might seem obvious that the height of the planting is important, it is also a very good way to start on the positioning of your plants. For example in a shrub border, before putting down any plant names do a simple outline of the high and low areas as illustrated in Fig 51. This will enable you to get the essential framework correct and restrict the choice of plants within those areas of the borders.

At this stage you will also want to consider the shape and form of the plants and decide whether you wish to harmonise the planting or create a contrasting foliage effect. Here

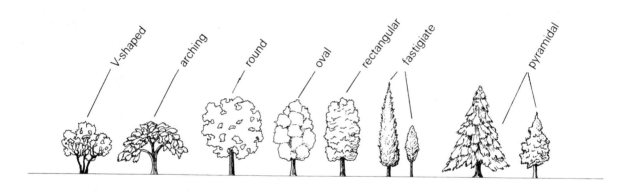

FIG 52 *Diversity of shape and form in trees and shrubs*

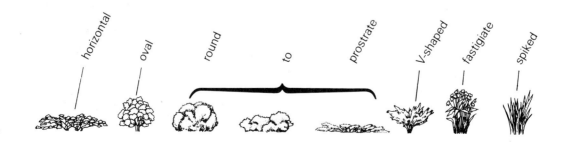

one can consider the range of foliage textures with bold leaves of hostas in contrast with grass-like foliage of hemerocallis (day lilies), and arundinaria (bamboo), or the pinnate leaves of mahonia. Having arrived at the overall design effect you require there are a few other important considerations.

Colour in the planting scheme The amount of vivid colour one uses in a garden is very much a personal choice. However, the following notes may be useful to avoid an unplanned colour display and the possibility of a well arranged planting scheme being ruined by one coloured plant clashing with another and detracting from the scheme as a whole. Firstly, there are some wonderful shades of green which can be very effective without including any colour at all. Grey foliage plants are extremely useful, not only for their cool tranquil effect, but also because adjacent colours become stronger compared with them. The repetition of some plants throughout the garden will also add real strength to a design. Grey foliage is again particularly useful. Repeating a brightly coloured flower will also prevent it from becoming an isolated focal point. Greens and reds together will tend to make colours appear much brighter. Red is a difficult colour to use as it tends to dominate. Similarly, pure white flowers are also difficult to blend with other plants as they tend to have a very contrasting effect. Off-white or cream is much easier. Some of the prettiest gardens are those where soft, subtle colouring has been used.

Although flowers and autumn colour can be planned to provide interest throughout the year, it is generally better to plan one border for one period of the year, and another for another, rather than over mix the flowering periods, resulting in the planting never looking really effective at any one time of the year.

Ground-smothering When we think of plants which suppress weeds, we tend automatically to consider those plants generally termed 'ground cover'. These are plants that grow horizontally, spreading or creeping along the ground. However, when you are

FIG 53 *Overall effect based on plan in Fig 51*

very tall

tall

medium

planning your planting design it is worth considering all those shrubs, large and small, that cast so much shade that weeds are unable to survive beneath them, for example, *Cornus alba* varieties, *Viburnum plicatum* 'Mariesii', *Mahonia japonica, Prunus laurocerasus* 'Zabeliana', all have this effect. These larger shrubs are in fact superior in many ways to the lower-growing ground covers, in which larger perennial weeds occasionally develop; a certain amount of weeding work is usually needed. Having said this, the ground-smothering effect of the larger plants of course only develops once they are reaching maturity. The weed problem is at its worst in the early years of the development of the planting scheme and it is therefore desirable to have a balance of ground covers, planting quick growing (even short lived) low ground cover to be effective in the early years, eg *Euphorbia robbiae, Stachys olympica, Lamium maculatum* varieties. These plants may die out naturally or simply be suppressed by the larger plants in due course.

Planting density is another difficult area and one which tends generally to be dictated more by the garden owner's patience rather than rigid horticultural guidelines. All too often one sees gardens packed with plants: large shrubs 2ft (600mm) apart, trees only 2m apart and so on, all to gain an instant effect. It is of course possible to do this satisfactorily provided that those plants that will be retained in later years have been planned in their correct positions and that one is prepared to remove the temporary plants when they start to compete with the main planting. We tend to plant out gardens aiming at a good effect within 3–5 years and in many respects this is a very short period and open to some criticism (but nothing like the criticism from an impatient client!). Good maintenance is really the key to the success of any garden. (Refer to chapter 6). The real art is the knowledge of when to prune, when to move plants that are becoming too large and to combine colours and shapes successfully. The initial design structure must of course be

right at the outset. Also, the long-term plants and the short-lived ones should be in the right positions to avoid gaps initially, and to avoid these developing later as the garden matures.

Finally, above all, your planting design and choice of plants must not only survive but flourish in the garden if it is to look good. There is no point in nurturing a plant that in its wild state grows in moist shady conditions and expecting it to look well in bright sunlight, and perhaps even in unsuitable soil. The knowledge of selecting those plants which will flourish in different situations wet or dry, shady or exposed, is of vital importance and we will discuss it in great detail later in chapter 7.

TRANSFERRING THE DESIGN TO THE GROUND

The joy of having prepared a well and accurately planned garden, as a scale drawing, is the setting out and reality on the ground. You will need, ideally, some setting out pegs 5cm sq × 30–45cm (2in sq × 12–18in), but garden canes are quite adequate at this stage; the simplest and most accurate way to set about the task of positioning the major points, and corners of the main garden features, is to follow the same principles used to undertake the garden survey (chapter 2) ie making a base line across the plot and measuring from various points along it.

Mark up a copy of your plan, whilst inside in the warm, with the principal dimensions to save unnecessary time outside and possible mistakes. You will probably be relieved to learn that however well you have done your planning work, when you come to measure it out on the ground something invariably does not fit. However professional, not only garden designers, but even architects and engineers cannot escape the inevitable unforeseen differences. It is at this stage advisable to look over the garden you have set out and be critical. Perhaps make some alterations where something is quite obviously wrong, but beware, have confidence in your design. Sometimes on initial setting out, areas can seem smaller or larger than they will actually appear when constructed and the planting has grown to give the vertical height and scale. (If it looks good on paper it more than likely will look good on completion.)

The construction of the garden from this point is essentially a matter of craftsmanship and attention to good, sound constructional and planting techniques.

THE INHERITED GARDEN

There was a time when the family home was lived in for a generation or more. Today, with a general increase in mobility, many people move houses several times within a few years. We are far more prepared to accept the necessity to move to find the right job or be posted to another area. We are, therefore, at every house move inheriting not only a new house that needs to be re-decorated, but also a garden. The real difference between the move to the new house and the new garden is quite simple. People leave their personal possessions, the plants they have collected in their gardens; this can be a benefit, but also a major problem. There may be excellent features in the garden which you have inherited, but, inevitably, much you will wish to change. Looking back at the gardens we have done in recent years, remarkably few were in fact gardens which had to be designed completely from scratch. Sometimes a change has been requested simply for the sake of change, or perhaps a change of circumstances, for example the family grows up and leaves home, the vegetable garden is too big, the herbaceous border prone to weeds and ineffective, shrub borders overgrown. We are actually most often brought in to sort out the inherited garden and particularly to solve many daunting problems, frequently involving extensions to the house or installation of swimming pools or tennis courts. (We discussed the 'inherited garden' in general terms in chapter 2.) In this section, however, we will look in more depth at

specific areas and how to adapt certain parts of the garden.

First impressions of the garden you inherit are well worth jotting down: note your likes and dislikes at the earliest opportunity. If this is not done we all tend to become accustomed to our surroundings, accepting them as the norm, and you may miss the opportunity to make good improvements.

It may be that you have had the garden for some time and have simply become bored and dissatisfied with it; perhaps we can help in this section to look at ways of improving it.

Criticising your garden

Criticising your own garden can be a very useful exercise in establishing the important areas that could be improved. Unfortunately, it is not always easy to do. You may have a garden which is generally good, everyone tells you it is lovely, but you know somehow that it is not quite the garden you would like it to be. The problem is in identifying exactly where improvements can be made. You may have been to gardens open to the public, admired them, but not known on arriving home, why yours does not have the same appeal or atmosphere.

In Chapter 2 (p29) we list the majority of the features that could be included in the garden. Going through this list may help in identifying any short-falls particularly with reference to the gardens that you have visited. You may have noticed a number of definite features such as focal points, statues, terracotta pots, sundials and seats – could you perhaps do more in this way? Think too of the way you are using your garden. Is there sufficient room for sitting out and entertaining, would you use your garden more if you could make space for different activities? Does the garden feel a little cramped and would a greater feeling of space be an improvement? Creating the illusion of space can often be achieved by dividing the garden and restricting the view. Surprisingly, a totally open, empty garden may appear smaller than it is, particularly if it is a long narrow garden.

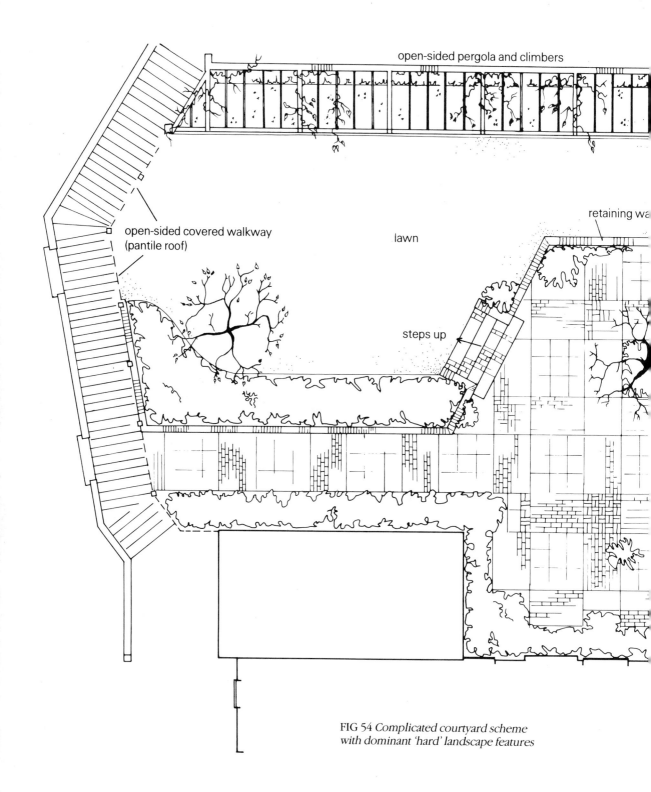

open-sided pergola and climbers

open-sided covered walkway
(pantile roof)

lawn

retaining wa

steps up

FIG 54 *Complicated courtyard scheme
with dominant 'hard' landscape features*

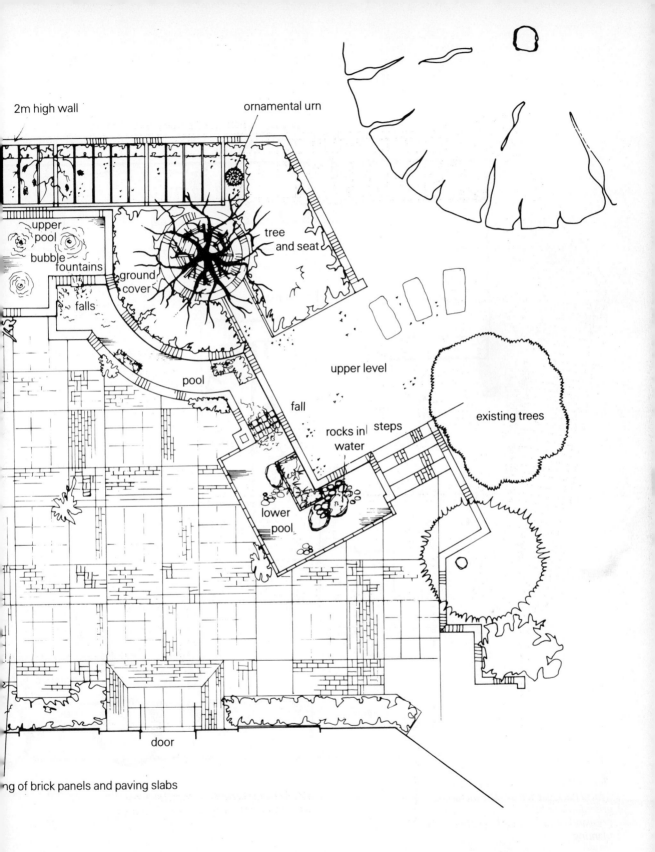

2m high wall

ornamental urn

upper
pool

bubble
fountains

tree
and seat

ground
cover

falls

pool

upper level

fall

existing trees

rocks in
water

steps

lower
pool

door

ng of brick panels and paving slabs

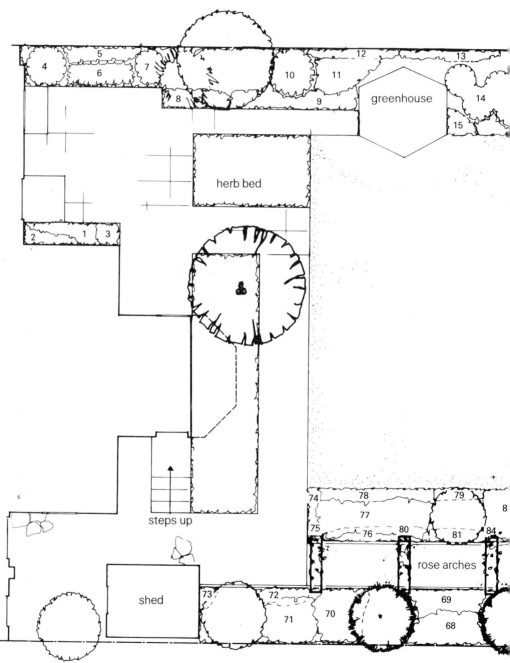

4
5
6
7
8
10
11
12
13
14
15
9
greenhouse

herb bed

2 1 3

steps up

74 78 79
77
75 80 81 84
76

8

rose arches

73 72 69
71 70 68

shed

FIG 55 *More general scheme showing typical back-garden design, including greenhouses, herb bed, vegetable plot, pool and terrace, linked together by the planting*

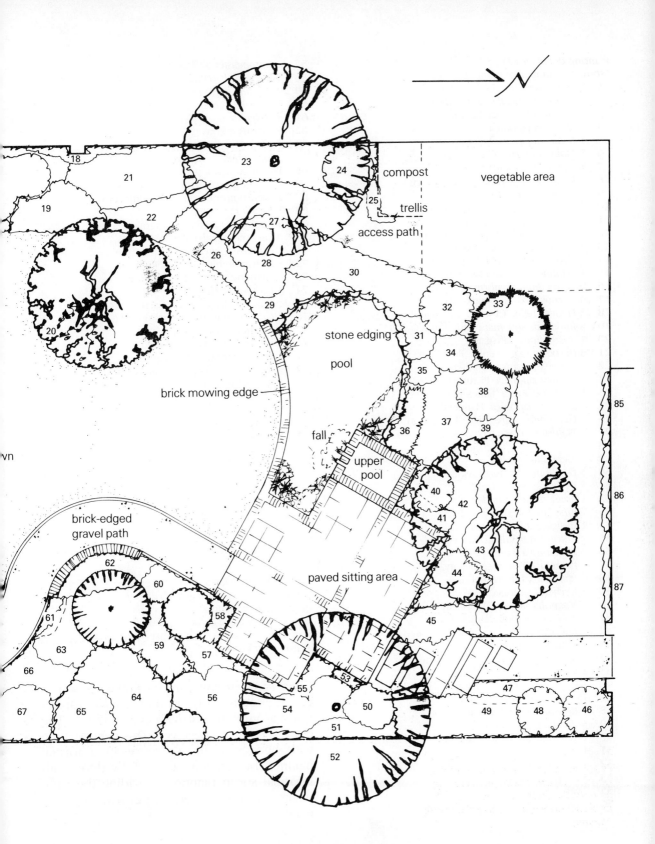

N

18
21
19
22
23
24
compost
vegetable area
25
trellis
27
access path
26
28
30
29
32
33
stone edging
31
pool
34
35
38
20
37
39
brick mowing edge
36
85
fall
upper
pool
40
42
brick-edged
gravel path
41
43
62
60
44
vn
58
45
61
59
63
57
66
64
56
55
53
67
65
54
50
47
51
49
48
46
52

117

Planting details for Fig 55
(showing number of plants used)

1	5	*Hemerocallis* 'Pink Damask'
2	1	*Clematis viticella* 'Abundance'
3	1	*Skimmia japonica* 'Rubella'
4	1	*Mahonia japonica*
5	1	*Lonicera japonica* 'Repens'
6	5	*Molinia caerulea* 'Variegata'
7	1	*Skimmia japonica* 'Nymans'
8	5	*Epimedium x youngianum* 'Niveum'
9	7	*Alchemilla mollis*
10	1	*Philadelphus coronarius* 'Aureus'
11	3	*Hypericum x moseranum*
12	1	*Hedera colchica* 'Sulphur Heart'
13	1	*Parthenocissus henryana*
14	4	*Hydrangea serrata* 'Grayswood'
15	1	*Daphne cneorum* 'Eximia'
16	9	*Epimedium x rubrum*
17	3	*Cornus alba* 'Elegantissima'
18	2	*Hedera helix* 'Chicago Variegated'
19	3	*Juniperus squamata* 'Blue Carpet'
20	1	*Rose filipes* 'Kiftsgate'
21	3	*Berberis x ottawensis* 'Purpurea'
22	4	*Spiraea japonica* 'Goldflame'
23	3	*Aucuba japonica* 'Picturata'
24	1	*Garrya elliptica* 'James Roof'
25	1	*Lonicera japonica* 'Halliana'
26	6	*Geranium endressii* 'A. T. Johnson'
27	5	*Waldsteinia ternata*
28	3	*Callicarpa bodinieri giraldii*
29	7	*Alchemilla mollis*
30	3	*Escallonia* 'Apple Blossom'
31	5	*Bergenia* 'Silver Light'
32	1	*Amelanchier canadensis*
33	7	*Vinca minor* 'Bowles Variety'
34	1	*Indigofera heterantha*
35	1	*Cotoneaster salicifolius* 'Gnom'
36	7	*Iris sibirica* 'Perry's Blue'
37	3	*Potentilla* 'Primrose Beauty'
38	1	*Photinia x fraseri* 'Robusta'
39	1	*Berberis temolaica*
40	1	*Magnolia stellata* 'Water Lily'
41	7	*Acaena microphylla*
42	5	*Euonymus fortunei* 'Emerald Gaiety'
43	3	*Viburnum tinus*
44	7	*Agapanthus* Headbourne Hybrids
45	2	*Viburnum tinus*
46	1	*Ceanothus* 'A. T. Johnson'
47	15	*Cyclamen hederifolium*
48	1	*Kolkwitzia amabilis* 'Pink Cloud'
49	3	*Photinia glabra* 'Rubens'
50	1	*Mahonia japonica*
51	1	*Pyracantha* 'Orange Glow'
52	1	*Gleditsia triacanthos* 'Sunburst', standard
53	3	*Fuchsia* 'Chillerton Beauty'
55	7	*Stachys olympica* 'Silver Carpet'
56	3	*Philadelphus* 'Manteau d'Hermine'
57	2	*Cotoneaster salicifolius* 'Gnom'
58	5	*Iris pallida dalmatica* 'Variegata'
59	9	*Hemerocallis* 'Golden Chimes'
60	3	*Santolina chamaecyparissus*
61	3	*Helianthemum* 'Wisley White'
62	5	*Cytisus x kewensis*
63	3	*Cistus* 'Silver Pink'
64	2	*Elaeagnus x ebbingei* 'Limelight'
65	1	*Acer griseum*
66	3	*Potentilla dahurica* 'Abbotswood'
67	1	*Viburnum plicatum* 'Grandiflorum'
68	1	*Escallonia* 'Iveyi'
69	5	*Euonymus fortunei* 'Emerald Gaiety'
70	3	*Fuchsia magellanica* 'Versicolor'
71	1	*Cotinus coggygria* 'Royal Purple'
72	3	*Helianthemum* 'Wisley Pink'
73	3	*Hemerocallis* 'Golden Chimes'
74	3	*Lavandula* 'Hidcote'
75	1	*Rosa* 'Madame Alfred Carriere' (climber)
76	7	*Geranium wallichianum* 'Buxton's Variety'
77	3	*Capanula portenschlagiana*
80	1	*Rosa* 'Dublin Bay' (climber)
81	3	*Ajuga reptans* 'Atropurpurea'
82	3	*Hebe brachysiphon* 'White Gem'
83	5	*Festuca glauca*
84	1	*Rose* 'Handel' (climber)
85	1	Cherry 'Morello' (fan trained)
86	1	Apple Cox's Orange Pippin (espalier)
87	1	Apple James Grieve (espalier)

FIG 56 *Design using a variety of separate features and areas: formal herb garden, ornamental fountain garden, pergola, Japanese courtyard garden, and small vegetable/fruit garden. The conservatory is a converted Victorian glasshouse*

Given some divisions, restricting the view can give the impression that an extensive garden is just around the corner – even if it isn't. The eye can easily be deceived. This may be done with hedges, trellis or fence in a formal manner, but equally successfully done with informal shrub planting providing the right plants are used to form a permanent dense effect.

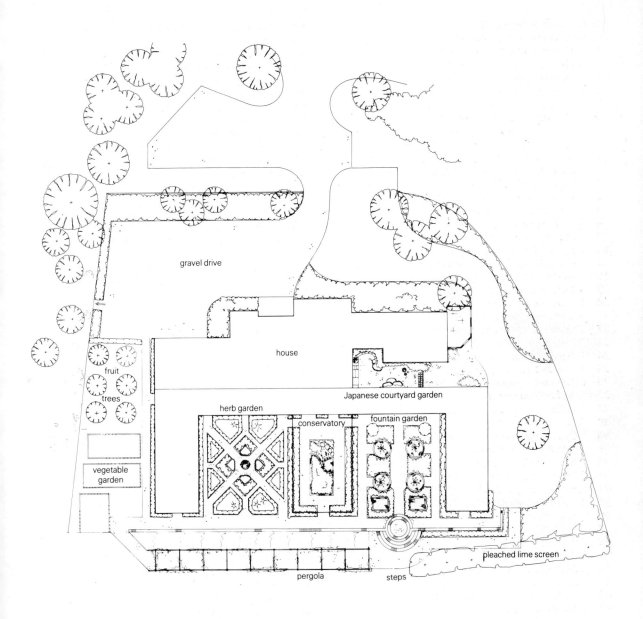

gravel drive

house

Japanese courtyard garden

fruit

trees

herb garden

conservatory

fountain garden

vegetable garden

pleached lime screen

pergola

steps

You may well have inherited the very basic old-style house garden, such as shown in Fig 57 which is really offering very little apart from its lawn as a play area and a vegetable garden. Fig 58 shows the same plot incorporating the best of existing features, but adding considerable interest and potential use to the owner. The same design principles would be used in amending an existing garden as would have been used had you started from scratch. The first part of this chapter details how to go about this exercise. You may well find that your existing garden does include most of your requirements, but their arrangement is poor, the sitting area perhaps too far from the house, or shaded for part of the day. Certainly the area immediately adjacent to the house, particularly the

119

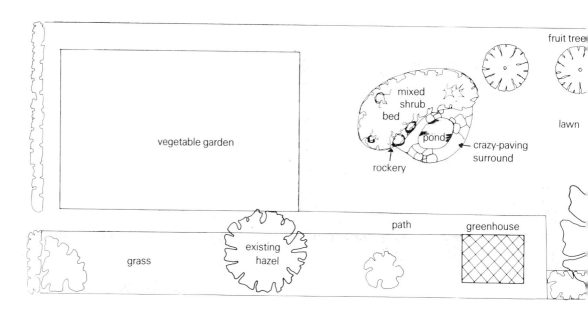

FIG 57 Unimaginative, high-maintenance garden with narrow, peripheral planting beds and few features

FIG 58 The same plot, redesigned to create interest and be labour saving

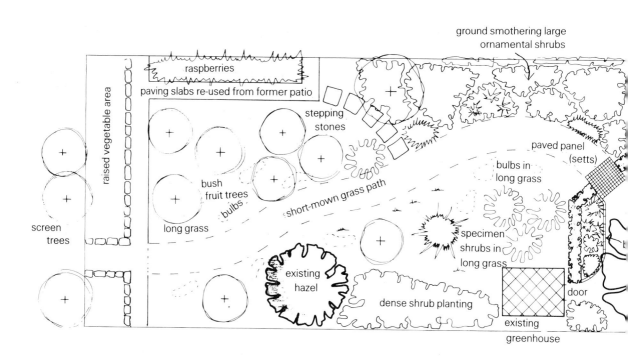

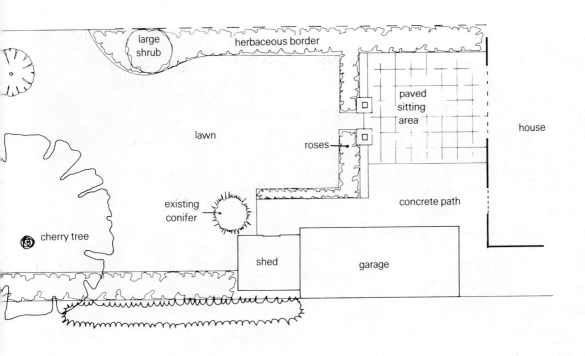

large
shrub

herbaceous border

paved
sitting
area

house

lawn

roses

concrete path

existing
conifer

cherry tree

shed

garage

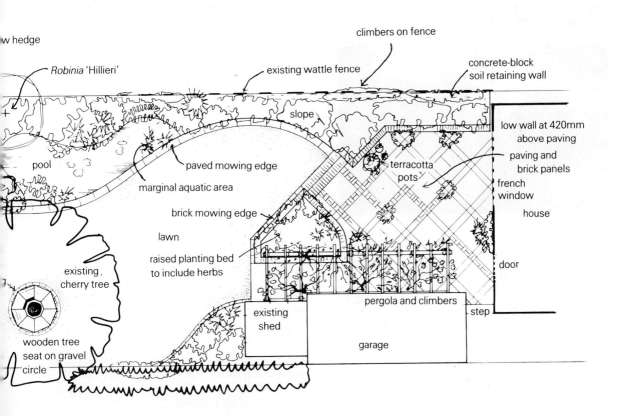

climbers on fence

w hedge

Robinia 'Hillieri'

existing wattle fence

concrete-block
soil retaining wall

slope

low wall at 420mm
above paving

pool

paved mowing edge

terracotta
pots

paving and
brick panels

marginal aquatic area

french
window

brick mowing edge

house

lawn

raised planting bed
to include herbs

door

existing,
cherry tree

pergola and climbers

step

wooden tree
seat on gravel
circle

existing
shed

garage

An award winning scheme constructed by Hillier Landscapes shows the use of bubble fountains, old mill wheels and multi-coloured bricks

The gentle rolling landscape viewed from over a ha-ha in this garden illustrates the subtleness required for successful soil mounding

This small garden area shows a wide diversity of foliage contrasts

living room and the kitchen should form a direct link to the garden. This is a critical area and you want to be able to look out of the house and be encouraged to venture out and use the garden.

We have mentioned the importance of considering the possible features to include in the garden, but discretion must of course be shown as it is quite easy to go too far. Is your garden too fussy, are there just too many things in it, making it too busy and restless? It may be that there are too many conflicting ideas; a formal pool and an informal pool, rockery, rose garden, heather garden, etc, all of which do not satisfactorily blend together. The overall theme must work and perhaps some simplification would be beneficial.

If you are a keen gardener or plantsman you know how difficult it is *not* to buy plants when you see something interesting, and then you have the problem of finding where to put them. Over a period of time the garden can become cluttered and bitty. Your original colour schemes possibly become eroded; a careful look and re-arrangement of the plants from a colour point of view is the only real solution.

Plants rarely stop growing. They may slow down in maturity, but they are always gradually striving to increase their plot, this is after all what makes gardening so fascinating. However, your garden will gradually become overgrown unless the appropriate action is taken on a regular basis to maintain the garden in peak condition. From time to time it is necessary for good positive criticism of how the planting has grown, and this should be followed by some substantial (even drastic) action and re-arrangement. This can often work wonders.

If you have any photographs of the garden taken a few years previously these will help to identify the major changes. Because we are living with the garden year in year out, we tend not to notice these changes and photographs will immediately point them out. There remains just one further and important possibility as to why you may feel unhappy with your garden – you may be bored with it. Why not make a change? No need necessarily to change the whole garden, but come up with something new that no one has ever seen before! Brighten up the dull shady corner, move things around a bit. We do it inside our houses, why not outside?

SOLVING THE PROBLEMS OF THE INHERITED GARDEN

The Wilderness of neglect

The garden that has been neglected can be a real source of inspiration – to use Estate Agents' jargon 'house (or garden) in need of further renovation and offering enormous scope for improvement', for which of course you need to fork out an extra few thousand pounds. But like the house, the garden too should have amongst the scrubby plants and weeds, a few old trees and large shrubs to give the sense of character and maturity that only time can provide. In 'house' terms these might be considered as the beams or period details. Even an old tree stump could be furnished with climbers.

The important thing to avoid is wading in 'with machete in hand' desperate to tidy the place up a bit. A careful inspection of the plants to identify those that are important and if there are a number of them, labelling them with a hanging label, raffia or some such material will be most helpful. As mentioned earlier in this chapter when surveying the garden for replanting it is better to keep anything remotely suitable for retention at this stage. Some plants may be small enough to move and can be used elsewhere – chapter 2 (p29), these must also be labelled and this can best be done in the summer when the identification of the trees and shrubs will, of course, be much easier. It is quite likely that there will be self-sown shrubs and trees such as buddleia, willow (shrubby sallows) and birch, which are more difficult to distinguish from their garden varieties when dormant. Unfortunately, it is inevitable that some very good or unusual shrubs will be either grow-

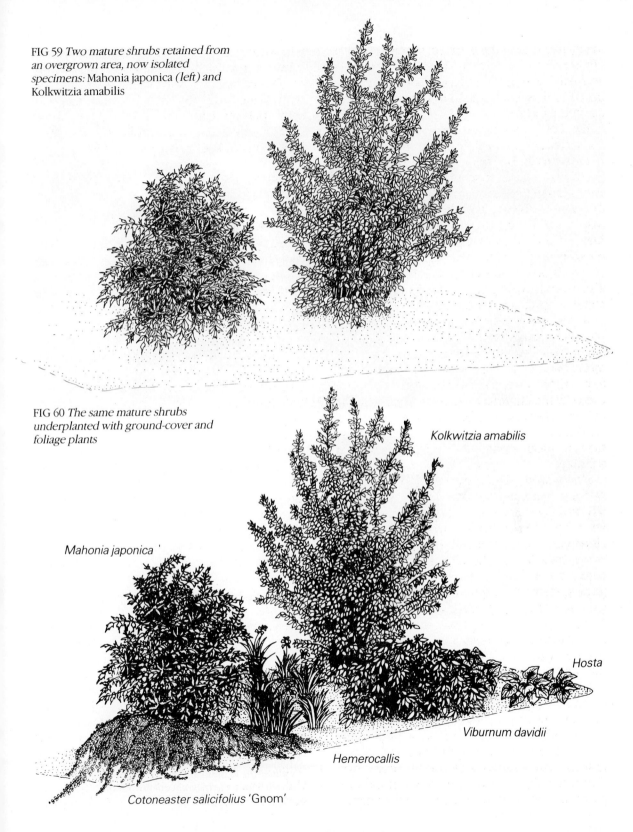

FIG 59 *Two mature shrubs retained from an overgrown area, now isolated specimens:* Mahonia japonica *(left) and* Kolkwitzia amabilis

FIG 60 *The same mature shrubs underplanted with ground-cover and foliage plants*

Kolkwitzia amabilis

Mahonia japonica

Hosta

Viburnum davidii

Hemerocallis

Cotoneaster salicifolius 'Gnom'

A lush planting of green and white – other colours would spoil the effect. The cow parsley heads of Giant hogweed (Heracleum mantagazzianum) are the dominant plant

Delightfully soft, subtle colouring in a long border

Although only hardy in the mildest localities the Echium at Ventnor Botanic Garden shows the magnificent flower and foliage structures plants can offer

ing into each other or over-shadowing one another, and will have to be sacrificed. You will need, therefore, to weigh up the merits of each, particularly the life-span of the shrubs in question. Effort should be made to retain worthy mature (or maturing) shrubs that are widely spaced, to form the 'bones' of a new planting scheme. This is often possible by removing (and often resiting) several less desirable shrubs. The isolation of the exposed specimens will help to show their shape and form in contrast with their neighbours and the new planting. The mature shrubs will give the new planting scheme an instant effect which otherwise would not be possible.

If your garden, or part of it, is very shaded by trees, it may be necessary to remove some, but do bear in mind that good tree surgery can reduce the shading effect without losing the trees or affecting their beauty. This is dealt with in chapter 6. Having labelled all the plants you wish to retain, then and only then, a ruthless frame of mind is necessary to deal with the rest.

Only too often we encounter the relatively recently planted garden that has been over-planted, badly arranged, full of good young specimens, including perennials. In this case a note of all suitable plants should be made for inclusion in a new planting scheme. However, be prepared to throw away or give to friends those plants that do not fit the scheme as to include them could be detrimental to the overall effect you are trying to achieve.

The unfortunate paving

Everyone's tastes in colour and materials are different. In the garden one of the more expensive 'ground covers' is paving. Quite frequently a problem crops up where a large expanse of paving has been laid by the previous owner, but it is either multi-coloured, bright pink, or has a poor finish to it, otherwise it may be perfectly well laid and structurally very sound. It might even be tarmacadam or concrete. Rather than cart it

all the way to the tip, there are some other options which might be considered. If the area is not to be the main sitting out area, where tables and chairs are likely to be used, loose shingle could be spread over it to form an attractive and weed-free surface (it would require edging). Alternatively the surface could first be sprayed with tar followed by a blinding of small pea-shingle. Plants look particularly good spreading over gravel and pockets could be excavated for additional planting within this surface.

If you have inherited some reasonably good paving, but not quite attractive enough for the main sitting area, lifting these and re-using the slabs, incorporating brick panels could be considered. Even if you do decide to repave the whole thing, the slabs could be used elsewhere, perhaps in the vegetable garden and, at worst, broken up as hardcore for use as foundations, even this can be a money-saver.

Boundary problems

Unfortunately, every garden owner seems to have problems with garden boundaries at one time or another. On moving into a new house and garden there is inevitably some form of conflict, often over ownership of the hedges, who cuts the top and to what height? That aside, if you do inherit a garden that is overlooked, or you wish to screen an unsightly more distant object, the right choice of planting can be a problem (see also Screening, pp200–6).

If you have a long narrow garden, providing it is not too exposed and you do not wish to have a timber fence all the way round, consider the option of using plastic coated chain-link fencing, which although unsightly when used on its own, it can be attractively planted with ivy. The ivy (*Hedera*) will rapidly cover the chain-link fence, never to be seen again. Use the *Hedera helix* varieties for hardiness and speed of growth. To add a little colour, try some variegated varieties, such as 'Goldheart'. In this way a very thin evergreen hedge can quickly be achieved

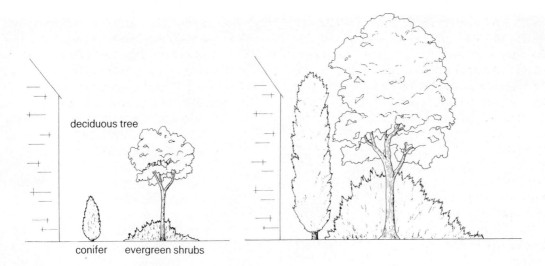

FIG 61 *Coniferous screen with deciduous
trees and evergreen shrubs*

without loss of space.

Possibly the most common enquiry made
to our Landscape Department is by the
customer who wants to plant an instant tall
evergreen screen to block out the nextdoor
neighbour. The only sensible answer to this
request is quite simply that it cannot be done.
Large evergreens move extremely badly, they
are committed to a full-leaf exposure with
transpiration all year, unlike the deciduous
plants, and are therefore prone to desiccation. Even in winter when the soil is wet the
plant will be unable to take up adequate
water without a fully established root system
due to the cold. Even plants purchased at
medium size usually suffer a check in growth
when moved. The smaller plant, however,
will settle in more quickly, grow more
rapidly and usually overtake larger transplanted specimens. It is possible to provide
high-level screening instantly for at least the
summer months, using deciduous trees,
these can be transplanted up to 4.5m (15ft)
high without using any specialised moving
equipment. They do need slightly better
securing, as detailed in Chapter 5, p153. Even
in winter the leafless branches will provide a
certain amount of screening. If evergreen
planting is required, a conifer hedge can be
planted as a backcloth and other shade-
tolerant evergreens beneath the canopy of
the deciduous trees. The eventual effect
therefore also has the advantage that the
conifer hedge itself is screened during the
summer, and all year at low level (Fig 61).

You may have inherited a tall coniferous
hedge in your garden, but although doing an
admirable screening job you consider it to be
forbidding, dark and ugly. If there is no space
to screen with the trees and shrubs, try
growing vigorous climbers into it. The
Virginia Creeper (*Parthenocissus quinquefolia*) looks superb in the autumn with its
brilliant red colouring against the dark green
conifer. Similarly in the spring, *Clematis
montana*, or later in the summer *C.
rehderiana*, and vigorous roses such as 'Kiftsgate' or 'Wedding Day', will look particularly
effective. *Vitis coignetiae*, with its large
impressive leaves, will also rapidly grow into
a conifer hedge.

On the newer housing developments we
are often faced with the garden already
completely fenced in, looking extremely
harsh and liable to remain so for a few years
until the garden planting has developed. In

The remains of a dead tree have been retained and planted with golden ivy

these circumstances we would suggest a combination of bold shrub and hedge planting for the long-term effect, interspersed with sections of fence clothed with rapid-growing climbers. The secret is, (a) to provide substantial training wires at the time of planting the climbers, this ensures that they grow rapidly from the word go, and (b) to choose the right climbers for the aspect chosen, particularly for their vigour. In chapter 7, Wall Shrubs and Climbers, the range of climbers are discussed. As stand-by plants for rapid growth and their evergreen nature use *Lonicera japonica* Halliana and *Hedera helix* varieties for the bulk planting.

A garden of weeds

Inevitably, when you inherit your garden you will be faced with a weed problem. What do you do with a herbaceous border that has reverted to weeds, apart perhaps from a few tough plants like golden rod (*Solidago*) which have themselves taken on the form of a weed and become a menace. The weeds will undoubtedly include all the worst enemies, such as ground elder, bindweed and the like. In these circumstances it will be impossible satisfactorily to dig out all the weed roots, and attempts to do so would be unnecessary given the chemicals available to us. Even if there are some plants you would like to keep, their roots will be intertwined with weed roots and unless they are rare, or irreplaceable, it is usually best to sacrifice them in the clearance. Rare plants should be lifted (with weed root) and retained in a suitable corner situation (or container) to await propagation. The only solution to the border itself is to allow a full growing season and to repeatedly spray the area with chemicals such as glyphosate (Roundup or Tumbleweed). (Refer to chapter 6 for detailed information on weed control and mulching.) A little patience is well rewarded to be sure that all weed growth has been killed. Chemical weed control is likewise often essential where a rockery has been allowed to overgrow. Rockeries are so difficult physically to keep

weeded at the best of times. If the area of rock is too large, consider the planting of large ground (and rock) smothering plants that will also smother the weeds, for example *Juniperus squamata* 'Blue Carpet' or *J. horizontalis* varieties, *Cotoneaster microphyllus*, cistus and many many others. For suggestions on ground-smothering plants, refer to Chapter 7, p196. Before planting these subjects however, the areas should be sprayed to get rid of the weeds to allow these plants to establish.

The over-large garden

In the Victorian era if you had a large garden you also had the money to support it. You would have had as many willing and inexpensive gardeners as were necessary. Today it is a different story and whether you like it or not, you must be a 'DIY' enthusiast. Even a smaller garden can become a burden, our circumstances can change and we may no longer have the time to spare, or when we get older we may not have enough energy to do the work. There are many quite simple alterations that can be made to make the garden more labour-saving. Do also consider the possibility of completely redesigning, this could be most useful and produce a very different garden taking account of the new requirements and restrictions. The way you would plan the garden now may be very different from a few years ago, see chapter 2. Obviously you may need to employ a landscaping firm to undertake the more major alterations, but the initial cost will be recovered in the long run by saving on employing labour to deal with the garden when it has got out of hand.

The principal alterations could include reducing the total number of plants or features that need the most attention, ie those that need staking, tying, pruning, and hedges that need frequent trimming. Consider, therefore, doing away with rose beds, herbaceous borders and annual bedding areas. This does not mean that some of these subjects cannot be included, but that they should only be small groups amid more permanent groundcover areas both shrubby and herbaceous.

We would also highly recommend the simplification of your planting into bold groups of one plant rather than a mixed planting, this will reduce maintenance. Not, however, to the extreme of the industrial type of planting we see in and around our towns, but it is much easier to look after a group of one plant than a mixture.

The shrubaceous border, chapter 7, could replace the herbaceous border, or if the herbaceous border is essential it too can be made easier to maintain. A stone mowing edge could be added. As an additional aid, narrow paving may be used to divide the border into sections to give better access. The paving will not show during the summer as the plants spread.

Reduce the area of short-mown lawn. Hours of valuable time and money can be lost to the lawn. (Chapter 2 p12). With the arrival of the ride-on mower much of the short grass could be converted to longer grass areas, and spring bulbs and wild flowers could be added to the garden scene. Cutting will be required far less frequently. Bold planting of large shrub borders goes one step further in terms of reducing the maintenance in the long term. (Chapter 2, p13.) If your area of grass is small, consider the possibility of replacing it with shingle (washed gravel) and sell the mower. (Chapter 4, p96.) If the lawn is large and to replace it all as gravel would be too much, perhaps the introduction of just part of the area in gravel and planting would at least reduce the lawn area.

Make the short-mown lawn easy to mow
The sooner the mowing is done, the sooner the gardening can begin. Many garden lawns, particularly those whose shape was never actually planned, but resulted from the space that was left, will have difficult corners and slopes. Square corners are far from perfect, curves are much easier. If you can take the mower all round the perimeter of the lawn

without stopping more than once or twice, this is ideal. To do away with the corners and difficult slopes will mean more planted area but if ground-smothering plants are used the maintenance will be reduced still further. Trimming the edges is a tedious and lengthy job and the installation of a brick or paved mowing strip will save a lot of effort as the mower cuts all the grass to the edges, and plants which otherwise over-hang the grass are not damaged. This method is also excellent where grass abuts walls.

The paving must be very slightly below the lawn surface to prevent the mower snagging. If the level is wrong the edging problem is back, the grass needs then to be edged to avoid hitting the paving! You might also consider enlarging the mowing edge making it sufficiently wide to become a path.

Further ideas
Finally, in chapter 6, Management and Maintenance, there are a variety of ideas discussed and a 're-think' on how to treat different areas of the garden. For example, would it be prudent to reduce the vegetable garden area to a minimum and perhaps grow a few bush fruit trees, making the smaller vegetable garden area more ornamental?

Problem plants
If you discover that few of your plants are thriving in your inherited garden, the first possible cause that comes to mind is the soil. It may simply be very impoverished, it may be too wet and mostly clay, or dry, chalky and shallow. We discuss the soil in detail in chapter 3 and show how it can be improved. Certainly, the poorly drained garden is a problem, and land drainage should be considered. However, for most other situations the problems are usually those associated with an unsuitable choice of plants for the position. Sun-loving plants will not thrive in the shade and vice-versa. However, for every situation there are groups of plants one can use. In chapter 7 we discuss and list plants suitable for dry shady places, wet sites and

A stone mowing edge is an ease to maintenance and allows the foreground plants to spread freely to their natural shape

hot dry sites. There are also important maintenance considerations (chapter 6) such as the necessity of keeping an adequate grass- and weed-free area around each young tree if successful growth is to be achieved.

Inspection covers

The newly built house and garden area you inherit may often be rather featureless, apart from the rubble and a fine collection of specially positioned inspection covers. They are invariably in the most inconvenient places and, at the time of your arrival, the focal points of the garden. There are several means of disguising these, depending upon their location and the proposed design of the garden. If an inspection cover occurs in an area which you would like to pave there are specially made recessed lids available, and your paving can be cut to size and fit inside a frame. However, even these are still quite obviously visible as the inspection covers that they are. An alternative is actually to lay the paving over the inspection lid and leave the paving unpointed in order that the slabs may be lifted. If necessary, you can often lower the lid by the removal of a layer of the bricks that support it. For other hard landscape areas, such as paths, the inspection covers may be disguised by taking a shingle (washed gravel) path over them but you must remember to make a note on your plan of their positions. Putting a garden ornament over the top is another possibility, but if the site is not ideal for the position of a garden ornament this tends to draw attention to the fact that there is a manhole cover beneath. If possible, the easiest solution is to incorporate them into planting areas (see chapter 7 for lists of suitable spreading plants and diagrams of planting arrangements).

The steep garden

It is lovely to have a magnificent view, but to do so might also involve inheriting a very steeply sloping garden. With such a garden comes the problems of maintenance and plant establishment. Terracing in the garden,

wherever possible, will help enormously. A number of dwarf retaining walls will be less oppressive than high walls, (see also p76). Wood palisading is another option as illustrated in the photograph on p94. However, these are both expensive and are not always practical. On a slightly less steep slope, railway sleepers, if available, can be satisfactory as their bulk holds them in place. The steep, unmowable slope is a problem and in chapter 7, we discuss how ground cover planting can be used and which species are particularly effective. On an extremely steep slope, cultivating the soil may not be possible, and the 'L' shaped planting bays discussed in chapter 7 may be difficult to achieve. In this event we would suggest using 1.8m (6ft) long treated tree stakes to make 1.2m (4ft) long planting bays, the points of the stakes being cut off to make the supporting pegs. To prevent the soil from being washed away a fine-meshed matting material such as 'Terram', or other similar material, should line the base and front side of the planting pocket (Fig 62).

FIG 62 *Planting pockets on a steep bank*

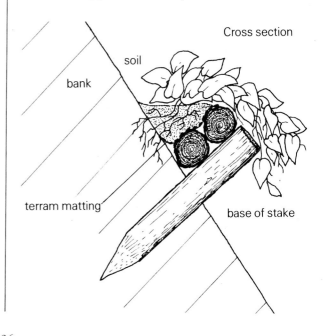

Cross section

soil

bank

terram matting

base of stake

THE SMALLER GARDEN

The small garden, or garden space, is in many ways easier to plan than a larger one. The space restriction automatically rules out many features enabling one to concentrate in more detail, and possibly greater imagination, on the chosen requirements. As the plants used in the small garden space are seen more closely they gain an extra importance and interest, each individual leaf and its shape and texture is noticed rather than the overall shape of the plant alone. The effective use of contrasting foliage, such as hostas, grasses and bamboo, grouped together, can greatly enhance the small garden planting scheme. Floral colour may not in fact be of prime importance. Likewise, the hard landscape materials – bricks, paving slabs, cobbles and pebbles – can almost be treated as individuals.

One of the pitfalls when designing the small garden is trying to achieve too much, including too many features. A good, clear, but simple statement is likely to be more successful. By trying to include too many features the scale can easily go wrong, you

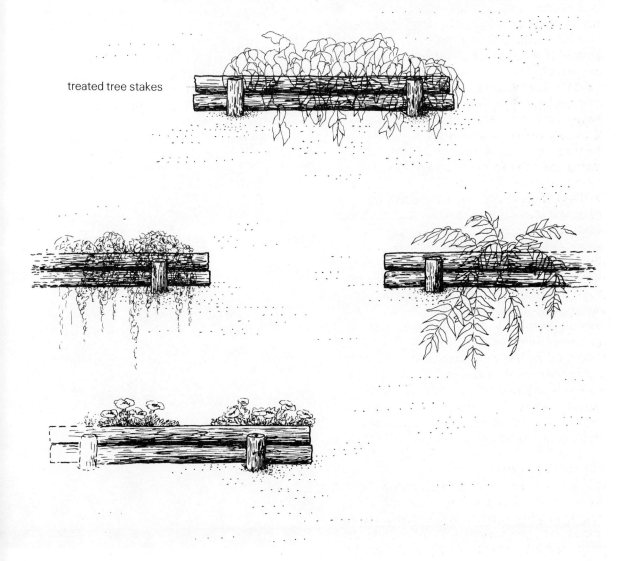

treated tree stakes

A sunny bank clothed with spring bulbs,
Anemone blanda *and* Narcissus
pseudonarcissus

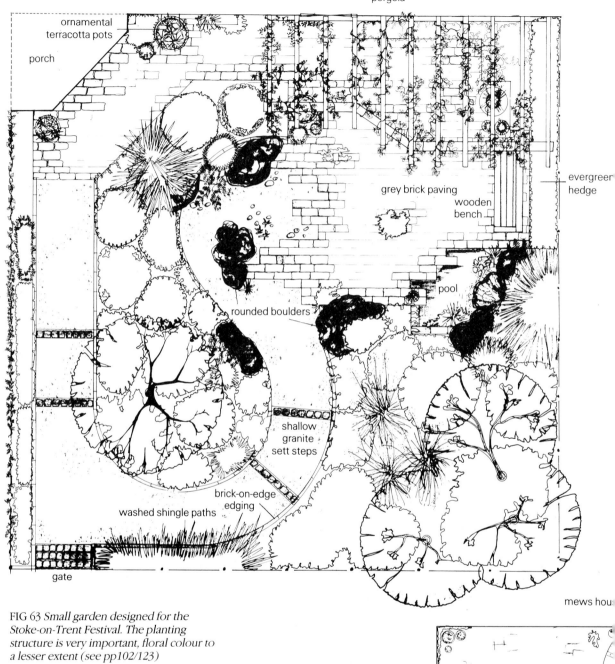

pergola

ornamental
terracotta pots

porch

evergreen
hedge

grey brick paving

wooden
bench

pool

rounded boulders

shallow
granite
sett steps

brick-on-edge
edging

washed shingle paths

gate

mews hou

FIG 63 *Small garden designed for the*
Stoke-on-Trent Festival. The planting
structure is very important, floral colour to
a lesser extent (see pp102/123)

water feature

lead statue feeding wa
into upper pool, and
onto lower cobble-fille

140

cannot scale down a larger garden into a small space, the result would be both a visual and physical mistake. Paths still need to be a comfortable width to walk along and the spaces for chairs, table and people not too cramped. The principles of designing the small garden are entirely the same for any size of garden.

An all-the-year-round floral colour display can be difficult to achieve. In very small gardens even to try to do so may be detrimental resulting in a garden that is never effective at any one season. It is, therefore, better to get the overall structure of planting and foliage right and then concentrate on colour at certain times of the year. For summer, choose individual plants that have a long-flowering season, with the roses for example, 'Ballerina', *Rosa chinensis* 'Mutabilis', in association with Hidcote Lavender, and the common *Alchemilla mollis*, are very satisfactory. Evergreen shrubs, such as mahonia and viburnum provide additional strength.

FIG 64 *Typical small London plot designed to be simple, effective and easily maintained*

Vegetables in the smaller garden

It could be argued that, particularly where space is limited, there is little point in sacrificing ornamental flowering plants for vegetables and fruit which can easily be purchased from a shop. However, some fruit and vegetables are never better than straight from the garden and others are unavailable in the shops. When planning the vegetable areas, try to keep these small, avoiding big gaps when crops are harvested. Many vegetables are themselves ornamental, like the runner bean, (introduced to this country as an ornamental climber, not as a vegetable), which can be trained on trellis, on a fence or on pyramids made from three or four bamboo canes tied together at the top. Other vegetables, such as red lettuce or beetroot can give colour as well as food. The herbs and vegetables could be surrounded by dwarf box or lavender as an edging, all making the vegetable garden more attractive, but adding considerably to the work. Bush fruit trees (grafted on dwarfing root stocks) and espalier fruits, grown against a wall or fence, can be useful and effective, at the same time saving space. With careful planning all can be included in the design with the other ornamental planting.

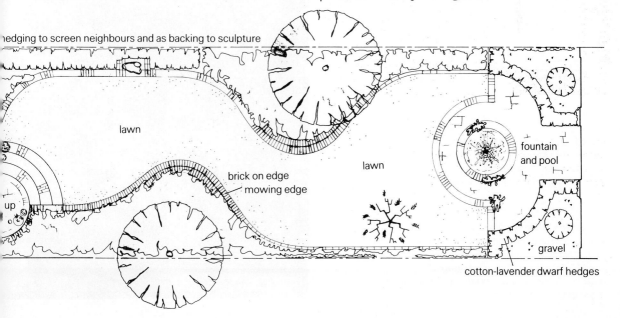

hedging to screen neighbours and as backing to sculpture

lawn

lawn

brick on edge
mowing edge

up

fountain and pool

gravel

cotton-lavender dwarf hedges

The foliage effect is very important to this small garden area

These York stone paving slabs have been arranged in a radial fashion, each stone clearly shown up by the surrounding gravel. Where only a small quantity is required, expensive materials such as York stone become possible

5
PLANTING AND ESTABLISHMENT

To achieve a rapid and successful establishment of trees, shrubs and plants, thorough and generous ground preparation is essential; this cannot be too strongly stressed.

Frequently trees, shrubs or plants may be seen struggling slowly to establish themselves in inhospitable circumstances – a perimeter border which has borne a jungle of scrub growth, eg snowberry (symphoricarpus) with brambles and self-sown sycamore and ash seedlings for many years, will be choked with the roots of the previous plants even after clearance of top growth; invariably stumps of trees or large shrubs are left to regenerate and to become a major competition with new plants or, if dead, encourage the development of the dreaded honey fungus (*Armillaria*) on the rotting wood and the root left in the ground. There is even greater competition for food and moisture in closely mown or rough grass areas: trees or shrubs introduced here with the minimum of preparation will take two or three times as long to establish – if they survive – owing to competition with the grass. Smaller shrubs, roses and herbaceous plants are unlikely to survive at all.

Ideally, in garden circumstances, the entire perimeter border, planting area or island bed should be dug 45cm (1½ft) deep. If chalk or gravel sub-soil is encountered, it should be replaced at least over the site of each tree or shrub with good loamy top-soil. Roots and stumps of previous plantings should be removed in the course of this preparation. To help with large stumps, you can hire a stump-chipping machine which will reduce stumps of most sizes to sawdust, going below ground to a depth of up to 45cm (1½ft). These are now available in several sizes, from hand-pushed small models to tractor-mounted versions requiring generous access and room to manoeuvre.

In practice we often compromise, preparing borders of this nature, after clearance of stumps and as much root as possible, by a combination of rotovation to a 20cm (9in) depth and hand-digging of corners or small areas missed by the rotovator.

Particularly on poor soils, individual sites for trees and shrubs within borders or cultivated areas should be further prepared for a minimum width of 1m (3ft) for shrubs, and 1.2m (4ft) for trees and larger shrubs; introduce well-rotted farmyard manure, good compost and a slow-release fertiliser well mixed with the soil at the base of each 45cm (1½ft) excavation.

PREPARATION OF TURF OR ROUGH GRASS AREAS

Glyphosate weed killer (Roundup or Tumbleweed) is most useful to kill off a turf area prior to rotovation or hand digging. This herbicide, absorbed by green parts of the plant, is a non-residual type and is translocated back through the system of the plant to kill the roots as well as the top growth. Any glyphosate reaching the soil is quickly inactivated and the ground not rendered toxic to a subsequent crop. A month is necessary for the complete action of the glyphosate weed killer during the winter months or in times of low temperature, half this time being adequate during the warmer summer months. The land may then be successfully rotovated and hand dug with deeper preparations for trees and large shrubs, as already suggested. As it rots down, the dead turf adds humus and root fibre to improve the texture and fertility of the soil.

When planting in isolated sites in turf or rough grass, or in any position where the whole area is not cultivated, it is recommended that sites should be not less than 1.2m (4ft) wide cultivated to 0.6m (2ft) for each tree or large shrub and 1m (3ft) wide and 0.5m (1½ft) deep for smaller shrubs. In addition break up sub-soil at the base of the hole. Unless planting is to take place immediately, it is wise to backfill prepared planting holes, particularly on clay or badly drained soils or in areas with a high water table, as in such circumstances they will tend to fill with water and remain so for several weeks in winter. Special pipe drainage from tree pits in clay soils may be necessary – individually dug holes can act as wells or soakaways and kill roots by drowning.

Indeed the complete cultivation of border areas if at all possible is strongly advised – weaving between shrubs or small trees 1.2–2.4m (4–8ft) apart in an area of rough grass or lawn can be frustrating and time consuming for the weekend gardener, with limited time and an appreciation of unimpeded mowing! Furthermore, even with adequate prepara-tion, the grass remains (or re-invades the plant site) as a serious competition taking the lion's share of food and moisture from the soil in the vicinity; inevitably at some point trees and shrubs will suffer impact from the lawn mower, receiving damage to the base of their stems, which at best delays their establishment and at worst can kill them.

However, isolated widely spaced tree or large shrub sites in lawn or rough grass areas must be accepted to some extent in most gardens and here a generous cultivation area should be maintained free of grass and weeds for at least three years following planting.

Generally, small shrubs, roses and herbaceous plants in particular are demanding of nutrients and will quickly deteriorate without them. Well rotted farmyard manure is especially beneficial in the early stages, both as a source of nutrient and as a mulch, particularly when combined with peat or pulverised bark. Again, the best performance from roses and herbaceous plants will only be obtained on sites where there is deep and thorough cultivation in conjunction with generous manuring.

To sum up, the more thoroughly and diligently you prepare and maintain your borders and planting areas the better will be the results in rapid establishment and good consistent growth in the following years.

PLANTING

When to plant

The planting of most hardy subjects can be carried out safely at any time during open weather from late October until March in the case of deciduous open ground trees, shrubs and plants, and from early October until May for evergreen trees and shrubs, provided that proper and careful attention is given after planting. Ideally evergreens and conifers are best planted by the end of December or in April or May when desiccation of foliage is less likely. Open weather in the dead of

Hosta fortunei *'Aureomarginata' makes a*
perfect ground-cover foil for the cutleaf
Japanese maple Acer palmatum *'Nigrum'*

winter is better for planting hardy subjects than a bad day in November or March. Hardy deciduous container or pot grown plants may be planted at any time, providing that watering is attended to and that the pot full of roots is thoroughly moist before planting, whatever the season. They should, however, *never* be planted when frozen.

There are many most desirable trees and shrubs, for instance from California and South America, which are borderline hardy in our climate and will be decidedly vulnerable to frosts and freezing winds while they are still small. For these, spring planting or late summer and early autumn (August–September) is advised. Even then, temporary protection against spring frosts with polythene sheet, hessian or branches of conifer or evergreen hedge positioned around the new plant is usually necessary, and again probably in the following winter if exceptionally severe weather is forecast. If spring planting is missed, establishing half-hardy subjects in late summer/early autumn has its advantages; with free rooting into warm soil the new plant becomes hardened and acclimatised, and better able to withstand the low temperatures of late autumn and hard frosts of winter.

Having attended closely to preparation of ground or planting site and discussed the season of planting you now come to the equally important, if not vital, part of the successful planting operation.

Plant selection and purchase

At the Garden Centre, examine critically those plants which are offered to ensure they are new, fresh, vigorous stock, attractive to look at if not in flower, well furnished in the case of shrubs. Ensure that they are adequately moist with not too many roots through the bottom of the pot. Reject plants which show yellowing or diseased foliage or have premature leaf drop. Reject pot-bound plants or those in pots which are too small for the size of the plant or shrub they contain – such plants are often very top-heavy. Test the weight of the plant – an exceptionally heavy pot may well be waterlogged and contain dead or dying roots, while an unnaturally light-weight pot may have a bone-dry centre, equally to be avoided.

Delivery or collection If you are planning a border or area of your garden or have a professionally-produced planting plan, it is most desirable to place an order with the nurseryman for plants not normally available container grown from the nurseryman's garden centre. Such plants will normally be available between September and April or May, dug from the open ground and root-balled or with roots protected by moist straw or similar material, with an outer cover of plastic or burlap. Allow at least four weeks for delivery, or three weeks for collection from the nursery premises. In the meantime it is well worth preparing beds, borders or individual planting sites in advance, backfilling where necessary. Planting can then proceed on receipt of plants with the minimum of delay.

How to plant

Nursery stock, whether field grown (bare-root or root-balled in soil) or container grown is produced today by most good nurserymen to exacting standards of size and quality (British Standard BS3936). If correctly handled and planted it has every chance of successful establishment.

Bare-root trees, shrubs and roses should reach you individually wrapped, or a number bundled together, with roots packed with moist straw or similar organic material and then enclosed in hessian or plastic film which is secured to the stem of the plant or plants.

If weather conditions allow, plant within a few days of receipt – if delayed longer than about a week, temporary storage or 'laying-in' may be required (see p153). If you are able and ready to proceed with the planting operation, do not unpack the bundle until the hole or holes are ready to receive the plants, and certainly do not expose bare roots to cold winds – it doesn't take long to kill the fine root fibres so essential for quick establishment. As planting proceeds, use the damp packing material and hessian to cover roots after unpacking.

If possible choose a fine calm day for the operation when the soil is in a workable (friable) condition. Hole-out in the prepared site or area, at least 15cm (6in) greater than the width and depth of the root of the tree or shrub to be planted.

Feathered and standard trees will require a stake, ideally round, 5–7cm (2–3in) in diameter treated with preservative and this should be positioned after holing out. It should be driven with a large wooden mallet or 'Drival' so that it is of sufficient depth to be very firm in the sub-soil. Recent research

(Arboricultural Research Note 40/82/ARB 'Tree Staking' by Derek Patch, Forestry Commission Research Station, Alice Holt Lodge, near Farnham, Surrey) advocates the consideration of short stakes (say 0.5 to 0.6m [1½–2ft] above ground) used with a single purpose-made tree tie at the top of the stake, rather than taller stakes supporting the length of a standard stem 1.5m (5ft), as has long been the custom. The short stake method stabilises root and lower part of stem, allowing the remainder of the young trees to sway naturally in the wind and thereby develop a strong wind-resistant trunk (see Fig 65). However, larger heavy, extra heavy standard or semi-

FIG 65a *Correctly staked and secured tree, using the short-stake method. The buckle-type adjustable tie is at the very top of stake, with a nail to prevent it slipping down, and there is a weed-free or mulched area of at least 1m (3ft) in diameter*

FIG 65b *Badly staked tree. Slipping ties will result in a wound at the top of the stake, and there is no weed-free area*

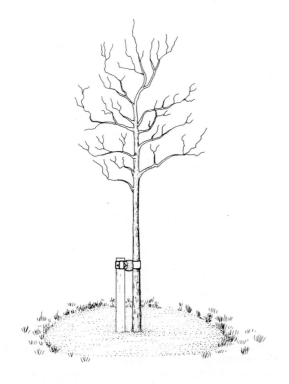

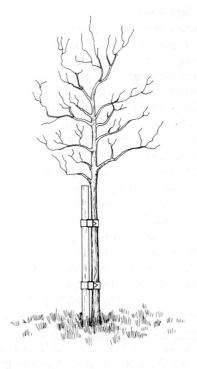

nail

FIG 66 *Detail of tie, with nail through the belt into stake to prevent slipping*

mature trees may require specialised staking or guying. (See also Figs 67 and 68).

Have on hand in a wheelbarrow suitable organic matter, such as coarse peat, pulverised bark or tree planting compost. If the material has no nutrient in it, as is the case with bark or peat, the addition of a compound fertiliser, such as Growmore, or even better a slow release fertiliser, such as Enmag or Vitax Q4 (or rose fertiliser with a slow-release action) can be added to the compost and well mixed in readiness to apply to the open hole and around the roots of the tree or shrub when planting. This is particularly advantageous if the local soil is not of a fine friable nature.

Finally, before positioning the tree or shrub in the hole, trim any roots which appear damaged in lifting. If the shoot system seems large in comparison with the roots, some pruning of the top growth may be beneficial in encouraging establishment of deciduous subjects by reducing the amount of top growth the roots have to support.

The act of planting is perhaps best carried out with an assistant to hold the tree or shrub at about the correct position in the hole so, with backfilling, the soil level will be the same as the previous nursery soil mark on

The rewarding sight of a well planted rowan, Sorbus scalaris

150

the stem. Initially every effort should be made to spread the root system evenly so that it is not congested within the planting hole. Take great care not to position the plant too deeply or too shallowly. As a mixture of fine soil and compost, with fertiliser, is slowly backfilled, the assistant should agitate the plant gently up and down, in order to filter the fine soil and compost between the fibres of the roots. The plant at the correct level should be well firmed in with the full weight of the body behind the heel. Further backfill to the soil mark on the stem and secure tree ties where appropriate.

Root-balled trees, shrubs and conifers should be planted in a similar manner in the prepared border or planting site. First excavate a hole to an estimated correct depth, allowing for a finished level to the nursery soil mark on the stem of the tree or shrub. If there is a depth of loose soil in the planting hole, light firming of this will be necessary before positioning the root-balled plant, in order to avoid settling or subsidence. Be careful also to ensure that any budding or grafting union at the base of the stem of the tree is not buried in. Such a union should normally be 5.0–6.0cm (2–2½in) above the finished soil level. The soil-retaining material (usually hessian or plastic net) should be removed with care, after positioning in the hole. With large heavy root balls, cut away such material from top and sides of the root-ball – if hessian (jute) or biodegradable plastic it can remain under the root-ball to rot down. Firm in thoroughly. Heavy, extra heavy or semi-mature trees are often root-balled (or supplied in large containers) and will require staking or guying, particularly in exposed positions. Double staking with heavy-duty plastic or reinforced rubber hose or ties is a good method which avoids damage to roots by driving in stakes through the root-ball or adjacent to the trunk. An alternative method useful for the largest specimens is the use of multiple wire or hawser guys (usually three) with tree branches protected by a rubber reinforced

hose where contact is made (see Fig 68). Such wire or hawser guys ideally will require U-bolts top and bottom and turnbuckles on each guy which will be secured at the base to a short stake of preserved wood 5×5cm (2×2in) wide and 60cm (2ft) long, driven at an angle towards the tree.

Container grown nursery stock Today a very wide range of trees, shrubs, conifers, roses, herbaceous plants, grasses, ferns and alpine or rock plants are available, container or pot grown for planting the year round, though drought conditions at mid-summer and frost and snow at mid-winter are best avoided. Such plants are today grown in peat or bark-based composts with nutrients added which in time become exhausted. It is very important to ensure when planting that there is a generous supply of fertile fine top soil, mixed say on a 50/50 basis with coarse peat or bark or a good planting compost, well laced with compound or slow-release fertiliser (if not present in the planting compost). The object of this generosity is to encourage the plant to root into the surrounding area and establish itself more rapidly. A mass of pure peat or bark surrounding the root of the container plant is indeed as undesirable as is a planting site of unimproved local soil which may be clayish, gravelly or chalky.

It is equally important to ensure that every container grown plant is adequately moist before it is placed in the ground – after handling a number of plants one soon realises that this or that specimen is unusually light in weight in comparison with others of the same size. The suspect container should be at once submerged in a bucket of water until air bubbles cease – it is usually not good enough to apply water from the top. If the centre of the root-ball has become dry, the peat will remain dry following planting, even in winter, and eventually the plant will fail to establish and die.

As with root-balled plants, firming of loose soil at the base of the planting hole may be necessary to avoid excessive settling.

Remove or cut away the plastic container

and examine the roots of the plant – a specimen in good condition should show a good proportion of active, usually white root on the surface. These should be gently teased away from the shape of the pot in order to encourage them to grow out into the surrounding generously prepared soil. If you find the plant to be excessively pot bound or showing a large quantity of dead or dying inactive roots, reject it or put it aside to be exchanged. Having firmed the plant well into the ground, a light shallow covering of top soil or compost will be necessary. In most circumstances, a mulch of pulverised bark, black polythene or coarse peat is desirable following watering in. Again, as with root-balled trees, where necessary double staking will be appropriate for container grown standard or feathered trees.

Temporary storage – 'laying-in or heeling-in'
Weather in the British Isles, in particular, can be variable and unpredictable during the winter planting season. Nurserymen may despatch your order in good open weather conditions and a lengthy period of frost and snow may well set in before planting is possible. Temporary storage of hardy bare-root and balled deciduous and evergreen trees and shrubs can usually be found in barns, sheds or unheated garages. Slacken ties on shrubs (particularly evergreens) which are tied in bundles, but do not unpack at the root (unless known to be dry – in which event submerge the roots in water before repacking). Equally, good sheltered storage can often be found amid long estab-lished rhododendrons or like large ever-greens. Straw, bracken frond, coarse bark, sawdust or similar material can be used to

FIG 68 *Guying a semi-mature tree*

Skimmia laureola – *a shade-tolerant small shrub with fragrant flowers and leaves; there are male and black-fruited female or hermaphrodite forms*

prevent cold winds desiccating roots and freezing root balls and containers. Stand container grown plants upright, ideally on a soil, peat, sand or other absorbent surface, rather than concrete or stone, and maintain moist, but prevent from freezing as suggested above for root-balled plants.

Perhaps due to building delays or to flooding or other unusual causes, a planting area cannot be made ready for several weeks, even months, following receipt of plants – regrettably this happens all too often – then with such exceptional delays it is desirable to 'lay-in' bare-root trees, shrubs (including roses) and balled evergreens. Take out a trench at least a foot deep in a sheltered cultivated area, say vegetable garden, where there is good workable soil. Unpack bundles and plant temporarily in the trench, spacing each shrub reasonably from its neighbour and spreading roots, filtering fine top soil and peat between the root fibres (as with permanent planting) before 'heeling-in' very firmly and finishing off with fine soil to the nursery mark on the plant. Be careful to avoid air pockets in this process and water in thoroughly, particularly in February or March when an upsurge of spring sap is due and the plant will rapidly desiccate without adequate water at the roots.

FURTHER ESSENTIALS TOWARDS SUCCESSFUL ESTABLISHMENT

Pruning of newly planted woody subjects

Establishment of trees and shrubs, particularly those which are late planted as bare-root (open ground) stock larger than standard size or which are used in exposed situations, will be assisted by thinning or pruning back of top growth by up to one third. While one is perhaps reluctant to do this as the planted height of the tree is obviously influenced, this pruning may, nevertheless, often prevent a substantial natural die-back or complete failure to establish of late planted large nursery stock.

Root growth

Earlier in this chapter we have laid considerable stress on the need for adequate ground preparation and careful and efficient planting. Equally, aftercare or maintenance following planting is of great importance.

Plant roots have two main functions – firstly to provide anchorage and support for the aerial portions of the tree, shrub or plant, and secondly to extract nutrients and moisture from the ground and translocate these through the systems of the plant, thereby promoting establishment and growth. Most bare-rooted trees and shrubs suffer damage to their roots in the lifting and transplanting process and growth of new root is essential in order to ensure establishment in the new site.

With trees planted at 1.5–1.8m (5–6ft) or more in height, as already advised, stakes are necessary to stabilise the base of stem and prevent the wrenching of the existing roots in the ground with subsequent inhibition of new root formation. Furthermore the ability to regenerate a new permanent root system, as opposed to a rather short-lived root system able to absorb water and nutrients temporarily, depends very much on the nature and genera of the tree involved; for instance most poplars, willows and maples adapt well and regenerate good root systems with rapidity, enabling them to be moved successfully as quite large trees. Other genera, notably birch, beech and oaks rapidly lose their power to make permanent new roots.

Therefore, in addition to adequate firming at planting time, combined with stability of the root system by staking as necessary, we can give the new transplant the best possible chance by ensuring that there is adequate moisture in the vicinity of the roots from early spring onwards and throughout the summer. This is best achieved by careful attention to watering, controlling the weeds which compete with transplants for food and moisture and by applying suitable mulches to moist, weed-free soil over the root area.

Watering

Watering-in following the planting of container grown and bare root trees, shrubs and conifers is a vital operation, particularly in the spring of the year. A standard tree or large shrub or conifer will require at least one bucketful of water to settle the soil around the roots or rootball, and to ensure that there is adequate moisture present when the plant puts out its new roots with the advancing of spring. If substantial rain is not evident, this should be repeated say weekly during spring or early summer, when the plant exhibits its greatest water demand. Overhead spraying with clear water in the evening following a warm day or periods of drying wind would also be beneficial in assisting establishment.

Mulching

5cm (2in) of an open textured material, applied to the root (cultivation) area of a tree, shrub or conifer can be of great value in conserving moisture and hence reducing frequency of watering in times of drought. Coarse peat, half rotted leaves, garden compost, well rotted farmyard manure or a mixture of these are all useful as mulches. However, a coarse grade of pulverised pine bark (such as Cambark 100) is effective as an open textured and long lasting mulch and has the added bonus of an attractive and pleasant brown appearance. Bark is clean and easy to handle and allows convenient application of water, fertiliser, etc to the root area of the plant, while discouraging the growth of weed and repelling such troublesome garden pests as slugs and snails.

Tree ties, tree guards and tree shelters

Tree Ties – Today's purpose-made tree ties undoubtedly provide an effective and efficient means of securing a tree to its stake. The use of string, rope or other materials is to be firmly discouraged. The modern rubber or plastic belting/buckle type tree tie (Tom's or Rainbow) usually has a rubber or plastic spacer to separate the tree from the stake and thus prevent friction or damage to the stem. However, a tree tie must initially be correctly positioned; if one only is used on a short stake this should be at the very top of that stake. If positioned more than 5cm (2in) from the top of the stake and insufficiently tightened, the natural flexing of the head of the tree can result in a serious wound to the stem at the point of contact at the top of the stake. If this condition is allowed to persist, the head of the tree may well snap at this point. It is equally important to ensure that the tree tie – particularly of the buckle (Rainbow) type is fixed to the stake by a single galvanised nail through the eyehole usually provided – otherwise the buckle can slacken off and the tree tie drop down the stake, creating the situation described above (see Fig 66).

An essential after-care task is the examination and adjustment of tree ties once or twice a year and particularly before commencement of spring growth. Neglect of this can result in strangulation and serious damage to stems or the breaking and necessary replacement of the tree tie belting.

Tree Guards Protection against cattle, horses and sheep grazing in park land has always traditionally been by means of heavy post and rail tree guards, ideally not less than 1.2m (4ft) square and up to 1.8m (6ft) in height. In such circumstances this type of protection remains the best method of preventing heavy animals damaging trees, conifers and shrubs by browsing, bark rubbing or stripping and by trampling of root areas – an important factor often overlooked. More ornamental, heavy metal tree guards, usually about 0.5m (1½ft) in diameter are occasionally seen in park land of country estates, but these are relics of the past and would be prohibitively expensive to manufacture today in quantity.

Rabbits and hares, and to an increasing extent, deer, are often a problem in gardens in rural areas. The damage they do by browsing bark, stripping and fraying and (in the case of rabbits) burrowing into roots of newly planted tree transplants, shrubs, roses and conifers is considerable.

There is now a legal requirement to control rabbits where present and certainly a high population in any area is to be avoided. Specialised and expensive fencing is often necessary to protect valued collections, fruit and conifer plantations or arboreta from browsing deer, perhaps invading from nearby woodland.

Fortunately, plastic net tree guards (Netlon) in a variety of sizes have been developed in recent years which give a considerable measure of protection against these animals. In rural garden circumstances, they may well replace the more expensive galvanised wire mesh (Weldmesh) tree guards which may still have application against vandalism in particular in public places and in urban and suburban situations. Plastic net tree guards are made from tough light-degradable black polyethylene with a mesh structure up to 25×35mm (1× 1⅜in), cut conveniently from a continuous length and rolled to various widths to protect a wide range of shrubs, tree transplants and conifers. The plastic mesh may be cut to various height from 0.6m (about 2½ft) to 2m (6ft). The guard thus formed is usually stapled to one or more rough sawn or round wooden stakes, positioned to support it. Further details and information are given in Arboricultural Research Note 5/83/WILD.

Tree Shelters In recent years research by the Forestry Commission has been carried out into the manufacture and use of vertical plastic tube structures, generally from 8–15cm (3–6in) square and primarily used to improve survival, establishment and growth rate of young broad-leaved tree transplants (such as oak) under forestry conditions. Although not beautiful the system seems to have proved successful, so far, and its use is spreading throughout Britain; the trees rapidly produce a straight stem and are adequately protected from rabbits and deer and from exposure to wind while small, until

growth reaches the top of the tube – usually 1.2m (4ft).

For those planting trees in woodland circumstances or in exposed gardens where they perhaps wish to establish choice or rare subjects available only as small plants, less than 1m (3ft) high, consideration should be given to the use of plastic tree shelters. There are a number of manufacturers, among them Correx Tree Shelters (Corruplast Ltd, Correx House, Moreland Trading Estate, Bristol Road, Gloucester GL1 5RZ) which offers shelters in green or brown as well as translucent, rigid polypropylene, UV stabilised for a long life of five to eight years. Trees which are often very slow in growth and difficult to get through the baby stage (eg nothofagus, holly and sessile oak have greatly benefitted).

Weed control
As stressed earlier, the maintenance of planting sites and areas free of invading weeds and grass is of the greatest importance in the establishment and good growth of trees, shrubs, conifers and roses, and indeed of all cultivated plants. Starting with clean cultivated ground, free of perennial weed and weed roots, particularly of dandelion, ground elder, couch, dock, etc, is essential – annual weed is relatively easy to deal with and on a small scale the hoe still has a place here. Once an initial crop of annual weeds is removed, mulching with bark or similar material or with black polythene is the best method of maintaining planting sites and areas free of competing weeds. Ground cover plants can further assist if planted into weed-free or mulched areas.

Black polythene Although often excluded from ornamental plantings on aesthetic grounds, medium gauge black polythene sheeting has considerable value in weed control for up to three years among newly planted roses, shrubs, ornamental and fruit trees as well as bushes and hedging plants. In addition it has the advantage of retaining moisture and promoting good growth and more reliable establishment of young plants, both woody and herbaceous.

Chemical weed control   Chemical means of weed control in these days are many, complicated and continually advancing. For the amateur, however, several products are now well established as reliable and effective, if sensibly and intelligently applied. These are described in the next chapter.

Keeping records

If you have your own or a professionally produced garden plan, it will be worth keeping a garden record book in relation to this plan in order to record changes, deaths, replacements, date of planting, etc.

Equally, a record for seed sowing, noting dates of germination and potting on and for dates when cuttings were made and inserted – the source of origin of seeds and cuttings is often worthwhile noting, particularly if the plant is uncommon or rare.

When you visit gardens which are open it is worth having a notebook to record plant associations or details of any particular planting scheme which impresses you.

Labels and labelling

There are now a number of systems available, almost every system has some disadvantage as well as a number of advantages. Temporary labelling both outside and under glass is important as this will detail not only the name of the plant but the record of seed sowing, cutting taking, etc and what is written should last at least several months. Temporary labels in seed pot or hung from the plant are usually plastic of 8–15cm (3–6in) long, white or green, but could be wooden, and of similar dimensions, painted white on one side. Names written with black pencil (2B) will last a reasonable length of time – longer on wood if used firmly pressed on to half dry white undercoat paint. A modern waterproof marker pen like Pentel Marker MS50 is reasonably non-fading as well as waterproof but are not permanent on all surfaces.

Permanent labels – these are now available in metal (aluminium), laminated plastic and ceramic (stoneware).

Andrew Crace Designs of Bourne Lane, Much Hadham, Hertfordshire, SG10 6ER, offer four sizes of 20 gauge aluminium labels to hang from tree or shrub or with stem to push into the ground. A special jig enables the punching of letters and numbers to form the name, etc. These are certainly permanent, but not very beautiful. The same firm also offers a very useful label – an updating of the earlier Hartley labels made of anodised and etched aluminium – which may be written upon in ordinary pencil or chinagraph, the name lasting rather longer than on plastic or wood. Several companies, notably Dolphin Labels, 25 Church Road, St Marks, Cheltenham, Glos GL51 7AL and Annamarie Beresford, Little Chantry, Hurston Close, Findon Valley, Worthing, Sussex, offer engraved to order plastic laminate labels, black with white lettering. These are most frequently seen in botanic gardens, arboreta, horticultural colleges, etc. They can be hung or positioned on metal stems or wooden posts. (See Fig 69.)

While metal and plastic laminate labels especially engraved to order are inevitably more expensive, MacPenny Nurseries of Bransgore, near Christchurch, Dorset, offer a simple and inexpensive plastic label, with a hole at one end for hanging and pointed to insert in pots. This label is of flexible white plastic, matt black on one side, and a metal stylus is provided to score or print the name in white on the black side. These labels are effective, reasonably permanent and unobtrusive in the garden, though easily dislodged or blown away if not attached to the plant.

Finally, very attractive round or oval ceramic (stoneware) plant labels, 5–9cm (2–3½in) in diameter approximately are made to order by Towy Pottery, Rhandirmwyn, Llandovery, Dyfed, South Wales, SA20 0NR. The plant name is inscribed in black lettering and a stone/white glaze is applied before firing. There is a hole for the label to be hung

FIG 69 *Engraved plastic-laminate plant labels and ceramic (stoneware) labels*

if desired. Being stoneware they are very strong and, short of taking a hammer to them or dropping them from a great height onto a hard surface, they are almost indestructible. These labels are particularly attractive near the house in the vicinity of patios or pergolas and are not expensively priced considering the work involved. They are well worth the understandable delay in production which is dependent on the firing of the pottery kiln, at one or two monthly intervals. (See Fig 69).

TOOLS AND EQUIPMENT

As one would expect, there is now a great variety of tools and gadgets, manual, electric and motorised, available for the garden owner to use. The need for basic hand tools remains, however, and the purchase of reliable good quality spades, forks, hoes, trowels and allied tools is a most sensible investment towards efficient and successful garden creation and maintenance. High quality hand tools of recent manufacture usually carry a five year guarantee and are well designed and a pleasure to handle and use. Often the business end is made of heat-treated carbon steel, the blades coated with epoxy-polyester for additional protection, or stainless steel of a high grade, with wooden or light weight aluminium shafts.

Several leading manufacturers now offer an ingenious multi-change range of clip-on tool heads used in conjunction with snap-lock aluminium handles up to 1.3m (4ft 3in) long to accommodate various hoes (draw and Dutch) and rakes (for seed bed preparation or lawn scarifying). It is also possible to fit a curved blade pruning saw to this length of shaft – most useful for pruning work in trees. A shorter T-handle system incorporates edging irons, lawn edge trimmer, trowel, weeding fork, etc. Such systems can be stored in the smallest of garden sheds where space may be strictly limited. A tidy minded person would enjoy arranging hooks and shelves to accommodate such a collection. Good quality secateurs and long-handled pruners or loppers are also essential for most gardens where shrubs, trees and fruit trees are grown.

The owner of a larger garden will have a need for some electric or motorised equipment. Apart from lawn mowers an electric hedge trimmer will be essential to supplement hand shears if hedges are extensive. The motorised strimmer is most useful for clearing around tree bases and removing herbage from difficult corners which are missed by the lawn mower. If trees abound, a smaller chainsaw is a desirable tool to have in your garden shed, particularly if you have a wood burning stove to use the wood resulting from tree prunings – larger operations conducted by the local tree surgeon usually result in a heap of cord wood to be logged up. Great care should be exercised when using a chainsaw as they can be lethal.

Larger lawns with surrounding deciduous trees may call for the use of a leaf sweeper (a wheeled vehicle which collects leaves into its hopper when pushed over lawns, paths or paved areas).

Similarly a powered cultivator reduces extensive hand digging in vegetable gardens – or you may prefer to hire if you consider this once a year operation does not justify the expense of purchase. A wheeled fertiliser applicator is a useful device if you need to apply fertiliser or moss-killer evenly to a substantial lawn – but again hiring is possible even from the company who sell you the fertiliser or moss killer dressings.

Choose your lawn mower with care to suit the size and nature of the grass area it is likely to have to deal with; seek specialist advice which is usually available from the vending company. If you like to see traditional stripes on your lawn you will require a cylinder mower, available in a number of sizes from 0.5m (about 18in) to about 1m (36in) in width cut and powered by electricity or petrol engine. If the finish is less important to you, a rotary type machine will be appropriate with a similar range of sizes and means of propulsion and usually a variable height of cut. Finally, the hover type so popular today enables one to mow informally in a variety of locations from odd corners to long grass areas and particularly to deal efficiently with otherwise unmowable bankings.

In conclusion, essential garden equipment should also include such items as a wheelbarrow (consider one of the newer 'ball barrows'); a knapsack or smaller pump-up type sprayer for weedkiller, insecticide or fungicide application (if you have several fruit trees, half or fully grown, a knapsack sprayer will be needed at least for winter wash spraying and probably at other times); unless the rainfall is heavy in your district, the knitted braided hosepipe (15-year guarantee) is a good investment, together with an oscillating sprinkler for lawn and vegetable garden areas in particular. One or two watering cans (usually plastic these days) and fitted with sensible roses, fine and coarse, will be necessary to transport water to patio containers, and for planting and maintaining newly-planted trees, shrubs, roses, etc.

The above items are essential for the reasonably efficient running of today's garden, whether small, medium or large – in addition a great many gadgets and labour-saving devices are available, usually from garden centres, designed to make life easier and gardening more pleasurable. These range from wooden clogs and gardeners' gloves to knee pads and gardening aprons – the sort of items that make excellent birthday or Christmas presents for dedicated gardeners.

6
MANAGEMENT AND MAINTENANCE

In the earlier chapters the emphasis is on making the most of the natural features of the garden by assessing the site, design and planning, site preparation and on the mechanics of planting. This chapter should be read in conjunction with the earlier chapters at the design stage but the main intention is to provide information on the management and maintenance of a garden from the stage when the plans have been executed until the garden has matured and is ripe for re-designing.

The twin heading of management and maintenance covers two different aspects of this stage. Maintenance includes the operations involved in keeping the garden, or a garden feature, in first rate order. These operations will include control of weeds, application of fertilisers and feeding, watering, dealing with fungal or insect pests, disposal of waste and periodic activities such as pond cleaning and path maintenance. Maintenance is thus activity based.

Management involves the taking of decisions, such as to employ time saving ideas, when to replace a shrub or tree or to thin out overcrowded plants or divide herbaceous plants, what grass cutting policy and equipment to use, and aspects such as what

pruning regime to use on shrubs. Management, therefore, is decision based.

However, these two aspects are closely inter-related and need to be considered together.

WEED CONTROL
Weed control is the removal of unwanted plants. Generally, there are two reasons for removing weeds, firstly because they are judged unsightly, and secondly to remove competition for water and nutrients needed by the intended plants. A species may be a weed in one part of the garden and a plant in another and the best definition of a weed is a plant out of place. Mulching is used as a means of achieving weed control and also as a method of improving the soil conditions for the benefit of the favoured plants. Mulching an area can also make it look more pleasing and set off the plants (see p43).

Aspects of weed control are discussed in chapter 3, features of the biology of weeds on

The exquisite bells of Rhododendron *'Lady Roseberry'*

p56 and the need to remove competing vegetation on p57. Methods of weed control include mechanical methods, herbicides and mulches.

Mechanical methods of weed control

Mechanical methods include digging, hoeing, rotovating, cutting and pulling the weeds. In *digging* the soil is turned over and the weeds growing on the surface are buried, where, deprived of sunlight, they should rot down and incorporate organic matter into the soil. Digging, however, is not a fool-proof method of weed control for several reasons. Where there are weeds with perennial underground stems or rootstocks capable of making new growth, eg couch grass, docks or bindweed, turning the soil over is unlikely to kill the weeds. Some weeds, eg groundsel, are still capable of setting seeds even after being buried (although the seeds will not germinate until they are brought to the surface at some later stage). Existing weed seeds in the newly exposed soil surface will now be capable of germinating. Also digging near to existing plants is likely to damage their root systems and reduce growth (although where the plants are making rampant vegetative growth, this might encourage flowering). Digging is a useful method for turning over the soil prior to planting and as a way to remove spot weeds, eg docks, but is limited in its value in an established bed or border. Where a perennial weed is present, a proportion of the weed's root or underground system can be removed by forking through the dug soil; this is unlikely to give satisfactory control but will reduce the vigour of the weeds and make it easier to control them with a herbicide application to the new growth.

Hoeing involves cutting the weeds off at just below ground level. This can be very effective in dry weather, as the severed tops of the weeds wither and die. However, in wet conditions, the weeds may be able to re-root into the soil. Also, in wet weather it may be difficult to hoe effectively, as the soil may cling to the hoe (stainless steel tools are much better in this respect). The frequent turning over of the top few centimetres of soil will continually expose new weed seeds to the right conditions for germination, and if a prolonged period follows when it is impossible or impractical to hoe, a healthy flush of weeds may develop. Hoeing can be a technique useful on bare conditions where perennial weeds are absent and as a therapeutic form of gardening, combining activity with a useful end product.

A *rotovator* can be used as a hoe to keep the top few centimetres of the soil loose and friable and to chop up germinating seedlings and established weeds. This can be an effective method of weed control in specific situations where the plants are spaced so that a rotovator can be used between them. As with deep digging, too deep cultivation can restrict plant growth, as will accidental damage to the base of the plants. Using a rotovator is less dependent upon weather conditions than using a hoe, but if the ground is sticky, it can damage the soil structure.

Cutting of weeds is often advocated when establishing woodland. Certainly rampant weed growth can cause the death of plants by competition and by smothering them. However, research shows that cutting weeds, especially grasses, may actually increase the competition they put on the plants; this includes the close mown grass near the base of a tree or shrub. In gardens the weeds should never be allowed to grow rampantly over plants and all plants will do better (newly planted trees and shrubs especially) with an area of at least 60cm (2ft) diameter, preferably 1.2m (4ft), kept free of all competing vegetation. Cutting woody weeds a few days prior to using a herbicide can reduce the quantity of herbicide needed.

Pulling weeds is useful where only the occasional weed is present, on intricate features such as a rockery, or where the weed is about to seed and other methods will entail the release of the seeds. It is often necessary where a weed has established within a plant.

Chemical weed control

Herbicides are chemicals which can be very effective in controlling weeds and save much time and effort. However, when misused they can be a danger to the operator and kill off valuable plants; it is for these reasons that some people deprecate their use. If used with care they are safe and effective, valuable tools in the garden. They must be stored safely, out of the reach of young children, and in many cases in a frost-free environment (as several of them are sold as formulations which will be altered and rendered ineffective by freezing). They should only be used in accordance with the recommendations given on the label.

Herbicides divide into two categories: contact herbicides and residual or persistent herbicides. *Contact herbicides* enter the plant by contact with the tissues, primarily leaves and shoots, onto which they are applied. They may either kill only the portion of the plant to which they are applied or they may be moved, or translocated, through the plant to other tissues. Contact herbicides will have no lasting effect and will not kill the weeds which may start to germinate a few days after the herbicide is applied. They are most useful for clearing ground before planting and for spot treatment of weeds amongst established plants. Care must be taken only to apply the herbicide to weeds, not to valued plants; this is especially true with translocated herbicides.

Contact herbicides have to gain entry to the plant through the leaf surface or cuticle layer. This normally takes some time and most contact herbicides require several hours without rain for effective penetration. Also, there has to be sufficient foliage to take up a lethal dose of the herbicide. Contact herbicides are most useful during the spring, summer and autumn months. They are less effective against weeds with thick waxy cuticles, as found on many evergreens, or where the foliage is wilted due to drought conditions.

Residual or persistent herbicides kill weeds following uptake from the soil, normally by the roots. They are applied to the soil surface and become bound into the soil. As they are more or less insoluble in water, they remain in the top few centimetres of the soil, persisting for a number of months. They can be used selectively to control germinating weeds because the roots of established plants tend not to be in the very top few centimetres of the soil (except grasses), whereas nearly all germinating weeds initially root exclusively in this zone. Also, a germinating seedling is rather fragile, requiring less herbicide to kill it than an established plant. Persistence is a function of the quantity applied and of the rate of breakdown of the chemical in the soil.

Persistent herbicides should only be applied when soil conditions are suitable. For most, this means that the soil must be moist or that adequate but not very heavy rain must follow application. If conditions are dry, this can usually be engineered by gently watering the garden. Persistent herbicides are rather slow in acting. Several, however, can be applied to the soil during the winter period.

Residual herbicides function by creating a shallow surface layer of soil which contains the herbicide. Total weed control is only effective whilst the layer of treated soil is intact. Any activity which breaks this layer will reduce the effectiveness of the herbicide. Particularly, persistent herbicides are not compatible with pulling weeds or with hoeing and it is better to spot treat any weeds which develop with a contact herbicide. If it is necessary to plant a shrub or tree into an area treated by a persistent herbicide within the likely period of its persistence, the top 10cm of soil should be removed from the planting pit and not used for backfilling. It is especially important not to bury treated soil whilst the herbicide is still active, as this will make it available to the roots even of plants which are normally tolerant to the product, and will also slow down the rate of breakdown of the herbicide.

Methods of application

Several methods are available, each with some advantages and disadvantages. Most herbicides are applied as a water-based solution or suspension, usually either by a pressurised sprayer or from a watering can. Using a watering can tends to be rather imprecise and wasteful of the herbicide; however, it is a very convenient method for a small scale use and there is little risk, with care, of the herbicide drifting in the wind. If using a watering can for application of herbicides, it is sensible to have one solely for this purpose; this removes the risk of killing plants because the can was not properly washed out. Using a pressurised sprayer is more economical of the herbicide but does require more care. Most pressure sprayers cannot be used when there is any appreciable wind due to the risk of drift of the chemical. Whatever equipment is used, it should be thoroughly washed out after use and made-up but unused batches of herbicide should not be kept; several formulations are corrosive if left in the equipment and others become ineffective.

Granular formulations of some herbicides are available. These can be applied by special devices but within the garden the usual method is a 'glorified' pepperpot. This is a small canister with holes in the top. The granules are shaken over the area of ground to be treated. The advantages of granular applications are that there is no risk of drifting and the herbicide can be placed through existing vegetation; any granules lodging in the foliage or shoots can be gently knocked to the ground, unlike with water-based formulations where the herbicide will remain on the foliage of any plant. Water-based applications can be used for both contact and persistent herbicides but granules can only be used for persistent ones. Also, with granular formulations, the soil conditions must be suitable for the granules to breakdown and release the herbicide to the soil. This usually means it must be sufficiently moist, but one commercial herbi-cide, which may become available for garden use, requires low soil temperatures for it to be bound into the soil and be persistent.

No herbicides will control all weeds with the same degree of efficiency. If a certain herbicide is used for a prolonged period, there is a tendency for a population of weeds with some resistance or tolerance to that herbicide to develop. It is, therefore, quite a useful idea to alternate between herbicides or between methods of weed control to prevent this.

How much to apply?

With any herbicide, it is sensible to apply just sufficient to achieve the intended result. With contact herbicides, applying an excess usually only results in the wastage of the extra amount. With persistent herbicides, over-dosing may turn an efficient selective herbi-cide into a general killer and lead to leaching or lateral spread of the herbicide through the soil. It is necessary, therefore, to work out accurately how much herbicide should be applied to a given area. The manufacturer's label recommendations will give details of the dosage and dilution rate and these recommendations should always be followed in all respects. The area to be treated with one loading of the watering can, sprayer or pepperpot can be worked out from these instructions. An equivalent area should then be treated to judge the rate at which the product should be applied. With water-based systems, an area of paving can be sprayed. The trial spray, however, does not need to be with the made-up herbicide; plain water, or with a coloured dye, can be used to judge the rate of application. With granular herbicides, the accompanying leaflet will often show the density of granules needed to achieve effec-tive control. This rate can be checked by applying the granules to a clean and dry area of paving or a sheet of polythene and then sweeping up the granules afterwards.

What to apply?

The following notes are on a selection of the

herbicides available to the general public. This is a shorter list than are available to commercial users and, with time, a wider range of products may be released for amateur use. These notes are believed to be correct at the time of going to press. In each case, the manufacturer's label recommendation must be consulted, both as regards use and safety considerations. Always take care to prevent herbicides reaching valued plants.

Weedout or Clout (*Alloxydim sodium*) is a contact herbicide which is grass specific, ie it only controls grasses. It does not harm other plants if used as recommended. Of grasses, it will kill a number of species, but vigorous ones like couch grass (*Agropyron repens*) are not killed but checked for the season of application. It is available as a water-based formulation which is applied in late spring or early summer before the grasses have made substantial growth. Its main use is to control grasses in areas of herbaceous plants, ground cover and amongst small shrubs.

Rootout or Amcide (*Ammonium sulphamate*) is a very effective herbicide for killing stumps and is easily translocated through the root system. It will also assist the decay of the stumps, as it degrades into an ammonia fertiliser, encouraging decay fungi. It can be used to control other plants and is available as water-soluble crystals.

Dalapon is a contact herbicide which will effectively control grasses. It is available either as a water-based formulation or as granules with Dichlobenil. It is used to kill couch and other grasses prior to cultivation and can be used with established shrubs but is less generally useful (and potentially more damaging to other plants) than Glyphosate. When applied to clear ground, six to eight weeks should elapse before cultivation and twelve weeks before replanting. If used to kill grasses between existing shrubs, twelve rainfree hours are needed for uptake by the grasses and the foliage should not be sprayed to run-off, or the plants may be harmed by uptake from the soil.

Casoron G (*Dichlobenil*) is a persistent herbicide applied in granular form. It is useful for controlling weeds in shrub beds and around trees. At the lower recommended dose rates, it will control germinating weeds and a number of established weeds. As the rate is increased, a greater range of weed species is controlled. At high rates, however, damage to plants is possible, particularly if the granules are allowed to lodge against the base of the stem. It is generally recommended that Dichlobenil should not be used on plants until they have been established for two years. It is usually applied in February/March, when the soil is moist and it will then give season-long control. However, damage can occur if the soil is not moist or a very dry period follows application.

Round-up or Tumbleweed (*Glyphosate*) is a contact herbicide which is translocated throughout the plant. It is very effective against grasses and many broadleaved weeds. It is applied to live foliage and absorbed into the plant, where it interferes with respiration. The rate of entry into the leaf is slow, and it is important that at least six hours without rain follow application, or it will be washed off. It is useful for killing weeds prior to cultivation and for spot treatment of weeds in shrub beds or around trees. Glyphosate is particularly useful for killing perennial weeds with underground rhizomes or grass areas. It is rather slow in action, taking from one to three weeks or so in summer to kill plants; consequently it is of little value against annual weeds, such as groundsel, as they can ripen viable seeds before the parent weed is killed; also, it will not prevent germination of the next crop of weeds. Spray must not be allowed to drift onto plants, as treating a small area of a susceptible species can kill or damage the entire plant. If any accidental spraying of plants occurs, quickly wash the spray off the foliage or cut off the sprayed branch. On contact with the soil, it is quickly neutralised by the soil fauna.

Glyphosate has a very low mammalian toxicity (ie it is scarcely poisonous). As a result, it can be applied safely by two methods other than those detailed above. It is available as a proprietary product mixed with a gelling agent to give a consistency similar to wallpaper paste (Tumbleweed gel). This is painted onto weeds and can be used in intimate mixtures of plants such as on rockeries, to remove weeds from lawns, or to treat a weed growing through a plant. The low mammalian toxicity means that there is no danger to pets or children eating the gel off plants. Glyphosate can also be applied using a weedwiper. This is a tool consisting of a wick attached to a reservoir of herbicide. Proprietary Tumbleweed should only be diluted with two parts of water for use in a weedwiper. The wick is wiped across weeds, applying a small dose of the herbicide. Both these methods can be used in dry, windy conditions with no risk of drift.

Ronstar (*Oxydiazon*) is a contact herbicide and will cause damage to foliage to which it is applied. However, it is persistent in the soil and kills germinating weeds as they push through the treated surface layer of soil. It can also be useful for controlling bindweed as it operates as a chemical hoe, killing the shoots as they emerge through the treated layer of soil from the underground root system (although not killing the rootsystem).

Weedol (*Paraquat*) is a contact herbicide. It has a high mammalian toxicity and the commercial formulation is covered by the Poisons Act. Nevertheless, provided the product is used in accordance with the manufacturer's label recommendations, it is a useful product. It is not translocated within the plant and therefore will not kill plants with extensive root systems. Its only real advantages over the much safer (to people) herbicide glyphosate are that it will kill weeds fairly quickly by disrupting photosynthesis and therefore can be used on annual weeds such as groundsel with some success, and it is quickly absorbed through the leaf cuticle, making it less susceptible to rain washing it off the foliage. As with glyphosate, it is quickly rendered ineffective on contact with the soil.

Simazine is a persistent herbicide which remains in the top 2–5cm (1–2in) of the soil. It is usually applied as a water-based suspension (which means that the tank or watering can should be gently agitated to keep it suspended in water). It can be used to keep an area clear of weed for several years if sufficient is applied, but at low dose rates will control germinating weeds without harming established plants. It is normally sold for amateur use for keeping paths clear at dose rates which are too strong for use amongst plants. However, if applied at lower dose rates of 2kg (4.4lb) product (which is 50% simazine) per hectare (2.5 acres) in a minimum of 200 litres (44 UK gall) of water on light soils, rising to 4kg (8.8lb) product per hectare (2.5 acres) on heavy soils, it should cause little damage to most plants (to treat an area of 100 square metres (120 sq yd), ie 10×10m (11×11yd), on a light soil 20gm (4.7oz) of simazine should be applied in 2–5 litres (½–1 UK gall) of water). At these dose rates, germinating seeds of most weeds will be controlled for up to 7 months. Slight overdosing will usually cause chlorotic foliage on plants, higher over-dosing may kill. Some of the formulations for keeping paths clear include other herbicides, such as Aminatriazole, and cannot be used amongst shrubs.

2,4-D and other Lawn herbicides, eg MCPA, mecoprop, dichlorprop, fenoprop and dicamba, are sold for the control or elimination of broadleaved weeds in lawns. These are all growth regulators. At the recommended dose rates, they do not adversely affect grasses but cause uncontrolled growth of broadleaved plants. Initially this shows as twisted and distorted leaves, followed by the death of the weed. Although usually sold as lawn herbicides, they can be used to kill broadleaved weeds in other places in the garden and 2,4-D is effective against bindweed. However, they can cause damage to all trees and shrubs, and 2,4-D is sold as part of a 'cocktail' of herbicides for the control of brushwood. 2,4-D is also volatile and in hot weather it can cause damage to nearby or overhead trees and shrubs.

A number of products are sold for the control of moss in lawns. These include lawn sand, which contains sulphate of iron and ammonium sulphate; these will also act as contact herbicides to broadleaved weeds.

Mulching

A mulch is a layer of material covering the soil surface. Mulches are used to control weeds and moisture loss from the soil, to improve soil conditions, especially for certain plants, and to give a background against which some plants can be displayed. The effect of a mulch is to prevent the loss of moisture from the underlying soil whilst letting rainwater percolate downwards, and to smother any weeds which germinate on the soil surface. Many weed seeds will only germinate in response to light, so the covering effect of the mulch keeps them dormant. Any seeds which germinate on the surface of the mulch can either be pulled or sprayed, whilst some mulching materials will provide little or no sustenance for the germinating weed. Using a mulch is an attractive option where you do not wish to consider the use of herbicides, or where you want to restrict the use of herbicides. However, a mulch will also give a buffer layer around a plant, making the use of herbicides that much safer.

A mulch needs to let air be exchanged between the soil and the atmosphere, otherwise the soil beneath will become dead. Mulches do not show footprints in the same way that bare earth does and therefore access paths for maintenance and for the enjoyment of plants are not needed with a thick organic mulch. However, with some materials, birds and animals may scatter the mulch about whilst searching for worms.

Mulches should be put onto clean soil in a layer at least 5cm (2in) and preferably 10cm (4in) thick. Thinner layers, except for sheet mulches discussed below, are unlikely to achieve any improvement. The activity of earthworms and the decay of organic mulches will slowly incorporate the lower layer into the soil, so the mulch will need to be topped up with an occasional topdressing; this is needed even with gravel mulches. However, topping up the mulch should not be needed with many groundcover plants once these have covered the soil surface. Organic mulches can be used as a means of applying nutrients to a bed, either from the decay of the leafmould or from fertiliser added to the mulch. With small plants, such as groundcover plants and heathers, care must be taken to ensure that the plants are not swamped by the mulch. Mulches which will heat up, eg grass mowings (which are generally unsuitable unless mixed with other materials as they tend to form too dense a mat on their own), should not be built up into too deep a layer, especially not close to the stem of plants, as the heat generated as they decompose may cause damage.

The commonest mulches are composed of organic materials like peat, pulverised conifer bark and leafmould. Organic mulches will last for from one to three years for peat and leafmould to upwards of five years for pine bark. These are the best mulches for species such as rhododendron which naturally root into the surface layers of leafmould. Regular topdressing will keep a thick surface layer for these plants and most mulching materials will also maintain the soil acidity. A thick organic mulch will keep the soil cool for these and other plants which like cooler conditions. Organic mulches are also beneficial for adding organic matter or humus to the soil, which is needed to keep the soil fauna and flora functioning well and recycling nutrients. In shrub beds, fallen leaves can be left to add to the mulch.

Mulches can be made out of gravel. The grade of gravel used should be around 2cm (.8in) in diameter, or washed shingle. Gravel mulches can be very effective for displaying dwarf conifers and scree and rockery plants. When first applied, they look rather stark but the colour should soon mellow.

Sheet materials can also be used for mulches. The best material is 500-gauge black polythene, but bituminous roofing felt can also be used. The material needs to cut out all light, or weeds will germinate beneath it, partly negating the benefit of the mulch. Black polythene is often recommended for vegetable plots but can also be effectively used to hasten the establishment of woody plants; it is especially useful in out-of-the-way sites, which are easily neglected when it comes to watering and weed control and where the unsightliness of the polythene is not an eyesore.

Sheet materials, such as black polythene, will last for around three years before ultra-violet sunlight causes them to fail (at which stage they should be removed before they blow everywhere). They will control water loss better than other mulching materials, whilst there are normally sufficient holes around the plants to permit rainwater to percolate and for the exchange of gases. Unlike the above mulches, they heat up quickly and will give higher soil temperatures. This makes them very useful for plants which need to be encouraged to grow away in the spring, such as vegetables or strawberries.

Polythene sheeting can be held down using stones or clods of earth but it is much easier to bury the edge in the soil. A slit is made with a spade some 8–10cm (3–4in) in from the outline of the sheet; the spade is then used to push the edge of the sheet into this slit. When this is done on all four sides, the sheet should be held firmly in place, although if large, some clods in the middle will help. If used around a newly planted tree, a slit should be made so that the sheet can be laid around the plant; ideally, the sheet used should be at least 1m (3ft) in diameter for a young tree.

A colourful combination for a sunny, dry aspect. The white flowers of Cistus 'Elma' *contrast well with the dark-red climbing rose 'Park Direktor Riggers', and the mauve* Nepeta x faassenii *in the background*

FERTILISERS, MANURES AND FEEDING

This section looks at whether additional nutrients should be provided as part of the management of a garden, and if so, how they should be made available to the plants. The stages involved in considering this are: (a) What nutrients are needed by the plants? (b) Are they already available in sufficient quantity in the soil? (c) If they are not, what are the ways to provide them?

Specific requirements for nutrients

The nutrients needed by all plants, both major nutrients and trace elements, are discussed in Chapter 3 (see pp42–6). However, they are needed in different amounts by plants, depending both upon species and the stage of growth. Rhododendron, for instance, need calcium just like other plants, but they are adapted to situations where there is very little calcium available to the plant and the excess present in many soils acts as a poison and prevents the uptake of other nutrients. Species of hydrangea will grow on both acidic and alkaline soils, but it is only on naturally acidic soils that the best blue flowers are developed. This is because of the availability of aluminium ions at low soil pHs (see p43) and their unavailability at higher pHs. In both these examples, improvements in growth can be achieved by giving nutrients in a form adapted to let the plant absorb the necessary ingredients despite the soil pH. Some plants are sensitive to the quantity of a nutrient present in a soil. Rhododendron and members of the Ericaceae do not flourish on soils with high nitrogen levels; members of the Proteaceae, eg embothrium, need soils with low levels of phosphate.

Plants grown for fruit effect will have a higher requirement for potassium and phosphorus than plants grown for foliage, when proportionately more nitrogen is needed. Feeding a plant grown for fruit, therefore, with a high nitrogen fertiliser may result in vigorous vegetative growth but little or no fruit formation. Giving extra fertiliser may reduce the attractions of the plant. Where the beauty of the plant is in the large bold foliage, as with an ailanthus or paulownia coppiced annually, nutrients are needed in good quantity for the best effect.

It is also important to consider where the nutrients in the soil are going. This is not the place to consider the whole range of natural inputs and outflows of nutrients from a soil (eg loss of nutrients by leaching and gain from nutrients in rainwater or from the breakdown of bedrock) but the topic should be briefly considered. Where produce is being harvested from the site, either as fruit or vegetables, these often contain a disproportionate amount of the total nutrients in the plant. To maintain production, these nutrients should be replaced. Similarly, where leaves or mowings are being continually removed from site, there is an outflow of nutrients which need replacing. However, nutrients can be 'lost' to the system by being tied up in permanent tissues, such as the woody bole of a tree.

How fertile is your soil?

The next point is to find out whether there are sufficient nutrients available for the plants in the soil. There are two practical ways of doing this, by having the soil tested and by observing plants already growing on the site.

It is possible to have the soil tested commercially by a number of firms, or alternatively small kits can be purchased. These will give an approximate indication of the relative fertility of the soil. Before using any figure or recommendation gained by soil testing, you should consider the type of plant you will be growing in the area. The recommendations usually given with the types of soil testing kits available in many garden centres are appropriate to most vegetable plots but are too rich for shrub beds and a number of plants.

Observation of plants growing on the site can be a very effective way to gauge the fertility of the soil. It requires a modicum of knowledge as to what the plant should look like, but comparison with the same plant in a neighbour's garden will go a long way towards answering whether extra nutrients are needed. If the plants in your garden have much smaller leaves and poor fruit compared to others of the same form elsewhere, it is likely that yours are deficient in some nutrient (although you should first consider the possibility of a fungal infection to the roots). If however, they are large, leafy and barren, it is likely that your plant has too much nitrogen and either no fertiliser should be applied, or only potassium and phosphorus should be given. The simplest cases are where the plants are showing some deficiency symptom. These are discussed in Chapter 3 (p42–4) and can be controlled by the addition of the appropriate fertiliser.

Where there are no plants growing on the site, it is possible to obtain an indication of the fertility of the soil from observing weed species. For example, sheep's sorrel (*Rumex acetosella*) indicates a very acidic soil or surface layer, as does natural ling or heather; nettles indicate freely available nitrogen. These and other indications can be gained from reference to a wild flower book which gives details of the natural ecology of the weeds or wildflowers.

Most gardens soils are not short of nutrients, although additional fertiliser given as a balanced feed at a low rate will often encourage better all round growth. The main exceptions to this are where special groups of plants are being grown, such as rhododendron, and on very acidic or alkaline sites, where nutrient availability may be affected by the pH. The effect of pH on the availability of nutrients is discussed in Chapter 3 (p43). The application of lime can be used to raise the pH and that of sulphur to lower it.

Application of nutrients

There are several ways in which nutrients can be applied to a soil or plant; these include manures, mulches (see above) and chemical or artificial fertilisers.

Manures

These are made from waste products, either from the composting of garden refuse or from animal droppings mixed with straw. Spent mushroom compost or spent hops are also available. Farmyard manure is a messy material but a number of products are on the market where the manure has been dried and made more convenient to handle. Manures are variable in the quantity of nutrients they contain and they should not be used in too generous a layer at one time. For a well rotted farmyard manure or garden compost, a layer from 2–5cm (1–2in) thick should be spread over the soil surface, except for plants which are gross feeders, such as asparagus or roses which will tolerate up to 10cm (4in).

With most plants, it is important to use well rotted manures; raw or fresh manures can cause three sets of problems. There may be an excess of ammonia in raw manures such as pig slurry and chicken waste which in a raw state will scorch or poison the soil. Where there is fresh organic matter present, such as straw, the soil bacteria which break this down into humus will use nitrogen and other nutrients from the soil and cause a short-term deficiency. Thirdly, where the manure has not been properly composted and has not reached a sufficient temperature to kill weed seeds present, they will germinate giving a beautiful flush of weeds! However, manures are useful for adding organic matter or humus to the soil, which assists the natural processes working for soil fertility.

Artificial fertilisers

These do not have the drawbacks of being particularly messy or smelly but they do not add humus and it is much easier to scorch the plants by adding too much. Also, artificial fertilisers will have the effect of either making the soil more acidic (usually) or more alkaline (less often), depending upon how the fertilisers are formulated. This can be used to advantage, eg where the soil pH is slightly too high for optimum growth of plants (such as roses) the use of ammonium sulphate formulations to provide nitrogen will tend to make the soil more acidic. In other circumstances, the use of lime may be needed to restore the pH, such as where cabbages are being grown.

There are several different ways to apply artificial fertilisers. Most are sold as balanced formulations containing a range of the major nutrients and described as, eg, 12:9:8, showing that the fertiliser will give 12 parts of nitrogen (N) (either as ammonium or nitrate – this is given on the label), 9 parts of phosphorus (P) and 8 parts of potassium (K) per unit applied. It is possible to purchase the ingredients singly. Formulations giving trace elements are also available.

Granular fertilisers should be spread evenly over the soil at a rate of around 50–60gm per square metre (2oz per square yard). This should only be carried out when the soil is moist and generally should be applied in the spring. If the soil is dry, the fertiliser will not enter the soil and may either scorch the plants or be washed away next time it rains. With granular fertilisers which are applied in the autumn, there is likely to be a considerable loss of nutrients due to leaching; applications at this time of the year should average a third of the above figure. Formulations giving a slow release of the nutrients are available and allow a larger initial application with little risk of either scorching or leaching.

Fertilisers can also be applied in liquid solution. There are advantages in that the nutrients are in a form immediately usable by the plant, in fact they can be given direct to the foliage as a foliar application, and there is a much lower risk of loss of nutrients from leaching. The drawback is that it is less easy to know precisely how much is given. However, this should not be much of a problem where the liquid feed is given as part of a regular watering regime. Diluters are available which will give an appropriate solution when used with a garden hose and a small reservoir of fertiliser.

WATERING

Water is an essential ingredient in plant growth and must be available to the plant in adequate quantity. Emergency watering in mid summer may keep the plant alive until next year but will not create an effective display and the need for it may result in poor growth, flower and fruit next year as well. Also, in many parts of the country, when there is a hot dry summer, a general water shortage develops, and the use of water in the garden is restricted or prohibited.

The time to ensure that there is sufficient water available for plant growth is before there becomes a shortage. The first action in preventing plants from dying due to lack of water is good planting practice and the control of water loss, either directly from the soil or by competing weeds. Weed control and effective mulches will go a long way towards achieving this objective.

There are occasions where watering will be needed. These are with newly planted stock, especially container-grown trees planted in full leaf during the growing season, and when there is a very dry summer.

When watering an area, give a good soaking once a week or fortnight rather than a light application every day or so. The heavy application will rewet the soil, leaving a reserve of moisture in the soil which can be tapped by the plant over the coming days. This will encourage the roots to spread into the soil and exploit it to the full. Applying a little and often will not adequately wet the soil and the lower portion will remain dry whilst the surface layer is regularly wetted. The effect of this will be to prevent the plant's roots growing into the lower soil and restrict them to the top portion; when the regular watering is omitted for any reason, the plant will quickly exhaust the reserves and wither. There is little risk of over-watering a plant in the open ground with a weekly watering (although over-watering is a very real threat to plants in pots or tubs).

During June and July, the potential weekly loss of water from a square yard (0.9sq m) of ground is equivalent to a layer approximately one inch (2.5cm) in depth, or 20 gallons (91 litres). This is the amount which should be given each week during these months to replace that lost by evaporation through the plant's foliage or from the soil surface. During May and August the corresponding figures are 15 gallons (68 litres) per square yard, and 10 gallons (45 litres) for April and September. In practice, the soil will retain a reserve of moisture and with established plantings, the above volumes of water need not be given for the first week or two when there has been no rain. Also, with some plants, a slight shortage during late summer may encourage flower bud initiation.

The best way to provide the above quantities of water is by a sprinkler system. The oscillating models will give a better and more even coverage than the rotatory versions. Late afternoon or overnight are the best times to apply water, as there is no risk of the foliage of sensitive plants being scorched and the cooler temperatures will result in less loss due to evaporation. A rain gauge is useful for measuring the volume of water applied, or for recording the weekly rainfall total. Individual plants can be watered with a watering can, but this will involve several fillings to give sufficient water; a hose pipe *at a gentle pressure* is more effective for individual plants.

Newly planted stock can need extra attention. This is especially so during the winter period with container-grown evergreens – they can dry out during cold dry periods – and with container-grown shrubs planted when in full leaf. Here the plant has been receiving regular watering during the time in the nursery or garden centre and the volume of compost around the roots is unlikely to keep the plant healthy for more than a few days or so in the absence of watering. Such newly planted stock will need extra watering, probably every second or third day for the first fortnight, and then reduced to a weekly or fortnightly watering as above. In these circumstances, the extra waterings are intended not to rewet the soil in the potential rooting area but to moisten the compost around the plant's roots whilst they extend out into the soil; a couple of gallons (9 litres) from a watering can (with a weekly full watering) should be appropriate. (See also planting container grown nursery stock, p152.)

PEST AND DISEASE CONTROL

Individual gardeners adopt approaches to pests and diseases ranging from the *laissez-faire* attitude of enjoying the natural history aspects of bugs and fungi, to a scorched earth policy of total elimination. The latter technique can work on a few specific pests and is necessary for some vegetable crops. Fortunately, with ornamental plants, only the occasional pest or disease becomes a serious problem. However, the range of ornamental species which can be grown make a detailed discussion of this aspect of horticulture beyond the scope of this work. The reader is referred to the following book which provides further information on this aspect, *Collins Shorter Guide to the Pests, Diseases and Disorders of Garden Plants* by Stefan Buczacki and Keith Harris (Collins).

When using chemical methods to control any pest or disease, it is important to follow the general recommendations given under herbicides above, and also the precautions advised by the manufacturer of the product.

Deer, rabbits and similar animals may be very attractive but can cause considerable damage in a garden. The best method to limit damage is to fence them out; other techniques, such as shooting, are rarely practical within a garden. Chemical repellents are not totally effective and are rather unsightly. However, where fencing is not feasible, they may be of relevance. More details can be found in *Chemical Repellents* by H. Pepper, Forestry Commission Leaflet 73.

Rabbits can cause damage by eating small trees and new shoots and by burrowing. They can be excluded by a fence. This should be

TEMPUS

badger gate

180 × 250mm door

40 × 75mm frame

270mm high by 270mm wide

FIG 71 *Bottom 15cm of wire is turned out and covered with soil to prevent rabbits burrowing beneath it. If the fence crosses a badger path, damage to the fence can be avoided by putting in a badger gate which is hinged at the top and too heavy for a rabbit to open*

FIG 70 *Rabbit/deer fencing. Where the fence also marks a property boundary, stakes may be needed at closer spacing, down to 5m*

150mm

constructed, as shown in Fig 70, using wire netting with a mesh size of 3cm (1¼in) and a height of 1m (3ft 6in approx). The lower 15cm (6in) should be buried facing outwards, which will reduce the risk of rabbits burrowing in from outside. The wire will need to be supported by a stake every 3–4m (10–13ft).

Deer cause damage by either eating the foliage or using trees and large shrubs as rubbing posts to remove velvet from the antlers or for territory marking. Although they can damage a wide range of plants, those most affected include hybrid tea roses, where the young blooms are a choice delicacy. An option, therefore, is to avoid the use of such plants or to enclose the rose garden within a deer-proof fence, rather than the entire garden. To be effective a deer-proof fence must totally enclose the protected area.

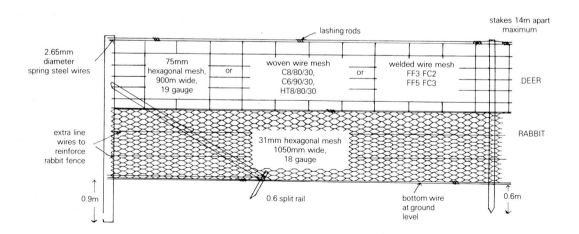

Depending upon species of deer, the height of the fence will need to be 1.2m (4ft) (roe deer) to 1.8m (6ft) (red or fallow deer), although it can also serve as a boundary fence. Fig 70 shows the construction of a deer- and rabbit-proof fence. Badgers can cause serious damage to deer and rabbit fences. Badger gates can be constructed where a problem is found to exist, as shown in Fig 71.

More information on fencing against animals is given in Forestry Commission Leaflet 87, *Forest Fencing*.

Other animals, such as squirrels, and birds can be troublesome but can be difficult to exclude, except from vegetable frames.

TREES

Tree maintenance consists of removing stakes and ties, as well as some tree surgery, such as removing damaged or diseased branches or controlling growth. Aspects of pruning for fruit production are not considered in this book.

Removing stakes and ties

Staking and tying a tree is discussed in detail in Chapter 5 (see pp148–53). A stake is only needed to hold the tree's roots in place whilst it becomes established; a stout stake should not be used to support the crown of a tree, as this leads to delayed thickening of the stem, and frequently to disaster during strong winds. (If support of the stem is needed, a bamboo cane will provide it). If the tree has been carefully planted and weed growth controlled, the function of holding the roots firm should no longer be needed after the second winter, although in very exposed locations, a further year may be necessary. Spring is the best time to remove a stake and tie. At this season the tree will be making active root growth and when it first comes into leaf it will only carry a small crop of leaves; during the summer, it will strengthen the trunk and should be capable of withstanding the autumn gales. If the stake is removed in late summer, the quantity of foliage will be much larger and there is a risk of the tree being damaged by late summer or early autumn gales before the stem has adjusted to the change. If removing a stake at other times of the year, it is a wise precaution to thin out the crown of the tree to reduce the area of foliage. When removing a stake, it is usually better to saw it off at ground level; this risks the stake rotting away and possibly infecting the tree, but the disturbance which will follow the forced removal of a stake will usually cause more harm.

With fast growing trees, it is important to check that the tie is not constricting the stem, or the stake rubbing against it. The tie, or top tie if more than one has been employed, should always be within 5cm (2in) of the top of the stake so that there is no prospect of the tree rubbing against it. Plastic tree ties usually expand safely in the warm temperatures of summer and only rarely cause constriction of the stem, but webbing based ties can be far more damaging and should be loosened as the tree grows.

Tree surgery

The purpose of tree surgery is to prolong the safe life of a tree and to control its development. The following account is intended to give an outline of tree surgery relating to small trees. More information on aspects of tree surgery can be found in the *Hillier Book of Tree Planting and Management* by Keith Rushforth and *Tree Surgery – A Complete Guide* by Peter Bridgeman, both published by David & Charles. When it comes to work in large trees, the reader is strongly advised to consult a professional arboricultural consultant or employ a qualified tree surgeon. The Arboricultural Association (Ampfield House, Ampfield, Romsey, Hants, SO51 9PA) publishes a list of consultants and approved contractors, and the Institute of Chartered Foresters (22, Walker Street, Edinburgh, EH3 7HR) produces a *List of Members in Consultancy Practice*.

Practical tree surgery in the garden will involve removing branches which are un-

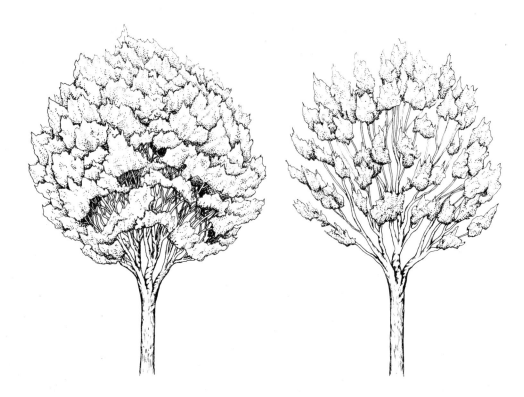

FIG 72 *A hornbeam before and after thinning to remove dead, diseased or damaged branches and to reduce density. Foliage will develop more evenly the following spring*

healthy or create a poor branch structure and controlling the growth of trees so that they give the best return for the space they occupy.

Diseased and damaged branches should be removed because they can lead to further disease and dieback of branches. Where two branches rub against each other, the bark at the point of contact will be damaged, permitting the entry of decay fungi, and in a strong wind one may snap off at the point of contact, which acts as a fulcrum. It is also sensible to remove branches which cross from one side of the crown to the other, as if left they will create a tangled mass of branches in the crown (see Fig 72).

Dead branches should always be removed. If they are left, there is the risk of decay fungi entering the tree but, more seriously, they will fall to the ground at some time and could cause injury or damage in so doing.

Trees will often grow larger or denser than originally intended, or a large growing tree will have been planted where there is insufficient space for its full development. In these circumstances, there are several ways to control the growth of a tree. None is as satisfactory as having the right tree for the site but, as replacing a tree involves a loss of amenity until the new tree grows, pruning is often preferable.

The traditional approach of lopping off the branches, giving a pollarded tree is *not* the solution. This causes the tree to grow very vigorously from the cut surfaces and the new

Contrasting barks: (centre) the peeling mahogany bark of Betula utilis, *(left) the scaly bark of a young* Tsuga dumosa

FIG 73 *The dense mass of regrowth from pollarding may appear acceptable during the summer but is ugly in winter and will lead to decay at the cuts. Reducing the number of regrowth shoots (right) may reduce the density of foliage and shade, but is still very ugly*

growths will quickly become as large as the original, and often cast an even denser shade. If the process is repeated, decay soon sets into the cut surfaces, making the new growths unsafe.

Where the shade cast by a tree is too dense, the effective solution is to thin out the crown of the tree. This involves removing a proportion of the branches whilst retaining the present natural outline. As none of the branches are cut back hard, the amount of regrowth is much less, therefore the tree takes longer to become as dense as it was originally (see Fig 72).

The difference between lopping and thin-ning out a tree can be illustrated for syca-more (*Acer pseudoplatanus*). On its own this will make a tree ultimately as much as 20m (65ft) tall but from approximately 10m (33ft) high, the rate of upward growth of a tree in the open slows down markedly as it starts to flower and seed. If a 15m (49ft) tree is lopped back to 10m (33ft), it will regrow at the rate of a metre a year for several years, until it is 15–18m (49–59ft) tall; only then will it start to flower and fruit but by this time it is larger and casting a denser shade than a tree which was thinned out when 15m (49ft). The thinned tree will continue to flower and fruit, and consequently grow only slowly.

Where a tree is spreading too wide, its spread can be reduced by 'drop-crotching' or crown reduction. This involves retaining the present natural shape but on a smaller crown. The process is similar to thinning. Long extending branches are cut back to a crotch or side branch and because there is live foliage beyond the point of cutting, there is little dense regrowth (see Fig 74).

Removing a Branch When removing a branch for any reason, the aim should be to cut it so that natural healing is assisted. A tree has a system of defences which involves laying down a series of barriers to the entry of decay fungi. If these natural barriers are breached, decay is more likely and healing slowed. Normally, at the base of a branch there is a natural swelling or collar. This is closer to the stem on the top side and further out on the lower side. This collar shows up more clearly in some species, such as white-beam (*Sorbus aria*), and is illustrated in Fig 75. The objective is to cut just outside the line of this collar. Where there is no obvious collar, the cut should be made at the angle shown in the diagram. This will involve making a cut nearly at right angles or trans-versely across the branch, and therefore the area of exposed wood will be less than if the branch is cut off flush with the stem.

In the branch to be removed is a large one, ie over 5cm (2in), it should be removed in two stages involving three cuts. The first cut is an under-cut some 30cm (12in) from the collar and penetrating approximately a quarter to a third of the way through the branch. This cut is designed to prevent the branch tearing back down the stem when it is cut through. The second cut is made just beyond the first cut and removes the branch. The stub is then removed in a third cut just outside the collar (Fig 75).

The tree will cover the cut surface by making callus growth from the cambium tissue, that is the layer of actively growing cells between the wood and the bark by which all radial growth is made. Protecting this layer of cells from drying out will hasten callusing. However, research by the Forestry Commission has shown that treating the central part of the cut surface with a tree paint can hasten decay. The recommendation, therefore, is to apply a protective treatment, either latex, bitumastic or any water-repellent material which does not harm plant tissues (eg vaseline or lanolin) to the zone around the cambium layer and to leave the central

FIG 74 *Deep-crotching to reduce the spread without altering basic appearance*

FIG 75 *Removing a branch, leaving a clean wound which will soon heal. Cut 1 prevents the limb tearing a strip of bark off the tree. Cut 3 is made just outside the collar or swelling where the branch joins the trunk*

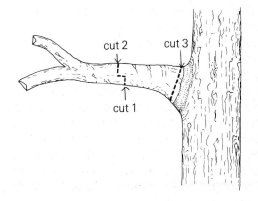

part of the wound untreated. If this sounds too complex, it is better to leave the wound open to the air than to cover the entire surface.

TREES AND THE LAW

Trees impose a legal liability upon their owners. This is part of the same requirement that you are responsible for any damage caused through your negligence by something you have brought onto your land and then allowed to 'escape', eg tree, fence or dangerous animal. To avoid any possibility of negligence, you should inspect all the trees in your garden at least once a year, checking for broken, dead or diseased branches which may fall down and cause injury or damage, and signs of weakness, such as fungal bodies arising from the stem or directly from the roots. Arboricultural Leaflet no 1, *External Signs of Decay in Trees*, published by the Forestry Commission, gives valuable advice on inspecting trees. If in doubt the advice of an arboricultural consultant should be sought.

If a tree grows over the boundary of a property, it may cause a nuisance and the occupier of the land is entitled to cut it back to the boundary (but no further). As this is often not the best place to make the cut (see above) negotiations with the neighbour are called for to avoid ugly stubs which may lead to disease. The cut portion remains the property of the tree's owner and must be returned.

TREE PRESERVATION ORDERS

Trees are also covered by aspects of planning legislation. The local authority may place a tree preservation order upon the trees on any land. This requires that their consent is obtained prior to any felling or cutting, except in certain circumstances. The most significant of the exemptions is where the tree is unsafe, where the requirement is to inform them of any works carried out; also you are free to remove deadwood from the tree without reference to the local authority.

The responsibility for unsafe trees remains with the owner of the tree. A tree preservation order cannot be made upon fruit trees. If you are in a conservation area, you must give the local authority six weeks' notice of any tree works, except for the above exemptions. The intention is that this allows the local authority to consider whether a preservation order should be placed upon the trees. If any order is not made, you may carry out the proposed works within the next two calendar years. If your trees are subject to a preservation order, or you live in a conservation area, you should consult the local authority or an arboricultural consultant for advice. If you do not live in a conservation area or the trees in your garden are not covered by a preservation order, you are free to treat them as you wish. There are certain constraints on felling trees for timber but they do not concern trees in gardens.

SHRUBS

Maintenance of shrubs involves keeping the plants and the ground around them in good order, eg by weed control and fertiliser applications, and controlling the growth so that the optimum pleasure is obtained from the bed or individual specimen plant.

Controlling the growth will vary depending upon species and location. Most shrubs do not need annual pruning, but many will be more attractive for it. The purpose and consequences of the pruning need to be considered before the plants are cut back.

The purpose of pruning is to control the shape of the plant, to increase the beauty of the flowers, fruit, foliage or bark, and to remove diseased or potentially disease carrying portions.

Keeping a shrub healthy

This involves the removal of weak, damaged, dead or over-crowded shoots. In this way

This may tree has been beautifully overwhelmed by the flowers of Rosa longicuspis

potentially damaging decay fungi which gain entry to weak shoots, etc, can be prevented from growing back into the healthy ones, and the number of places where damaging insects can hide can be reduced. This aspect of pruning would include prompt action to remove a dying shoot which shows during the growing season. When cutting out diseased material, always make the cuts into sound or healthy wood well beneath the diseased portion which should be promptly burnt. With some diseases, eg Fireblight and Dutch elm disease, the organism responsible is likely to have penetrated some distance below the obvious signs and removal of the branch from its point of origin is advised. When cutting diseased shoots, it is good practice to sterilise the knife or secateurs used by wiping them on a rag soaked in methylated spirits, ideally after each cut. This will reduce the chance of transferring the cause of the infection to a new branch or plant next time the tool is used.

Controlling or reshaping a shrub
Many of the more vigorous shrubs will grow into small trees or become very wide spreading with time. They therefore need pruning to keep them within the space allotted or to rejuvenate an old plant.

The technique for reducing the spread of a shrub is similar to that for trees in that too great a reduction will lead to excessive regrowth, defeating the objective. If a branch extends too far in one direction, it can either be reduced to a suitable crotch (see 'drop-crotching' above) or should be removed from the base. Indiscriminate hacking back will usually give a mediocre result of a tangled mass of leafy new shoots.

An overgrown shrub can be rejuvenated by cutting it back either to ground level or to low down on the stem. Most, but not all plants, will coppice or regrow following this treatment and will make useful plants in less time than if a new specimen is planted. Subjects where this is a useful technique include lilac (Syringa) and mock orange

(Philadelphus) but it can also be used on overgrown plants of buddleia, holly, corylus, yew and other similar large shrubs. It will not work on conifers (there are rare exceptions) and many evergreen shrubs do not respond that well, eg hebes and camellias may sometimes fail to regrow. If a large shrub is in poor health, cutting it back may rejuvenate it but where the plant is diseased, eg at the roots, it will often fail.

Suckers from the roots are a natural feature of many shrubs, eg *Rubus cockburnianus*, but in species which are propagated by grafting onto a rootstock, they will be growths from the rootstock. If they are left, they will often be more vigorous than the choice plant and swamp it. They should be removed from the lower stem or root system where they originate; cutting them off at soil level will only encourage their proliferation. The simplest method is gently to force a spade down between the stem and the sucker until it is in the crotch and then to pull the sucker with one hand and lever the spade away from the stem with the other.

Variegated plants will often produce patches where there is no variegation, just plain green foliage. As with suckers, these must be removed before they dominate and ruin the plant.

Pruning to enhance attractiveness
There are several different ways to prune shrubs. The variations between the techniques of pruning are primarily related to the season or timing of the operation and the type of wood on which the desirable characteristics of the plant are displayed. Which technique is appropriate depends upon the growth characteristics of the particular shrub and also upon what is desired of it. Similar plants in one genus may require very different pruning regimes to flower to best effect, eg different buddleia and clematis. The first requirement is to know which species you have and when it will flower. If you are not familiar with a plant in a newly acquired garden, it often pays to wait and see what it

does before pruning.

The simplest group of shrubs to prune are those which flower in late summer on the current season's growths, eg *Buddleia davidii*, caryopteris, *Clematis tangutica*, *C. jackmanii*, fuchsia, hypericum and indigofera. These plants can be cut back to old wood in late winter or early spring and most will give larger or more strongly coloured flowers than if left unpruned. All the flowering plants in this group will give a display without pruning and this will be earlier in the season than occurs on pruned plants, although the plant's habit may not be as attractive.

Plants grown for the effect of the winter bark of one-year-old twigs, eg *Cornus alba*, *Rubus cockburnianus* and *Salix alba* 'Chermisina', or for bold summer foliage, such as coppiced plants of ailanthus, paulownia and *Cornus alba* 'Elegantissima', will produce longer and more brightly coloured twigs or larger leaves than unpruned plants. These too should be cut back hard in late winter.

Many plants flowering in the early part of the season, usually up to late June, do so from flower buds laid down during the previous summer. Examples are *Buddleia alternifolia*, *B. globosa*, *Clematis montana*, *Rosa* species and rambler roses. With these, it is disastrous to prune them hard in late winter, as all the coming season's flowers will be thrown away. They should be pruned as soon as flowering has finished. Pruning will entail the removal of the shoots which have just flowered so that vigorous young shoots can replace them and develop next year's flowers. Pruning of these plants should not be severe. Also, with several plants, eg specie roses and *Berberis x stenophylla*, the fruits are an attractive part of the display, and this aspect will be lost by pruning.

Similar to the above group are many shrubs which, whilst flowering on the previous year's growth, produce most flowers on short spur growths off two-year-old shoots. Examples include deutzia, forsythia, kolkwitzia, philadelphus, ribes and weigela. In these plants, the pruning needs to be carried out on a three-year cycle. After flowering, the two-year-old shoots are removed and the current year's shoots selected to replace them; this will usually involve thinning out the number of current and previous and one-year-old shoots.

Many smaller evergreen plants do not respond to any pruning or are rather touchy. These include items such as cistus which can only be pruned when young. Brooms, such as cytisus, genista and spartium, and most conifers, such as chamaecyparis and x cupressocyparis, can only be cut back into wood which is still green; if you cut into old wood, the plant will die back. These items can only practically be pruned to retain a shape.

The Wisley Handbook *Pruning Ornamental Shrubs* gives advice on the cultural requirements of many shrubby species.

How to prune shrubs

Pruning cuts should be made just above a bud. The cut should be at a slightly oblique angle across the stem; start level with the bud but on the opposite site. The cut should be

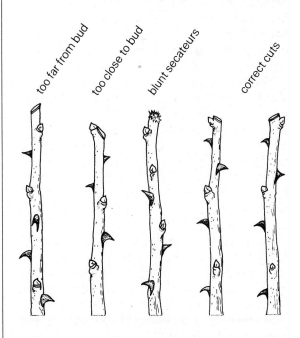

FIG 76 *Pruning cuts on a shrub or rose*

185

close to the bud, but not so close that the bud is damaged. Cuts should be clean and crushing of the twig should be avoided. Fig 76 shows examples of correct and incorrect pruning cuts.

Pruning cuts can be made by a variety of tools. The most effective is a sharp pruning knife but this needs skilled handling for best results. Most pruning is carried out using secateurs. The best models are the scissor-type, in which a sharp cutting blade is drawn across the edge of a non-moving or static blade; the static blade can cause slight compression of the plant tissues, so it should be positioned against the portion of shoot to be discarded. Anvil secateurs are the other type, in which a sharp blade compresses the twig against an anvil. This type causes more damage to the twig but they will tackle thicker shoots and the damage is generally acceptable. Pruning saws and shrub pruners are useful where the diameter of the shoots is large.

HEDGES

Maintaining a hedge is largely a matter of correct cutting or trimming; however, fertilising should not be forgotten, as a large quantity of foliage is removed each year. Hedges fall into two types, formal and informal ones.

Informal hedges, such as a boundary or partition planting of *Rosa rugosa* or *Potentilla fruticosa*, do not require clipping so much as periodic pruning to restrain the shape of the hedge. With items like *Rosa rugosa* the hedge should be cut back nearly to ground level in early spring, as this species flowers on the current season's growth, but with the potentilla only a minimum of pruning is desirable, as it mainly flowers on the previous season's growth.

With a formal hedge, the objective should be to keep it fully furnished to the ground (Fig 77). This can be achieved by making the base wider than the top. This will allow light to reach the lower part of the hedge and also help it withstand the elements, especially

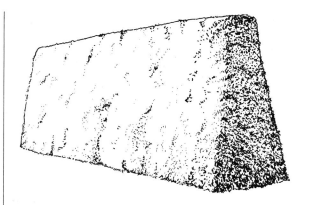

FIG 77 *Correct profile for a durable hedge, furnished to ground level*

The bold foliage of Rhododendron arizelum *makes a fitting backcloth for its splendid large flowers*

wind and snow. Too many hedges are the reverse, much broader at the top and bare at the base.

When to clip a formal hedge will depend upon the species used. Vigorous plants, such as *Crataegus monogyna* (may, hawthorn or quickthorn), *Ligustrum ovalifolium* (privet), *Lonicera nitida*, or dwarf hedges, such as *Buxus sempervirens* (box), will need clipping every four to six weeks during the growing season if they are to look their best. Slower growing hedging plants, such as *Carpinus betulus* (hornbeam) and *Fagus sylvatica* (beech), will normally only need a single trim in late July/August, although in certain seasons, a late flush of growth may need removing later. Conifers such as *Taxus baccata* (yew) and *Thuja plicata* (western red cedar) and evergreens such as *Ilex aquifolium* (holly) and *Prunus laurocerasus* (cherry laurel) should be clipped once in late August or early September; if they are clipped earlier in the season, there is the danger that a late flush of growth will not ripen before the autumn frosts and damage may ensue.

A chemical, marketed by ICI as 'Cutlass', is available which can be sprayed onto certain hedges after the first cut of the year which will largely obviate the need for further trimming. Take care not to spray it onto other garden plants.

Hedges can be clipped using powered hedge trimmers or shears and these tools are satisfactory for most hedging plants. However, for large-leafed evergreens, such as *Prunus laurocerasus*, secateurs should be used; hedge trimmers will cut or mangle many leaves which will remain as an eyesore on the hedge for many months.

GRASS AREAS

The following suggestions are intended for situations where the grass areas are for family play or to set off the surrounding planting, rather than where a perfect lawn is intended. Many books give detailed prescriptions for making and maintaining perfect lawns – if that is your desire.

Grass maintenance activities will include mowing, feeding, aerating the soil, and weed control.

Mowing

This has a pronounced effect both upon the appearance and the composition of the lawn. When the grass is actively growing in early summer, it may need cutting once a week or every ten days. At this season, the maximum length of time it can safely be left, if a lawn effect is required, is a fortnight. At the beginning and the end of the growing season, and usually during dry periods from July/August on, the grass will not need such frequent cutting and a fortnightly cycle should be adopted.

The frequency and height of cutting will determine the species of grass and other plants present. Where the cut is made close to the soil surface, only plants able to grow from the base will survive and flourish; this will include certain species of grass but also plants such as plantain, daisies and moss. If the grass is cut longer, other species of grass are able to survive, whilst daisies are less able to do so. Very close mowing, ie with the blades set at only 15mm (.6in) or less above ground level, will induce a larger crop of weeds and moss, as even the grasses are unable to cover the ground effectively. The optimum cutting height for weed control and general durability under the influence of children or grandchildren is where the mower blades are set at 20–25mm (0.8–1in). Also, where the grass is let grow this long, the frequency of cutting needed to maintain an attractive appearance drops slightly!

Lawns do not have to be cut close and frequently. In the right circumstances, very attractive meadow lawns can be created by only cutting the grass two or three times a year. In a meadow, wild flowers such as snake's-head fritillary, wild orchids, cowslips, vetches and cranesbills can flower and seed if the area is only cut periodically; with intensive mowing, these plants are soon eliminated or reduced to sterile plants. The above examples of meadow plants all flower at different times of the year and if an area is to be managed to give a meadow lawn, the timing of the cutting needs to be correlated with the flowering and fruiting season of the meadow herbs present. If you wish to grow a variety of such plants, giving a succession of flowering times throughout the summer, the different areas must be cut at different times. With bulbs, such as daffodils or snake's-head fritillary, the area must not be cut until June, or the bulbs are unlikely to flower satisfactorily next year and will not naturalise. With flowers such as vetches, cranesbills or wild orchids, an early cut no later than the beginning of April can be given to tidy up the area, with the next cut in late July or September. What should be avoided is cutting at different seasons in following years, as this will hinder the development of a flora suited to one particular mowing regime. Apart from the attractions of the meadow flowers, meadow lawns require substantially less effort to maintain! They will look attractive and cared-for if a half metre wide strip is regularly cut around the edges and paths.

Mowers cut either by a revolving cylinder or a rotating blade. Cylinder mowers are better where a neat effect is required and the grass cuttings removed from site, whereas rotary mowers are faster and will tackle longer grass or wetter conditions. Mowers are discussed in more detail in chapter 5 (see pp160–1).

Feeding

This is necessary to maintain a heavily used or frequently mown lawn in good order. The regular removal of the mowings means an effective loss of nutrients from the lawn and these need replacing if the grass is to flourish. A wide variety of fertilisers are sold specifically formulated for use on lawns. Two different types of fertiliser are often used. An autumn feed, with relatively more phosphorus and potassium to nitrogen, is given to promote healthy growth prior to the ravages of winter. In the spring a heavier

application of a formulation with more nitrogen is given.

Where a meadow lawn is intended, little or no feeding should be given. Most of the attractive wild flowers have a preference for a lower level of nutrients and are swamped by grasses where too much fertiliser is applied. In these situations, the removal of the periodic mowings will gradually alter the nutrient status of the ground in favour of the meadow plants.

Aeration

Where worms are controlled or where the soil gets trampled and compacted, eg by the playing of games, aeration will be necessary. The purpose of aerating the soil is to relieve compaction and improve both the drainage of moisture through the soil and the oxygen available to plant roots. A compacted lawn will take a long time to dry out following rain and the grass will grow much less well, tending to look scraggy (but needing less cutting!).

Aeration can be carried out using several different tools. The simplest is a fork, which is pushed into the ground and lifted slightly, to create a space around the prongs. Mechanical tools which will perform the same function are available. Some of these make holes in the turf with a solid tine, as with the fork, or have a blade which makes a narrow slit. These methods work effectively, although they compress the soil as the tine is inserted. A more effective technique is to extract a core of turf and soil using a machine with hollow tines. Because these remove a core of soil, they cause less additional compaction, which is relieved as the soil expands to fill the space left by the removal of the core. The cores can either be left to weather down (as happens to earthworm casts) or removed and grit brushed into the holes to give a long-term improvement in drainage. Aeration should be carried out from late autumn into winter and the lawn not used during the period after treatment.

Where earthworms are not present in

quantity, there is often a build-up of organic matter on the soil surface from the roots of grasses or old mowings. This can harbour disease and make mowing difficult. It can be removed either using a strong garden rake or a machine designed for the purpose. The ideal time for this operation is either in the autumn or after the first cut in spring.

Weed and moss control

In a lawn weed control will consist of removing unwanted weeds, such as daisies or moss. Lawn herbicides are discussed in the section on herbicides above. They are invaluable in removing certain weeds. However, any respite gained may only be temporary, especially if some aspect of management is favouring the weed at the expense of the grass. For example, raising the height of mowing will act against daisies and reduce their numbers.

Moss can be a particularly troublesome weed to control. Moss killers will give some respite but several other things should be done at the same time to make any lasting effect. Moss will flourish where the soil is permanently damp, such as when it is shaded for much of the day, or drainage is poor; it will also grow better where either the soil pH is low or the nutrient status is low. The complete cure, therefore, involves killing the moss with a suitable herbicide and removing the remains from the soil using a rake; feeding the grass with an appropriate fertiliser and raising the pH if necessary; improving the natural drainage by aerating the soil; and, if practical, reducing the shading of the lawn.

HERBACEOUS BORDERS

Apart from general aspects of gardening, such as weed control and fertilising, maintaining a herbaceous border involves dividing the plants when they grow too dense, staking the lankier sorts and cutting them back in autumn.

Many herbaceous plants will act as effective forms of ground cover and therefore swamp

Unless irrigated, lawns perform badly in times of drought, whereas drought-resistant shrubs, such as Lavandula angustifolia *'Hidcote' and deep-rooted perennials like* Alchemilla mollis *(background) will flourish*

most weeds. *The first essential, therefore, is that the border is weed free from the time of planting,* as it is easier to keep difficult weeds out than to eradicate them when they are established amongst the roots of a perennial plant. Herbicides such as Clout (Alloxydim sodium) for control of grasses and Tumbleweed gel for spot treatment by painting onto the foliage of weeds (see above) are useful weapons in the armoury. Residual herbicides are generally not so useful as herbaceous plants are far less tolerant of them than shrubs are. Where woody weeds become established, these can be removed with a fork. The application of a mulch, such as conifer bark, between the crowns of the herbaceous plants can greatly assist in keeping the bed weed free.

Many of the taller growing herbaceous plants will need supporting, otherwise windy weather is likely to see them broken or bent. An individual stake or cane is appropriate for the tall single stems of delphiniums and hollyhocks. For plants which make a mass of stems to a metre or so, a cage effect is more suited. This can be made from string stretched around three or four bamboo canes, or be a plastic or wire mesh cylinder which is placed around the crown before growth starts in the spring; another alternative is to use peasticks, pieces of branched brushwood. Whichever form of staking is applied provided it is the correct height for the plant, ie 20–50cm (8–20in) shorter than the average height of the plant, growth before flowering will soon hide the supporting structure.

After the plants have died back in late autumn, the dead portions can be cut off and removed to the rubbish tip or manure heap. Any woody weeds can also be removed at this stage and a mulch or manure dressing applied in the spring. There is no need to rush into cutting back the dying foliage as often it can be attractive, even when brown or covered with hoar frost in the winter.

Many herbaceous plants will grow very vigorously once well established. If left alone, they will tend to suppress each other and the quality of flowers will go down. Most plants in the herbaceous border will make a better display if they are lifted once every three years during the dormant season. The older and weaker parts of the plants are discarded and only the vigorous young portions re-planted at the initial spacing. This action will also allow any perennial weeds which are establishing themselves in the bed to be removed, or sprayed, and for compost or manure to be worked into the soil. It is also an opportunity to control the spread of the more rampant members of the border.

Herbaceous borders are often considered a dying form of gardening, as they are prone to invading weeds such as ground elder, they require a large input of labour to give good (spectacular) results and give little benefit over the winter period. There is a tendency to combine the herbaceous and shrubby borders together to give 'shrubaceous' borders. The plants suitable for these associations are discussed further in chapter 7. They need to be the more vigorous species, such as alchemilla, dicentra, geranium, hellebores, hostas, hemerocallis, pulmonaria and waldsteinia, with widely spaced but not too vigorous shrubs. The shrubs can provide support for some of the herbaceous plants and give a winter element to the design. The main management consideration is that care is needed in the use of herbicides and most persistent ones cannot be used.

GROUNDCOVER

Groundcover plants make a close and dense layer of vegetation over the soil surface, preventing weeds from becoming established. Initially, weed-free ground is essential, as the plants will take a couple of seasons to cover the ground fully and will not suppress established perennial weeds, such as couch.

Groundcover plants include shrubby species, such as *Rubus tricolor* and *Hypericum calycinum*, which remain green all winter, and herbaceous plants, such as hostas

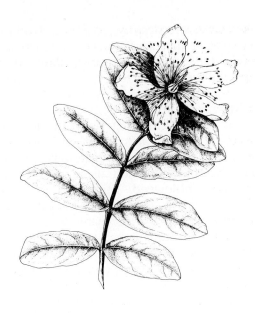

FIG 78 *Foliage and flower of* Hypericum calycinum

and geraniums. The annual maintenance is slightly different for the two groups.

Herbaceous plants should have the dead tops removed after they have died down. This should be carried out in late autumn or over the winter. Any woody weeds, such as brambles, should be dug out at the same time; any regrowth should be painted with Tumbleweed gel in early summer. Any bare patches, eg where plants have died, should be replanted at the same time, using surplus plants from another area. Despite leaving the ground surface bare and uncovered over winter and spring, the flush of growth in the spring is usually sufficient to kill any weeds which germinate over winter.

Woody groundcover plants will benefit from a periodic trim. With most, this should be carried out in early spring and the plants will quickly re-cover the ground. It does not need to be an annual operation. Plants like heathers will benefit from the old flower heads being removed after flowering, ie in the autumn for the summer flowering ones, and in late spring for the winter flowering heathers. Some woody groundcover plants also tend to spread outside the confines of the allotted space and will need regular cutting. This is particularly so with vigorous plants like *Rubus tricolor* which makes long growths to 2m (6½ft) in a season and will tip layer the ends of the shoots.

Some groundcover plants, eg *Hypericum calycinum* and hemerocallis, will spread by underground root suckers. The perimeter of the area may need to be dug once a year to prevent spread.

Groundcover will benefit from the occasional feed, but apart from herbaceous ones, should not need mulching once established, as the natural leaf litter is usually left *in situ*. Most forms of groundcover will last ten to fifteen years before needing to be replanted or divided.

PONDS

Once a pond is established, its maintenance will involve three aspects: these are protecting the fish, controlling weed growth in the pond, and preventing other plant debris from entering the pond.

The main threats to fish come from cats and herons. These can be controlled in several ways. At the design stage, the pond can be built so that the water level is 25cm (10in) below the bank level. This will make it difficult for these predators to fish effectively, but can look unsightly, as if the pond has a leak! Completely covering the pond with wire netting will largely prevent predation but makes a mockery of having fish in the first place and should not be considered; in such circumstances, more pleasure can be derived from a fish-free pond, enjoying the effect and appearance of the water and wildlife such as dragon and damsel flies. A more effective method of reducing feline and heron predation is a strand of wire placed approximately 25cm (10in) above soil level and within 15cm (6in) of the edge. A single strand is effective against herons, but where cats are a problem, several strands may be needed. From a distance, the wire will not be obtrusive.

The most effective way to safeguard the fish is to make the pond as large as practical and to use marginal plants to distance the edge from the open water; this will also allow a wider range of fish and plants to be grown. Larger ponds will involve using a polymer sheeting material or concrete to make the pond, as preformed ponds are usually too small. However, remember that claws can damage sheeting materials and these need protecting by a layer of mud or stone at vulnerable points. Pond construction is discussed in Chapter 4.

Vigorous weed growth needs controlling to prevent it swamping the pond. This will apply to marginal plants, aquatics and items such as lilies. Fast growing items like aquatic weed will need to be controlled as they become too rampant but marginal plants and lilies are better controlled in autumn or early spring, ie after or before new growth is made, as the appearance of the pond will be temporarily affected. In each case, the excess growth should be removed. Plants from the actively extending end of the clump should be used to replace any bare areas. With lilies, 15cm (6in) long tips of the rhizomes should be kept and repotted and the older woody parts discarded.

Algae will often turn the pond rather green and murky in early summer. This is a natural process and normally the water clears after a few weeks, although where there are many fish or the pond is small, this may take some time. An appropriate number of submerged aquatics (oxygenators) will help to speed clearance. (See Chapter 7.)

The pond should be kept free, as much as possible, from falling leaves and other debris. As these decompose, they will absorb oxygen and will cause the water to turn stagnant and foul. This is especially a problem where small ponds are situated close to trees and shrubs. Most ponds, however, will accumulate some leaves and debris and it will usually be necessary to clean out the pond every third year or so. This should be an early spring job, before the plants have started into growth.

Take care not to destroy the larvae of damsel and dragon flies and transfer the fish and weeds, etc, into a temporary tank whilst emptying the pond.

PATHS

Weeds need controlling on paths for two reasons, they are unsightly, and they will cause damage to the path materials. Existing weeds should be killed using a herbicide such as Tumbleweed. This is sprayed onto the exposed foliage and is translocated into the root system. With many weeds, one application is sufficient, but with some, eg bindweed, dock and creeping thistle, several applications may be needed to achieve control.

When existing weeds have been controlled, or no weeds currently occur, the path should be treated with a residual herbicide, such as simazine. This will prevent the germination of weed seeds. Other materials, such as sodium chlorate, can be used, but these may be moved laterally by rain and will damage surrounding plants and lawn margins.

Slimy growths, eg algae, on paving stones can be very dangerous, although not causing any damage to the path itself. They will form wherever the path remains damp, such as when shaded by tall vegetation or buildings. If the former is the cause, redesigning the garden can reduce the problem. Slimes can be controlled by washing the path with phenol or chlorine based disinfectants eg Jeyes Fluid.

WASTE DISPOSAL

Any human activity seems to generate an inordinate quantity of waste material and gardening is no exception. Most of the waste will be in the form of organic matter, eg clippings and mowings, but polybags and chemical containers will also feature. Inorganic waste should be placed in the rubbish bin but much organic matter can be usefully recycled to the benefit of the garden.

The prime method to recycle waste is

through the compost heap. Here the material is rotted down by soil bacteria and turned into manure. As the material is put onto the compost heap, it should be chopped as small as possible and mixed up. The addition of a nitrogen fertiliser, such as ammonium sulphate or one of the compost starters available from garden centres, will hasten the decay process and enrich the compost. The material in the heap should be moist but not wet and the heap will need protecting from rain. Heat from the decomposition process should raise the compost to a temperature which will kill weed seeds. The outer few centimetres of the heap will not become as hot, and to avoid putting weed-ridden manure on the ground the heap should be turned or the outer layers can be put aside and used to start the next batch. The time taken to make usable compost will vary from three or so months during the summer to six months or more over winter.

Lawn mowings are generally too small and dense to make good compost on their own, but if mixed with leaves or straw will have the right consistency.

Garden waste can be chopped using an electrical shredder, which will make materials such as prunings suitable for inclusion in the compost heap, or as a woody mulching material for immediate use on shrub beds.

Not all clippings, etc are suitable for recycling. Diseased portions of plants, along with soil containing a disease organism, such as honey fungus, or phytophthora, should either be burnt or dispatched to the rubbish bin or local civic amenities tip.

A bonfire is a useful method of getting rid of woody or diseased material. However, in many parts of the country, they are not allowed under the Clean Air Act and a neighbour's bonfire can be a source of irritation and dispute. Bonfires should only be used for waste which cannot conveniently be disposed of in other ways. They should be positioned so that smoke does not blow over the fence or across a road. Letting the waste material dry out will reduce the amount of smoke created, as will an efficient, hot fire. Care must also be taken to ensure that flames from a bonfire do not damage plant foliage, nor sparks fly off and set light to your neighbour's thatched cottage or polythene greenhouse. Material such as leaves should never be burnt. Apart from creating too much smoke, this is a waste of a useful mulching or composting material. Also, plastics and used chemical cartons should not be burnt, as they may release poisonous compounds.

7

CHOOSING PLANTS FOR THE DESIGN

FIRST CONSIDER YOUR SOIL TYPE

Of prime consideration when selecting plants is the soil type in your garden, particularly whether it is acid – below pH 6.5 or alkaline or limy/chalky – above pH 7.0.

At around pH 7.0, usually known as neutral, certain shrubs or trees which are usually associated with acid soil will perform reasonably well, although perhaps not growing as large or living as long as they would on soil of lower pH. Here we might include *Hamamelis* (witch hazel), *Cytisus* (brooms), winter-flowering heathers (*Erica carnea* cultivars), certain magnolias, *Castanea* (sweet chestnut) and *Eucryphia*, among a few others frequently planted.

Most trees, shrubs and plants which grow satisfactorily on an alkaline or chalky soil will perform equally well on a neutral or acid soil.

It makes good sense to avoid plants unsuited for your soil – particularly the larger trees and shrubs which are important to the structure or design of the garden. The plant lists, and other references in this book, state whether plants are lime-hating (calcifuge). Principal examples of lime-hating plants are members of the Ericaceae (with the notable exception of *Arbutus*) such as rhododendrons, and azaleas, heathers (*Calluna, Erica,*

Daboecia), Kalmia, Leucothoe, Pernettya and Vaccinium, or the plants such as Camellias, which in nature grow on peaty or sandy soils. Lime-hating trees include, unfortunately for those on chalky soils, such beauties as *Halesia* (snowdrop tree), *Liquidambar* and *Nyssa* (tupelo).

Also, there are several *lime-tolerant* trees and shrubs normally grown for their autumn leaf colour which are not recommended on chalk and limestone soils because their autumn leaves often shrivel or turn brown instead of displaying vivid hues of orange or scarlet as they would on acid soil. Particularly guilty are *Acer davidii* and *A. rufinerve* (snakebark maples) and *Cercidiphyllum japonicum*, the kadsura tree, but this tendency can vary from garden to garden within the same district. However, it is a comfort for those who garden on limy soil that *Sorbus sargentiana*, most of the sumachs (*Rhus*), many deciduous berberis, and *Euonymus alatus* and *E. europaeus* colour reliably and brilliantly in the autumn on the poorest of shallow soil over chalk.

Herbaceous and alpine plants for display and for groundcover are generally less troublesome over soil, but among the calcifuge plants commonly found in gardens are certain autumn-flowering gentians, lupins and meconopsis. On the other hand, white or grey foliaged plants which secrete chalk from glands on their leaves, such as dianthus (pinks and carnations), encrusted saxifrages and gypsophila seem happier on an alkaline soil; so do lavenders, artemisias santolinas, osteospermums (*Dimorphotheca*) and helianthemums, perhaps because of the sharp drainage the chalk soil affords.

Raised or retained beds (or islands) for lime-hating plants

Although it is frequently stressed that plants unsuited to the soil of your garden should be avoided, people who have grown up with rhododendrons and azaleas since childhood are sometimes reluctant to relinquish them in their new gardens in chalk or limestone districts. An old nurseryman had a jingle: 'A rhododendron set in lime is like a curate doing time', and it has to be accepted that rhododendron bushes as large, vigorous and happy as is usual on acid land are not possible or practical on alkaline soil, however much one may dose them with expensive chemicals, such as Sequestrine. However, if you really must grow such lime-haters in a chalk garden, you can build a properly sealed-off raised and retained bed, fill it with a few cubic metres of special peaty lime-free compost, and grow a few of the smaller more compact rhododendrons – such little gems as *R. calostrotum* 'Gigha', *yakushimanum*, 'Bluebird', 'Jenny' and 'Princess Anne' to name but a few of the many suitable ones now available.

It will dry out less in summer if it faces north or west, where often it can form a focal point of colour and interest from the house. Heathers for flower and foliage at all seasons can be added as groundcover, with other small calcifuge plants – for instance the delicious *Gentiana sino-ornata* or one of its hybrids would extend the season with spectacular autumn flowers.

Usually in chalk or limestone districts the public water supply is alkaline too; a white deposit on leaves is proof of this. In such localities it is worth installing one or more water-butts to catch rainwater for use on the lime-haters in your raised bed.

A semi-shaded site is preferred for evergreens, rhododendrons and pieris. Heathers (*Erica* and *Calluna*) should be well clipped after flowering to maintain a compact condition.

Retaining walls should be 30–60cm (1–2ft) high of natural walling stone (sandstone or granite is best). Peat blocks, if available, are also very suitable. Seal off alkaline soil with 5cm (2in) of sand then a sheet of polythene, perforated for drainage. Infill with 15cm (6in) of coarse lime-free drainage material before adding at least 30cm (1ft) of lime-free peaty compost. Small rocks may be positioned between plants if desired. Draping alpine plants such as phlox, aubretia, helianthemum, thymes, etc may be built into the wall during construction. Low growing ground covers should be sited about 30cm (1ft) apart each way between the specimen shrubs.

This arrangement is also adaptable without sealing off for lime-tolerant dwarf conifers and shrubs with low growing cover plants (thyme, campanula, phlox, etc) and dwarf bulbs. Any well drained fertile soil.

Free-draining soil

Before we leave the question of soils and plants suitable for them, mention should be made of light sandy, free-draining soil encountered in many districts, and heavy, badly drained, often clay, soil, hopelessly wet in winter and hard baked and cracking in summer.

While a large number of trees, shrubs and plants will adapt to an amazingly wide spectrum of soil conditions, some shallow-rooted subjects will suffer in severe summer droughts on light sandy soil, but survive on shallow well-drained soil over chalk – this has been well illustrated by the performance of birch and beech on these two types of soil during the record hot summer and drought of 1976. In spite of its limitations in other respects, the moisture stored in the porous

FIG 79 *Raised and retained bed or island for calcifuge plants (see also plan)*

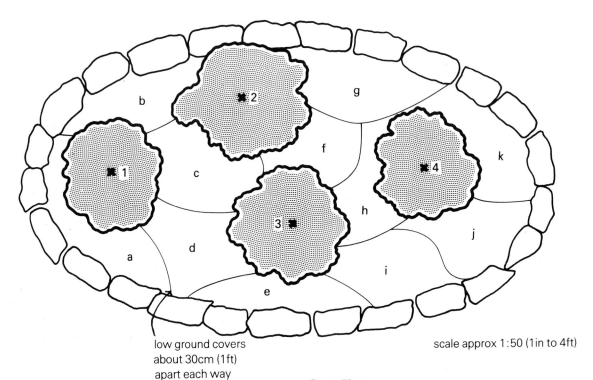

low ground covers
about 30cm (1ft)
apart each way

scale approx 1:50 (1in to 4ft)

79a *Plan for raised bed*

Specimen Shrubs

1 *Rhododendron yakushimanum* (pink opening white, mid-late H4)
2 *Rhododendron* 'Princess Anne' or 'Curlew' (yellow, mid, H4)
3 *Rhododendron* 'Blue Bird' (violet blue, early H4) or 'Elizabeth Hobbie' (scarlet translucent, early H4)
4 *Pieris japonica* 'Little Heath'

Cover Plants

a *Gentiana sino-ornata* 'Mary Lyle' (white)
b *Gentiana sino-ornata*
c *Erica carnea* 'Foxhollow'
d *Gaultheria procumbens*
e *Erica cinerea* 'Atrosanguinea Smith's Variety'
f *Calluna vulgaris* 'Kinlochruel' (double white) or 'Robert Chapman' (bronze leaves)
g *Vaccinium vitis-idaea*
h *Calluna vulgaris* 'J. H. Hamilton' or 'Mullion'
i *Phlox* 'Chattahoochee'
j *Erica carnea* 'Myretown Ruby'
k *Daboecia cantabrica* 'Porter's Variety' or 'Praegerae'

chalk proved a life-saver for these trees, among others.

In the milder districts and in many coastal areas, shrubs and trees with grey foliage do well in very porous soils. Many of them are of Mediterranean origin – *Cistus, Elaeagnus, Halimium, Phlomis*, rosemary, lavender, *Artemisia*, etc.

Moist situations

Few plants, trees or shrubs are tolerant of permanently badly drained or waterlogged situations. It is worthwhile to organise some form of drainage and to then dig in copious quantities of humus, farmyard manure or other bulky organic material in an effort to improve texture and aeration. River or waterside situations are different, however – suitable for several trees and shrubs that one normally finds in such circumstances, such as willows (*Salix*) in both shrubby and tree form, a large diverse and fascinating genus, alder (*Alnus*), dogwood (*Cornus*), sea buckthorn (*Hippophae*) and tamarisk (*Tamarix*).

Soil Tests   Unless you wish to grow vegetables or fruit extensively, expert comprehensive soil testing and analysis seems superfluous. The presence of sand, peat, chalk or limestone is usually fairly obvious, but in borderline cases, and there are many, use an inexpensive soil-testing kit to determine the pH of your soil – the degree of acidity or alkalinity. Also note the plants in nearby countryside: if heather or bracken, or in wooded areas the 'wild' rhododendron, *R. ponticum*, are growing there, the soil will be acid. The wild clematis (old man's beard) in the hedges usually indicates an alkaline soil, as does the presence of native shrubs of chalk downland, particularly yew, box, wayfaring tree and spindleberry.

CONSIDER ULTIMATE HEIGHT AND SIZE

As important in the long term as selection of plants that suit your soil is the careful consideration of their likely ultimate size, particularly of trees and the larger shrubs – everything always grows bigger than you expect. There may be a tendency today to treat a small garden as you might a room, 'redecorating' or refurnishing it after eight or ten years, a task often carried out anyway if the property changes hands. Nevertheless, we all have some responsibility when we contribute major items, such as trees, to the local landscape – whether rural, urban or suburban – for these being suited to their surroundings and able to go on providing a framework for the garden for many years. We may not live long enough to see a tree in maturity or we may move on to another garden, but someone will have to face any problem our tree may cause, such as blocked drains from invading roots, impoverished soil, damage to house foundations, exclusion of light from the windows or heavy shading of the garden, or even merely the blocking of gutters with copious quantities of autumn leaves. Had a smaller tree been selected or a more appropriate site chosen, perhaps none of these problems would have arisen.

In urban gardens many of us have inherited difficulties caused by planting carried out by our predecessors a hundred years ago or more, when few trees other than forest species of ultimate large size were available. The noble stature of such trees as oak, beech, lime, even sycamore, are still much admired and valued by architects today as part of the urban scene, but they bring their problems. In ordinary gardens it is better not to plant these major trees, which are best suited to parkland or a few really spacious gardens where there is room for them to grow to their full stature without being heavily pruned or lopped, with the loss of their natural grace and beauty. Where such trees exist, some compromise may be reached, by having a few branches removed, the heads thinned and shaped, and crowns lifted – work for a skilled tree surgeon with the technical know-how, sophisticated equipment and an artistic eye.

Today there are many delightful small trees to choose from, and we can keep to those with an eventual height of say 4.5–9m

(15–30ft), or at most to medium-size trees with eventual height of 10–18m (33–60ft), in small gardens in urban areas, and particularly near buildings.

For such important plantings, make a careful study of ultimate sizes, spread and shape when considering how they are to be placed and spaced. In later years it may be better to remove every other tree (or to suggest doing this to those who buy your property) rather than rely on heavy pruning or lopping, which so spoils the natural form and beauty of individual specimens. Most garden trees, such as cherries (*Prunus*), ornamental crab (*Malus*), rowan and whitebeam (*Sorbus*), thorns (*Crataegus*), should be spaced initially, allowing for mature growth, at least 6–8m (20–26ft) apart. With sensible planting of a variety of medium to large shrubs in between them, trees at this spacing should have adequate room to develop shape and form.

CONSIDER THE CLIMATE

In the British Isles we can grow an enviable range of plants, trees and shrubs. Most gardeners, particularly those who are plantsmen or collectors, will put in some from Mediterranean countries, from Australia, New Zealand and South America, and in most areas they will over-winter successfully – in most years. Such plants provide the diversity and richness of our gardens and it is a pity to exclude them solely on the grounds that they cannot be guaranteed hardy in our climate. With well-considered siting and good drainage the possibilities are remarkable. Certainly it would be a pity to be without such shrubs as *Ceanothus*, *Pittosporum*, *Cistus* and *Hebe*, *Phlomis* and *Helichrysum*, although severe winters will undoubtedly take a toll on them.

For important focal points reserved for a permanent specimen tree or shrub, however, choose a species known to be hardy in your area. When borderline-hardy shrubs which are well established do succumb in a severe winter, it is usually only after they have given

five or ten years of good service and replacement plants will usually develop with amazing speed, if the stump and roots of the dead plant are entirely removed and the site thoroughly cultivated and manured. Remember that a great many borderline plants will survive and do well even in cold areas if given the protection of a south or west facing wall and nearby sheltering evergreens. Particularly for new plantings, the additional protection of bracken, straw, leaves and hessian or plastic covers can be given in hard spells. A caring owner should be prepared to go to this trouble for several winters until the plant is thoroughly established and has reached a reasonable size. Plastic or hessian covers are best used for the period when the most severe weather can be expected, usually the months of January and February. In new gardens in exposed areas, it is worth delaying planting tender or borderline-hardy subjects, until you have successfully established some hardy evergreens (see Screening, p201) to create some shelter for them.

HARDINESS ZONES OF THE BRITISH ISLES

1   *Hardy to very hardy plants needed if winter survival is vital*
    Central England from Yorkshire in the North to Oxfordshire in the South and the Highlands of Scotland, away from the coasts. To survive without special protection, plants need to be hardy enough to withstand −15° to −18°C (5–0°F).

2   *Moderately hardy plants required*
    The remainder of England, Scotland and Wales, apart from extreme West Wales, Isle of Man and South-west Scotland, South-west coasts and Cornwall and the Isle of Wight. In Ireland, most of the north and east of the island away from the coast. To survive, plants should be hardy enough to withstand −12° to −15°C (10° to 5°F).

3   *Half or semi-hardy plants should survive*
    The remainder of Ireland, apart from the

far west and South-west coastal districts, Cornwall, West Wales, the South-west coasts of England, Isle of Wight, Isle of Man and South-west Scotland – these are the areas influenced by the Gulf Stream and plants should survive if able to withstand temperatures as low as −6°C (21°F) at worst.

4 *Tender plants*
Far coast districts of West and South-west Ireland, the Isles of Scilly. Plants which are not hardy below −1°C (30°F) are possible here.

With winter protection, plants hardy in Zone 3 may well be possible in Zone 1, particularly if carefully sited on well-drained soil; and of course, all plants which are hardy in Zone 1 will be equally hardy in Zone 4.

PLANTS FOR SOLVING PROBLEMS

Screening

Plants can rapidly screen off undesirable objects, such as distant pylons, the neighbour's washing, nearby tin sheds, distant or not-so-distant housing which has mushroomed seemingly overnight, or that speci-

FIGS 80a, b *Evergreen screen giving interest of shape and form, with variegated and colour changing foliage (plan view below)*

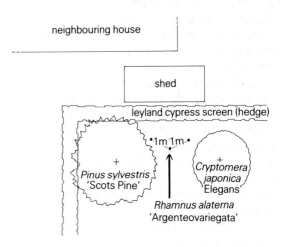

ally annoying focal point on which one's eye often settles – the neighbour's second-storey window which overlooks your lounge and patio! Well chosen, these screening plants, albeit with some gentle pruning and shaping, need never outgrow their situation and can also be most attractive in the garden scene.

Too often conifers that will ultimately become forest-size (thuya, cupressus and chamaecyparis) are used, all too soon blocking sunshine, endangering roofs and becoming too tall to clip or restrain – or being ruined by splaying after a heavy snowfall. The ubiquitous Leyland cypress (x *Cupressocyparis leylandii*) is useful as a temporary screen, and is indeed clippable to form a dense evergreen hedge to any reasonable size above 2.4m (8ft), but it is very demanding of space and will impoverish the soil, particularly if unrestricted. If it is planted in association with other slower-growing screening plants which in the course of time will take over, then the Leyland cypress can later be reduced to hedge size or even removed in some cases. As an alternative to Leyland Cypress *Thuja plicata* 'Fastigiata' is both neater and more adaptable to regular clipping although slower in growth. To provide a most attractive evergreen screening plant, try – at least 1.8m (6ft) away from your Leyland cypress planting – the rapid-growing and strikingly variegated *Rhamnus alaterna* 'Argenteovariegata' which will attain up to 3m (10ft) in sheltered garden conditions. It will also appreciate the shelter of the cypress and look well against it. In cold or exposed districts (Zone 1) use *Ilex aquifolium* 'Argenteomarginata'. In pleasing contrast, suitably spaced off, you could add *Cryptomeria japonica* 'Elegans', a conifer whose juvenile growth assumes a red-bronze hue in the winter, this handsome conifer can reach 6m (18.5ft) or more (but watch for splaying in snow). Our native Scots pine (*Pinus sylvestris*) is slow-growing but it forms a charming small tree if its growth is stopped at 3.6m (12ft) or 4.6m (15ft), making a spreading elegant head of arching evergreen branches

and patience is rewarded. Hampshire's New Forest has a liberal sprinkling of Scots pine, and isolated specimens of just this shape and form may be seen almost anywhere in clearing or heathland; extra large container-grown specimens are often available from specialist nurserymen for immediate effect.

Substantial boundary screening of busy roads, railways etc needs to be solid, heavy-leaved, dense and evergreen to help with sound as well as vision blocking. Cultivars of the broad-leaved holly (*Ilex x altaclerensis*), *Viburnum rhytidophyllum* and its splendid vigorous new hybrid from the USA *V. x rhytidophylloides* 'Alleghany', with elephant-ear leaves, form tall 3–4.5m (10–15ft) large-leaved evergreens effective in flower and berry. Also frequently planted as a substantial evergreen screen are the common laurel and Portuguese laurel (*Prunus laurocerasus* and *P. lusitanica*), and the latter is to be preferred for its greater tolerance of most soils, including shallow chalk ones, and its greater resistance to disease. The geographic form for the Azores Islands, *P. lusitanica azorica*, is especially good, with rapid growth, handsome reddish young leaves and arching habit.

Or, as a welcome substitute for the over-planted Leyland cypress, try an excellent, dense, close-growing, bright green cypress requiring little clipping: *Chamaecyparis lawsoniana* 'Green Hedger'.

For compact medium-height screening, choose hardy evergreen shrubs which are known to adapt well as hedge plants and may ultimately grow satisfactorily to 2.5–4m (8–12ft). Useful plants here include *Aucuba japonica* cultivars, *Cotoneaster lacteus, franchetii, C. franchetii sternianus* and *C. glaucophyllus vestitus; Elaeagnus x ebbingei E. x ebbingei* 'Limelight' and *E. macrophylla; Osmanthus x Osmarea burkwoodii;* Pyracantha (disease-resistant varieties) and *Viburnum* 'Pragense'.

Often a height of 3½–4½m (12–15ft) is adequate for screening; there is no point in using taller plants, which must block some of the sunshine coming to your garden. If you

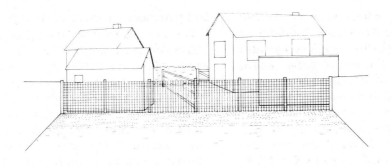

FIGS 81a, b, c *Low-level boundary screening using large growing evergreen or semi-evergreen cotoneasters – showing before, after and plan views. Cotoneaster salicifolius, glaucophyllus vestitus, 'Cornubia' and 'Rothschildianus' perform well in this situation, their berries giving winter colour*

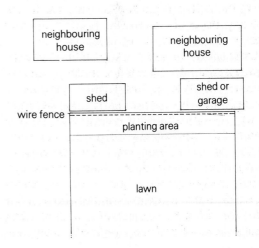

have enough room, large-growing coton-easters, which are evergreen (or semi-ever-green), are ideal for such low-level screening; they also provide good spring flower and spectacular autumn berry in yellow, red or pink. *Cotoneaster* 'Cornubia', 'Pink Champagne', 'John Waterer' or 'Roths-childianus' are all fast-growing with arching branches. They will spread as wide as they grow high 3–4½m (10–15ft), but their beauty is lost if they are heavily pruned so space them as widely as possible for best results.

Screening Inspection Covers One other type of screen planting, usually low, is needed in most gardens – the covering of at least one metal drain-inspection cover usu-ally about 60×50cm (2×1½ft) or more, while leaving it still accessible when need arises. If a septic tank of the latest 'giant bottle' type has been installed there is little restriction over planting, but with the older type involving large concrete tanks at or just below ground level, it is necessary to ensure there is enough depth of soil – ideally at least 30cm (1ft) – to support suitable shrubs. With older installations that do not have modern plastic piping, it is also vital to avoid water-seeking species, such as willows and dog-woods, for their roots will inevitably find faults or cracks in the pipes and may ulti-mately block them. These conspicuous metal covers can frequently be incorporated into border areas, which may be curved suitably to include them. If left isolated near the borders, these covers can be both an eyesore and an impediment to mowing.

If, however, a cover is well isolated in the lawn area, then an island bed is usually possible. Make it any reasonable size so as to incorporate the cover and shrubs which provide a focal point of colour and interest. Relatively low-growing shrubs or conifers which are both evergreen and of spreading and dense habit, but not armed with prickles (avoid berberis, pyracantha and holly in particular) are suitable. Sometimes a group of three to five plants of one variety of prostrate juniper or cotoneaster will screen a cluster of two or three covers.

A more generous planting area would allow the grouping of several varieties of shrubs to produce a focal point of interest at all seasons. Hardy evergreen shrubs and conifers of low-spreading habit are appro-priate for this; remember that ivies can creep as well as climb! The following list suggests some suitable for all fertile soils and for most situations in sun or semi-shade. (Hardy ever-green shrubs of compact but taller growth are suitable if the site allows.)

Shrubs of low growth for screening inspection covers (predominantly ever-green)
> *Cotoneaster conspicuus decorus, C. sali-cifolius* 'Gnom' and *C. salicifolius* 'Repens'; *C. microphyllus* and *C. microphyllus coch-leatus*
> *Euonymus fortunei* 'Coloratus', 'Emerald Gaiety' and 'Emerald and Gold'
> *Hebe* 'Marjorie', *H.* 'Mrs Winder' and *H. pinguifolia* 'Pagei'
> *Hedera helix* 'Little Diamond', 'Ivalace' and 'Manda's Crested'
> *Mahonia japonica*
> *Prunus laurocerasus* 'Otto Luyken'
> *Senecio* 'Sunshine'

Conifers for screening inspection covers (Fig 83)
> *Juniperus horizontalis* cultivars and *sabina* 'Tamariscifolia' (and 'New Blue') and *J. squamata* 'Blue Carpet' and *chinensis* 'Mordigan Gold'
> *Microbiota decussata* (related to juniper)
> *Pinus mugo pumilio*
> *Tsuga canadensis* 'Bennett' and 'Prostrata'

Inspection covers in shaded areas
> *Buxus microphylla* and *B. sempervirens*
> *Hedera helix* 'Buttercup', 'Hibernica' and 'Gold child'; *H. colchica* 'Dentata Variegata'
> *Sarcococca humilis*
> *Pachysandra terminalis* and *terminalis* 'Variegata'
> *Prunus laurocerasus* 'Zabeliana'
> *Mahonia aquifolium* 'Apollo'

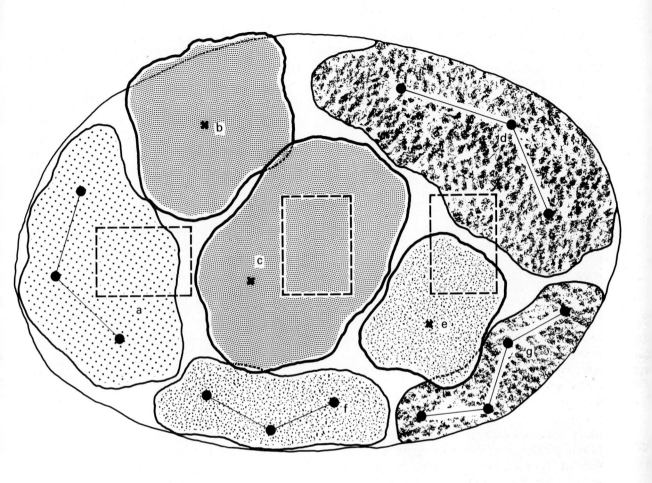

And for heavily shaded sites
Aucuba japonica cultivars
Skimmia japonica cultivars
Euonymus japonicus 'Macrophyllus Albus'
Danae racemosa

Shrubs for screening inspection covers
For flower, foliage and berry all year in sun or semi-shade
Viburnum tinus 'Eve Price'
Elaeagnus x ebbingei 'Limelight' and 'Gilt Edge'
Escallonia 'Donard Radiance'
Lonicera nitida 'Baggesen's Gold'
Cotoneaster salicifolius floccosus
Osmanthus x burkwoodii

FIG 82

Screening of drainage or septic tank inspection covers in a lawn area
Use dwarf to medium evergreen shrubs to form a feature of colour and year-round interest of flower, berry and grey or variegated foliage, while keeping the covers reasonably accessible. Sun or semi-shade in all fertile soils.

a 3 *Lonicera nitida* 'Baggesen's Gold'
b 1 *Viburnum tinus* 'Eve Price' or 2 *davidii*
c 2 *Cotoneaster salicifolius floccosus* or *lacteus*
d 3 *Senecio* 'Sunshine' (greyi Hort.)
e 1 *Elaeagnus x ebbingei* 'Limelight' or 'Gilt Edge'
f 3 *Euonymus fortunei* 'Emerald Gaiety'
g 4 *Euonymus fortunei* 'Emerald 'n' Gold' or *Hebe pinguifolia* 'Pagei'

FIG 83 *Screening of inspection cover using prostrate junipers*

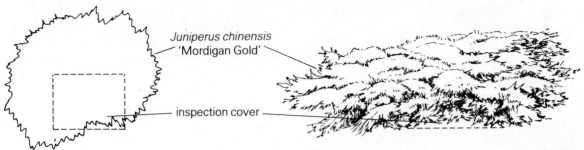

Juniperus chinensis 'Mordigan Gold'

inspection cover

Among others, *Juniperus chinensis* 'Mordigan Gold' or *sabina* 'Tamariscifolia' and 'New Blue' are ideal for this task: they do not get too large, and they leave access for grass cutting and to inspection cover, etc

Elaeagnus x ebbingei, *provides evergreen screening at Bath University*

Screening of inspection covers: Euonymus fortunei 'Emerald Gaiety' and Mahonia japonica

Plants for difficult banks

Steep, unmowable banks are frequently a problem. Ground covering and mound-forming shrubs can be used with advantage to cover them in an attractive and labour-saving manner. Assuming at least 22cm (9in) of reasonably good top soil is present, often covered with coarse grass, it is customary today, to kill off the grass with a translocating herbicide, such as glyphosate (Tumbleweed/Roundup). Then after the necessary wait to allow the weedkiller to act, remove the dead grass, leaving the roots intact, and the bank is then ready to prepare for planting. Plant into the base of 'L'-shaped stations cut into the bank. The more generously the sites are prepared, the better establishment and growth will be. Rainwater draining down the banks should run into the L-shaped level station and into the roots of new plants rather than running to waste down the bank.

One species frequently used is the invasive *Hypericum calycinum* (Rose of Sharon), also *Cerastium tomentosum* (snow-in-summer), *Rubus tricolor, Vinca major* (greater periwinkle) or *Hedera helix* 'Hibernica' (Irish ivy). On acid soils heathers may be used or *Gaultheria shallon.* Either of these can be planted at 3 to 5 per square metre, or yard, and will quickly colonise to form solid and impenetrable planting, often inhibiting

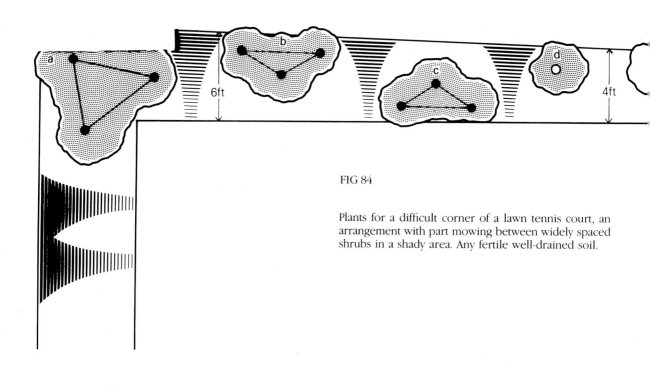

6ft

4ft

FIG 84

Plants for a difficult corner of a lawn tennis court, an arrangement with part mowing between widely spaced shrubs in a shady area. Any fertile well-drained soil.

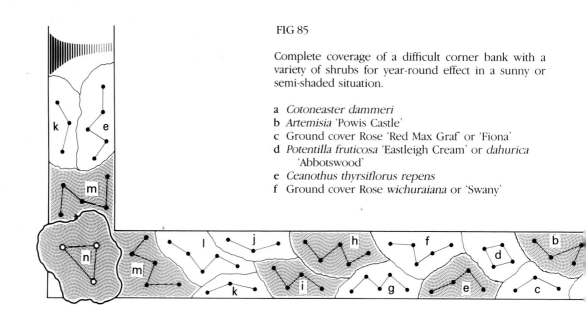

FIG 85

Complete coverage of a difficult corner bank with a variety of shrubs for year-round effect in a sunny or semi-shaded situation.

a *Cotoneaster dammeri*
b *Artemisia* 'Powis Castle'
c Ground cover Rose 'Red Max Graf' or 'Fiona'
d *Potentilla fruticosa* 'Eastleigh Cream' or *dahurica* 'Abbotswood'
e *Ceanothus thyrsiflorus repens*
f Ground cover Rose *wichuraiana* or 'Swany'

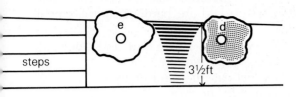

a *Pyracantha* 'Soleil D'Or' or 'Orange Glow'
b *Prunus Laurocerasus* 'Zabelliana' or 'Otto Luyken'
c *Stranvaesia davidiana* 'Pallette' or *Pyracantha* 'Sparkler'
d *Buxus sempervirens* or *Skimmia laureola* (male)
e *Acer palmatum* 'Dissectum' or 'Dissectum Crimson Queen'

g *Genista hispanica*
h *Hebe pinguifolia* 'Sutherlandii' or *rakaiensis*
i *Hebe recurva* or *albicans* 'Red Edge'
j *Hypericum moseranum* (or *moseranum* 'Tricolor' in mild areas)
k Ground cover Rose 'Bonica' or 'Max Graf'
l *Potentilla fruticosa* 'Elizabeth' or *fruticosa* 'Longacre'
m *Cotoneaster salicifolius* 'Autumn Fire' or *salicifolius* 'Gnom'
n *Buddleia davidii* 'Nanho Purple' or *Juniperus* 'Grey Owl'

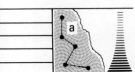

scale 1:100 (approx 1in to 8ft)

growth or smothering any newly planted small tree or shrub associated with it. Such a planting is undoubtedly of low maintenance and useful on path sides and in areas less important visually. In more prominent situations – say the banks surrounding a disused tennis lawn or a swimming pool, a more varied planting seems desirable, perhaps associating groups of shrubs of like character and vigour with wider spacing of 50cm–1m (1½–3ft) – varying with the size and strength of the shrub proposed – to completely furnish the bank.

Some useful hardy shrubs and conifers for this task are listed below, suitable for sun or semi-shade in all fertile soils. In most cases, unless the areas involved are very small, groups of three of a kind or more are recommended. It is possible to build up plantings of colour and effect throughout the year.

Shrubs for banks

Artemisia 'Powis Castle'
Choisya ternata and *ternata* 'Sundance'
Cytisus praecox 'Allgold'
Genista hispanica and *G. lydia*
Hebe albicans and cultivars; *H. recurva*, *H. salicifolia* 'Spender's Seedling', *H. rakaiensis*, *H. pinguifolia* 'Sutherlandii'
Cotoneaster adpressus 'Praecox'; *C. salicifolius*, and *floccosus* and 'Coral Beauty';
Potentilla cultivars, particularly 'Elizabeth', 'Tangerine', 'Eastleigh Cream' and 'Abbotswood'
Rosmarinus officinalis 'Severn Sea'
Senecio 'Sunshine'

Shrub roses for banks

Mound-forming and ground-covering shrub roses include *R. x paulii*, 'Raubritter', 'Max Graf', 'Red Max Graf', 'Bonica', 'Rosy Cushion', 'Pheasant', 'Swany', *wichuraiana* (semi-evergreen).

Taller shrub roses with arching branches are, particularly: *R. rubrifolia*, 'Canary Bird', 'Fritz Nobis' and 'Gypsy Boy'.

Many others will adapt to this task. This list is more intended to point you in the right direction.

Sometimes it is possible to part-mow a bank from the top with a hover-type mower. In this event, groups or focal points of planting can be introduced say 2–3m (6–10ft) or more apart with mown grass between. Particularly useful for this specimen style of planting are any of the following:

Conifers for banks

Juniperus chinensis 'Pfitzeriana' and other cultivars and *J.* 'Grey Owl'

Pinus mugo pumilio and *P. strobus* 'Prostrata'

Picea pungens 'Procumbens'

Dwarf and medium size shrubs for banks (those asterisked are particularly tolerant of shade)

Acer palmatum 'Dissectum' and cultivars*

*Buxus sempervirens**

Buddleia davidii 'Nanho Purple'

Cotoneaster horizontalis

Ceanothus thyrsiflorus 'Repens'

Prunus laurocerasus 'Otto Luyken'*, 'Zabeliana'* and 'Schipkaensis'*

Pyracantha 'Soleil D'Or', 'Golden Dome'

*Skimmia laureola**

Tamarix cultivars

Genista lydia, *for difficult banks*

'Red Max Graf', an ideal ground-cover rose for banks

For difficult banks in shade, Prunus laurocerasus *'Otto Luyken'*

SHRUBACEOUS BORDER AND ISLAND BEDS

We seem at last to be moving away from the conventional herbaceous border so popular in the 1920s and 1930s and so labour intensive, with its choice of plants requiring staking, tying and frequent lifting and splitting. Gardeners must be thankful for the shrubaceous border – produced by a sensible system of planting using widely spaced shrubs of various sizes, with a carefully chosen infill of mainly dwarf or medium height herbaceous perennials, which are either ground-covering or self-supporting and largely of easy culture once established. By using shrubs to give 'bones' or a more natural and permanent structure, the shrubaceous planting offers another dimension, lacking from the conventional herbaceous border which was traditionally cut down annually at the end of October 'to tidy the garden' for the winter. We are able to introduce carefully chosen specimens, often evergreen shrubs, widely spaced to show their natural character and elegance and adding year-round interest of leaf, flower and often berry. Herbaceous plants chosen to associate with them should combine beauty of flower and foliage with reasonable permanence and ease of maintenance. Circumstances frequently seem to dictate that borders are located on garden boundaries and backed by wall, fence or hedge. But why not a shrubaceous island bed introducing a few carefully chosen shrubs or conifers to the excellent herbaceous island bed? (The latter was the brainchild of renowned herbaceous specialist Alan Bloom.) The drawings below illustrate a suggested shape and planting for shrubaceous borders and a shrubaceous island bed with planting to give a year-round effect on all fertile soils, whether acid or alkaline.

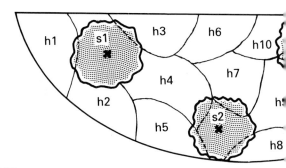

FIG 86

SHRUBACEOUS BORDERS

These borders are designed to cover an area up to approximately 20m × 2–2.5m (60ft × 6–8ft) but are adaptable to smaller or larger areas.

Site herbaceous plants at 30–45cm (1–1½ft) apart within groups of three to five plants of a kind and spaced off at least 45–60cm (1½–2ft) from the base of newly planted shrubs. Some adjustment or thinning of herbaceous plants and pruning and shaping of shrubs may be necessary as the plants grow to maturity, the herbaceous plants maturing more quickly. Avoid closer planting of the shrubs.

South facing or in open sunny position, all soils
* Evergreen
Shrubs
* S1   *Viburnum tinus* 'Gwenllian' or 'Eve Price'
* S2   *Yucca filamentosa* 'Bright Edge' or 'Variegata'
  S3   Shrub Rose 'Frulingsmorgen'
* S4   *Daphne retusa* or *x burkwoodii*
* S5   *Ceanothus veitchianus* or *Eucryphia glutinosa*
* S6   *Hebe pimeleodes* 'Quick Silver' or *albicans* 'Pewter Dome'
  S7   *Rosa moyesii* 'Geranium'
  S8   *Magnolia stellata* 'Water Lily'
* S9   *Elaeagnus pungens* 'Dicksonii' or 'Frederici'

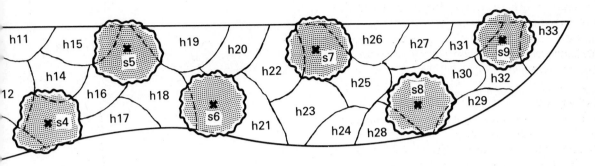

fence or hedge

Herbaceous Perennials

h1	*Euphorbia polychroma*
h2	*Geranium endressii* 'A. T. Johnson' or 'Wargrave Pink'
h3	*Crocosmia* 'Lucifer'
h4	*Santolina neapolitana* 'Edward Bowles'
h5	*Helianthemum* 'Wisley Pink' or 'Firedragon'
h6	*Kniphofia* 'C. M. Prichard' or 'Shining Sceptre'
h7	*Delphinium* 'Summer Skies' or 'Blue Fountains'
h8	*Gypsophila* 'Rosy Veil'
h9	*Aster novae-angliae* 'Alma Potschke'
h10	*Hemerocallis* 'Pink Damask' or 'Stafford'
h11	*Lythrum salicaria* 'Firecandle'
h12	*Stipa calamagrostis* (grass)
h13	*Geranium* 'Johnson's Blue'
h14	*Salvia nemerosa* 'Superba'
h15	*Lysimachia punctata*
h16	*Nepeta* 'Six Hill Giant'
h17	*Alchemilla mollis*
h18	*Agapanthus* 'Headbourne Hybrids'
h19	*Aster x frikartii*
h20	*Hemerocallis* 'Golden Chimes'
h21	*Aster novi-belgii* 'Little Pink Beauty'
h22	*Polygonum campanulatum* or *bistorta* 'Superbum'
h23	*Helictotrichon sempervirens* (grass)
h24	*Geranium* 'Ann Folkard' or *macrorrhizum* 'Ingwersen's Variety'
h25	*Delphinium* 'Lamartine'
h26	*Achillea* 'Moonshine' or *filipendula* 'Coronation Gold'
h27	*Euphorbia griffithii* 'Fireglow'
h28	*Rudbeckia fulgida* 'Goldsturm'
h29	*Iris pallida dalmatica* 'Variegata'
h30	*Aster amellus* 'King George'
h31	*Kniphofia* 'Bressingham Hybrids'
h32	*Lavandula* 'Hidcote Variety'
h33	*Ruta graveolens* 'Jackman's Blue'

Hardy perennial plants for groundcover and to associate with trees and shrubs

Of the multitude of hardy herbaceous perennials available, some are more suitable than others to associate with shrubs or even shrubby trees to form an important constituent of today's 'shrubaceous' borders. To qualify they should be reasonably hardy and long-lived once established, thereupon requiring the minimum of attention: while lifting, splitting and replanting will not be entirely eliminated, plants requiring frequent division or propagation should be avoided in such a planting where the accent is on low maintenance. One might think that this will rule out a host of old favourites, but this is not so, indeed, they are often in that position because they have good constitutions and have persisted well, often in circumstances of neglect. A worthwhile hardy herbaceous perennial should have reasonable vigour and good groundcovering potential, but not be invasive. Ideally, plants should be selected not only with regard to a satisfactory blend of flower and foliage, but also in respect of their stature in relation to the widely spaced specimen shrubs which are an important part of the border. Such specimens should be planted as large as possible and, assuming all planting is carried out at the same time in a

FIG 87

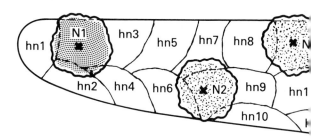

North facing or in a shaded situation
*evergreen

Shrubs
*N1	*Rhododendron cinnabarinum* 'Concatenans' (or *Ilex aquifolium* 'Golden Milkboy')
N2	*Hydrangea* 'Preziosa' (or 'Geoffrey Chadbund')
N3	*Acer palmatum* 'Bloodgood'
*N4	*Berberis verruculosa*
*N5	*Cotoneaster lacteus* (or *Sambucus racemosa* 'Plumosa Aurea')
*N6	*Weigela praecox* 'Variegata' (or 'Rubidor')
*N7	*Daphne bholua* 'Jacqueline Postill'
N8	*Acer palmatum* 'Dissectum'
*N9	*Mahonia japonica*
*N10	*Rhododendron* 'Winsome' (or *Viburnum* 'Anne Russell')

Herbaceous Plants
hn1	*Alchemilla mollis*
hn2	*Geranium wallichianum* 'Buxton's Variety' (or 'Johnson's Blue')
hn3	*Astilbe* 'Bressingham Beauty'
hn4	*Bergenia* 'Ballawley'
hn5	*Anemone hybrida* 'Queen Charlotte'
hn6	*Hosta* 'August Moon' (or *fortunei* 'Aurea')
hn7	*Campanula latifolia* 'Brantwood' (or 'Gloaming')
hn8	*Kirengeshoma palmata*
hn9	*Helleborus foetidus*
hn10	*Brunnera macrophylla* 'Variegata' (or *macrophylla*)
hn11	*Ajuga reptans* 'Burgundy Glow'
hn12	*Aconitum septentrionalis* 'Ivorine'
hn13	*Lysimachia clethroides*
hn14	*Paeonia* 'Sarah Bernhardt'
hn15	*Dicentra eximia* 'Alba' (or 'Luxurians')
hn16	*Phlox paniculata* 'White Admiral'
hn17	*Astilbe taquetii* 'Superba'
hn18	*Hosta* 'Royal Standard'
hn19	*Lamium* 'Beacon Silver' (or *Pulmonaria saccharata* 'Pink Dawn')
hn20	*Epimedium rubrum*
hn21	*Liriope muscari*
hn22	*Astrantia major* 'Sunningdale Variegated'
hn23	*Astilbe* 'Irrlicht'
hn24	*Phlox maculata* 'Alpha' (or 'Omega')
hn25	*Campanula lactiflora* 'Prichard's Variety'
hn26	*Bergenia* 'Silver Light'
hn27	*Hosta undulata*
hn28	*Helleborus orientalis*
hn29	*Rodgersia aesculifolia* (or *tabulensis*)
hn30	*Paeonia* 'Karl Rosenfield'
hn31	*Aconitum* 'Bressingham Spire'
hn32	*Cimicifuga ramosa* 'Atropurpurea' (or *racemosa*)
hn33	*Phlox paniculata* 'Starfire'
hn34	*Anemone hybrida* 'White Queen'
hn35	*Helleborus lividus* 'Corsicus'
hn36	*Campanula alliarifolia* 'Ivory Bells'
hn37	*Astilbe* 'Fire' (or 'Fanal')
hn38	*Hosta* 'Halcyon' (or 'Elegans')
hn39	*Epimedium x warleyense* (or *perralderanum*)
hn40	*Gentiana asclepiadea*

FIG 88

SHRUBACEOUS ISLAND BED
Dwarf and slow growing conifers; dwarf compact shrubs and herbaceous ground cover plants for all fertile soils, in an open, but not exposed situation. Viewed from all sides the island bed is more effective if mounded up to 15cm (6in) proud of surrounding lawns.

Conifers
C1	*Chamaecyparis lawsoniana* 'Green Globe' or 'Pygmaea Argentea'
C2	*Pinus mugo* 'Ophir' or *parviflora* 'Adcock's Dwarf'
C3	*Juniperus communis* 'Hibernica' (or 'Sentinel')

Shrubs
S1	*Ceanothus* 'Blue Mound' (or *thyrsiflorus repens*)
S2	*Viburnum davidii*
S3	*Berberis thunbergii* 'Pink Queen' (or 'Rose Glow')
S4	*Daphne x mantensiana* 'Manten' (or *tangutica*)

Herbaceous perennials and ground cover
hi1	*Geranium* 'Ann Folkard' (or *sanguineum lancastriense*)
hi2	*Artemisia maritima canescens*
hi3	*Sedum* 'Autumn Joy'
hi4	*Hakonechloa macra* 'Albo-aurea' (grass)
hi5	*Aster* (dwarf) *novi-belgii* 'Audrey'
hi6	*Lavandula spica* 'Rosea'
hi7	*Paeonia officinalis* 'Alba Plena' (or 'Rosea Plena')

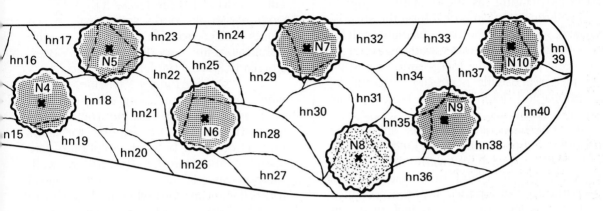

hi8   *Ruta graveolens* 'Jackman's Blue'
hi9   *Helianthemum* 'Jubilee'
hi10   *Helianthemum* 'Mrs C. W. Earle'
hi11   *Salvia nemerosa* 'Lubeca'
hi12   *Gypsophila* 'Rosy Veil'
hi13   *Iris pallida dalmatica* 'Variegata'
hi14   *Lavandula spica* 'Hidcote' (or 'Munstead')
hi15   *Euphorbia polychroma*

hi16   *Santolina chamaecyparissus nana (corsica)*
hi17   *Stachys macrantha*
hi18   *Vinca minor* 'Bowles' Variety' (or 'Gertrude Jekyll')
hi19   *Waldsteinia ternata*
hi20   *Molinia caerulea* 'Variegata' (grass)
hi21   *Helianthemum* 'Wisley Primrose'
hi22   *Polygonum vaccinifolium*

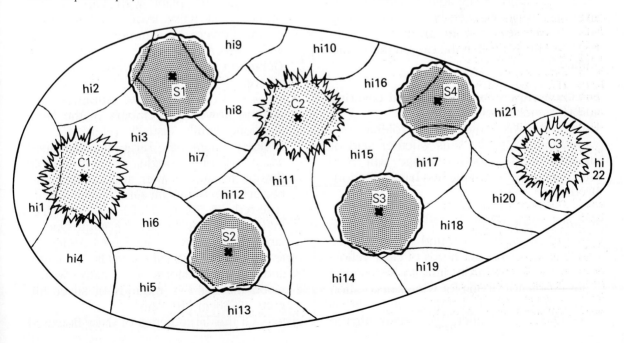

prepared area, shrubs should be planted at least 60cm (2ft) distant from vigorous herbaceous planting, as these mature quickly and will tend to swamp or inhibit the shrubs' growth. While most herbaceous plants will be of low stature occasional variations in height or accent points in the foreground or middle distance are usually necessary – aconitum, kniphofia and delphinium are typical plants for such situations.

Most herbaceous perennials should be grouped in threes or fives of a kind, 30–45cm (12–18in) apart each way within the group. It is worth having island beds and borders prepared well in advance and in accordance with the advice on this subject given in chapter 5 under Planting and Establishment. Incorporation of well-rotted farmyard manure and a slow-release fertiliser will ensure rapid establishment and good growth. The planting should be easily maintained and should provide colour and interest at all seasons. Even within the limitations mentioned above there are plenty of hardy herbaceous perennials – indeed almost too many – to choose from and certainly enough to satisfy most tastes. Any discrepancies in arrangement are easily adjusted in the next planting season, or even beforehand during the growing season if the ground is consistently moist, as is often the case in the British summer.

Selection of perennials for ground covering and to associate with shrubs

Unless otherwise noted, all are tolerant of a wide range of fertile soils whether acid or alkaline (limy). Good drainage will help with overwintering of the less hardy or short-lived.

Achillea 'Moonshine'
  A yarrow with year-round silver filigree foliage and large flat heads of clear yellow flowers effective from June to August and invaluable for drying for winter decoration thereafter. 60cm (2½ft). *Filipendulina* 'Gold Plate' is taller, has green filigree foliage and large dense heads of golden flowers retaining their colour well when cut and dried 1–1.5m (3½–5ft).

Aconitum – Monkshood – spiky easily grown plants effective in summer, with delphinium-like hooded flowers. 'Bressingham Spire' (violet-blue) and *A. x bicolor septentrionalis* 'Ivorine' (ivory white) are excellent, about 90cm (3ft).

Agapanthus The hardy Headbourne Hybrids 60cm–1m (2–3ft) are superb for their umbels of china blue or violet-blue, late summer and autumn flowers. A well-drained site is necessary. Select good forms if you can – buy when in flower from a garden centre or nursery. A large white-flowered variety *A. campanulatus* 'Albus' is less often seen and well worth acquiring and is hardy.

Ajuga Forms or cultivars of our native bugle (*A. reptans*) make excellent ground cover, particularly in moist conditions. 'Atropurpurea', bronze-purple leaves; 'Burgundy Glow' has purple leaves becoming wine-red as the season advances, and edged with cream and pink. Both 15cm (6in).

Alchemilla mollis (Lady's mantle) is a popular clump-forming plant with large round, pleated, soft hairy leaves and greenish-yellow flowers in summer. Blends well with *Nepeta* (catmint) or blue hardy *Geranium*. 25cm (9–12in). Succeeds everywhere.

Anemone x hybrida Late summer and autumn flowering members of the large anemone family, usually referred to as Japanese anemones. Large saucer-shaped white or pink single or semi-double flowers in late summer and autumn, particularly 'Bressingham Glow' semi-double rose-red, 35–50cm (1½ft); 'Queen Charlotte', single pink, 60cm (2ft); 'White Queen' large single white, about 1m (3–3½ft).

Artemisia maritima f. *canescens* is a beautiful and non-invasive form of our native Wormwood making low mounds of silver filigree. 25–30cm (10–12in).

Aster Of this large genus of daisy-flowered

plants the well-known Michaelmas daisies are most common. Regrettably these are often marred by mildew and can be unreliable in their performance, though some of the smaller dwarf hybrids are rewarding. Instead try the dwarf compact disease-free *amellus* cultivars, notably 'King George', brilliant ultramarine blue, 60cm (2ft) and the very beautiful hybrid *x frikartii* with large peacock blue flowers with orange centres, 80cm (2½ft) prominently featured at Hidcote and other National Trust gardens; cultivars of *A. novae-angliae* are also disease-free and distinct in habit and foliage, particularly the new 'Alma Potschke', a compact newcomer with startling salmon-rose flowers on branching heads, about 1m (3ft); among dwarf Michaelmas daisies, *A. novii-belgii* 'Audrey', mauve-blue, 30cm (1ft) and 'Little Pink Beauty', 40cm (16in) are particularly good value.

Astilbe The herbaceous spiraeas, with their conspicuous brightly coloured plumes contribute a brilliant display in July and August; deep moist soil will produce the best results. Good cultivars are 'Bressingham Beauty' deep rich pink, about 1m (3ft); 'Fire' an intense salmon-red, 60cm (2ft) and 'Irrlicht' snowy-white, with dark tinted foliage, 50cm (about 1½ft).

Astrantia major Masterwort – is a vigorous, easy plant for semi-shade, with attractive, long-lasting pale green flowers, usually tinted pink or red, 60cm (2ft).; *A. major* 'Sunningdale Variegated' is a beautifully marked selection of this species, its handsome lobed leaves conspicuously splashed with cream and yellow, the typical umbels of flower following as a bonus later in the summer, as the variegation ages to green.

Bergenia An indispensable plant for shrubaceous planting with roundish leathery evergreen leaves, a winter or early spring flower. An adaptable plant for shade. Some first-class hybrids of German origin include 'Ballawley' ('Delbees'), with leaves attractively tinted red in winter and bright

pink flowers in March or April, about 30cm (1ft); 'Evening Glow' ('Abendglut') with copper-coloured winter leaves and deep crimson-purple flowers in May, 30cm (1ft); and 'Silverlight' ('Silberlicht'), white-flowered, aging to pink, 30cm (1ft).

Brunnera macrophylla (*Anchusa myosotidiflora*) can best be described as a large leaved perennial forget-me-not, useful as ground cover and very pretty in May and June with its bright blue flowers. There is a scarce form 'Variegata' with leaves splashed creamy-white which is well worth seeking out. Shelter from cold wind is desirable. 50cm (1½ft).

Campanula Of the large family of bell-flowers there are several appropriate for our planting in shrubaceous borders and island beds, notably *alliarifolia* 'Ivory Bells' – particularly tolerant of shade it has rosettes of soft hairy grey-green heart-shaped leaves, from which come arching stems of creamy-white flowers, effective for a long period between June and August; *lactiflora* is taller, but also useful in this setting. Its flowers can be variable in colour and the best forms usually available are 'Prichard's Variety', violet-blue, and 'Loddon Anna', soft lilac-pink. Both are 1.2–1.5m (4–5ft); *latifolia* is a form of our native giant bellflower, very striking with stout erect stems and large pendulous flowers, particularly 'Alba' (white) and 'Brantwood' (violet-purple), both 1.2m (4ft). Both *lactiflora* and *latifolia* cultivars are useful to give height between shrub specimens.

Crocosmia Exciting and garden effective Montbretia-like plants with spiky or sword-like leaves and summer flowers in startling shades of red, orange and yellow; newer hybrids include 'Lucifer' – a brilliant large orange-red is robust in growth to about 1m (3ft) while 'Emily Mckenzie' 60cm (2–2½ft) has deep orange flowers with mahogany coloured throat and 'Citronella' is lemon yellow 60cm (2–2½ft). Protect corms from hard frost.

Delphinium can also be used to good advant-

age, particularly the dainty Belladonna hybrids, generally shorter, with smaller flowers, than the more conventional large-flowered hybrids. Seed-raised plants of varieties like 'Cliveden Beauty' single 1m (3ft); 'Lamartine' violet-blue 1.5m (5ft) and 'Summer Skies', sky blue, 1.5m (5ft), may show some variation in flower, but usually within acceptable limits. Vegetatively-propagated cultivars of delphinium are scarce today in nurseries. Some of the old named varieties are becoming conservation items for collectors or connoisseurs.

Dicentra (*Dielytra*) (Dutchman's breeches or bleeding hearts) are excellent in shady situations, providing dainty fern-like, usually glaucous foliage; *eximia* 'Alba' has white and 'Luxurians' deep rose flowers on graceful stems. From the shape of the flowers you see how this plant earned its common name; the larger taller *spectabilis*, while striking in flower, has the disadvantage of dying down after flowering and leaving a hole in the border!

Epimedium (barrenwort or bishop's hat) the latter name referring to the delightful flowers is an excellent groundcover plant, its flowers daintily poised on slender stems with the young leaves in spring; the foliage remains as pleasing groundcover, adding a bonus of autumn tint. Among a number of species and hybrids the following are particularly rewarding: *perralderianum*, an Algerian species with bright yellow flowers in arching sprays and glossy green leaves with prickly edges, 25cm (10in); *x rubrum* with crimson flowers and good autumn leaf colour, 30cm (1ft); *x warleyense*, a lovely and distinct hybrid with coppery-red flowers, 25cm (10in) and particularly the doyenne of the genus *x youngianum* 'Niveum', a very beautiful little plant with bronze young leaves and glistening white flowers, on slender stems, 15cm (6in).

Shrub roses and herbaceous planting at Mottisfont Abbey Rose Garden, Hampshire

Euphorbia Of the many spurges, the following two are appropriate for our task and are usually readily available: *polychroma* produces bright yellow bracts in early spring, forming mounds 45cm (1½ft) in height; *robbiae* (Mrs Robb's spurge) is mildly invasive, but excellent groundcover, with dark evergreen rosettes on erect stems and bright yellow flower heads, up to 45cm or 50cm (about 1½ft). *E. griffithii* 'Fireglow' is perhaps the most colourful of the hardier spurges quickly forming large clumps up to 80cm–1m (about 3ft) high, surmounted in May with brilliant flame-coloured bracts contrasting well with the bright green foliage.

Gentiana We usually think of gentians as low-growing mountain plants, but *asclepiadea*, the willow gentian, is an admirable plant for our purpose, with graceful arching stems and clusters of gentian-blue flowers in the axils of the leaves in late summer. There is a white form 'Alba'. Both reach 60cm (about 2ft). Willow gentians are a great feature in the wild garden at Wisley.

Geranium The cranesbill or true hardy geranium are among the most colourful and useful of groundcover plants, and associate magnificently with shrubs; colourful and beautiful in both leaf and flower in sun or shade, even dry shade. Among the best and most perpetual are 'Ann Folkard', golden yellow foliage and magenta flowers 30cm (12in); *endressii* 'A. T. Johnson' or 'Wargrave Pink', silvery pink 45cm (1½ft); 'Johnson's Blue' with deeply cut foliage and clouds of bright blue flowers throughout the summer; *macrorrhizum* 'Ingwersen's Variety', aromatic foliage, compact neat habit and shell pink flowers from May to July, 35cm (14in). There is also a white-flowered form. And, finally, the popular, if slightly tender, *wallichianum* 'Buxton's Variety' with beautiful cup-shaped violet-purple flowers with white eyes, from July to September. About 30cm (1ft).

Gypsophila paniculata 'Rosy Veil' Essentially a plant for well-drained sunny positions, where it will form excellent groundcover to about 30cm (1ft). The mounds of grey foliage are covered throughout the summer with dainty double pink flowers and are as useful for cutting as the flowers of its taller relatives.

Helianthemum Strictly a dwarf ground-covering shrub, this has always been considered with herbaceous perennials. The sun roses or rock roses are indispensable sun-loving groundcover plants for the foreground of well-drained border or island bed. A small plant will rapidly make a 60cm (2ft) wide mound or more of green or grey-green evergreen foliage, often completely covered in summer with brilliant, usually saucer-shaped flowers, in a remarkable range of colours. There are one or two good double forms. As a genus they are not long lived, but clipping when flowering is over to maintain a compact habit will keep them going for some years. They are excellent value. Some of the best cultivars are nummularium 'Amy Baring', clear orange, compact; H. 'Firedragon', orange-flame; 'Jubilee', double primrose yellow; 'Mrs C. W. Earle', double scarlet; 'Rhodanthe Carneum', pale pink with orange base and silvery-grey foliage; and 'Wisley Primrose' and 'Wisley Pink' with single flowers and grey foliage.

Helleborus A group of magnificent shade-loving early-flowering plants which include the well-known Christmas roses, (*H. niger*) with pure white summer-shaped flowers from December to March, 30cm (1ft), and the Lenten Rose (*orientalis*), usually available in a mixture of colours from white and crimson to purple with delightful spotting and flecking; the cup-shaped blooms hang on stems of up to 45cm (1½ft) from January to March. Our native *Helleborus foetidus* is a most rewarding plant, significant throughout winter, with panicles of green, purple-tipped nodding blooms above mounds of deeply cut evergreen leaves, 60cm (2ft). Equally evergreen, the Corsican hellebore *lividus corsicus* forms clumps of leathery and spiny glaucous leaves, copper-tinted when young; apple-green saucer-shaped flowers are produced in quantity in February and March. This is an outstanding plant. Both *foetidus* and *lividus corsicus* make an important contribution to the winter garden scene.

Hemerocallis (day lily) is a clump-forming, long-lived herbaceous perennial, useful early in the year for its distinctive clumps of graceful, fresh green, arching leaves and during summer for its long succession of trumpet flowers borne in clusters. Moist soil is to be preferred. Hybridists, particularly in the USA have worked extensively on this genus; among the many cultivars available are three distinct and outstanding varieties, 'Golden Chimes', deep yellow, 60cm (2ft); 'Pink Damask', reflexed deep pink flowers, 75cm (2–3ft) and 'Stafford', deep crimson with greenish-yellow throat, 75cm (2–3ft).

Hosta The plantain lily is considered by many the most handsome and desirable of all herbaceous plants. It offers superb arching leaves in summer and erect stems of pendulous tubular or trumpet-shaped flowers from mid-summer to autumn. Hostas will thrive in any fertile soil in sun or shade, providing it is moist. There has been great interest in recent years in Britain and the United States in selecting and breeding interesting new cultivars. The late Eric Smith, Hillier's herbaceous propagator in the 1950s and early 60s, bred a number of new hybrids involving the late-flowering species *H. tardiflora* and contributing in no small measure to the popularity of the genus. Some of his hybrids are now being extensively propagated, and specialist societies promote the genus enthusiastically. Among the many species and hybrids commercially available in Britain, the following are particularly outstanding: 'August Moon', a recent American introduction, with large golden-yellow leaves which hold their colour well throughout the summer, even in a sunny situation. Flowers are pale mauve, 60cm (2ft); *crispula* although now scarce remains one of the choicest and most elegant of variegated species; 'Elegans' (*sieboldiana* 'Elegans'), has some of the largest leaves of any hosta, corrugated and silvery-grey, 60cm (2ft); *fortunei* 'Albopicta' is most striking in May and June, when its clumps of broad oval leaves are bright yellow with a contrasting green edge. The flowers are lilac in July and August, 50–60cm (1½–2ft); 'Frances Williams' is an outstanding cultivar, in effect 'Elegans' with unusual beige-yellow variegation and mauve flowers from June to August, up to 1m (3ft); *lancifolia* is quite distinct with small clumps of narrow, shining deep-green leaves and quantities of lilac or violet flowers from July to September – a splendid contrast with the larger-leaved species; 'Royal Standard' is a hybrid of *plantaginea*, with pale green prominently-veined leaves and scented white tubular flowers in late summer and autumn; 'Thomas Hogg' has deep green leaves with broad creamy-white margins and remains one of the most reliable variegated varieties. The flowers are deep lilac in June and July, 60cm (2ft); *undulata* produces neat clumps of leaves with wavy margins and prominent central white variegation; 'Halcyon' is an Eric Smith *tardiana* hybrid, forming mounds of bright silvery-grey leaves of good substance and deep lilac flowers in July and August, 45cm (1½ft); *ventricosa* 'Variegata' one of the best and most handsome of all variegated hostas has large, shining, heart-shaped leaves generously edged with gold. Unusual deep-blue flowers are produced in July and August. About 90cm (2–3ft).

Note that slugs and snails will cause great damage to the hairless unprotected leaves of hostas. Wage war with slug and snail pellets, and liquid slug killer, if you wish to enjoy your hostas at their best. These pests are most active in moist warm summer weather.

You can have the best of both worlds by associating hostas with some of the best daffodil varieties which can be planted in groups on the fringes of the clumps. After they have performed in the early spring, the dying foliage of the daffodils is covered by the arching leaves of the hostas.

Iris Of this large and diverse genus a select few species and varieties are particularly useful and effective in shrubaceous borders – *I. foetidissima*, the native Gladwyn iris is remarkably shade tolerant. Its evergreen leaves and showy scarlet seeds in winter well compensate for its dingy lilac blue flowers; its cultivar 'Variegata' has leaves longitudinally striped creamy white; both attain 60cm (2–2½ft); *pallida dalmatica* 'Variegata' is indeed a very striking plant throughout the growing season, its blue-grey sword-like leaves, generously striped creamy white; *p. d.* 'Aurea Variegata' is a scarcer plant with golden variegated leaves; both have excellent large mid-blue flowers – well worthy of a sunny well drained focal point, *unguicularis* (*stylosa*) the lavender blue, winter flowering Algerian iris is well known and indispensable for a hot dry sunny position; its cultivar 'Mary Barnard' is a much improved free-flowering form worth seeking out.

Kirengeshoma palmata A typical native of Japan, its elegant palmate foliage, reminiscent of the Japanese maple. In late summer and autumn, tubular, waxy, canary-yellow bell flowers appear poised on stems up to about 1m (3ft) high. A moist and shaded situation is desirable.

Kniphofia (*Tritoma*) the red hot poker or torch lily is of great value as an accent point in foreground or middle distance, and to provide a bold effect. In some species the yucca-like foliage is evergreen or near evergreen; *caulescens* with bicolor flowers of buff-yellow and salmon-red in June, set

Shrubaceous planting associations, in a south facing area of Bodnant Gardens, North Wales: Eucryphia glutinosa *with* Achillea 'Coronation Gold', Anaphalis triplinervis *and* Potentilla x tonguei

Shrubaceous planting associations in a north facing border. Sambucus racemosa 'Plumosa Aurea' *with* Anemone x hybrida 'Queen Charlotte'

against broad, glaucous foliage is a distinct and worthwhile species, about 1m (3ft). A delightful dwarf species *galpinii* is invaluable for its late, saffron-orange flowers produced in September and October amid grass-like foliage, 50–80cm (2–2½ft). An ever-changing range of named hybrids in many shades and combinations of yellow, scarlet and orange are offered today by nurserymen. 'C. M. Prichard' bronzy-orange 1.85m (5–6ft); 'Little Maid' yellow shading to ivory-white 60cm (2½ft) and 'Shining Sceptre' golden orange 1m (3ft) are excellent new varieties.

Lamium (dead nettle) is excellent ground-cover; *maculatum*, spotted dead nettle, has a prominent central white stripe to its leaves and pink-purple flowers in May. It can be invasive and may require some controlling. 'Beacon Silver' with smaller bright silvery leaves with narrow green margins, and pink flowers is much less invasive and no more than 10cm (4in).

Lavandula A familiar and much-loved garden plant. Lavender makes excellent dwarf hedges and associates well with stonework and rose plantings, and can also be used effectively in groups in the fore-ground of shrubaceous borders or island beds. Essentially a maritime plant, it succeeds almost anywhere in well-drained conditions and an open sunny site. All species and varieties are aromatic, and there is now some variation in colour and habit. In addition to the familiar *angusti-folia* (*spica*), the old English lavender, notable cultivars are 'Alba' with narrow grey-green leaves and white flowers on erect stems in June, about 1m (3ft); 'Hidcote' ('Nana Atropurpurea') perhaps the most popular, certainly the most compact form; with narrow grey-green leaves and dense violet spikes, 60cm (2ft); 'Munstead', which can best be described as a compact dwarf form of the old English lavender, producing typical lavender-blue flowers in early July; and to complete the colour range, a neat, compact, narrow-leaved form 'Rosea' with lavender-pink flowers in July, 60cm (2ft); *vera*, the Dutch lavender has distinctly broader grey leaves with lavender-blue flowers and is of robust growth, up to about 1m (3ft).

Liriope muscari A shade-tolerant member of the lily family, making clumps of arching evergreen grass-like foliage. Grape-hyacinth-like violet-purple spikes of bell-shaped flowers appear as late as September and October. A useful and unusual groundcover plant worthy of wider use, 45cm (1½ft).

Lysimachia (loosestrife) is excellent ground-cover and a spectacular flowering plant; *clethroides* forms clumps of graceful arching stems terminating in racemes of white clethra-like flowers from July to September. The long willowy leaves tint well in the autumn, about 1m (3ft); *nummularia* Creeping Jenny makes most useful low groundcover in shady places or on moist banks. A familiar cottage-garden plant, its bright yellow flowers show up well against the dark green leaves. There is also a yellow leaved form 'Aurea', 5cm (2in); *punctata* is taller and very conspicuous with whorls of bright yellow flowers in July and August. It associates well with *Lythrum*, purple loosestrife, growing well in moist border or waterside conditions, 1m (3ft).

Lythrum (purple loosestrife) is a British native that in selected forms makes showy border plants and is excellent by water. *L. salicaria* 'Firecandle' produces spikes of bright rose red in July and August, 1.5m (5ft). A more dwarf plant, *virgatum* 'Rose Queen' has bright rose-purple flowers, not usually exceeding 60cm (2ft).

Nepeta x faassenii (*mussinii* Hort.) – catmint – is a familiar and invaluable edging and groundcovering plant, with aromatic grey foliage and spikes of lavender-mauve flowers produced from May to September. 'Six Hills Giant' is slightly taller and hardier. Associates well with *Alchemilla mollis* and is best in a sunny, well-drained condition; spring planting is recommended.

Ophiopogon planiscapus 'Nigrescens' Distinct and unusual as low-growing groundcover, with blackish-purple evergreen leaves in grass-like tufts, small white flowers in late summer and then black berries. Adaptable to sunshine or shade, 10cm (4in).

Pachysandra terminalis A most useful evergreen, shrubby, carpeting plant; toothed leaves are clustered at stem tips. Small whitish flowers are produced in February and March. 'Variegata' is the form with silver-variegated leaves. Both make reliable, if slow, groundcover in shade.

Paeonia Paeonies are much loved and long-lived garden plants for sunshine and semi-shade. Established clumps produce spectacular double or single flowers from the end of May until the beginning of July. The foliage often tints crimson in autumn. Among many varieties usually available, the following are particularly notable for their large scented blossoms; 'Bowl of Beauty', large semi-double, deep pink with creamy centre; 'Duchesse de Nemours', double cream, fading white, fragrant blooms; 'Karl Rosenfield', double, deep crimson; 'Sarah Bernhardt', apple blossom pink, double.

The old fashioned cottage garden paeonies, so reliable and spectacular in flower each year, are regrettably not scented; *officinalis* 'Alba Plena', double white; *o.* 'Rosea Plena', double pink and *o.* 'Rubra Plena', double, deep crimson, all attaining about 75cm (2½ft); *peregrina* (*lobata*) 'Sunshine' is distinct with large, single salmon-orange flowers in May, 75cm (2½ft).

Phlox The border phlox, with their wide range of colour are among the most desirable of plants, particularly for moist semi-shade, producing fragrant blooms from July to September. Regrettably they are not without problems and sometimes are not the easiest plants to establish. Check before buying that container-grown plants do not bear signs of eelworm infection – usually evident in poor brittle growth and puckered, distorted leaves. Excellent, well-tried varieties still commercially available include: *maculata* 'Alpha', with tapering spikes of pink flowers, 80cm (2–2½ft) and the following *paniculata* (*decussata*) varieties: 'Dodo Hanbury Forbes', clear pink, 1m (3ft); 'Harlequin' with leaves variegated creamy-white and violet flowers which contrast well, 1m (3ft); 'Marlborough', compact habit and purple flowers, 1m (3ft); 'Prince of Orange', large orange panicles, 60cm (2ft); 'Sandringham', large pink flowers with darker centre 75cm (2½ft); 'Starfire', perhaps the best red available, about 1m (3ft); and 'White Admiral', the best white variety now available, 75cm (2½ft).

Polygonatum x hybridum (Solomon's seal) has white hanging bell-like flowers and graceful arching stems clothed with pointed ovate leaves. A familiar and invaluable plant for the shadiest of conditions under trees.

Polygonum A large and varied genus containing many weedy plants of no horticultural value, as well as a number of rampant plants suitable for waterside and naturalising. Hardy species particularly appropriate for shrubaceous borders include *bistorta* 'Superbum', a compact large-flowered form of our native bistort, producing long cylindrical spikes of bright pink flowers in July and again in September, 60cm (2ft); *campanulatum*, mildly invasive, but controllable and well worthy of a border position, with grey-green pointed leaves and pale pink flowers over an extended period in summer, 1m (3ft); *vacciniifolium* forms mats of wiry trailing stems, conspicuous well into the autumn with spikes of bright pink flowers, 15cm (6in) and excellent low groundcover.

Potentilla Although most people think of potentillas as shrubs, there are a number of worthy herbaceous species and cultivars which make excellent, showy free-flowering groundcover, notably *nepalensis* 'Miss Willmott', with sprawling masses of straw-

berry-like foliage and carmine-pink flowers throughout the summer, 30–50cm (1–1½ft) and 'Gibson's Scarlet', with large single vivid red flowers and a similar habit, 50cm (1½ft).

Pulmonaria (lungwort) is a most attractive and useful spring flowering, shade tolerant groundcover plant: *angustifolia Azurea* has gentian blue hanging bells and associates well with the common primrose, 15–25cm (6–10in), while *saccharata* has white marbled foliage and flowers of variable colour from pink to blue; *rubra* 'Bowles' Red' and *s.* 'Pink Dawn', both 25cm (10in) are selected for their distinct flower colours. Forms of *saccharata* showing exceptional silvery-leaf variegation are worth seeking out and can be most effective in shady areas – one has been named 'Argentea'. Pulmonarias are useful in dry shade.

Rodgersia Handsome plants for moist soil in sun or shade, notable as much for their distinct and variable foliage as for their complementary spikes of white or pink flowers, produced in June or July. They associate well with waterside plantings: *aesculifolia* has horse chestnut-like leaves and white flowers, 1.2m (4ft); *pinnata* 'Superba' has bronze-tinted pinnate leaves and clear-pink flowers, 80cm (2½–3ft). *tabularis* is very distinct, with flat parasol-like pale green leaves and spikes of creamy-white flowers, 80cm (2–2½ft).

Rudbeckia The cone flower or black-eyed Susan are easy and effective border plants, particularly *fulgida* 'Goldsturm' (*sullivantii* 'Goldsturm'), a fine plant with stiff stems and masses of golden, black-centred daisy flowers with pointed petals from July to September, 75cm (2½ft).

Ruta graveolens 'Jackman's Blue' A much-improved selected form of the long-cultivated medicinal herb rue. Bright yellow flowers contrast well with the glaucous

Alchemilla mollis, Geranium endressii
'A. T. Johnson' and Hosta 'Elegans' as
ground cover beneath Cordyline australis

blue, much divided, foliage which is pungently aromatic when touched. Prune back in the spring to maintain a compact habit, 60cm (2ft).

Salvia The hardier herbaceous and sub-shrubby species of sage are among the most effective groundcovering and decorative plants for the border. They include the common sage, *officinalis*, with aromatic grey-green foliage and blue-purple flowers, much valued as a pot herb. Several cultivars have variegated or coloured leaves, particularly 'Icterina', variegated green and gold, and 'Tricolor' of more compact habit and less robust growth, its leaves splashed with creamy-white and suffused with purple and pink, up to 60cm (2ft). *S. nemerosa* 'Lubecca' ('Compacta') has dense spikes of rich purple flowers in the summer. A compact form of an old border favourite, 50–60cm (1½–2ft).

Santolina The lavender cottons are invaluable, dense, low-growing evergreen shrubs with usually grey foliage and dainty button-like yellow flowers. They associate well with sages and lavenders and are best in a dry sunny situation. *S. chamaecyparissus* (*incana*) has densely woolly, silver-hued foliage and lemon-yellow flowers, 50–60cm (1½–2ft); the Corsican form of this, *S. c. nana* (*corsica*), is distinctly more compact, about 30cm (1ft); *pinnata* 'Edward Bowles' has less dense finely divided grey-green foliage and primrose-yellow flowers, 60cm (2ft); *virens* (*viridis*) has a dense, rounded habit with vivid green, almost thread-like leaves, contrasting well with bright lemon-yellow flowers, 60cm (2ft).

Sedum Most of the smaller-leaved species of this large family are suited to the rock garden, but larger-leaved kinds make good border plants for sunny situations, their late summer and autumn flowers are attractive to butterflies and bees. Among the best available are 'Autumn Joy', with large long-lasting salmon-pink flowers, bronze tinted in September and October,

about 50cm (1½ft) and 'Ruby Glow', a first-class plant of lax habit; deep ruby-red flowers appear well against the blue-grey foliage, September to October, about 25cm (10in).

Smilacina racemosa A handsome plant, reminiscent of Solomon's seal and liking similar shady conditions. Distinct in its panicles of creamy-white flowers in May and June, 60cm (2ft).

Stachys Several species make excellent groundcover, notably *macrantha* (*Betonica grandiflora*) or betony. It is a vigorous and effective groundcover plant with broadly ovate, downy leaves and large rosy-violet hooded flowers in spiked whorls in May and June – worthy of wider planting, 50cm (1½ft). The more familiar *olympica* (*lanata*) – lamb's tongue – has silvery-grey felt-like leaves, and spikes of purple-pink flowers in July. The non-flowering form 'Silver Carpet', 10–20cm (4–8in) is the best form to plant for effective grey groundcover in dry sunny situations.

Tiarella (foam flower) makes excellent groundcover in shady places and is not invasive. Spikes of white flowers in feathery masses are produced in May and June, 25cm (10in).

Vinca (Periwinkle) popular, much planted, trailing evergreens which thrive in sun or shade. While *major*, greater periwinkle, is a rampant grower suitable for unsightly banks, its variegated form 'Variegata' ('Elegantissima') is less invasive and brightly margined creamy/white. Both have bright blue flowers from May to September, and attain about 50cm (1½ft). *V. minor*, the lesser periwinkle, makes neat and pleasing groundcover and is much smaller and more prostrate. Of a number of cultivars the following are particularly rewarding in flower; 'Bowles Variety', single azure-blue; 'Gertrude Jekyll', with glistening white flowers, well worthy of the name it bears; and 'Variegata' with leaves marginally variegated creamy white, and blue flowers.

Waldsteinia A most useful low and effective carpeting plant of the strawberry family. Neat carpets of trifoliate hairy leaves persist well; bright yellow flowers in the spring make a pleasing contrast, 10cm (4in). Sun or semi-shade.

PLANTS FOR SPECIAL FEATURES

Courtyards, terraces and patios

Most gardens today have a sitting area – sometimes no more than a few concrete slabs, probably facing south and sunny, it is hoped. More favoured gardens have a patio or terrace of patterned paving, perhaps relieved with areas of brick and gravel. A few people are proud possessors of a courtyard, paved with natural stone, where there may be areas of warm sunshine or cool shade and shelter from the wind. Design and construction of these desirable features are discussed elsewhere (p78–9). Here suitable plants are recommended to complement such areas – shrubs, shrub roses, associating herbaceous plants and, perhaps, a small tree to delight the eye and provide colour and interest at all seasons when viewed from the house. Scent of flower and foliage is very important; the ultimate shape, size and vigour of shrubs and plants must be considered in order to make an interesting and effective blend. Of course, many of the essentially hardy, compact or smaller-growing subjects considered in the Plant Profiles, chapter 8, and in the list of shrubs and plants for shrubaceous borders are equally appropriate here, but in these sheltered walled areas against the house, we can grow, with a good chance of more permanent success, a considerable range of borderline hardy shrubs, plants and climbers which may not be possible elsewhere in the garden. When planting it is worth ensuring that there is good drainage and there is adequate space to accommodate the wall shrubs and plants you wish to grow. A well-prepared border is best given as much width as can be spared and is so much better than a single slab or less removed for one wall shrub or climber.

Paved areas invite the use of tubs, pots, urns and similar ornamental containers; while these are frequently used for annuals for spring or summer display, permanent planting is certainly possible, but should be carefully chosen – variegated evergreens, some which can be clipped to any reasonable shape and size are suitable choices.

The following is a carefully considered selection of suitable plants to choose from, including some newer introductions – there are many more possibilities:

Climbers for sunny walls

Where there is adequate height or space between windows, *climbing* or *pillar roses* often provide scented and perpetual or recurrent flower. Particularly good value are:

'Aloha' – deep rose-pink, perpetual.
'Iceberg' – the climbing edition of perhaps the most popular white rose.
'Dublin Bay' – double recurrent, deep red.
'Marigold' – vigorous, early, gold with a bronze sheen.

Clematis will often blend in well with roses and live happily with them, particularly the less vigorous large-flowered hybrids for example 'Henryi', creamy-white with two periods of flower and 'Hagley Hybrid', soft shell-pink from June to September; include also some of the species, notably:

C. *alpina* 'Frances Rivis' – blue with white centre; *alpina* 'Ruby' – purple-pink intermittently through summer
C. *macropetala* 'Maidwell Hall' – the best deep blue form of this double-flowered species
C. *montana* 'Tetrarose' – a superb hybrid of compact strong growth, lilac-rose flowers and bronze foliage
C. *rehderiana* – delightful cowslip-scented, pale yellow bell flowers in late summer and autumn

Climbers and shrubs for shady walls

Honeysuckles (*Lonicera*) can provide good coverage and satisfying fragrance, particularly:

Lonicera x americana – pale to deep yellow with purple tint in June and July.

L. periclymenum 'Graham Thomas' – a superb selection of the common woodbine, worthy of the name it bears. Regrettably not all honeysuckles are as fragrant as this one.

Variegated ivies which are self-clinging are also excellent to brighten shady walls:

Hedera canariensis 'Gloire de Marengo' provides silver-grey white variegated foliage, and *H. colchica* 'Dentata Variegata' creamy-yellow marginal variegation to their large leaves, while variegated forms of our common ivy (*H. helix*) can be most effective for smaller areas of wall, and notably 'Glacier', silvery-grey leaves with white margin, and 'Goldchild', among many others which has leaves margined yellow.

As space permits, wall shrubs trained to trellis or wire and suitably pruned are of good value as background shrubs – dwarf planting is seen to good advantage against them. Consider particularly:

Ceanothus arboreus 'Trewithen Blue', with its large leaves and deep blue spring flowers, makes a superb wall shrub for patio or courtyard.

For the shadier wall, *Pyracantha* 'Soleil D'Or' with orange-yellow fruits or new, cream-variegated *P. coccinea* 'Sparkler', its leaves pink tinted in autumn, are suitable for a low wall or balustrade.

Robinia hispida 'Macrophylla', the large-leaved form of rose acacia, is a shrub best grown against a sunny wall or fence, where its brittle branches can be well supported. Clusters of rose-pink pea flowers are spectacular at mid-summer.

Cytisus battandieri Moroccan broom – is justifiably popular and an excellent wall shrub, with pineapple-scented cone-shaped clusters of yellow flowers, seen well against the silky grey foliage in July.

Helleborus lividus *'Corsicus'* (argutifolius)

Hosta crispula, *one of the most elegant of variegated species, though now scarce*

The scarce cultivar 'Yellow Tail' has extra long spikes and a more compact habit.

Solanum crispum 'Glasnevin' is an easy and rewarding semi-evergreen climber for sunny fence or wall, yellow-centred purple-blue flowers are produced generously throughout the summer and autumn.

Shrubs for patios and courtyards

The following is a short list of some most desirable shrubs for this task most of them dwarf, mound-forming or of compact habit. Do not plant too closely and consider the ultimate size of the shrub, even allowing for some pruning.

Many familiar plants, for example, *Choisya ternata, Cistus x purpureus, Convolvulus cneorum, Daphne x burkwoodii,* or one of the many hebes, will perform the useful task, if set at the base of climbing rose or clematis, of covering unsightly leggy stems. A climbing plant, particularly clematis, will also appreciate the shading of its root and lower stem and respond with enhanced performance.

Key (Sh) = Shady site desirable
(A) = Acid soil essential
(E) = Evergreen
(T) = Good for tub or container

Abelia – particularly *chinensis,* 'Edward Goucher' and *x grandiflora* (Semi-E)
Abeliophyllum distichum
Acer palmatum 'Dissectum' cultivars (Sh) (T)
Acer palmatum – Japanese Maples – 'Benimaiko' and 'Butterfly' and *japonicum* 'Aureum' (Sh) (See Plant Profiles, chapter 8.)
Camellia – among the multitude of varieties available notably outstanding are *japonica* 'Adolphe Audusson', blood-red with prominent golden stamens; *x williamsii* 'E. T. R. Carlyon', a good late-flowering semi-double to double pure white, and 'Tiptoe', silvery-pink semi-double of bushy upright habit (A) (E) (T)
Ceanothus 'Blue Mound' (E)
Choisya ternata and 'Sundance' (E)
Cistus – sun roses (E) – particularly *x aguilari* 'Maculatus', 'Anne Palmer', 'Peggy Sammons', *x purpureus,* 'Silver Pink' and *x skanbergii.* Good drainage essential.
Convolvulus cneorum (E) one of the finest grey-foliaged plants for a patio.
Daphne – many of the species and cultivars, and particularly *bholua* 'Jacqueline Postill'

(E), *x burkwoodii* semi-(E), *cneorum* and cultivars (E), *collina* (E), *x mantensiana* 'Manten' (E), *odora* 'Aureomarginata' (E), *retusa* (E).
Euonymus – several species and cultivars, particularly the following evergreens which are adaptable to sunshine or shade and will climb a low wall: *fortunei* 'Emerald Gaiety', 'Emerald 'n' Gold', 'Silver Queen' (T) (E).
Fabiana imbricata 'Prostrata' (E)
Fuchsia – many hardy cultivars, particularly 'Chillerton Beauty', 'Genie', 'Lady Thumb', 'Mdme Cornellisen', 'Sharpitor', 'Versicolor', 'Prosperity' and 'Tom Thumb' (T) (Sh).
x Fatshedera lizei (E) and (Sh).
Hebe – many species and cultivars (E) particularly *albicans,* and its new cultivars 'Pewter Dome' and 'Red Edge'. 'Blue Clouds' flowers from June to December; *colensoi* 'Glauca'; *x franciscana* 'Variegata' 'Great Orme'; *pimeleoides* 'Quick-silver'; *recurva; salicifolia* 'Spender's Seedling' (T).
Helichrysum (E) – particularly *serotinum* the curry plant, *italicum* and *splendidum.*
Hedera (E) – including some ivies relatively new to commerce, mound-forming, some variegated and some quite different – 'Bird's Foot', 'Ivalace', 'Little Diamond', 'Manda's Crested' (Sh) (T).
x Halimiocistus (E) *wintonensis* and 'Merristwood Cream' and *Halimium ocymoides* (E).
Hydrangea – many species and cultivars (Sh) (T). Some exciting and compact newcomers include *arborescens* 'Annabelle', 'Ayesha', *involucrata* 'Hortensis'; in the hortensia group, 'Ami Pasquier' and 'Madame Emile Moullière'; in the lacecap group, the unique 'Geoffrey Chadbund', a remarkable light red unaffected by differing soils; 'Seafoam' and 'Tricolor' as much for its variegated leaves as for its flower; *paniculata* 'Praecox' for July flower and 'Tardiva' with its stiff erect spikes in October; *sargentiana* for its bold foliage and 'Preziosa' and *villosa.*

Hypericum – of the many St John's worts very rewarding and less frequently planted are *beanii* 'Gold Cup' with its arching branches, and *kouytchense* with its bright red fruits.

Mimulus aurantiacus (Shrubby Musk) (E).

Myrtus (E) – particularly the new *apiculata* 'Glanleam Gold' (T) and *communis* 'Tarentina' (T).

Nandina domestica and 'Nana Purpurea' (E).

Ozothamnus (E) *ledifolius* and *rosmarini-folius* 'Silver Jubilee'.

Paeonia suffruticosa superb varieties of the Moutan Tree Paeony are available – double or semi-double in pink, red and white.

Perovskia atriplicifolia 'Blue Spire'.

Philadelphus – (mock orange), particularly 'Belle Etoile', 'Manteau d'Hermine', 'Sybille'.

Phlomis (E) *chrysophylla, fruticosa, italica*.

Phormium (E) (New Zealand flax) has many exciting forms with highly coloured and variegated leaves, which have been introduced recently from New Zealand. The larger ones are excellent in the patio border, while weaker growers make excellent tub or container plants: take care that they do not get frozen in winter in a container – they can be put into the garage or cold greenhouse for the hardest weather period. Among the best are *cookianum* 'Tricolor' and 'Cream Delight', 'Dazzler', 'Maori Sunrise', *tenax* 'Sundowner' (T) and *t.* 'Variegata'.

Photinia (E) *x fraseri* 'Red Robin'.

Phygelius (E) Hillier's Peter Dummer has produced a range of exciting new hybrids, outstanding are *aequalis* 'Yellow Trumpet', 'Devil's Tears', 'Moonraker' and 'Winchester Fanfare', all making excellent patio plants.

Pieris (A) (E) – particularly *formosa forrestii* 'Jermyns', *japonica* 'Little Heath' – a new compact and bushy plant with white margined leaves and coppery young growth; *j.* 'Variegata' and 'Bert Chandler' (T).

Pittosporum (E) – well worth a carefully chosen sheltered site; *eugenoides* 'Variegata', 'Garnetti', 'Tom Thumb' and 'Warnham Gold' (T).

Potentilla – of the many available try particularly *arbuscula* 'Beesii', *fruticosa* 'Eastleigh Cream', 'Elizabeth', 'Red Ace' (Sh), 'Tangerine' (Sh).

Prunus tenella 'Fire Hill'.

Punica granatum 'Nana' (Dwarf Pomegranate) (T).

Rhaphiolepis x delacourii 'Coate's Crimson' (E) (T).

Rhamnus alaterna 'Argenteovariegata' (E).

Rhododendron (including *Azalea*) (A) (E) (Sh) (T) – Among the multitude of species and cultivars available today, particularly of note for compact dwarf growth, interesting leaf and reliable flower are: *calostrotum* 'Gigha', *dauricum* 'Midwinter', *nakaharae*, for its brick-red late flowers and the incomparable, irresistible *yakushimanum*. Among the hybrids are 'Brocade', 'Curlew', 'Elizabeth Hobbie', 'Humming Bird' and 'Winsome'. There is a large range of dwarf evergreen Japanese azaleas to choose from – particularly good are: 'Blaauw's Pink', 'Kure-no-yuki', 'Rosebud' and 'Vuyk's Scarlet'.

Rosmarinus officinalis 'Severn Sea' and 'Tuscan Blue' (E) (T).

Skimmia japonica cultivars (E) (Sh).

Sarcococca humilis (E) (Sh).

Spiraea japonica 'Goldflame', 'Shirobana', 'Alpina'.

Viburnum (Sh) *davidii, x juddii, tinus* 'Eve Price'.

Yucca – including variegated cultivars of *filamentosa* and *flaccida*.

Zenobia pulverulenta (A) semi-(E) (Sh) – a little-known shrub with aniseed-scented white blooms in pendulous clusters and bloomy grey-blue leaves and young shoots. Worthy of wider planting.

Roses for patios and courtyards

Roses, particularly shrub roses, including old fashioned, bourbon, china and hybrid musk, are invaluable for flower and fragrance near

Hosta fortunei *'Albopicta'*

the house. Some of the best and most compact and free-flowering include:

Species roses 'Agnes', *chinensis* 'Mutabilis', *ecae* 'Helen Knight', *gallica* 'Versicolor', (Rosa Mundi), *rugosa* 'Fru Dagmar Hastrup'.

Bourbon roses – 'Coupe d'Hebe', 'Gipsy Boy' and 'Zephirine Drouhin'.

Hybrid musk are well represented with 'Ballerina', 'Buff Beauty' and 'Penelope'.

Modern shrub roses with 'Golden Wings', 'Frühlingsmorgen', the excellent new 'Graham Thomas' and 'Marjorie Fair', (red with white eye) and 'Scarlet Fire'.

Old fashioned roses, so desirable for their scent – 'Celestial', 'Charles de Mills', 'Fantin Latour', 'Maiden's Blush' and 'Quatre Saisons Blanc Mousseux'.

New patio roses bred with this setting in mind are neat, compact disease-free, usually with groundcovering potential and marvellous in the foreground, and in association with grey foliage shrubs like lavender, *Santolina* and *Helianthemum*. Try particularly: 'Elegant Pearl', single creamy-white; 'Gentle Touch', pale pink hybrid tea blooms in clusters and Rose of the Year 1986; 'Robin Redbreast', dark red with white eye, bushy and spreading and 'Sweet Magic', double golden-orange – joint Rose of the Year, 1987.

Groundcovering, these free-flowering roses are often listed confusingly under ramblers or modern shrub roses; particularly notable and reliable are 'Nozomi', single pearly pink, prostrate growth; 'Rosy Cushion', large single pink flowers with ivory centres; 'Bonica', rose pink, recurrent, cupped blooms, mound-forming, slowly to about 75cm (2½ft); 'Raubritter', semi-double, silvery-pink of low mounding habit, well featured at Mottisfont Rose Garden; 'Fairy', a delightful groundcovering rose with small shiny leaves and sprays of rose-pink flowers from July until the late autumn is particularly well displayed at the Royal National Rose Society's Gardens near St Albans.

Hardy perennial groundcovering plants for patios and courtyards

Below are listed some good companions to live-in with your shrubs – again many of those listed under plants for shrubaceous borders are equally appropriate here – so we take the opportunity to stress those which are less hardy or require shelter afforded by patio areas.

Acaena – (New Zealand Burr) the grey-green *buchananii* and the bronze-leaved *microphylla*, with its startling red spiny burrs, make excellent carpeting or paving plants 5cm (2in).

Acanthus mollis latifolius The architect's plant fits well in these conditions.

Agapanthus (Lily of the Nile) particularly the Headbourne Hybrids, is also excellent in tubs or containers.

Alchemilla mollis (Lady's mantle) needs no introduction.

Artemisia absinthium 'Lambrook Silver' associates so well with the shrub roses as does the shade-tolerant –

Campanula alliarifolia 'Ivory Bells' and the taller *persicifolia* 'Telham Beauty', its rich blue flowers attaining about 1m (3ft).

Carex morrowii 'Evergold' is strikingly variegated and does well in moist semi-shade.

Crambe cordifolia is one of those bold plants grown as much for its foliage effect as its huge panicles of white gypsophila-like flowers in June and July. Up to 2m (6ft).

Crinum Well sited in deep soil in a sunny border *C. x powellii* is permanent and beautiful with its pale-pink trumpet flowers, excellent for flower arranging.

Crocosmia Although montbretia-like this has large sword-like leaves and sprays of trumpet flowers in vivid colours in summer and autumn. Notable varieties are 'Citronella' (lemon-yellow) and 'Lucifer' (flame red).

Dianthus Most gardeners would not be without the well-loved pinks of our cottage gardens. The native Cheddar pink *gratianopolitanus* (*caesius*), with fragrant single pink flowers in May and June, is gardenworthy, as is x *allwoodii* 'Doris', a perpetual flowering double shell-pink and 'Mrs Sinkins', the common fragrant double white are invaluable for edging paved areas.

Diascia Some of this spectacular group of plants from the highlands of South Africa are proving reasonably hardy in well-drained sunny conditions. They can be brilliant en masse in varying shades of pink. A number of species and cultivars are available and, as yet, names may be a little confused, but all are excellent value. Particularly distinct are 'Ruby Field', which produces a long succession of pale pink-lipped flowers rising from ground-hugging mats of green leaves, to about 25cm (10in) while *rigescens* is taller and more vigorous, possibly less hardy and has spikes of soft-pink flowers, in arching sprays; continuous from June to October.

Dicentra (Dielytra) (Dutchman's breeches and bleeding heart). All are beautiful and happy in shady spots.

Dierama pulcherrima The wand flower has graceful arching stems carrying hanging bells of pink or white trumpet shaped flowers in summer, up to 1.2m (4ft).

Dictamnus albus The burning bush, a beautiful and unusual plant, is so called because the inflammable oil exuded by glands on the flower stalks will ignite on warm summer evenings. The type plant has white flowers, and *purpureus* (*D. fraxinella*) purple or rose-red, 60cm (about 2ft).

Dimorphotheca (Cape marigold or Star of the Veldt) see *Osteospermum*.

Euphorbia The hardier members of the spurge family are superb plants for patio or courtyard in sun or semi-shade particularly *polychroma*, a mound-forming plant with bright yellow bracts in early spring, about 50cm (1½ft); *wulfenii* is a handsome evergreen shrubby spurge with glaucous blue foliage and large heads of buff or greenish-yellow flowers in spring and early summer, 1.2m (4ft).

Geranium The cranesbills fit in excellently with courtyard and patio planting in sun or shade and notably *endressii* 'A. T. Johnson', silvery-pink; *macrorrhizum* 'Alba' (white) and 'Ingwersen's Variety' (shell pink) 35cm (1ft 2in); 'Johnson's Blue' 50cm (1½ft) is particularly fine in association with shrub roses.

Hellebores and *Hostas* are equally at home here, as they are in shaded shrubaceous borders and in moist situations.

Kirengeshoma palmata, with its nodding, waxy, pale yellow bells in autumn and maple-like palmate leaves, requires a similar moist, shady situation. 1m (3ft).

Lamium maculatum 'Beacon Silver' gives excellent low, silver-variegated groundcover.

Lavatera olbia 'Rosea' – the tree mallow – is spectacular throughout summer, with its large pink hollyhock-type flowers and grey downy leaves. A sunny situation is necessary and plenty of space. It will make 2m (6ft) by 1m (3ft) wide.

Liriope muscari has evergreen grass-like foliage and purple flower spikes in autumn, 50cm (1½ft).

Nepeta x faassenii Catmint is as useful here as *Alchemilla mollis* with which it associates well.

Nerine bowdenii The nerines are South African bulbous plants for the base of south-facing walls, they produce welcome and beautiful pink lily-like trumpets from September to November. 'Fenwick's Variety' is the best form. They are a magnificent and permanent planting, and look well with grey groundcover, such as *Helianthemum* 'Wisley Primrose' *Stachys olympica* 'Silver Carpet', or *Acaena buchananii*.

Oenothera missouriensis The prostrate evening primrose with fragrant, large soft yellow blooms from June to August. Slightly tender, 25cm (10in).

Ophiopogon planiscapus 'Nigrescens'. Its blackish-purple leaves are unique and ideal in patio areas.

Osteospermum (*Dimorphotheca*) (Cape marigold, Star of the Veldt). There are a number of distinct and showy species and cultivars, excellent value in full sun on a well-drained soil. Winter protection may be necessary for some; they also make superb pot or container plants; *barbariae* has aromatic foliage and unique pink daisy flowers with burnished bronze reverses; 'Buttermilk', pale yellow, and *ecklonis*, white above and purple beneath, are sub-shrubby and excellent, about 60cm (2ft).

Origanum vulgare (marjoram) and in particular 'Aureum' the golden-leaved form of the herb, bright and aromatic, goes well in paved areas, about 25cm (10in).

Penstemon Easy sun-loving plants producing large quantities of tubular foxglove-like flowers throughout summer. Very rewarding are the dainty 'Evelyn', fine pale green foliage and pink red-flushed flowers and 'Garnet', a larger grower with brilliant wine-red blooms throughout the summer, about 50cm (1½ft).

Potentilla The herbaceous varieties, particularly *nepalensis* 'Miss Willmott', are appropriate here.

Pulmonaria saccharata (Lungwort) is excellent in a shady spot.

Rudbeckia fulgida 'Goldsturm' (black-eyed Susan) is a sun-lover.

Ruta graveolens 'Jackman's Blue'.

Salvia officinalis, the common Sage, and its variegated and purple-leaved cultivars.

Santolina (lavender cotton) is a good grey plant with fine filigree foliage.

Scabiosa – particularly the Caucasian scabious *caucasica* 'Clive Greaves' and its white form 'Miss Willmott', both superb for cutting, look well in patio areas among the shrubs and shrub roses. Less commonly seen, *S. rumelica* (*Knautia macedonica*) is well worth a place with its deep rich crimson flowers throughout the summer. These scabious all reach about 60cm (2ft).

Schizostylis coccinea Although mildly invasive, the Kaffir lily is an invaluable autumn-flowering plant, with gladiolus-like flowers from September to November; 'Gigantea' ('Major') is a fine, large-flowered crimson form and 'Mrs Hegarty' a clear rose-pink, 50–60cm (1½–2ft).

Stachys olympica 'Silver Carpet' is the non-flowering version of the silvery-grey lamb's tongue, 10–20cm (4–6in).

Thymus The 'thymes' are excellent in paved areas; try particularly some selected forms of our native chalk downland plant *drucei* (*serpyllum*), which are transformed into sheets of colour throughout the summer; 'Albus', the white-flowered form; 'Coccineus', rich crimson; and the grey leaved 'Pink Chintz', with shell-pink flowers, 2.5cm (about 1in); 'Porlock' is essentially a dense, low, hummocky shrub to about 25cm (10in), covered in pink flowers in May and June. All thymes are aromatic and forms of the lemon thyme *x citriodorus*, and common thyme *vulgaris* are both favourite flavouring herbs; *vulgaris*

'Aureus' has bright yellow foliage and *x citriodorus* 'Silver Queen' has effective white variegation, 25cm (10in).

Verbascum The mulleins are handsome in foliage and flower and although not long-lived, self-sown seedlings appear pleasantly in unexpected places. Most have handsome large leaves, particularly *bombyciferum* ('Broussa') white woolly and yellow flowers. 'Gainsborough', canary-yellow spikes; and 'Pink Domino', rose-pink with darker centre. All 1–1.2m (3–4ft) or more and effective spiking up between the shrubs or in sunny paved areas.

Veronica The speedwells are the herbaceous rather than shrubby veronicas (for these see Hebe) (A). Of the many species and cultivars perhaps the most rewarding for courtyard and patio is *austriaca* 'Crater Lake Blue', a reliable plant with long spikes of vivid ultramarine blue, June to August, 30cm (1ft).

Waldsteinia ternata An excellent carpeting plant with golden-yellow flowers.

Hardy ornamental grasses and ferns

These are assured of suitable homes in courtyards and patios. Of those described in our Plant Profiles (chapter 8) the following grasses are appropriate for *sunny situations*, *Festuca glauca, Helictotrichon sempervirens, Stipa calamagrostis* and *S. gigantea*.

For *shadier situations*: *Hakonechloa macra* 'Aureola' ('Albo-aurea'), *Milium effusum* 'Aureum' – (Bowles golden grass), and *Molinia caerulea* 'Variegata'.

Most smaller-growing ferns can be effectively sited where they can enjoy a cool, moist rootrun, perhaps in shady courtyard or patio, notably:

Adiantum pedatum (Maidenhair fern) Can be successful in a draught-free moist and shady area.

Athyrium (lady fern). *Blechnum* (hard fern). *Phyllitis* (*Scolopendrium*) (hart's tongue).

Polystichum setiferum 'Plumoso-divisilobum' The soft shield fern is particularly magnificent in a paved setting.

Diascia *species, spectacular plants for a*
well drained, sunny site

Fuchsia *'Madame Cornelissen'*

Small shrubby trees and shrubs for courtyards, terraces and patios

A small tree in patio or courtyard is often a necessity for shade or desirable as an effective and important focal point. Many of the larger shrubs reach proportions of small trees, some may be pruned or tailored to fit quite small areas.

Those suitable, and available, come in two groups: Firstly those provided by nurserymen or garden centres, with straight standard stem usually 1.5–2m (5–6ft) and small-formed head of branches. Some varieties are 'top-work grafted' on the stem of another variety, in order to attain an effective standard tree (std) more quickly.

Such specimens should be carefully staked and the graft protected until the growth of new tissue has made the union strong. Suckers from the stem or base or in the vicinity of the graft union should be immediately removed. Many of the trees in group form weeping or semi-weeping specimens and a few are of fastigiate or upright growth. These are marked (f):

Acer palmatum 'Dissectum' and cultivars. (Std)

Acer platanoides 'Globosum' – a compact form of Norway maple and *pseudoplatanus* 'Brilliantissimum'. (Std)

Caragana arborescens 'Lorbergii' an elegant form of the Pea Tree with narrow grass-like foliage and 'Walker' a similar fine-leaved variety but of weeping habit. (Std)

Cotoneaster 'Hybridus Pendulus' (E) and *salicifolius* 'Gnom' (E). (Std)

Malus 'Red Jade' and 'Van Eseltine' (f).

Morus alba 'Pendula' (weeping white mulberry).

Prunus 'Amanogawa' (f); *yedoensis* 'Shidare Yoshino'; 'Kiku-shidare'.

Robinia 'Hillieri'.

Salix caprea 'Kilmarnock' (the weeping Kilmarnock willow); *purpurea* 'Pendula' (Std) (the weeping purple osier).

A number of the smaller-growing species and cultivars of rowan make excellent small, compact trees, particularly:

Sorbus aucuparia 'Fastigiata' (f); *cashmiriana* with white fruits; 'Ethel's Gold' with amber fruits persisting into the New Year; *vilmorinii* with rose-red fruits and an elegant habit.

The second group of small trees for patios comprises plants which may slowly reach the proportions of a large multi-stemmed shrub or small shrubby tree. Many have the advantage of being evergreen and reveal great diversity of habit, foliage and flower. However, they are frequently slow in growth and are rarely available supplied above 1m in height; they will consequently take some years to become effective as a small specimen tree or shrubby tree. They are less frequently planted, but none-the-less desirable for that specially important site. To help you make up your mind, you cannot do better than visit the Hillier Arboretum, RHS Gardens at Wisley, or Savill Garden near Windsor, to see the trees in mature or semi-mature form. Here is a select list of likely candidates:

Acer palmatum 'Bloodgood', 'Osakazuki', 'Seiryu' and 'Ribesifolium'.

Aesculus pavia 'Atrosanguinea'.

Albizia julibrissin 'Rosea'.

Aralia elata and variegated cultivars.

Arbutus unedo 'Rubra' (E).

Cornus 'Eddie's White Wonder' and 'Norman Hadden' (A) (semi-E).

Cotinus 'Grace'.

Embothrium coccineum lanceolatum (Chilean fire bush) (A) (E).

Eucalyptus niphophila (snow gum) (E).

Genista aetnensis (Mount Etna broom).

Halesia carolina (snowdrop tree) (A).

Hoheria glabrata and 'Glory of Amlwch' (semi-E).

Magnolia species and cultivars, particularly *x loebneri* 'Leonard Messell'; *salicifolia* 'Jermyns'; *sieboldii* or *wilsonii*.

Ptelea trifoliata 'Aurea'.

Weeping standard roses

A weeping standard rose can be used to make an effective and colourful formal specimen in the smallest of paved areas. It may require training on special umbrellas which are usually available from good garden centres. Weeping standard roses are usually 'top-work' grafted and suckers should immediately be removed. Some of the old favourites are frequently available, and some new cultivars are being tried with success.

Here is a selection giving a wide range of colour: 'Bonica', rose-pink, recurrent, 'Crimson Shower', 'Emily Gray', double, deep yellow, 'Fiona', bright red, 'Sanders White Rambler', and a long-established favourite 'Canary Bird', bright yellow with fern-like leaves.

DRY GARDENING

In the late 1960s at the Hillier Arboretum an area of sloping land, south of the house and in full sun, was landscaped and part retained with substantial rock boulders of Purbeck stone. The soil in this area is a good, deep acid loam, but this open and sunny area seemed an ideal situation to grow a wide range of conifers, shrubs and herbaceous plants from Mediterranean, Californian and similar areas where hot, dry conditions are experienced. Sharp drainage is of the utmost importance, particularly if these plants are to over-winter satisfactorily in our climate. Sir Harold Hillier therefore arranged that a considerable quantity of builders aggregate (about 2cm (¾in) downwards) was dug into the top 30cm of the area following clearance and weed killing. This improved the drainage considerably and a wide range of interesting conifers in all shapes and sizes, particularly dwarf forms of cedar, *Cryptomeria*, cypress, juniper, pine and *Tsuga* were planted together with the groundcovering shrubs associated with Mediterranean countries in particular. At a later date smaller ground-covering herbaceous plants were added, many associated with the rock garden. Over the years this planting has proved most successful and is full of interest at all times of the year. The dwarf and slow-growing conifers have matured, as have many of the specimen shrubs. A mulch of gravel has been added to make a pleasing and weed-free finish, the plants benefiting from the cool rootrun this affords.

Similarly at the Savill Garden, Windsor Great Park, in the late 1970s on the light, peaty Bagshot sand, a similar planting was initiated by John Bond, the keeper of the garden, using a south-facing slope which was a sun-trap between the trees sheltering the garden. This has proved a great success and is one of the main features today of the Savill Garden, suitable homes having been found for a very exciting range of shrubs, bulbous and herbaceous plants, hailing from the drier, sunnier temperate regions of the world, including South Africa and Australasia. Here many of the new interesting introductions from such areas are finding conditions to their liking.

If you have a sun-trap area in your garden which could be treated in this manner, we feel the planting could be most interesting and rewarding, particularly for the plantsman. A visit to both the Hillier Arboretum and Savill Garden will, we feel sure, confirm this.

Here is a short list of plants particularly appropriate to dry gardening:

Small trees

Depending upon the size area involved, you may not need more than three or four widely-spaced shrubby trees, and a choice might be made from any of the following:

Arbutus andrachne or x *andrachnoides* (Grecian strawberry tree) (E).
Caragana arborescens 'Lorbergii' – a form of the pea tree with narrow leaflets.
Colutea arborescens (bladder senna) with bright yellow flowers and bronze-coloured

inflated seed pods together all summer – a large shrub which can reach almost tree-like proportions.

Quercus suber, the cork oak, will grow satisfactorily in the south and be the envy of your friends and neighbours.

Rhamnus alaterna 'Argenteovariegata' – one of the best of all variegated evergreen shrubs.

Robinia 'Hillieri' – for its elegant habit and pink summer flowers.

Sophora tetraptera 'Grandiflora' – the best form of the New Zealand kowhai could be used if your garden is very sheltered or has a south or west facing wall.

Conifers making large upright shrubs or small trees

Cupressus macrocarpa 'Golden Cone' or 'Golden Pillar'; *sempervirens* 'Green Spire' and 'Swaine's Golden'.

Juniperus chinensis 'Obelisk'; *communis* 'Hibernica' (Irish Juniper); *recurva* 'Castlewellan'; *scopulorum* 'Blue Heaven'.

Pinus sylvestris 'Fastigiata' – a unique upright form of our native Scots pine.

Taxus baccata 'Fastigiata' – the Irish yew.

All of the above are evergreen.

Ginkgo biloba – Maidenhair Tree – a deciduous and unique conifer has a narrow conical form 'Tremonia', worthy of a place in the dry garden and worth seeking out.

To complement these, one or more evergreen conifers of more spreading or rounded habit could be chosen:

Cedrus libani 'Sargentii'.

Cryptomeria japonica 'Spiralis' (Grannies' ringlets).

Juniperus chinensis 'Blaauw' or 'Mordigan Gold'.

Pinus parviflora 'Adcock's Dwarf'.

Taxus baccata 'Summergold' or 'Semperaurea'.

Shrubs of mainly compact habit Dwarf to large shrubs which are likely to do well in these circumstances include:

Arbutus unedo 'Rubra' (E).

Artemisia 'Powis Castle'.

Atriplex halimus (semi-E).

Buddleia in considerable variety, particularly: *alternifolia* 'Argentea'; *davidii* 'Harlequin' and 'Nanho Purple'; 'Lochinch' and *x weyerana* 'Golden Glow'.

Caryopteris x clandonensis 'Heavenly Blue'.

Cassinia fulvida and *vauvilliersii albida*.

Ceanothus "Blue Mound"; 'Gloire de Versailles'.

Ceratostigma griffithii and *willmottianum*.

Cercis canadensis 'Forest Pansy'; *siliquastrum* (Judas tree).

Choisya ternata and 'Sundance'.

Cistus aguilari 'Maculatus'; *C. populifolius*; *Casiocalyx*, *C. pulverulentus* and *C. x skanbergii*.

Clerodendrum trichotomum fargesii for late-summer flower and blue autumn fruits.

Convolvulus cneorum.

Carpenteria californica 'Bodnant'.

Cytisus – brooms – in many species and varieties, notably: *nigricans*, *praecox* 'Allgold'; 'Minstead' (white-tinged lilac).

Daphne particularly *bholua* 'Jacqueline Postill'; *x mantensiana* 'Manten' and *tangutica*.

Deutzia setchuenensis corymbiflora.

Dorycnium hirsutum.

Genista aetnensis (Mount Etna broom).

Helichrysum italicum, *serotinum* and *splendidum*.

Hibiscus syriacus cultivars, notably: 'Blue Bird'; 'Diana', single white; 'Woodbridge', rose-pink with carmine eye.

Indigofera heterantha.

Olearia waikariensis.

Phlomis chrysophylla.

Perovskia 'Blue Spire'.

Phormium tenax and *cookianum* and cultivars.

Romneya coulteri (Californian tree poppy).

Tamarix species and cultivars.

Low growing sub-shrubs and herbaceous groundcover plants

These will blend together to make the type of maquis growth so familiar in Mediterranean areas. Besides the familiar lavender, rosemary, santolina and sage (salvia) could be included particularly:

Acaena (New Zealand burr).

Acanthus (architect's plant).

Agapanthus 'Headbourne Hybrids', *campanulatus* 'Albus'.

Artemisia absinthium 'Lambrook Silver', *maritima f. canescens*.

Ballota species.

Diascia – from the highlands of South Africa, are excellent value in full sun.

Eryngium – sea holly.

Euphorbia – particularly: *wulfenii, characias, griffithii* 'Fireglow' and *polychroma*.

Hypericum olympicum 'Grandiflorum'.

Lavatera olbia 'Rosea'.

Nepeta species and cultivars.

Osteospermum species and cultivars.

Penstemon 'Evelyn' and 'Garnet'.

Sedum 'Ruby Glow' and 'Autumn Joy'.

Stachys olympica.

Zauschneria – Californian fuchsia.

Ornamental grasses

As many enjoy a sunny well-drained situation, they should be included, particularly: *Festuca glauca, Helictotrichon sempervirens, Stipa calamagrostis* and *S. gigantea*.

Ornamental bulbs

Many bulbous plants naturalise well in such circumstances, particularly the ornamental onions (*Allium*) of which there are many species, some rather invasive. Acceptable for our purpose are: *albo-pilosum moly* (golden garlic), *rosenbachianum, siculum*.

Anemone fulgens and cultivars

Fritillaria do well in these conditions, notably the well-known *F. imperialis* (crown imperial) and *F. acmopetala; F. persica* and *F. pyrenaica*.

Galtonia candicans with its hanging white bells is useful for summer flower.

Nerine bowdenii 'Fenwicks Variety' with its spectacular heads of pink flowers, so useful for cutting as late as November.

Tulip species and cultivars

There are many other possibilities in the field of bulbous plants, and a specialist nurseryman, such as Broadleigh Gardens, Bishops Hull, Taunton, Somerset (Lady Skelmersdale) should be consulted.

DRY SHADE

Trees, shrubs and groundcover

In marked contrast, shade induced by a dense canopy of large trees, such as beech, is one of the most difficult situations to cope with in the garden. Here we may experience a dry situation made worse by the invading roots of the trees causing the shade. Inevitably there is drought which is difficult to contend with. Sometimes efforts are made to seal off roots by means of plastic sheeting or corrugated iron inserted in the ground, but it remains difficult to garden successfully. However, there are a number of tough evergreen shrubs that grow even in these circumstances. *Aucuba japonica* and its variegated cultivars will slowly attain 2m each way (6× 6ft). Generally lower growing, *Mahonia aquifolium* and cultivars will produce bright yellow flowers in spring to enliven the gloom. Less commonly seen and amazingly tolerant of dry shade is the Alexandrian laurel, *Danae racemosa*, and *Ruscus aculeatus*, butchers broom, with its curious dark green spiky leaves. Large red berries are borne by female or hermaphrodite forms. Shrubby evergreen groundcover is catered for by many of the ivy species and cultivars, particularly *Hedera colchica* 'Dentata Variegata' with its large broad leaves, generously margined with yellow. Although slow, *Pachysandra terminalis* and its variegated form is reliable here. *Vinca* – periwinkle – both *major* and *minor* make effective groundcover in shade, but will take longer to establish in very dry conditions. *V. minor* is the neater of the two. One of the most satisfactory shrubby groundcovers in dry shade is Irish ivy – *Hedera helix* Hibernica, with its bright shining leaves and dense permanent cover.

Our native evergreen holly – *Ilex aquifolium*, yew – *Taxus baccata* and box – *Buxus sempervirens*, and many of their cultivars, once established will be effective and tolerant in dry shade situations.

Herbaceous plants

Really successful herbaceous plants which are long-lived in this situation are few. Perhaps the most responsive and certainly the most rampant is the variegated form of 'yellow archangel' (*Lamiastrum galeobdolon* 'Variegatum') – not only is this luxuriant in growth, but is a very beautiful plant under the shade of trees, where its bright silver leaf variegation and yellow dead-nettle flowers show up well. Amazingly tolerant and very beautiful is the hardy *Geranium macrorrhizum*. Other species seem less successful and permanent. Many of the epimediums will colonise quite well, notably *E. perralderianum* and *x warleyense*. Once established, *Euphorbia robbiae* – Mrs Robb's spurge – seems to perform quite well and the clump-forming native Gladwyn iris, *Iris foetidissima* and its variegated form will provide welcome evergreen clumps of dark, shining leaves; its seed pods, which open in the autumn to display bright orange seeds are a delight for flower arrangers, but the dull mauve-veined flowers of early summer scarcely show up in the gloom.

Those desirous of delving more deeply into the fascinating subject of dry gardening should read the comprehensive work on this subject, *The Dry Garden* by Beth Chatto.

HEDGES

We have discussed screen planting in particular earlier in this chapter, p201–4. Undoubtedly hedge or boundary planting and screening are functional and are closely linked. In most gardens it is necessary to define a boundary and very often in the interests of privacy it needs to be dense, evergreen, and of a minimum height to achieve the screening required. A boundary hedge may also need to be reasonably proof against unauthorised entry of man or animals, such as dogs and farm stock (sheep and cows). Rabbits and deer are an increasing problem and special fencing is necessary here, in addition to the boundary hedge.

Hedges, whether formal or informal, should be composed of plants which respond satisfactorily to clipping or pruning – once mature the majority of hedges only require an annual clipping to ensure the necessary density of their growth (see under Management and Maintenance, chapter 6). Hedges need not be dull and functional, they can be beautiful in flower, foliage and berry. The range of plants adaptable for this purpose is remarkable, including forest trees, such as beech (*Fagus sylvatica*), hornbeam (*Carpinus betulus*) and the evergreen holm oak (*Quercus ilex*); among conifers the ubiquitous Leyland cypress (*x Cupressocyparis leylandii*) forms the fastest-growing evergreen tall hedge or screen; pines, such as *Pinus nigra*, the Austrian pine and *sylvestris*, the Scots pine make beautiful and functional evergreen screens; Western red cedar (*Thuja plicata* and *T. P.* 'Fastigiata') responds well to clipping; yew (*Taxus baccata*), perhaps not so slow in growth as generally supposed, is one of the finest of all evergreens for formal hedges within the garden, or on the boundary in urban areas.

A wide range of shrubs, both evergreen and deciduous, will make flowering and berrying hedges within the garden and on the boundary – from dwarf hedges of lavender and rosemary to taller hedges of berberis, cotoneaster, pyracantha, rhododendron, roses – both species and hybrids – tamarix and viburnum but avoid the straggly *Lonicera nitida* other than as a very low hedge form as a very fast-growing substitute for box, when it requires much clipping.

Preparation of ground and planting

Hedges are usually permanent features in the garden and the site they occupy should be well prepared, cultivated to a depth of 50cm (1½ft) and, ideally, a width of 60cm–1m (2–3ft). Well-rotted farmyard manure should be well dug into the base of the trench before backfilling, allowing for settlement before planting. Open ground loose-rooted deciduous hedge plants, such as thorn, beech and hornbeam are best planted in the autumn, and certainly no later than February. Many hedge plants are container grown in these days which certainly allows much flexibility in planting. A balanced, preferably slow-release type fertiliser, such as Enmag or Vitax Q4 should be added at planting time to the root area of the hedge, mulched with bark or well-rotted leaves. Attention to watering in the first and second springs following planting is essential, particularly with loose-rooted (open ground) transplants. The spacing for most subjects is 50–60cm (1½–2ft). A slightly wider hedge is possible if a staggered planting arrangement is adopted; for taller informal screens, plant in a staggered arrangement, 1–1.5m (3–5ft) apart.

In the following list of recommended trees and shrubs for hedging or screening, those followed by (B) are particularly appropriate for boundary planting. (E)=evergreen. HZ = Hardiness Zone (see p200).

Acer campestre – our native field maple (B) is excellent for rustic or tapestry hedges involving thorn, blackthorn, holly, etc.

Bright red young shoots and golden autumn colour.

Beech – see *Fagus sylvatica*.

Berberis – all are spiny, many evergreen, particularly good are: *gagnepainii* (E) forming an impenetrable evergreen hedge; *panlanensis* (E) an ideal compact low hedge, sea-green leaves; *x stenophylla* (E) (B) superb as an informal hedge of arching habit, orange-yellow flowers in spring; *thunbergii*, of neat compact habit, bright green leaves, rich red autumn colour; *thunbergii* 'Dart's Red Lady', a selection of *thunbergii* 'Atropurpurea' with deep purple foliage; *thunbergii* 'Atropurpurea Nana' makes an excellent dwarf hedge to about 50cm, purple foliage throughout the growing season; *verruculosa* (E) a fine hedge plant, lustrous green leaves are white beneath, flowers golden yellow.

Blackthorn – see *Prunus spinosa*.

Buxus sempervirens (E) – the traditional box of small to medium-size hedges, of dense habit when clipped: 'Handsworthensis' (E) (B) is taller, 'Suffruticosa' – box edging is the dwarf compact form for formal hedges and parterres.

Carpinus betulus (B) (hornbeam) excellent for formal hedges or boundary planting.

Chamaecyparis lawsoniana (E) (B) (Lawson cypress) is variable from seed; for a trimmed hedge it is better to plant a good proven cultivar such as 'Columnaris' blue-grey, or 'Green Hedger'.

Cotoneaster – of many possibilities, the following are particularly recommended: *franchetti sternianus* (E) (B), with small sage-green leaves silvery-white beneath, and abundant orange fruits in autumn; *lacteus* (E), a denser evergreen hedge, with oval leaves grey beneath and late-ripening red fruits, which frequently last until the New Year; *glaucophyllus vestitus* (E) (B), rounded leathery leaves, abundant flowers in July and red berries through the winter.

Crataegus monogyna (quickthorn, hawthorn or may) (B), the commonest and most reliable of hedges or screens for all soils.

x *Cupressocyparis leylandii* (E) (B) (Leyland cypress) much planted, extremely fast-growing hybrid cypress. Excellent tall hedge or screen for exposed gardens. Golden and variegated forms are now available including: 'Castlewellan', golden and 'Robinson's Gold', yellow foliage, golden-bronze in the spring. Tapestry hedges, green and gold make a pleasing variation.

Elaeagnus x ebbingei (E) (B) – a fast-growing evergreen, large leaves are silver beneath, wind-resistant and excellent for coastal gardens; 'Limelight' has a deep-yellow central blotch to the leaves and is equally vigorous.

Escallonia – many species and cultivars make good hedges in coastal areas, with abundant flower in summer and autumn. Hardier, reliable sorts include: 'Crimson Spire', 'Donard Radiance', 'Donard Seedling'; *macrantha*. Not for HZ1.

Fagus sylvatica (B) (beech) – a very popular hedging or screening plant. When clipped as a hedge it retains its russet brown leaves throughout the winter. The purple form, though scarcer, is also good for hedging.

Hebe x franciscana 'Blue Gem', an excellent dense, low hedge of rounded leaves, particularly recommended for seaside gardens. Not for HZ1 or 2.

Ilex x altaclerensis and cultivars (E) (B) – broad-leaved holly, and several of its forms, make excellent taller hedges and screens; *aquifolium* common holly is one of the best and densest of all evergreen hedges; stock-proof and impenetrable, it may be used formally or informally.

Laurel – common – see *Prunus laurocerasus*.

Laurel – Portuguese – see *Prunus lusitanica*.

Laurustinus – see *Viburnum tinus*.

Lavandula (E) (lavender) a popular low aromatic hedge for sunny situations, eg as edgings to borders of shrub roses: particularly 'Hidcote' or 'Munstead Dwarf'.

Ligustrum ovalifolium (privet) (E) (B) is perhaps the commonest of all garden hedge plants, and is easily managed. Long-

established hedges tend to be vulnerable to honey fungus; *ovalifolium* 'Aureum' – golden privet – is well known and much loved.

Lonicera nitida (E) – there are several forms of the shrubby honeysuckle: 'Ernest Wilson' with its tiny leaves makes a neat, very low hedge, almost a substitute for box, but needs clipping many times during the summer. Becomes leggy and unsatisfactory if grown above 1.2–1.5m (4–5ft) but its golden form, 'Baggesen's Gold', is as worthy in its way as golden privet.

Olearia (E) – for coastal areas in particular and sheltered garden inland the daisy bushes are excellent value, particularly *avicenniifolia*, pointed leaves, white beneath; *macrodonta* 'Major' – New Zealand holly – grey silvery leaves. Not recommended for HZ1 or 2.

Pittosporum (E) – again not reliably hardy inland, but a magnificent and fast-growing shrub for the boundary or within the garden, particularly in coastal districts: *tenuifolium*, with its wavy margined grey-green leaves, can be blended with several of its cultivars like 'Ella Keightley', 'Irene Paterson' and 'Purpureum' to give an attractive tapestry effect. Not for HZ1 or 2.

Pyracantha (E) (B) (firethorn) – makes impenetrable prickly hedges, with spring flower and autumn/winter berries. It is best to plant scab and fireblight-resistant cultivars such as *rogersiana* 'Flava' – yellow-fruited or P. 'Orange Glow', with orange-red berries, or 'Teton', with strong vertical growth and orange fruits.

Potentilla – several cultivars make excellent low-flowering hedges, particularly: 'Elizabeth', mid-yellow; 'Goldfinger', deep yellow; 'Primrose Beauty', pale yellow, grey-green foliage. Excellent to border the vegetable garden.

Escallonia macrantha *makes a good hedge in coastal areas*

Prunus – this large family which includes cherry laurel and the flowering cherries has a number of trees or shrubby trees which adapt well as hedges, particularly: *x cistena*, the purple-leaved sand cherry with white flowers in April and rich red foliage, makes a good low hedge; *laurocerasus* (E) (B) – cherry laurel, large long glossy leaves and a familiar plant, excellent as a tall dense screen; *lusitanica* – Portuguese laurel (E) (B), the best of the laurels, with dark green leathery and purple-tinted leaves; white flower spikes in June, excellent on chalk and alkaline soils. Several of its varieties are equally useful as hedge plants, notably: *azorica*, 'Myrtifolia' and 'Variegata'; *spinosa* (B) – blackthorn or sloe, a familiar and much-loved hedge plant with small white flowers on bare branches in March and bloomy black fruits (sloes) in the autumn. A dense, spiny impenetrable hedge.

Quercus ilex (E) (B) (holm or evergreen oak) makes an excellent hedge or taller screen inland or on the coast where it resists salt-laden gale. Not for HZ1.

Rhododendron ponticum (A) (E) (B) suitable as a large-scale bushy informal boundary hedge of medium to large size, denser than laurel, pale purple flowers in June; for acid soil only.

Rosa – many of the shrub roses make excellent hedges, some with an extended season of flower plus heps in the autumn, particularly: 'Canary Bird', bright yellow and fern-like foliage; *rubiginosa*, sweet briar or eglantine; *rugosa*, a very reliable hedge with recurrent flowers. The following cultivars are particularly good: *rugosa* 'Alba'; *r.* 'Fru Dagmar Hastrup'; *r.* 'Roseriae de L'Hay' and *r.* 'Rubra'. Hybrid musk roses of bushy habit are nearly perpetual flowering, particularly good are: 'Cornelia', coppery-pink; 'Felicia', salmon-pink and 'Penelope', shell-pink. Other hybrids particularly suitable include: 'Stanwell Perpetual', blush-white with greyish foliage and 'Schneezwerg', per-petual white flowers with orange heps.

Rosmarinus officinalis (E) (rosemary) the favourite aromatic shrub, has two forms particularly good for hedging: *officinalis* 'Fastigiatus' or 'Miss Jessup's Upright', which is vigorous and erect, and 'Severn Sea', low-growing and with arching branches and brilliant blue flowers. This makes an excellent hedge to border the vegetable garden without shading the crops. Nor for HZ1 or 2.

Taxus baccata (E) (English yew) is perhaps the best all-round evergreen hedge plant for formal purposes within the garden. It can be very long-lived, but likes a well-drained site in sun or shade; excellent on chalk.

Pinus nigra (E) (B) the Austrian pine, and *sylvestris* Scots pine, make excellent medium to tall boundary screens up to 3m to 5m (9–16ft).

Thuya plicata (*lobbii*) (E) (B) (western red cedar) a fast-growing conifer with fresh green foliage, pineapple-scented when crushed. Suitable when clipped as a formal hedge or as a tall screen. 'Fastigiata' is a narrow columnar form most appropriate for formal hedges.

Viburnum tinus (E) – one of the most popular evergreen winter-flowering hedges, good in coastal districts and towns. 'Eve Price', with pink scented flowers and carmine buds, has a neat compact habit. Not for HZ1.

Yew – see *Taxus baccata*.

WALL SHRUBS AND CLIMBERS

Boundary walls and fences and walls of houses and outbuildings frequently require beautifying, often there are unsightly pipes or large unbroken areas of brick to screen. This gives us an opportunity to grow many of the more spectacular flowering shrubs and climbers of borderline hardiness which may not be possible away from the warmth and shelter of a wall, particularly in cold districts.

One should endeavour to choose wall shrubs or climbers appropriate to the area to be covered – almost everything is likely to get bigger than you think and some restriction will be necessary; extensive pruning may reduce flowering potential. With a two· or three storey house where the space between the windows is not likely to be great, usually between 1–2m (3–6ft), a wall shrub or climber, or climbing rose adaptable to such narrow confines, should be considered. For instance on a south or west facing wall, *Fremontodendron* 'California Glory' or in very mild areas *Acacia dealbata* could be considered; a wisteria is frequently trained up a narrow area to fan out above and between the windows.

Suitable supporting wires strained through vine eyes, or trellis on batten, should be installed to cover the area it is desired to furnish.

Have due regard for the aspect of the wall when making your choice, and do not plant too closely, generally speaking, 2–2.5m (6–8ft) apart is about right. Here is a selection according to aspect: (E = evergreen)

For taller south- and west-facing walls and fences
Climbers
Actinidia kolomikta.
Campsis grandiflora and cultivars.
Clematis – particularly large-flowered hybrids – x *Jackmanii* 'Superba' and 'Huldine'.
Jasminum officinale and cultivars.
Passiflora caerulea (passion flower) (E).
Roses – climbing species and cultivars, notably: *Rosa banksiae* 'Lutea'; *brunonii* 'La Mortola'; and stronger growing cultivars, particularly: 'Easlea's Golden Rambler'; 'Mermaid' (E) – large yellow single; 'Madame Grégoire Staechelin' – large, rich deep pink; 'Souvenir de Claudius Denoyel' – large double crimson, recurrent. (Many produce fragrant flowers).
Schisandra grandiflora 'Rubriflora'.
Solanum crispum 'Glasnevin'.
Trachelospermum (E) *jasminoides* and *j.* 'Variegata'.

Wisteria sinensis and cultivars.

Wall shrubs
Abutilon vitifolium and cultivars (E).
Acacia baileyana and *dealbata* (mimosa) (E).
Buddleia colvilei 'Kewensis' and *crispa*.
Caesalpinia gilliesii.
Cytisus battandieri.
Escallonia 'Iveyi' (E).
Fremontodendron 'California Glory' (E).
Magnolia grandiflora (E) and cultivars flowering at a relatively early age such as 'Exmouth' and 'Goliath' which with generous cultivation may flower in 8 or 10 years from planting. This is the classic wall shrub for the two or three storey house, but does require 2–3m (6½–10ft) of width to make effective growth and display its large rusty-backed long leaves and immense highly-scented cream-coloured flowers produced throughout the summer.
Sophora tetraptera 'Grandiflora'.

For taller north- and east-facing walls and fences
(Many of these are equally good on south- or west-facing walls.)
Climbers
Akebia quinata (E).
Berberidopsis corallina (E).
Hedera helix cultivars (E).
Hedera colchica and cultivars (E).
Hydrangea petiolaris.
Lonicera (honeysuckle) most species and cultivars, particularly *L. japonica* 'Repens' (E) and *tragophylla*.
Parthenocissus, particularly *henryana*; *quinquefolia* and *tricuspidata* 'Veitchii'.
Pileostegia viburnoides (E).
Roses – several climbing and rambler roses perform well on north- or east-facing walls and fences, particularly: 'Aloha', 'Golden Showers', 'Gloire de Dijon', 'Maigold', 'Madame Alfred Carrière', 'Paul's Scarlet Climber', 'The New Dawn'.
Schizophragma hydrangeoides
Vitis (ornamental vines) particularly 'Brant' and *coignetiae*.

Wall Shrubs

Azara microphylla (E).

Camellia x williamsii and cultivars; 'Anticipation'; 'Donation'; 'E. T. R. Carlyon' (E) (A) – not on east-facing walls.

Chaenomeles japonica and cultivars, particularly 'Crimson & Gold', 'Knaphill Scarlet' and 'Pink Lady'.

Crinodendron (Tricuspidaria) hookerianum (A) (E).

Drimys winteri (E).

Eriobotrya japonica – loquat (E).

Garrya elliptica 'James Roof' (E).

Kerria japonica 'Pleniflora'.

Rhamnus alaterna 'Argenteovariegata' (E).

Pyracantha – choose disease-resistant species and cultivars (E).

For lower walls

For bungalows or one storey structures, garage walls, garden fences, wall shrubs and climbers of less vigour are required. Vigorous climbing roses and vines like *Parthenocissus quinquefolia* (Virginia creeper) will grow into gutterings and under roof tiles or slates; how often one sees the wrong plant used on low walls, heavy and continual pruning being necessary to restrict it. Some climbers and wall shrubs of moderate growth are included in the list below; some are also suitable for balustrades, low dividing walls within the garden or positions under windows.

For lower south- and west-facing aspects
Climbers

Clematis alpina and *macropetala* and cultivars; *C. tangutica*; *C. viticella* 'Alba Luxurians'; 'Kermesina' and 'Royal Velours'.

Eccremocarpus scaber.

Vitis vinifera 'Incana' and 'Purpurea'.

Trachelospermum asiaticum (E).

Wall Shrubs

Abelia 'Edward Goucher' (E) and *schumannii*.

Lippia citriodora (Aloysia triphylla) (lemon-scented verbena).

Callistemon citrinus 'Splendens' *linearis* and *salignus* (bottle brush) (E).

Ceanothus – many evergreen cultivars are suitable (E). Try *thrysiflorus var. repens* and 'Yankee Point'.

Cistus 'Anne Palmer'; 'Peggy Sammons'; 'Silver Pink' (E).

Coronilla glauca (E).

Corokia cotoneaster.

Pittosporum tenuifolium and cultivars (E).

Hebe x franciscana 'Variegata' (E).

For lower north- and east-facing aspects
Climbers

Clematis species and cultivars, particularly *cirrhosa balearica* (fern-leaved clematis); *montana* 'Tetrarose'; and large-flowered hybrid 'Nelly Moser'.

Hedera helix variegated cultivars, particularly 'Adam'; 'Goldchild' and 'Marginata Elegantissima' (E).

Jasminum nudiflorum (winter jasmine).

Lonicera japonica 'Aureoreticulata' (evergreen honeysuckle) (E).

Lonicera periclymenum 'Graham Thomas' and 'Serotina'.

Wall Shrubs

Chaenomeles (Japonica) – particularly 'Simonii' and 'Moerloosii'.

Daphne odora 'Aureomarginata' (E).

Euonymus fortunei 'Emerald 'n' Gold'; 'Silver Queen' (E).

Hydrangea serrata 'Preziosa'.

Hypericum rouytchense.

Jasminum nudiflorum.

Viburnum tinus 'Gwenillan' (E).

Climbers for pergolas

Pergolas constructed of well-preserved rustic poles or sawn timber, the uprights set 2–3m (6–9ft) apart make delightful features in the garden and good accommodation for the more vigorous climbers which often need considerable restriction on house walls and fences. It is usually sufficient to site a vigorous climber, such as wisteria or vine at every other upright; then, with well-prepared sites, growth will be adequate to cover roof beams and make a canopy of foliage and flower. Less vigorous, more upright growing climbers are frequently adaptable to furnish the uprights.

These are vigorous climbers, particularly suitable for pergola roof beams which may need wire between to afford adequate support: *Actinidia chinensis* (male and female), *Aristolochia macrophylla, Celastrus orbiculatus* (hermaphrodite form), *Clematis montana* cultivars and *C. tangutica. Humulus lupulus* 'Aureus' (Golden Hop), *Vitis coignetiae* and *Wisteria sinensis* and cultivars.

Climbers for pergola uprights, rustic tripods and arches

There are a number of climbers of moderate growth, particularly clematis, climbing roses and honeysuckles and ornamental vines, particularly adaptable for furnishing the uprights of pergolas, rather than the roof beams. Such plants also do useful duty on rustic tripods in shrubaceous borders or elsewhere in the garden and on the many rustic or plastic-covered wire archways that are used today. Do not forget to use a small mound-forming shrub, such as potentilla, hydrangea, hardy fuchsia, cistus or phlomis, or perhaps a group of hostas at the base of pergola pole or tripod – this not only looks better, but provides a cool rootrun for the climber, particularly clematis.

Try, clematis: *alpina* and *macropetala* cultivars; *C. viticella* 'Kermesina', and the large-flowered hybrids such as 'Comtesse de Bouchaud' – rose pink; 'Huldine' – pearly white; 'Niobe' – the best red; 'Perle d'Azur' – the best light blue.

Climbing roses include: 'Aloha', 'Climbing Iceberg', 'Dublin Bay', Climbing Pom Pom de Paris', 'Zephirine Drouhin' (Bourbon).

Vines include: *Vitis vinifera* 'Incana' and *v.* 'Purpurea'.

Scented honeysuckles: *Lonicera periclymenum* 'Graham Thomas'; *L. japonica* 'Aureoreticulata' (E) – with net-variegated leaves.

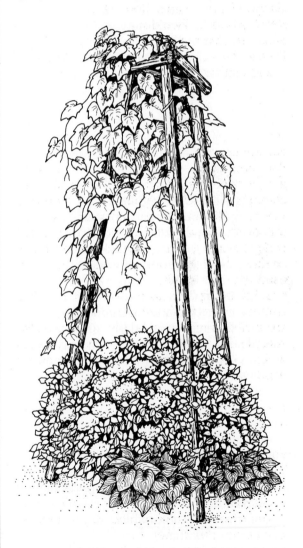

FIG 89 *Vine climbing a rustic tripod, with hydrangea and hostas at base*

251

ROCK GARDENS

Rock gardens remain popular as features in the modern garden and in public places. For devotees of the alpine plant, a well designed and constructed garden with bold pieces of preferably local stone is essential to accommodate and display a wide range of plants, essentially associated with mountain areas, and including dwarf bulbs, dwarf and slow-growing conifers and dwarf mound-forming or prostrate shrubs.

Alpine gardening is a vast subject and one of the world's largest horticultural societies, The Alpine Garden Society, exists to further the knowledge of alpine plants and to encourage their cultivation. Those wishing to go deeply into this fascinating subject cannot do better than become members of this Society (Secretary: Michael Upwood, Lye End Link, St John's, Woking, Surrey, GU21 1SW). Here we must regrettably confine ourselves to recommending dwarf and slow-growing conifers, dwarf shrubs and easy, reliable groundcovering plants to live in with them in a rock garden environment.

Most well-drained garden soils, with the addition of sand, grit and peat, if heavy, are quite suitable for general rock garden planting of this nature. More specialised conditions are required for many of the high alpines and rarities. It is, however, essential to ensure that the soil or compost is free of perennial weed, particularly ground elder and bindweed, which, if entrenched under rocks will be extremely difficult to eradicate. Although frustrating for most gardeners it is worth allowing several summer months to elapse after constructing a rock garden, in order to remove crops of weed and any perennial weed root before planting in the autumn or the following spring. After planting, a stone chipping mulch is both attractive and in keeping and the plants appreciate the cool rootrun. Varying sizes of gravels and pebbles are available which simulate scree conditions. Dwarf and slow-growing conifers and dwarf shrubs should be widely spaced, at least 1.5–2m (4½–6ft). Most will get larger than you think, and the beauty of their shape and form is lost if they are not well separated from neighbours. Groundcovering alpine plants help to set them off and to complete the scene, but can to some extent be depressed by the growth of the conifers and shrubs.

Dwarf and slow-growing conifers

There is now a very large range of these available. All are evergreen and make miniature spires, mounds, sprawls and carpets of blue, grey, green, silver or variegated foliage. While dwarf shrubs, many of which are evergreen, again have a diversity of shape and form, colour of foliage and flower.

Chamaecyparis lawsoniana 'Ellwood's Pillar'; 'Pygmaea Argentea'; 'Summer Snow'.
Chamaecyparis obtusa 'Nana'.
Chamaecyparis pisifera 'Aurea Nana'.
Cryptomeria japonica 'Spiralis'; 'Vilmoriniana'.
Juniperus communis 'Compressa'; 'Depressa Aurea'.
Juniperus conferta 'Blue Pacific'.
Juniperus procumbens 'Nana'.
Juniperus squamata 'Blue Star'.
Picea mariana 'Nana'.
Pinus mugo pumilio; 'Trompenburg'.
Pinus sylvestris 'Nana'.
Thuya plicata 'Rogersii'.
Tsuga canadensis 'Bennett'; 'Prostrata'.

This is but a small selection from many dwarf and slow-growing conifers, several are choice, uncommon and specially selected forms and may be seen to good advantage in mature or semi-mature state in the scree (dry) garden at the Hillier Arboretum. A visit there can be most rewarding and will help you to select those most appealing and appropriate for your rock garden planting.

Dwarf shrubs for rock gardens

Again, the choice is very large. Neat compact growth is important and generous spacings. Select from: (E) = evergreen

Anthyllis hermanniae.
Berberis thunbergii 'Atropurpurea Nana'.

Ceanothus 'Blue Mound' (E).

Cytisus procumbens.

Daphne species and cultivars, particularly: *arbuscula; blagayana; cneorum; mantensiana* 'Manten'; *retusa* (E).

Fuchsia 'Tom Thumb'.

Halimium ocymoides (E).

Hebe cupressoides 'Boughton Dome'; *pimeleoides* 'Quicksilver' (E).

Lavandula angustifolia 'Nana Alba' (E).

Nandina domestica 'Nana Purpurea' (E).

Parahebe catarractae (E).

Potentilla arbuscula 'Beesii'.

Rhododendron 'Curlew'; *impeditum*; 'Elisabeth Hobbie'; *yakushimanum* (some shade desirable) (A) (E).

Spiraea japonica 'Little Princess'.

Compact groundcovering rock plants or alpines

Generally, site in groups of three or more of a kind, 20–30cm (8–12in) apart, grouped between shrubs and conifers and to furnish crevices between the rocks. Heathers (*Erica, Calluna, Daboecia*) are also useful for this task. Acid soil is essential for all but *Erica carnea* and its cultivars. Most garden centres offer a good range:

Acaena species.

Ajuga reptans 'Burgundy Glow'.

Arabis ferdinandi-coburgii 'Variegata'.

Armeria maritima cultivars (thrift).

Aubretia in variety.

Campanula carpatica and cultivars; *C. portenschlagiana* (muralis) and 'Birch hybrid'.

Dianthus deltoides and cultivars.

Diascia 'Ruby Field' and others.

Dryas octopetala.

Gentiana septemfida.

Geranium dalmaticum; *G. sanguineum lancastriense.*

Gypsophila repens 'Rosea'.

Helianthemum in variety (E).

Lithospermum diffusum 'Heavenly Blue' (A).

Phlox douglasii and *P. subulata* cultivars.

Polygonum vacciniifolium.

Pulsatilla vulgaris cultivars (pasque flower).

Saxifraga (mossy) 'Pixie' (E).

Thymus citriodorus 'Aureus'; 'Porlock'; *drucei* (*serpyllum*) 'Coccineus'; 'Pink Chintz'.

Veronica prostrata (*rupestris*).

Waldsteinia ternata.

WATER GARDENS

In chapter 4 we discussed the siting, design and construction of pools and here the planting is considered.

Assuming that the water feature is in an open situation, hardy water lilies can be installed with every chance of success, particularly if the water warms up well in summer and is still. The use of a fountain will reduce the space available for successful culture of water lilies. Specialists in this field have a wide range of *nymphaea* (water lilies) available today in a variety of colours and sizes; select according to the depth of water. It is possible to grow delightful small water lilies in a very few inches of water and, at the other end of the scale, some of the large and vigorous growers will cover several square metres of a lake. However, most requirements are met by the following varieties which can be conveniently termed small growers with a surface spread of leaves and flowers of approximately 60cm (2ft).

Water lilies suitable for small ponds

Nymphaea odorata 'Alba' – white cup-shaped scented flowers; *odorata* 'Turicensis' has soft scented rose-coloured flowers with elongated petals; *N. alba* 'Froebelii' is the best and most free-flowering red for small ponds; 'Graziella' has flowers of subtle blend of apricot and orange.

For larger pools, the following water lilies have a surface spread of about 1m (3ft):

Nymphaea 'Gonnere' – goblet-shaped flowers of pure white; *odorata* 'W. B. Shaw' produces scented shell-pink flowers of good size, held well above the surface of the water; 'James Brydon' is one of the most popular of water lilies with rich carmine-pink flowers with a silvery sheen, succeeding in semi-shady situations where many would fail; *odorata* 'Sulphurea' has many-petalled clear yellow flowers, held well above the marbled leaves. The blooms remain open in the evening; 'Escarboucle' is perhaps the finest of all red water lilies and very free flowering.

Submerged oxygenating plants

These are an essential part of the planting of pool or lake; together with water lilies, the oxygenators help to reduce the incidence of algae (blanket weed) which is often so troublesome when establishing new ponds. Furthermore, a good supply of oxygenating weed helps to starve the algae of nutrients and reduce the incidence of cloudy or soupy water. Oxygenating plants should be installed at the rate of one per 60cm square (2sq ft), for pools of up to 9 square metres (100sq ft). They are usually supplied in bunches of unrooted stems with a small lead weight to cause them to sink. They establish more readily, however, if planted in coarse gravel or sand, perhaps retained by bricks on the pond bottom. A plastic seed tray or small purpose-made planting crate can be used to accommodate five or six bunches. Soil can be used but tends to discolour the water. Introducing fish too early in the life of the pond is often a mistake, as they may dislodge or consume oxygenating plants in the absence of other food. At least a month should elapse after planting before the introduction of fish, and then the insectivorous golden orfe is to be preferred.

Good submerged oxygenating plants include:

Callitriche verna (water starwort).
Ceratophyllum demersum (water hornwort).
Elodea densa.

Hottonia palustris.
Potamogeton crispus.
Ranunculus aquatilis (our native water buttercup) has masses of small white flowers on the surface.
Stratiotes aloides (water soldier) an unusual and interesting native oxygenator, with spiky leaves like pineapple tops, rising to the surface only to produce their curious white flowers.

Marginal trees and shrubs

In naturally moist soil and where there is adequate space there are a number of small or medium sized (usually deciduous) trees and conifers which can be effective if well spaced to allow for their ultimate growth. Large-growing willows, like *Salix* 'Chrysocoma' and most poplars, should be reserved for wide areas round spacious lakes and not used near ponds in small gardens where they will rapidly reach large size and need removal or heavy pollarding. There are also many suitable shrubs which can be seen to good advantage if they are well spaced between trees and associating marginal aquatic plants. Winter bark effects from shrubby willow (*Salix*) and dogwood (*Cornus*) can be particularly striking.

Trees for *smaller ponds* include:

Alnus glutinosa (alder) 'Imperialis' with finely cut foliage.
Amelanchier (snowy mespilus) – most species and cultivars.
Betula pendula (birch) and 'Darlicarlica' (Swedish Birch).
Populus tremula 'Pendula' (weeping aspen).
Salix (willow) – the smaller-growing tree species, notably *alba* 'Sericea'; *caprea* 'Kilmarnock' (the Kilmarnock willow); *daphnoides* (violet willow); x *erythroflexuosa* – twisted leaves and pendulous contorted stems; *pentandra* (bay willow).
and among conifers:
Taxodium ascendens 'Nutans'.

Trees for *large ponds and lakes only*. These are large growers requiring generous spacing:

Alnus cordata (Italian alder) and *glutinosa* (common alder).
Betula papyrifera (paper-bark birch); *nigra*; and 'Jermyns'.
Populus, particularly *alba* 'Pyramidalis'; *P. canescens* 'Macrophylla'; *P.* 'Eugenei'; *P.* 'Serotina Aurea'; *P. tremula* (aspen).
Quercus palustris (pin oak).
Salix (willow) – larger growers, notably *alba* (white willow); 'Basfordiana'; *alba* 'Caerulea' (cricket bat willow); 'Chryso-coma' (weeping willow); *fragilis* (crack willow); *matsudana* (Pekin willow) and its cultivars 'Pendula' and 'Tortuosa'.

and *conifers for large ponds and lakes*, include:
Taxodium distichum (swamp cypress).
Metasequoia glyptostroboides (dawn red-wood) and cultivars.

Waterside shrubs

Any of the following enjoy moist conditions and blend well near waterside. Some are less commonly seen and worthy of wider plant-ing: (A) Acid soil essential.

Andromeda polifolia and cultivars (bog rosemary) (A).
Cornus alba and cultivars – for variegated foliage Aurea (soft yellow); 'Elegantissima'; 'Spaethii'; 'Variegata'. For winter bark effects, *alba* 'Sibirica'; *stolonifera* 'Flaviramea'.
Hippophae rhamnoides (sea buckthorn).
Ledum groenlandicum (Labrador tea) and *palustre* (wild rosemary) (A).
Lindera benzoin (spice bush) (A).
Myrica gale (sweet gale, bog myrtle) (A).
Neillia species.
Physocarpus opulifolius (ninebark) and cultivars, including 'Dart's Gold'.
Salix – there are many suitable shrubby species of this diverse and fascinating genus, notably *alba* 'Chermesina' and 'Vitellina' when stooled for red and bright yellow winter bark effects; *elaeagnos* (hoary willow); *fargesii*; *hastata* 'Wehr-hahnii'; *helvetica*; *lanata*; *purpurea* 'Gracilis'; *repens argentea*.

and bamboos are useful by waterside:
Arundinaria.
Phyllostachys.
Sasa.
(see Plant Profiles, chapter 8).

Marginal aquatic plants

These add greatly to the character, interest and completeness of the pool. Many are adaptable from several inches of shallow water to permanently damp soil. In these days, planting instructions and depth of water are normally noted on the label of plants supplied by nurserymen or garden centres. Some first-class marginal aquatics include:

Acorus calamus 'Variegatus' – a striking varie-gated plant with iris-like leaves, striped cream and gold, about 60cm (2ft).
Alisma plantago-aquatica (water plantain) has large plantain-like leaves and whorls of pale pink flowers on branched stems, 60cm (2ft).
Butomus umbellatus (flowering rush) is a beautiful native plant with triangular rush-like leaves and rose-pink flowers, 75cm (2½ft).
Caltha palustris (marsh marigold or kingcup) a well-known native plant. The double-flowered form 'Plena' is more compact and a good garden plant, 30cm (1ft).
Glyceria maxima 'Variegata' (*aquatica* 'Varie-gata') is included in our Plant Profile of Ornamental Grasses. One of the most con-spicuous of variegated grasses, it adapts to moist soil or shallow water, 60cm (2ft).
Iris kaempferi – Japanese clematis iris is one of the many irises associated with water-side conditions. It is spectacular in June and July with varying shades and combina-tions of blue, purple and white flowers of

clematis-like shape. Acid soil preferred, 60cm (2ft); *Iris laevigata* will produce a similar effect and flowers of deep blue; tolerant of all soils, 60cm (2ft).

Lysichiton americanum – a striking plant with large yellow spathes, typical of the arum family, produced in April. Large lush green leaves follow the flowers. This and the white-flowered species *camtschatcense* are a great feature at the Savill Garden, Windsor Great Park.

Mentha aquatica (water mint) helps to keep the water pure and clear. It has sweet-smelling, bronze-purple foliage and clusters of deep lilac flowers, 30–45cm (1–1½ft).

Pontederia cordata (pickerel weed) has handsome spikes of blue flowers in summer and autumn, 45–60cm (1½–2ft).

Ranunculus lingua 'Grandiflorus' (great spearwort) a handsome plant; large lanceolate leaves and yellow buttercup flowers, 60cm–1m (2–3ft).

Sagittaria (arrowhead) has unusual leaves which give the plant its name, and our native species *S. sagittifolia* has whorls of white, purple centred, three-petalled flowers in June and July, 30–45cm (1–1½ft).

Scirpus tabernaemontani (bullrush) has two interesting forms, of moderate growth, suitable for ponds, 'Albescens', a tall plant with green and white variegated stems, 1m (3ft) and 'Zebrinus' with zebra stripes of green and white, about 1m (3ft).

Sparganium ramosum (bur-reed) is an unusual branched plant, most interesting when clothed with its green spiky fruits, which follow the heads of yellow flower, about 1m (3ft).

Typha (reed-mace or false bullrush). The charming dwarf species *minima*, with grass-like leaves and small brown pokers, is the best plant for the smaller pool. The giant reed-mace, *latifolia* erroneously known as bullrush can be a very invasive plant which, unless restrained, can colonise large areas of pond or lake.

Veronica beccabunga (brooklime) is an interesting fleshy native plant with bright blue flowers, 15cm (6in).

Zantedeschia aethiopica (arum lily) is an African species which will usually survive our winters if given at least 6in of water over its crown. It makes a striking contribution to the beauty of the pond margin with its large white spathes and large leaves.

Planting pool plants

May and June, are the most sensible times to carry out movement and re-establishment of aquatic plants, both water lilies and marginals. They move best when coming into active growth and when the water is warming up with the advent of summer. The planting season can continue into August if need be, but it is not advised later than this, as establishment will not be complete before the water cools and winter comes again. In these days plastic tubs and purpose-made baskets, with perforated sides provide an ideal method of accommodating water lilies and marginal aquatics in the concrete, fibreglass or butyl rubber pool. In natural ponds these containers can also be used to restrict the growth of water lilies where necessary, and stockades composed of preserved (tanalised) wooden posts or half posts driven into the bed of the natural pond, will restrict the advance of the more invasive marginal aquatics. Such treatment also serves to provide a neat finish to the edge of a natural pond or island in a pond. The standard water lily basket is 30×30×20cm (12×12×8in) with tapering sides. Unless set in mud at the bottom of the pond or surrounded by two or three courses of bricks on the bottom of the pool, they will tend to be top heavy and fall over. Good medium to heavy garden soil, with the addition of chopped turf, is a good mixture to use. Peaty, sandy or chalky soil should be avoided, as should soil-less compost or the use of farmyard manure or fertilisers, which will all tend to encourage the growth of algae and excessive growth of vigorous marginals and oxygenators. Containers for marginals in artificial pools are normally accommodated on a shelf around the edge. Here again, the commercial plastic planting crate, usually of smaller size and perhaps 15cm (6in) deep, with tapering sides, will need support with bricks unless a broad-based edition is available.

Waterside herbaceous plants

There are many suitable herbaceous plants, some, are described on p212 (Shrubaceous Borders), suitable for the soil adjoining natural pools, which will take an overflow or be naturally moist by capillary action or from a stream feeding the pool. Here we can accommodate, as space allows, such impressive specimens as: *Gunnera manicata* with its gigantic rhubarb-like leaves, 2m (6½ft) or more across on prickly stalks, and several species of *Rodgersia, Hosta, Hemerocallis; Peltyphyllum peltatum*, with its umbrella-like leaves, has pink flowers preceding the foliage in April; *Lythrum* and *Lysimachia* (purple and yellow loosestrife).

It is also possible to naturalise a considerable range of moisture-loving candelabra primulas which, if happy, will increase and colonise, particularly *Primula beesiana, bulleyana, denticulata, florindae, japonica* and *viallii*. For summer effect, astilbes, in variety, can be most effective. Spectacular planting can still be enjoyed by those possessing the natural pool, where the surrounding soil is moist. Regrettably, the present-day artificial pool of concrete, fibreglass or butyl rubber is sealed off from the local soil, which may be dry and unsuitable for such plants, unless a specially moist area can be contrived.

Further reading on this subject can be found in *Water Gardening* by Frances Perry, an old book, but packed with authoritative advice and information. An up-to-date book with detailed and practical coverage of most aspects of water gardens, their stocking and subsequent maintenance is the *Stapeley Book of Water Gardens* by Stanley Russell.

PLANT GROUPING FOR EFFECT

Plant groupings can achieve year-round impact of colour, shape, form and texture if carefully planned. Foliage, flower, berry, even winter bark can be effective. The great range of shrubs available today – evergreen and deciduous – extends from low ground-coverers to tall screeners. Conifers offer a bewildering if beautiful range of sizes, shapes and textures and with few exceptions are evergreen, evergrey, evergold – or even everbronze or everpurple! Variegation in deciduous and evergreen trees and shrubs and conifers can create satisfying and eye-catching effects too, particularly when used as a focal point.

It must be stressed, however, that it is most important to take account of the likely ultimate growth (as well as suitability for your soil) of the trees, shrubs and conifers chosen. Even allowing for pruning where this is desirable, these 'bones' of the garden scene should be well spaced to allow reasonably for their development, thereby achieving the impact they can create. Large-growing shrubs are often planted within 0.3m–0.6m (1–2ft) of one another or of a less vigorous shrub, because their foliage may happen to blend, or perhaps the owner has seen them so arranged at a flower show. The stronger will quickly engulf the weaker and if they both survive neither can develop satisfactorily.

Space garden trees or medium-height conifers at least 4–6m (12–20ft) apart; dwarf, medium or large shrubs should be 1.5–2.5m (5–8ft) or more apart. Ultimate growth is often greater than you imagine, particularly on heavy loams or clay. Between the trees and shrubs can be grown a fascinating range of associated planting, both shrubby and herbaceous, generally of a ground-covering nature. As well as low-growing shrubs, long-lived herbaceous perennials can be used, together with ornamental grasses, ferns and prostrate or mound-forming shrub roses and low-spreading conifers; site them between 0.3m and 1m apart (1–3ft) each way, often in groups of three or more of a kind, in order to ensure rapid coverage – closer for herbaceous plants, grasses and ferns and wider apart for roses and conifers.

Within the limits of soil, aspect and sensible spacing, the possibilities are infinite and the year-round interest, variety and artistic satisfaction that can be achieved from such a planting is boundless. However, in your planning have regard for colour blending as well as the vigour of your plants. Pleasing colour blends or contrasts are equally desirable when you arrange the groundcovers; these should be of similar vigour in order that weaker growers are not swamped or overrun by more lusty neighbours. Be warned, however, it is easy to be bitten by the 'plantsman bug' and to collect a great number of individually beautiful and interesting plants and shrubs, packing them in (often too closely), rapidly making a formless mini-jungle. (But it's fun!)

Elaeagnus x ebbingei *'Gilt Edge'*

FOCAL POINT PLANTINGS

These ideas should give effect for much of the year. They assume that background evergreen shrubs or a hedge are present (or can be planted) and are adaptable for most aspects in sun or semi-shade. Here the planting is confined to dwarf, medium or large shrubs in association with low-growing ground-covering plants, both shrubby and herbaceous, in a sequence of colour combinations.

Key

HP	= hardy perennial
HHP	= half-hardy perennial
DS	= dwarf shrub (0.3–0.6m) (1–2ft)
SS	= small shrub (1–1.5m) (3–5ft)
MS	= medium shrub (1.5–3m) (3–10ft)
LS	= large shrub (over 3m) (over 10ft)
ST	= small tree (eventual height 4.5–9m) (15–30ft)
MT	= medium tree (eventual height 10–18m) (33–60ft)
LT	= large tree (eventual height over 18m) (over 60ft)
GC	= suitable for use as ground cover
E	= evergreen

SCHEME (A) Red/purple with silver/grey foliage

To be used in association with pale-yellow, white or pale-blue or pink flowers:

Shrubs

Olearia macrodonta 'Major'	LS E (A1)
Cotinus coggygria 'Grace' or 'Velvet Cloak'	LS (A2)
Cornus alba 'Elegantissima'	MS (A3)
Senecio 'Sunshine' or *Artemisia* 'Powis Castle'	SS E (A4)

Herbaceous perennials and ground covers

Alchemilla mollis	HP (A5)
Geranium endressii 'A. T. Johnson' or 'Wargrave Pink'	HP (A6)
Hosta 'Elegans' or 'Frances Williams'	HP (A7)
Campanula lactiflora or *alliarifolia* 'Ivory Bells'	HP (A8)
Hemerocallis 'Golden Chimes' or *Helleborus foetidus*	HP (A9)

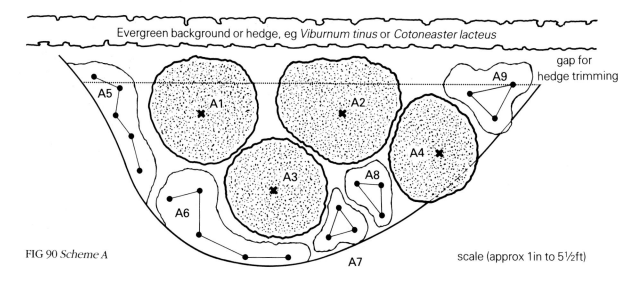

Evergreen background or hedge, eg *Viburnum tinus* or *Cotoneaster lacteus*

gap for hedge trimming

FIG 90 *Scheme A*

scale (approx 1in to 5½ft)

260

SCHEME (B) Golden/yellow and bronze/copper tinted foliage
Associated with yellow, orange or red flowers:

Shrubs

Sambucus racemosa	LS (B1)
'Plumosa Aurea' or 'Sutherland'	
Berberis thunbergii	MS (B2)
'Red Chief' (SS) or *Rosa rubrifolia*	
Choisya ternata	SS E (B3)
'Sundance'	
Physocarpus opulifolius	SS (B4)
'Dart's Gold'	
Euphorbia polychroma	HP (B5)
or *wulfenii*	

Herbaceous perennials and ground covers

Bergenia	HP E (B6)
'Evening Glow'	
Epimedium rubrum	HP (B7)
Crocosmia lucifer	HP (B8)
or *masonorum*	
Euonymus fortunei	DS E (B9)
'Emerald 'n' Gold'	

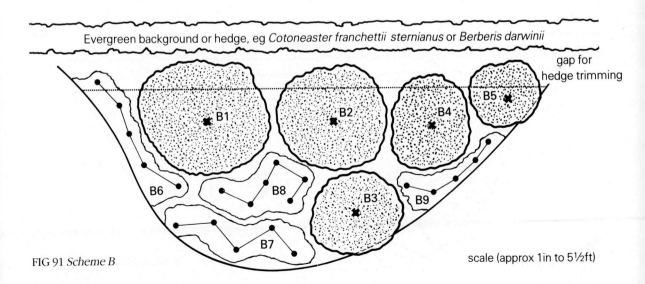

Evergreen background or hedge, eg *Cotoneaster franchettii sternianus* or *Berberis darwinii*

gap for hedge trimming

FIG 91 *Scheme B*

scale (approx 1in to 5½ft)

261

SCHEME (C) Silver and golden variegated foliage

This may be evergreen and deciduous and will go well with white, pink or blue flowers:

Shrubs

Cornus alternifolia	LS/ST (C1)
'Argentea' or *Aralia elata* 'Variegata'	LS/ST
Elaeagnus x ebbingei	LS E (C2)
'Gilt Edge' or 'Limelight'	
Weigela florida	SS/MS (C3)
'Variegata'	
Rhamnus alaterna	LS E (C4)
'Argenteovariegata'	

Herbaceous perennials and ground covers

Geranium	HP (C5)
'Johnson's Blue'	
Hosta	HP (C6)
'Thomas Hogg' or *undulata*	
Dicentra eximea	HP (C7)
'Alba' or 'Luxurians'	
Campanula persicifolia	HP (C8)
'Telham Beauty' or *alliarifolia* 'Ivory Bells'	

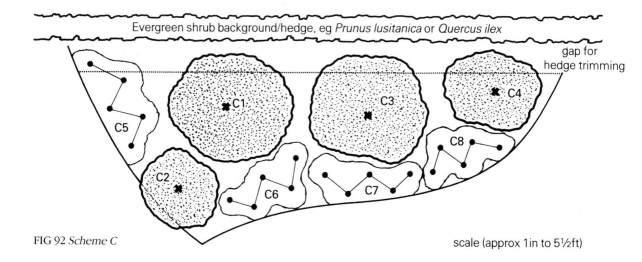

Evergreen shrub background/hedge, eg *Prunus lusitanica* or *Quercus ilex*

gap for hedge trimming

FIG 92 *Scheme C*

scale (approx 1in to 5½ft)

FIG 93 *Scheme D*

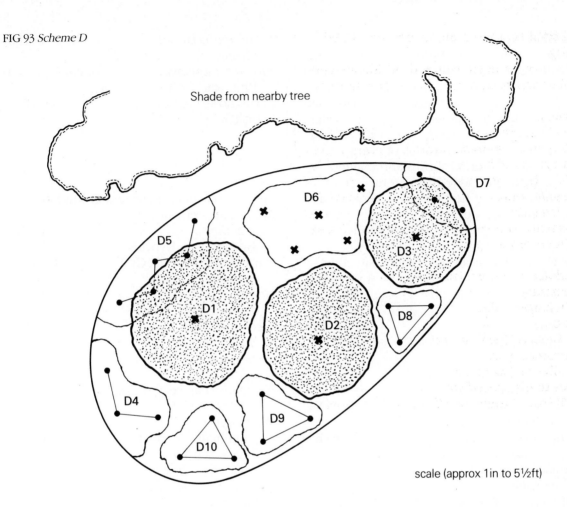

Shade from nearby tree

scale (approx 1 in to 5½ft)

SCHEME (D) Shades of green and pale-yellow leaves
To be associated with white, pale-yellow or blue flowers (for shaded areas):

Shrubs

Aucuba japonica	LS E (D1)
'Picturata' or *Euonymus japonicus*	
'Aureopictus'	
Viburnum opulus	MS (D2)
'Sterile' or *plicatum* 'Lanarth'	
Danae racemosa	DS E (D3)

Herbaceous perennials and ground covers

Gentiana asclepiadea	HP (D4)
Polygonatum x hybridum	HP (D5)
(Solomon's Seal)	
Vinca major 'Variegata'	HP E (D6)
Hosta fortunei 'Aurea'	HP (D7)
'Aurea'	
Kirengeshoma palmata	HP (D8)
Hakonechloa macra 'Aureola'	HP (D9)
('Albo-aurea') or *Milium effusum* 'Aureum'	
(Bowles' Golden Grass)	
Helleborus lividus corsicus	HP E (D10)

SCHEMES (E) TO (H)

Include shrubs with bold, large or heavily-lobed leaves providing interesting shapes and textures.

For a focal point by patio or island-bed planting, upright (fastigiate) trees or conifers may be cleverly contrasted with mound-forming or pendulous forms of evergreen or deciduous flowering shrubs and conifers. To these may be added a careful blend of ground-covering herbaceous perennials and ornamental grasses. Here are two suggested schemes appropriate to all well-drained soils.

SCHEME (E) for an open sunny situation

Shrubs and conifers

Phlomis 'Edward Bowles'	SS E (E1)
Juniperus scopulorum 'Skyrocket'	conifer E (E2)
Phormium tenax 'Purpurea' or 'Variegata'	MS E (E3)
Nandina domestica or *Photinia* 'Red Robin'	MS E (E4)
Thuja occidentalis 'Rheingold'	conifer E (E5)
Aralia elata or *spinosa*	LS (E6)
Modern Shrub Rose 'Heritage' or 'Mary Rose'	SS (E7)
Cryptomeria japonica 'Elegans Nana' or 'Spiralis'	conifer DS E (E8)
Juniperus squamata 'Blue Star' or 'Blue Carpet'	conifer DS E (E9)
Shrub Rose 'Rosy Cushion' or 'Raubritter'	DS (E10)

Herbaceous perennials and ground covers

Waldsteinia ternata	HP (E11)
Agapanthus 'Headbourne Hybrids'	HP (E12)
Shrub Rose 'Red Max Graf' or 'Fiona'	GC (E13)
Acanthus spinosus or *latifolius*	HP (E14)
Helianthemum 'Wisley Pink'	GC E (E15)
Penstemon 'Garnet'	HP (E16)
Santolina chamaecyparissus nana (*corsica*)	GC E (E17)
Alchemilla mollis	HP (E18)
Geranium macrorrhizum 'Ingwersen's Variety'	GC E (E19)
Cotoneaster salicifolius 'Gnom' or *dammeri*	GC E (E20)
Erica carnea 'Ann Sparkes' or 'Foxhollow'	GC E (E21)

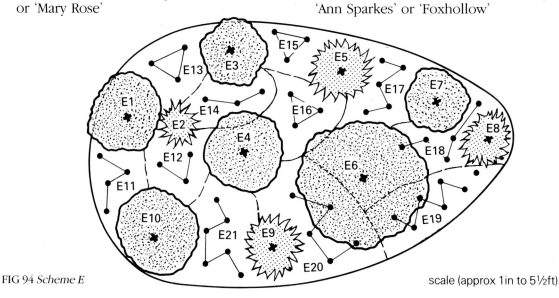

FIG 94 *Scheme E*

scale (approx 1in to 5½ft)

FIG 95 *Scheme F*

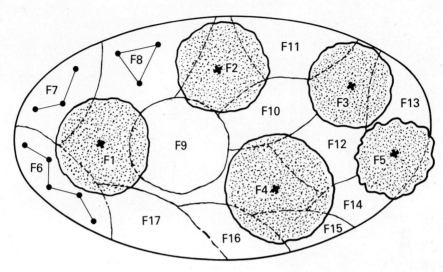

scale (approx 1in to 5½ft)

SCHEME (F) For a semi-shaded position
Shrubs

Hydrangea paniculata 'Tardiva'	MS (F1)
Rhododendron macabeanum (A)	LS/ST E (F2)
or *Ilex x altaclerensis* 'Lawsoniana'	
Hydrangea aspera or *villosa*	MS (F3)
Acer japonicum 'Vitifolium' or 'Aconitifolium'	LS (F4)
x Fatshedera lizei	MS E (F5)

Herbaceous plants and ground covers

Ophiopogon planiscapus 'Nigrescens'	HP (F6)
Hosta fortunei 'Aureo-marginata'	HP (F7)
Hedera helix 'Manda's Crested'	GC E (F8)
Rodgersia pinnata 'Superba'	HP (F9)
Cimicifuga ramosa 'Atropurpurea'	HP (F10)
Euphorbia polychroma	HP (F11)
Anemone x hybrida 'Queen Charlotte'	HP (F12)
Athyrium felix-foemina	fern (F13)
Hosta fortunei 'Albopicta'	HP (F14)
Bergenia 'Silverlight'	HP (F15)
Polystichum setiferum 'Plumoso-divisilobum'	fern (F16)
Hakonechloa macra 'Aureola' ('Albo-aurea') (grass)	(F17)

Agapanthus, *a near-hardy hybrid*
associated with santolinas at Ventnor
Botanic Garden, Isle of Wight

Disanthus cercidifolius, *a medium-sized*
shrub for acid soils which displays
spectacular leaf colour in late summer and
autumn – here in contrast with the yellow
autumn leaves of a young birch

SCHEMES (G) AND (H)

(G) proposes the use of shrubs and small trees giving exceptional displays of autumn colour of leaf and berry together with significant spring and summer flower. Effective shrubby or herbaceous ground covers are included; alternatives for alkaline gardens are suggested where acid soil (lime-hating) shrubs (A) are named in this arrangement.

(H) blends winter bark effects with variegated foliage and interesting ground covers to give colour at most seasons. Bulbs can be used to advantage in both of these schemes, particularly in association with hostas and many of the lower growing ground covers.

SCHEME (G)

Autumn colour of foliage and berry with spring and summer flower ((A) for acid soil only)

Shrubs/Trees

Disanthus cercidifolius (A)	MS (A)
(or *Rhus glabra* 'Laciniata')	
Euonymus alatus	MS (B)
Prunus 'Spire' (or *Photinia villosa* (A))	ST (C)
Berberis	SS (Semi E) (D)
'Parkjuweel'	
Fothergilla major (A)	MS (E)
(or *Hamamelis vernalis* 'Sandra')	
Prunus glandulosa	SS (F)
'Alba Plena'	

Ground covers – shrubby and herbaceous

Cotoneaster conspicuus 'Decorus'	DS(E)
(or *C. salicifolius* 'Gnom' PS(E))	(a)
Hosta	HP (b)
'Elegans' (or 'Frances Williams')	
Polygonum affine	HP (c)
'Donald Lowndes'	
Bergenia	HP (E) (d)
'Ballawley'	
Hosta undulata	HP (e)

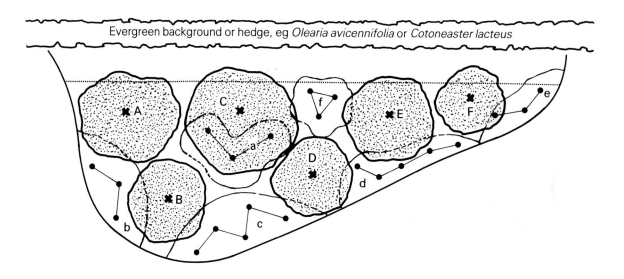

Evergreen background or hedge, eg *Olearia avicennifolia* or *Cotoneaster lacteus*

FIG 96 *Scheme G*

scale (approx 1in to 5½ft)

SCHEME (H)
Shrubs/small trees with winter bark effects

Some variegated foliage and ground covers and ferns with interesting foliage and flower (for sun or semi shade):

Acer griseum	ST (A)

(paper bark maple) (or *davidii* – snakebark maple)

Rubus cockburnianus	MS (B)
Cornus alba	MS (C)
'Variegata'*	
Euonymus fortunei	SS (E) (D)
'Emerald Gaiety' (or 'Emerald 'n' Gold')	
Cornus stolonifera	MS (E)
'Flaviramea'*	

(*stool/coppice periodically to maintain compact habit and brightly coloured shoots)

Ground covers and ferns

Hosta lancifolia	HP (a)
Hosta fortunei 'Albo picta'	HP (b)
Lamium maculatum	HP (c)
'Beacon Silver'	
Ajuga reptans	HP (d)
'Burgundy Glow'	
Alchemilla mollis	HP (e)
Osmunda regalis	fern (f)
(or *Phyllitis scolopendrium*)	
Vinca major	GC (E) (g)
'Variegata'	

These ideas can be extended if space permits to furnish larger borders or small 'theme' gardens – compartments within larger gardens, as seen so effectively at Sissinghurst Castle, Kent, and Hidcote Manor, Chipping Campden, Gloucester, in particular; also in many other National Trust and privately owned gardens opened to the public throughout the country.

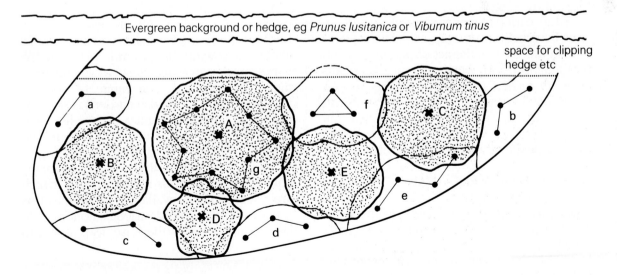

Evergreen background or hedge, eg Prunus lusitanica or Viburnum tinus

space for clipping hedge etc

FIG 97 *Scheme H*

scale (approx 1in to 5½ft)

8
PLANT PROFILES FOR THE PLANT-LOVER

To some, a garden is a setting, whether for the playing of games or the eating of barbecues, or for showing off the property to popular acclaim. Others think that anyone can design an attractive layout (or at least try to) but that gardening is a question of using and enjoying plants. Of course, both views have their limitations: a plantsman's collection may be too specialised to be beautiful, just as a functional landscape may be unwelcoming.

In the earlier pages, technical considerations have held most sway, subjects like how to plan the garden, the act of planting, shrub maintenance, and which colours of plants associate to best overall effect. This section of the book is not primarily concerned with these aspects, instead its starting point is the sheer enjoyment which can be gained from taking a passionate interest in plants.

WHY DEVELOP A PERSONAL COLLECTION?
A personal collection can provide the extra zest to gardening which comes from having something which few other people possess. Many of the plant genera or groupings discussed in the following pages include some very popular everyday items, such as roses or clematis. But the knowledge that 96% of all gardens contain hybrid tea or floribunda roses removes some of the impetus to grow them! After all, who really wants to be like everyone else? There are, of course, many more rose cultivars available than just hybrid teas and floribundas. A consideration of these, as well as the attractive species roses, provides an extra dimension to rose growing.

A personal collection is rewarding for the information it gives. Nearly every subject becomes more interesting as you know more about it. Growing the common plants in any genus means growing those which nurserymen have selected. The range of suitable plants available for British gardens is so large that no nursery can offer a complete list. Most of the plants in general circulation in the nursery trade are good and reliable examples of their species, but there are often many equally good forms or related species which are not commonly available. Sometimes this is because they are old varieties, no longer in fashion, sometimes they are too new and

Campanula latifolia 'Alba' grows well in moist and semi-shaded sites where it will naturalise

have not caught the eye of the right exponent of their group of plants. Quite a few, however, are actually better plants than those generally available but just difficult to propagate or needing that extra degree of cultural skill to show them to best effect.

Many of the commonest plants have been selected for their instant appeal, but what they gain in brilliance of colour or size of blooms is frequently matched by a loss of beauty and subtlety. Get to know a group of plants and you soon appreciate the potential of a wider range of forms, and can marvel at the different kinds of beauty offered by foliage, flower, fruit and habit.

PLANT PROFILES

The following essays each profile one genus of plants, such as clematis, or a special group of plants, eg grasses and bamboos. The object of each profile is to give an over-view of the genus. Each of the genera selected (and many promising genera have been omitted) contains a number of well known and common species or cultivars but also an attractive number of uncommon but desirable ones; these offer a range of characters or uses beyond those employed in the 'average' garden, yet the plants will still be recognised by most people.

The intention is not to give a series of prescriptions for the planting of this or that, rather to broaden the outlook and to encourage the development of a specialised interest in having a unique collection to give your garden an individual identity.

BERBERIS AND MAHONIA

Berberis and mahonia are so closely related botanically and between them offer the garden extremely handsome plants, that they are considered together. The major differences between the two is that mahonia is thornless (apart from the edges of its leaves) and has the larger pinnate foliage. All basically range in size from low spreading shrubs to large shrubs.

Dwarf forms

Of the low-growing types *Mahonia aquifolium* 'Apollo' is a particularly good spreading variety with deep golden-yellow flowers, an improvement to the type species which tends to be rather straggly in growth. *Mahonia repens* 'Rotundifolia' (growing to 60cm [2ft]) and *nervosa* (rarely attaining more than 30cm [1ft] in height) are two other dwarf growers. All the mahonias are evergreen as are approximately half of the berberis. Generally a very hardy group of plants with only a few exceptions. They will grow in almost any soil (except waterlogged) and they thrive in sun or shade.

Many of the berberis are low-growing and ideal as small evergreen ground smothering shrubs, particularly *Berberis candidula*, with small glossy leaves and bright yellow flowers. *B. x frikartii* 'Amstelveen', also small-leaved, mound-forming and shade tolerant. *B. x interposita* is vigorous and forms a dense rounded mound. *Berberis verruculosa*, although eventually a medium-sized shrub, this species is compact and slow-growing. *B. x stenophylla* 'Corallina Compacta' is a dwarf variety, rarely exceeding 30cm (1ft).

Floral effects

Although generally small in flower, berberis produce them in prolific masses, none more so than the common *Berberis x stenophylla* and its forms. The flowers, borne in April, crowd the branches. This plant makes an excellent hedge, magnificent when in full flower. To avoid cutting off the flower it is important to only cut the hedge during the early summer period. It will mean, of course, that there will be no berries. The dwarf-growing variety 'Coccinea' has pretty crimson buds that open orange. *Berberis darwinii* is another early-flowering species. *Berberis linearifolia* 'Jewel' has conspicuous flowers, scarlet in bud, opening bright orange, complementing the narrow, glossy, dark green leaves.

Mahonia flowers are undoubtedly the more spectacular. *Mahonia japonica* is the most popular of these, the flowers contrast well with its dark glossy deep green leaves. The long drooping racemes, 150mm (6in) and more long, are scented of lily of the valley in late autumn to early spring. This plant also has the merit of being shade tolerant. Its foliage spreads and covers the ground and this ability puts the plant in the category of an excellent ground smothering shrub, which is ideal for areas in the front garden where low maintenance evergreen foliage and all-the-year-round effect is such an advantage. There are a number of interesting good flowering hybrids both upright and lax: 'Buckland' has flowers 75cm (2½ft) long and 'Lionel Fortescue' 45cm (1½ft) long; 'Charity' is a particularly useful plant, its flowers are 35cm (1ft 2in) long. All produce flower in November and December, at a time when little else is in flower. They grow to almost tree-like proportions to 4m (13ft) and in maturity the bark on the stems is attractive. They have excellent architectural leaves, 30–60cm (1–2ft) long, with spiny leaflets. The flowers of common Oregan grape (*Mahonia aquifolium*) and its varieties are small and more rounded in shape.

Foliage

Certainly, for foliage, the mahonias do provide some marvellously architectural leaves, whereas berberis give us a wide range of colour, particularly the deciduous varieties in the autumn. Considering the summer foliage colour first, the purple-red foliage cultivars of *Berberis thunbergii* produce some of the most reliable purple leaves. *Berberis thunbergii* 'Atropurpurea' and its dwarfer form 'Nana' are the original purple varieties. There are selected forms now: 'Red Chief', rich wine-red in colour; 'Red Pillar', reddish-purple, now much in favour; 'Rose Glow', with its purple young leaves, mottled silver-pink and bright rose is an excellent plant that stands out in a planting scheme. The cultivar 'Aurea' has yellow leaves, becoming pale green by late summer. *Berberis temolaica* is a lovely plant to have in the garden, it is a vigorous medium-sized shrub. It is unusual, having glaucous foliage of a delightful grey-blue which is particularly effective in spring with its delicate pale-primrose flowers. The leaves remain pale blue throughout the season, taking on a pink tinge in autumn.

Of the evergreen species there are some handsome and barbarous specimens which will make excellent dense impenetrable hedges, ideal for deterring invasion from next door children. The best of these are:

B. francisci-ferdinandii is a vigorous, elegant, deciduous rounded shrub to 3m (10ft) tall with three-pronged spines up to 3.5cm (1.2in) long. It produces its yellow flowers on slender drooping racemes followed by large bunches of scarlet red berries.

B. valdiviana will quickly grow to 2m (6½ft) ultimately, achieving 3m (10ft). Like *francisci-ferdinandii* it is formidably armed with stiff three-pronged spines. The leaves are usually spineless, however, and are handsome large, leathery, polished and fully evergreen.

B. julianae is ideal as a hedging plant as it is dense and evergreen and forms an erect bush. It is extremely hardy, well supplied with spines. The flowers are slightly scented and the leaves are copper tinted when young.

B. panlanensis for smaller hedges is an ideal compact evergreen, to 1–1.2m (3ft 3in–3ft 8in), of neat growth, tinier leaves, sea-green in colour and spine-toothed. *B. hookeri* is of similar size and has dark glossy green leaves, glaucous-white beneath.

Berberis berries and autumn colour

Berries and autumn colour seem to go hand in hand in the berberis family, the best of which are 'Buccaneer', a brilliant autumn colour with clusters of large deep red berries; 'Bountiful', clusters of coral-red berries; *pruinosa* has blue-black berries covered with a white bloom. The pinkish-red egg-shaped berries of *B.* 'Georgei' are particularly effective, because they are not apparent until November. They will then persist until the end of January or early February, untouched by birds.

B. x rubrostilla is a most impressive autumn plant with beautiful translucent coral-red berries. For autumn colour all of the *Berberis thunbergii* varieties colour especially well.

BETULA (BIRCHES)

Silver birch (*Betula pendula*) is one of the commonest trees planted in gardens and can make a delightful specimen. It is renowned for silvery white bark, upright habit, with graceful pendulous branches, and a light, open crown of diamond-shaped leaves which turn yellow in autumn colour. Other birches include plants, not just trees, which compare favourably to it in foliage, bark and autumn colour although, to be honest, none has the grace of habit of the best individuals of silver birch. However, they are worthy of serious consideration, especially where you have room for more than one tree or where every other garden in the vicinity contains a monotony of silver birches!

Birches are normally considered as medium to large trees and most of the species and cultivars will grow 10–15m (33–50ft) tall, some to 25–30m (80–100ft) if conditions are absolutely perfect. However, they do not all grow as large, some not even a metre tall, and there are birches suited to most gardens.

The attractive features of birches include the bark (surely their strongest contribution), the foliage, especially in autumn dress, and the catkins in early spring. The seeds are also a valued food source for several birds, such as redpolls, siskins and tits. Bark ranges from the brilliant white of Paper and Jacquemont birches at one extreme to the mahogany bark of Himalayan birch at the other, with the silver white of silver birch somewhere in the middle. The bark may also be tight and smooth, as in silver birch, or peel off in large sheets, such as with Chinese red-bark birch. The leaves are usually light green and small,

Betula *'Jermyns' (at the Hillier Arboretum)* *showing catkins in spring and creamy white bark*

but in monarch birch they are large and lime-like, to 17cm (6½in). The catkins open in early spring before the leaves and when fully expanded the male catkins can be at least 15cm (6in) long in 'Jermyns'. Birches are also fairly fast-growing trees.

Birches will grow well on most soils, the main exception being heavy clays although they do not flourish on shallow soils over chalk. They are very much at home on sandy well-drained soils. Brown birch (B. pubescens) naturally grows on damp sites but is scarcely worth planting in a garden. Birches do not tolerate periods of drought and on dry soils watering is desirable in dry summers. The roots tend to be rather coarse and widespread and birches can be more difficult to move and establish than many other trees. Smaller trees are easier to move and more reliable; they will also grow away more rapidly than larger trees. The important considerations for successful establishment are to ensure that the plants are of good quality and that they are not allowed to dry out either before planting or afterwards, in other words follow good practice as discussed in chapters 5 and 6. Birches will bleed if cut during the late-spring period, at which time pruning should be avoided.

Birches are intolerant of shade and need an open position if they are to flourish. Also, although they cast a relatively light and dappled shade, they compete effectively for soil moisture and nutrients and do not make good overstorey trees. They are best planted where the bark and habit can be enjoyed, not to provide overhead shelter (although they give excellent *side* shelter) except to give dappled shade over a patio or sitting-out area.

Birches are not usually affected by serious insect or fungal pests although, like most trees, diseases such as honey fungus can kill them. Old trees are soon decayed by the birch polypore fungus but they are not long-lived trees, fifty years being a good life. They form associations with soil fungi and fruit bodies of these fungi, eg the fly agaric toadstool, are often found around the trees, especially on sandy soils.

Shrubby birches

Two shrubby species are commonly grown: *B. nana* (dwarf birch) is native to damp sites in upland parts of northern Britain. It makes a plant 60–120cm (2–4ft) tall with an upright habit. The deep green leaves are rounded and toothed and turn golden in autumn. In the garden it can be useful in wet soils, and to provide a contrast of foliage and habit in low shrubberies or with plants such as heathers (with which it is found in nature). The twigs are black and, needless to say, it does not grow large enough to have any bark feature. *B. medwediewii* (Medwediew birch) is taller growing and will make a rounded domed plant 5m (16ft) tall by 6m (20ft) in diameter. It has a short bole with a silvery grey-brown stem but it is grown primarily for the bright golden autumn colour, the handsome alder-like leaves, and the winter aspect of the glossy brown shoots with large bright green buds.

White-barked birches

B. pendula (silver birch) is, as discussed above, the commonest birch in gardens. The species shows some variability in habit and general quality, at its best it is almost unsurpassable, but poor individuals on sites which are too heavy can have little beauty. It also tends to grow too large for many situations, and often attains a height of 20m (70ft). 'Dalecarlica' is an excellent form. The habit is upright with only light branching on which are carried long pendulous branchlets; the leaves are deeply and attractively cut. 'Fastigiata' has a crown which is narrow at the base but broadens above, with erect sinuous branches. It may be suitable for sites where space is limited; however, it has none of the grace and charm of other selections and is of curiosity value only. 'Tristis' is a graceful form with a narrow erect habit and long-hanging curtains of branchlets. 'Dalecarlica', 'Fastigiata' and 'Tristis' will make tall trees. 'Purpurea' is a form with leaves which are deep purple. Because it has the characteristic open crown of silver birch it can look lost except against a strongly contrasting background, such as a golden cypress. 'Youngii' has pendulous branches and branchlets, forming a mound of weeping foliage. It only slowly, if at all, grows taller than the height to which it is trained but will spread 5–8m (16–26ft) in diameter. It is a useful weeping tree for a small garden.

B. papyrifera (paper birch) has a smooth bark which peels in thin paper-like layers, hence the above common name. Another one is canoe-bark birch – the framework of the original Canadian canoes was covered by sheets of its bark. The bark colour is often vivid white, much more so than in silver birch, with a creamy, pink or pale orange hue. The habit is rather stiff, making a small to medium tree with an open rounded crown. Var. *kenaica* is one of several varieties. It has a creamy-white to reddish-brown bark.

B. szechuanica (Sichuan birch, also known as *B. platyphylla* var *szechuanica*) has a rather gaunt aspect to the rounded crown. The leaves are heart-shaped or rhombic in outline, dark green above and rather glaucous beneath; they are relatively large and carried spaced on the branches. The striking feature of this tree is the chalky whiteness of the bark. It has such a generous coating of betulin, the waxy compound which gives many birches their white bark, that it can be rubbed off like whitewash or chalk from a blackboard.

B. maximowicziana (monarch birch) is renowned for having the largest leaves of any birch; they may be 17×12cm (6½×4½in), although 15×11cm (6×4in) is more usual. They are broadly ovate and deeply heart-shaped at the base, shiny rich green when mature but emerging a coppery or orange green and giving such a hue to the entire tree for several weeks. It makes a large tree 15m (50ft) tall or more, with a rounded open and broad crown. The mature bark is smooth and white with orange and pink zones.

B. ermanii (Ermans birch) is grown for the bark which in young trees is a good white, becoming creamy white with a pink or orange tinge and strongly peeling in older trees. Erman birch makes a medium-sized tree with neat leaves which turn a good golden yellow in autumn.

B. 'Fetisowii' is a hybrid of Polish origin. It forms a narrow erect tree and develops a chalky white peeling bark.

B. jacquemontii (Jacquemont's birch) is perhaps the best-known white-barked birch apart from silver birch. It makes an admirable small to medium tree with a really bright smooth yet peeling bark. The crown is upright, becoming rounded in older trees, and the leaves turn a good golden colour in autumn. This plant can be very attractive if used to create an avenue along a drive – the white bark will shine out in a ghostly way after dark in car headlights, or where garden lighting is contemplated. Botanically it is closely related to Himalayan birch and better treated as a subspecies of it. 'Inverleith' is the name given to a plant raised at the Edinburgh Royal Botanic Garden. It has a very white bark and makes a medium-sized tree. 'Sauwala White' is also selected for its white bark but has the added attraction of only making a small tree, probably less than 10m (33ft) tall. 'Jermyns' is a plant with creamy-white bark on the stem and main branches, giving way to orange-brown on the smaller branches. Apart from an excellent autumn colour, the male catkins in spring are longer than those of any other birch and give quite a display.

Coloured-barked birches

B. utilis (Himalayan birch) has an enormous range from Afghanistan to Western China. The western populations are often treated as a separate species (*B. jacquemontii*) or as a subspecies (see above) and differ from the typical form of Himalayan birch in the greater quantity of betulin in the bark, thereby making it a startling white. The typical form from the central Himalayas and western China has an equally attractive bark, although quite different in character. Here it is bright pink, mahogany or coppery-brown and peels in large thin sheets. The sheets remain partly attached to the bole and can give a mixture of colours when seen through sunlight. As with all trees with a peeling bark, this can be removed if you are tidy minded and do not like the shaggy effect, but on no account should the under layers be peeled off – as removal of these will leave a dark brown scar for many years. (See p 179).

B. albo-sinensis (Chinese red-bark birch) has one of the best non-white barks. The best form is the Werrington clone, raised from seeds collected by Wilson in western China under his number 4106 in 1910. This develops an orange peeling papery bark which has been likened to burnished copper and will attain large tree size. Almost as good is the variety *septentrionalis* which is more readily available and makes a narrower-crowned tree. Here the bark is dark pink or dark red with a white waxy bloom and peeling in large sheets to reveal chalky white beneath.

B. nigra (river birch) has a shaggy pinkish white bark with rhombic leaves which are medium green above, and paler with white soft hairs beneath. Older trees develop a dark, almost black bark.

B. alleghaniensis (yellow birch, also called *B. lutea*) has a bark which is a dull bronzy colour, and peels in small flakes. The best characteristic of this species is the really bright gold of the autumn colour, unsurpassed by any other birch. The twigs have a strong scent of oil of wintergreen, although this is only evident when the bark is scraped off. Yellow birch makes a tree of 10–15m (33–50ft) tall and has neat green foliage.

CEANOTHUS

Very beautiful, mainly blue-flowered, evergreen and deciduous shrubs or small trees, the species of ceanothus are native to the Pacific coast area of west and north America, where they contribute substantially to the 'chaperral' or dense brushwood vegetation found slightly inland from the sea. They are often known as Californian lilacs.

In the British Isles the ceanothus provides us with perhaps the most spectacular blue-flowered spring and summer flowering shrubs we can grow. They succeed on all fertile, well-drained soils, and are particularly suitable for south or west facing walls or free standing in sheltered walled or fenced gardens if associated with other dense evergreen shrubs. They are excellent seaside shrubs; some are of low mound-like habit and suitable for bankings and low walls. Regrettably none can be said to be absolutely and reliably hardy other than in the far south-west of England, Wales and Scotland or in Ireland; even in these favoured areas, as we have learnt in recent years, penetrating arctic winds in winter can seriously damage them, causing massive die-back of twigs and branches, notably of the evergreen species. However, where roots have not been severely frozen, well established specimens will usually regrow satisfactorily in the spring, particularly if new shoots are helped with foliar feeding. From observation it is likely the small-leaved species and cultivars will be somewhat hardier than those with larger leaves. However, the genus should not be looked upon as long-lived in Britain, and as replacements flower when young and are fast growing, the death of an older mature plant although disappointing, is not an irreparable loss.

Planting is best carried out in spring when danger of severe frost is over, early autumn being rather a second-best time, although it is usually successful for south or west facing sheltered wall sites in all but the coldest areas of the country; free-standing specimens planted in autumn will require winter protection in all but favoured coastal districts of the south and west.

Pruning The deciduous hybrids, such as 'Gloire de Versailles' and one or two of the late summer or autumn flowering evergreen hybrids ('Autumnal Blue' and 'Burkwoodii')

Ceanothus arboreus 'Trewithen Blue'

which flower on growth made that season, are normally pruned back in spring as new growth commences. Evergreen species and cultivars are pruned during summer when the flowers have faded. Those trained on walls should be pruned annually by cutting back laterals to within two or three buds of the previous year's growth if a neat compact mat-like wall coverage is desired.

Here is a short selection of some of the best and most reliable species and cultivars available arranged with regard to their best use in the garden.

Mound-forming or ground covering ceanothus

These are suitable for courtyard, patio and foreground planting and some are adaptable for furnishing bankings and festooning low walls and balustrades and for covering inspection covers. All are evergreen.

Ceanothus 'Blue Mound' lives up to its name, producing bright blue flowers in May and June. It is a small-leaved variety, possibly a variety of *C. prostratus*, a reasonably hardy creeping species with holly-like leaves from the Cascade and Siskiyou mountains where it is known as Squaw Carpet; although both of these seem moderately hardy *C. thyrsiflorus repens*, with pale blue flowers in early summer, is undoubtedly hardier and remarkably vigorous. It will furnish steep banks and is ideal for low walls. *C.* 'Yankee Point' is a promising, and as yet unproven, newcomer with deep blue flowers and larger leaves.

Taller-growing ceanothus

These are for training on south or west-facing walls or free standing in sheltered gardens. All are evergreen unless otherwise noted.

C. arboreus 'Trewithen Blue' – a tree-like habit and large, broadly oval leaves 5–10cm (2–4in) long characterise this fine species. Large panicles of deep blue flowers up to 13cm (5in) long are produced in April and May; it is suitable for tall walls.

The group of French-raised hybrids known as *x delilianus* are deciduous and mostly hardy and suitable as free-standing shrubs in sheltered gardens in all but the coldest areas, where they should be grown against walls of low to medium height. They are best hard pruned to the base each spring as they flower in summer and autumn on the current season's growth. Large panicles of flower show considerable variation of colour – among the most successful and popular are 'Gloire de Versailles', powder blue in large panicles, 'Henri Desfosse', violet blue and 'Perle Rose', carmine pink.

C. 'Puget Blue' is renowned for the brilliance of its deep-blue floral displays in spring and distinct in its small oval leaves with impressed veins. When grown as a wall shrub it will respond well to pruning to maintain a dense, close wall covering. *C. papillosus*, and its variety *roweanus*, is a beautiful and interesting species from the Santa Cruz mountains where it shows a variation in height between 1.5 and about 5m (5–16ft) and is notable for its sticky leaves with glandular teeth and wart-like excrescences. The lower more spreading *roweanus* has narrower leaves and deep blue flowers in late spring. This species is the parent of one of the hardiest and most spectacular of garden hybrids, the British raised 'Delight' which produces long racemes of rich blue flowers in spring. Derived from the hybrid *x lobbianus*, 'Southmead', a small cultivar of rather dense habit, is reasonably hardy and produces bright rich blue flowers in May and June. Of similar origin and flowering time is the popular hybrid *x veitchianus* with clusters of deep blue flowers up to 5cm (2in) in length; both will attain 3m (10ft) on a wall. *C. sorediatus* known in California as 'Jim Brush' is notable for flowering in both spring and autumn; consequently this species is most probably involved in the breeding of several popular and useful hybrids which produce their deep blue flowers in summer and autumn, particularly 'A. T. Johnson', flowering freely in both spring and autumn; 'Autumnal Blue' (the hardier) and 'Burkwoodii' with flowers in late summer and autumn.

C. thyrsiflorus has the distinction of being the hardiest evergreen species and can be successfully grown against a south wall in northern gardens of the British Isles. Free standing, it will grow rapidly up to 3m (10ft) or more; pale blue flowers are produced freely in the summer on maturing specimens, not always on young plants. The slightly tender cultivar 'Cascade' is thought to be a form of this species and makes a tall shrub with arching branches, very spectacular when in flower in the spring.

CLEMATIS

Clematis is a very popular group of plants, but despite this, few gardeners realise the full range available. Botanically, there are over 200 species in addition to the many garden hybrids. Clematis can be chosen to be in flower in any month of the year, whilst a few are attractive in fruit. They range from herbaceous plants to rampant climbers, with evergreen species as well as deciduous ones.

The commonest clematis in gardens are either the large flowered hybrids, such as *C. x jackmanii* 'Superba' and *C.* 'Nelly Moser', or the spring flowering *C. montana*. These are rightly highly valued for the striking displays they provide, but to limit the clematis you grow to this small band is to deny yourself some of the choicest of plants.

Firstly, though, consider the special merits and requirements of these plants. Most clematis are climbers and are very useful for covering walls, scrambling over trellis or through bushes and small trees. They can also be very effective in formal areas and borders grown on a pyramid of three stout stakes 2–3m (6½–10ft) tall, placed a metre apart at the base and tied together near the top. Clematis can be used to give an extra season of display to a flowering tree, such as when scrambling through a Magnolia, to brighten up a dull feature or add an extra element to heathers and dwarf conifers. Clematis like to have the flowers and foliage in the sun and the roots in cool and shady locations. They will therefore thrive best where these conditions are met; the general recommendation is to have the roots growing beneath a large stone or paving slab, and this will keep the soil beneath cool and moist. Many clematis will, however, grow and flower well in semi-shade and some, such as *C.* 'Nelly Moser', are better for it, as the flowers become bleached and pale in full sunlight. Some will grow well in deep shade, but few will flower well in these conditions.

In gardens clematis are mainly grown for the beauty of the flowers but in a number of species this aspect is augmented (in the case of the native old man's beard (*C. vitalba*) surpassed) by the fruits. These are in clusters and have long silky tails; when massed, they can give an effective silvery display in autumn and winter.

Another very useful characteristic is that they are highly resistant to honey fungus, thus making them suitable plants to grow where this disease is a problem. For instance, they can be used to cover a fence which has replaced a privet hedge destroyed by honey fungus, or to cover and beautify an old stump. Some clematis, mainly the larger-flowered hybrids, are susceptible to a wilt fungus, clematis wilt. This kills affected shoots, but rarely the whole plant.

Pruning

Clematis differ widely in the pruning needed for best effect. More than nearly all other common plants, they respond better to correct pruning, yet with inappropriate pruning some are merely a mass of foliage. In the garden, they can be classified into three cultural groups and reference is made to these groups in the following discussion.

Group 1 (1) includes all the early-flowering species such as *C. montana* or *C. armandii*. These produce the flowers from buds laid down during the previous summer's growth. They cannot, therefore, be pruned over-winter, at least, not if you want any flowers! With this group, it is not necessary to prune to promote flowers. Any pruning should be restricted to controlling rampant growth and encouraging the plants to retain young shoots near the base of the plant, rather than have just a twiggy mass of branches at the top. Pruning should take place immediately after flowering with these plants to give the subsequent shoots the longest possible growing season.

Group 2 (2) includes many of the garden hybrids such as 'Barbara Jackman' or 'Nelly Moser'. They produce the main flush of flowers from short shoots growing on the previous season's long growth. These growths should be spaced out and trained during the previous summer. Many of the plants in this category will also produce a flush of flowers at the ends of the current season's shoots, giving two seasons of display.

Group 3 (3) includes all the herbaceous species and several woody ones and these produce their flowers entirely at the end of the current season's shoots. Examples are 'Jackman Superba' and *C. vernayi*. These plants are usually hard pruned in February or March, cutting them back to within 30cm (1ft) of the ground (the herbaceous plants will naturally die back in the autumn and can be cut down then). Treated thus they respond by producing vigorous new shoots and plentiful flowers from mid summer onwards. The woody ones do not, however, have to be cut back and with plants growing through trees this is impractical; if left unpruned they will flower earlier in the season, although not so richly.

Clematis *'Heather Rushforth' bearing massed flowers in shade during July*

Herbaceous and subshrubby species

These are the Cinderella species of clematis. Perhaps not as showy as some of the others, they can be very useful either in the herbaceous and shrubaceous border or to cover the bare lower portion of a wall or trellis beneath taller-growing clematis. Generally, these plants do not cling to or entwine with other plants or supports.

C. heracleifolia (3) is the commonest herbaceous clematis and will grow to 0.75–1.5m (2½–5ft) tall. It has large bold trifoliate leaves and produces clusters of small scented hyacinth-like flowers from July to September from the ends of the shoots and from the axils of the upper leaves. The dead foliage in early winter is strongly scented. In the cultivar 'Wyevale', the flowers are mid blue, whereas in var. *davidiana* they are pale blue.

C. integrifolia (3) has entire leaves and produces nodding indigo-blue flowers in July. It makes a small compact plant to 70cm (2ft 4in).

C. x eriostemon 'Hendersonii' (3) has deep bluish purple bell-shaped flowers 5–6cm (2–2½in) across which are carried singly but in great number from July to September. It makes annual growths to 2–2.5m (6½–8ft), dying back to ground level in winter.

C. x durandii (3) also makes 2–2.5m (6½–8ft) tall. The flowers are 7–11cm (3–4in) across and dark violet-blue with contrasting creamy yellow stamens. They are carried from June to September.

C. x jouiniana 'Cote d'Azur' (3) is a vigorous hybrid between old man's beard (*C. vitalba*) and *C. heraceleifolia*. The flowers are pale lavender and carried from July through to September in large panicles 30–60cm (1–2ft) long. The stems are woody and persistent but do not twine. It will grow 2–3m (6½–10ft) tall and is useful for covering mounds, old stumps and the like.

Winter-flowering species

C. cirrhosa (1) is the only winter-flowering species in general cultivation. It needs the shelter of a warm south-facing or sheltered wall in most areas. The flowers are carried from December or January through to March and are 4–6cm (1½–2in) in diameter. They are nodding and creamy yellow with red-purple spotting within. The foliage is evergreen, turning bronzy over winter. *C. cirrhosa* var. *balearica* has the extra feature of deeply cut, fern-like leaves.

Spring-flowering species

C. montana (1) is the commonest of the spring-flowering clematis. The flowers are 5–6.5cm (2–2½in) across; they are borne singly from the axils of the cluster of leaves formed at the base of the new shoots in May and early June but in such profusion as to hide the foliage. It is a very vigorous climber, capable of attaining 9m (30ft) into trees, over shrubs and buildings and along telephone wires and similar items! It also has the ability to flower well in shade as well as in full sun. The wild plant in the Himalayas has white flowers and usually grows over shrubs where it looks very attractive in May. Usually this and similar species in pruning group 1 form a tangled mass of twigs, leaves and flowers. Alternatively, if they are cut back immediately after flowering, the long arching shoots can be allowed to drape over shrubs without smothering them and give an attractive display in spring. 'Alexander' is a form whose creamy white flowers (purer white in shade) are sweetly scented. 'Elizabeth' is a form with larger than usual pale pink flowers with an essence of vanilla scent. 'Grandiflora' is a selection which has larger white flowers, 6.5–7.5cm (2½–3in) across and is very effective on a north-facing aspect. Var. *rubens* is a Chinese variant of the species. It differs in the reddish-purple young shoots and petioles and the purplish foliage and has flowers which are rose-red, 6.5cm (2½in) across. It is an excellent plant, hence its universality. 'Tetrarose' has purplish-pink, scented, fleshy flowers up to 7.5cm (3in) across.

C. chrysocoma (1) is similar to *C. montana* and likewise makes a vigorous climber to 6m (20ft) tall. The soft pink flowers are carried in great abundance in May and early June, with a spasmodic crop later in the year.

C. **'Heather Rushforth'** (1) is a white-flowered relative of *C. montana* with large lustrous green trifoliate leaves and carries the flowers on long stalks above the foliage in July. They are 7–8cm (2¾–3in) in diameter and are scented of cinnamon. Best growth is from plants grown in shade.

C. alpina (1) makes a low-growing climber, rarely attaining more than 2–3m (6½–10ft), and is an admirable species for a low fence or the lower part of a wall. It is best in a semi-shaded position. The flowers, carried in April and May, are open nodding bells 2.5–3.7cm (1–1½in) long with usually pale to deep blue or lilac-blue sepals. (Clematis flowers do not have petals but the attractive coloured parts are sepals.) This and the following species are unusual in having a cluster of petal-like stamens (called staminoides) inside the ring of sepals and these are white, contrasting with the blue sepals. Each leaf has three sets of three leaflets. 'Frances Rivis' is a particularly good form, with deep blue and rather larger flowers. 'Ruby' is a selection with reddish-purple flowers and a white centre. 'White Moth' is a white-flowered selection.

C. macropetala (1) makes a climber to 3–4m (10–13ft) with prettily divided leaves. The flowers are composed of four petals and numerous staminoides which grade into the white stamens. 'Maidwell Hall' is a form with flowers pure blue. In 'Markham's Pink' they are rosy-mauve, flushed with purple at the base of the sepals.

C. armandii (1) is a vigorous evergreen species capable of attaining 6–9m (20–30ft) high in mild areas, although needing the protection of a wall or similar shelter in colder districts. The leaves are deep glossy green, in threes and 7–14cm (2¾–5½in) long. The 5–6cm (2–2½in) diameter flowers are produced in April and May in dense clusters. In 'Apple Blossom' they are white, softly flushed with pink, and the new foliage is bronze coloured. 'Snowdrift' has pure white flowers.

Summer-flowering species

C. campaniflora (3) is a vigorous climber to 6m (20ft). It has small bowl-shaped flowers only 2–3cm (¾–1in) across but carried in large numbers. They are white with a blue tint, and carried from July into September.

C. florida (3) is mainly represented in gardens by the clone 'Sieboldii' which has white flowers with purple staminoides, being likened to the passion flower. They are 8cm (3in) across, borne in June and July; it makes a climber to 2.5m (8ft). It should be given a sheltered south or west facing position.

C. texensis (3) is a small semi-herbaceous species. It can be very effective as a low climber scrambling through heathers, dwarf conifers and the like but is not reliably hardy and needs full sun. The flowers are tulip or bell-shaped and deep red or scarlet. 'Gravetye Beauty' is a hybrid with crimson flowers from July to September.

C. viticella (3) is a semi-woody climber to 4m but often dying down in winter. The flowers are around 4cm (1½in) in diameter, carried from July to September and have four to six spoon-shaped petals. It can be used in both full sunlight and shade. In addition to the following cultivars, several of the large-flowered forms (see below) belong to or derive from this species. 'Abundance' is a form with delicately veined soft purple flowers. In 'Alba Luxurians' they are white with a mauve tint. 'Kermesina' has crimson flowers and 'Royal Velours' has deep purple.

Autumn-flowering species

C. flammula (3) is a rampant climber attaining 4–5m (13–16ft). It has the most strongly scented flowers of any clematis and these are pure white, occurring in large clusters from August into October,

C. rehderiana (3) has fragrant flowers, smelling of cowslips. They are pale primrose in colour and carried in large erect clusters of nodding bells, 1.2–1.8cm (½–⅔in) long. It has bright green pinnate leaves and can grow to 8m (26ft) up a tree if not cut back.

FIG 98 *Fruit heads of* Clematis tangutica

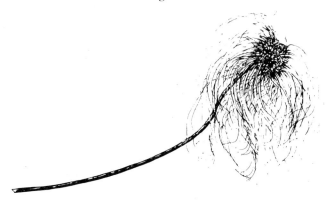

C. tangutica (3) has large lemon-yellow lantern-like flowers. These are carried over a long season, from late June to October. The sepals are thick and fleshy. It will grow and flower in full sun to shady sites.

C. vernayi (3) is commonly called *C. orientalis* but is not this species. It is known as the Orange-peel clematis because the sepals are very thick and fleshy, like orange peel. The flowers are open bells, from 2–4cm (¾–1½in) across and carried in August and September. The leaves are bluish green and deeply pinnate to bipinnate.

Fruit effect

Many clematis are very attractive in fruit when the fine hairs on the persistent styles give a silky effect to the seed heads. *C. alpina* is the first reliable species in fruit, lasting from June into the autumn before the seeds are shed. *C. tangutica* retains them longer over winter and with *C. vernayi* will be in both fruit and flower in the autumn. The native old man's beard (*C. vitalba*) gives a very effective display in hedgerows and can be used to hide unwanted eyesores. It is too vigorous for most gardens.

Large-flowered hybrids

These are mainly hybrids and have been selected for the size of the flowers, usually 10–15cm (4–6in) in diameter. They lose some of the charm of the species but can be used to give a bold display of colour, in several having two seasons of flower. The foliage is generally uninteresting. Most will make plants 3–4m (10–13ft) tall.

C. 'Barbara Dibley' (2) has flowers of a petunia red; it flowers in May–June and September. It is not suitable for north-facing locations.

C. 'Barbara Jackman' (2) has flowers of deep violet with a petunia or magenta strip running along the sepals. The flowers are 15cm (6in) across and carried in May and June. Do not use it on south-facing sites.

C. 'Beauty of Worcester' (2) has pale lavender or blue-violet flowers with creamy-white stamens carried from May to August.

C. 'Bee's Jubilee' (2) has blush-pink flowers with a paler central strip to the overlapping sepals, flowering May, June and August. It is not for a south-facing situation.

C. 'Blue Gem' (2) has sky blue flowers from June through to October.

C. 'Comtesse de Bouchaud' (3) is a free-flowering plant with soft rose pink flowers in July and August.

C. 'Dr Ruppel' (2) has flowers which have deep pink sepals with a carmine bar and yellow stamens and are carried from June to August.

Clematis *'Ville de Lyon'*

C. 'Elsa Spaeth' (2) has red stamens, contrasting with the large lavender-blue flowers which are borne in May–June and September.

C. 'Ernest Markham' (3) flowers from June to September, carrying glowing petunia-red rounded sepals with a velvety sheen. It is not suited to north aspects.

C. 'Hagley Hybrid' (3) has shell pink or rosy-mauve flowers with chocolate-coloured stamens. They are produced from June to September. It does not want full exposure to the sun, so shun south walls.

C. 'Henryi' (2) has large creamy-white flowers carried in May–June and August–September.

C. 'H. F. Young' (2) is a compact plant with wedgewood-blue flowers in May, June and August.

C. 'Huldine' (3) has pearly white flowers 5–10cm (2–4in) across from July to September.

C. 'Jackmanii Superba' (3) is the 'original' large-flowered hybrid. The flowers are dark purple, carried in profusion in July and August. It is suitable for conditions from full sunlight to full shade.

C. 'Lady Betty Balfour' (3) has purple flowers with yellow anthers and is late flowering, from the end of August into October. It does not suit a north-facing position and is best in full sun.

C. 'Lasurstern' (2) has deep lavender-blue flowers with white stamens. It flowers in May–June and August–September. It should not be put in full sunlight and is suitable for full or semi-shaded sites.

C. 'Marie Boisselot' (2) is perhaps the best white-flowered cultivar, with large pure white flowers with conspicuous yellow stamens. It flowers from June till the end of September and has better foliage than most cultivars.

C. 'Mrs Chomondeley' (2) is a vigorous plant which freely produces masses of light blue flowers from May to September. It is appropriate for semi shade and full shade conditions.

C. 'Mrs N. Thompson' (2) has pretty flowers with violet sepals with a scarlet bar and red stamens. It flowers May, June and August but should not be exposed to full sun.

C. 'Nelly Moser' (2) is a very popular cultivar but it should not be planted in full sun, as the flowers are quickly bleached to an off-white. In the shade they are mauvy-pink with a carmine bar and it will tolerate full shade. It flowers in May–June and August–September.

C. 'Perle d'Azur' (3) has light blue or azure-coloured flowers which are somewhat bell-shaped. They are carried from July to September.

C. 'The President' (2) has rich purple flowers which are silvery on the outside and produced from May to September. It is a reliable cultivar and suitable for positions in full sunlight as the flowers scarcely fade.

C. 'Ville de Lyon' (3) should be placed with either an east or a west aspect, avoiding both shade and strong sunlight. The sepals are bright carmine red with a deeper margin and it flowers from late June till August.

C. 'Vyvyan Pennell' (2) has double flowers in May and June but carries a flush of single flowers on the new growths in August. The sepals are lavender-coloured, suffused with purple and carmine in the centre. It should not be planted in shade or on a northern aspect.

C. 'W. E. Gladstone' (2) has very large flowers. These are pale blue with purple anthers and are produced from June until August.

C. 'Yellow Queen' (2) has primrose yellow flowers with yellow stamens in May and June. It should be planted where it faces east or west, avoiding both shade and full sunlight. It has better foliage than most of the above cultivars.

THREE CONIFER GENERA –
CHAMAECYPARIS, JUNIPERUS AND PINUS

It is a measure of their adaptability and beauty that more tree-growing conifers are planted in gardens than all other trees put together. Admittedly, many of these are used for hedging or for shelter but a substantial number are planted as specimen trees.

Conifers, however, are not just tall-growing species. A number are naturally low-growing in character and in cultivation all the conifer genera have produced a wide assortment of dwarf cultivars. As a group they provide a large reservoir of attractive plants with many possible uses in the garden and the three genera profiled here represent just a part of this resource.

Most conifers, including these three genera, are evergreen, remaining fully clothed with foliage throughout the year. They are hardy plants and thrive on a very wide range of soils, although some species do not do well, or at least not for long, on chalky soils. Coupled with an ability to withstand clipping, this makes them very suitable for hedges and screens which are needed for twelve months of the year. Although the pines (*Pinus*) are not appropriate for this purpose, their toughness and dense foliage make them excellent plants for shelterbelts and screens. The requirements for an effective shelterbelt are discussed on pp46–52. The foliage which forms the screen can also provide an excellent backdrop for planting, as well as visual separation between two areas.

As specimen trees, conifers provide height and scale to the garden, a wide variety of different foliage colours and textures, also features such as attractive barks, fruits and flowers. They provide homes for a wide range of wild animals, from insects which feed on them to safe nesting sites and roosting havens for birds.

Dwarf conifers offer the same attractive features that the larger-growing sorts provide but in a miniature scale making them appropriate for small gardens or small features in a larger whole. They include many character plants which give charm and maturity to a restricted layout and include some outstanding groundcover plants.

Conifers will grow on a wide range of soils: some are appropriate for very wet soils, including *P. contorta* of those discussed here, and also *Taxodium* (Swamp cypress) and *Metasequoia* (Dawn redwood); and some are suitable for very dry or sandy soils, especially all the pines. Many will also grow well on soils derived from chalk or limestone, including the cypresses (*Chamaecyparis* and *Cupressus*), junipers (*Juniperus*) and *Thuja*, but a number of pines and other members of the pine family are not long lived on these soils.

The foliage on pines is carried in bundles, called fascicles. These are short lateral shoots and contain two, three or five long leaves or needles. In the cypresses and junipers, the leaves are small and either minute and scale-like or short awl-shaped needles.

In the following pages, these three genera are discussed in alphabetical order under a number of headings, eg dwarf conifers, and noteworthy individual plants listed. More information on conifers can be found in *Conifers* by Keith Rushforth.

Conifer hedges
Of the three genera discussed here only *Chamaecyparis* is appropriate for general use in clipped hedges. Several junipers will tolerate clipping but do not grow sufficiently fast or large to make them really suitable. However, if you are planning an informal hedge, to mark a boundary or define a space but not totally to separate two areas, then several of the slower growing or dwarf cultivars of both *Juniperus* and *Pinus* could be used, such as *J.* 'Pfitzeriana' or *P. koraiensis* 'Winton', as well as similar dwarf forms of *Chamaecyparis*. Although making the best evergreen hedges, conifer hedges need more regular clipping than certain broadleaved hedges and if they are cut back so hard that there is little or no green foliage left on the plant, it will inevitably die.

Ch. lawsoniana (Lawson cypress) can make good hedges and will tolerate clipping. It is not as fast growing as Leyland cypress (x *Cupressocyparis leylandii*) but is better for light to medium shade (although *Tsuga heterophylla* [western hemlock], *Thuja plicata* [western red cedar] and *Taxus baccata* [yew] are much better for hedges in shade). Several of the cultivars selected for their narrow crowns can be used to make hedges which need less trimming, such as 'Allumii' with erect sprays of blue-green foliage, 'Columnaris' which has a narrow columnar habit with blue-green leaves, 'Kilmacurragh' whose leaves are a bright dark green and 'Lutea', with pendulous sprays of golden-yellow foliage. Be very wary of mixing two or more selected cultivars in one hedge or screen: in theory, having alternate plants or groups with different foliage colours or textures may sound attractive but the end result usually looks contrived and is rarely effective in the garden; the plants grow at differing rates and the colours do not naturally match in such formal situations.

Other *Chamaecyparis* species and taller growing cultivars can be used for hedges.

Screening, shelter and backcloth
Trees used for these purposes will be allowed or need to grow taller than a hedge. They will serve to cut out wind or sun (shelter), neighbours and other eyesores (screening) or light (backcloth). Obviously the one planting can easily achieve all three functions if correctly placed and planned. Aspects of shelter and the need for it are dealt with in Chapter 3 (see p50). When contemplating screening consider what exactly you wish to block out; if it is only your neighbour's ground floor windows the height required is much less than for a three storey block of flats. There is little purpose in planting trees which will reliably grow 20m (66ft) tall in 20 years (eg Leyland cypress) when you only need a screen 5m (16ft) tall, unless you have a masochistic desire to trim hedges. If the belt is going to have a role as backcloth to help display other plants whose foliage or flowers tend to get lost when seen against a bright sky (such as precocious flowering magnolia), the choice of foliage colour can be very important. Conifers offer a range of leaf colour unrivalled by other plants, especially in the blues and golds.

Chamaecyparis lawsoniana *'Pygmaea Argentea' used to brighten a dark corner in a heather bed*

Pinus sylvestris *in the New Forest – an isolated maturing tree with a rounded domed crown*

These colours, however, do not make the best backcloths, being too strong in themselves for most plants, although a golden conifer such as *Ch. lawsoniana* 'Lane' is the appropriate backdrop for a purple foliage such as *Betula pendula* 'Purpurea' or *Cercis canadensis* 'Forest Pansy'.

Ch. lawsoniana makes a very useful tree for these functions. The natural foliage colour is grey-green which is both restful to the eye and excellent as a backcloth. It grows somewhat denser than is desirable for optimum reduction of windspeed but is not so dense as to cause extra turbulence. It has a reasonable growth rate, averaging 30–50cm (12–20in) per annum over 20–30 years and is easily moved and often available at sizes up to 2m (6½ft).

Selected clones can be used for screens. Those with blue foliage include 'Allumii' and 'Pembury Blue' which is the best blue foliage form. 'Fletcheri' is a smaller growing plant with grey-green soft foliage. Plants with distinctive green foliage are 'Erecta' with a flame-shaped habit and erect bright green foliage sprays, 'Green Hedger' with ascending bright green foliage, and 'Pottenii'. 'Pottenii' may look interesting for a period with its very dense growth of sea-green foliage in feathery sprays but the veneer of foliage is shallow and if branches are dislodged as the tree grows older (which is inevitable especially in a shelter planting), the dead brown foliage beneath can look unpleasant. Forms with golden foliage include 'Hillieri', 'Lane', 'Lutea', 'Stewartii', 'Stardust' and 'Winston Churchill'. 'Lutea' is perhaps the most suited to shelter and screens (for a gold form) as the hanging sprays of foliage give an extra element to the display.

All of these selected forms, however, look excessively formal when used en masse. Seed-raised plants do not make such uniform features and this is usually an advantage, creating not just a screen but also a feature which changes with time and the seasons.

Ch. nootkatensis can be used but the very pronounced conical habit may be too strong for most situations.

Ch. pisifera has potential, especially in the cultivars with soft juvenile foliage, such as 'Plumosa' with yellowish grey-green leaves and 'Squarrosa' with longer blue-grey foliage. These make wider-spreading plants than Lawson forms, and consequently will need more space.

Junipers include a number of small trees which can be used for low screens, etc, where a top height of no more than 4–6m (13–20ft) in 10–15 years is required. They are perhaps too small and slow-growing for boundary screens but suitable for internal divisions in the garden. Several forms of *J. chinensis* are suitable for this purpose, such as 'Kaizuka' with its erratic and character habit. *J. scopulorum* has several forms with silvery or greyish blue foliage on broad upright small trees to 6–8m (20–26ft), such as 'Springbank' and 'Wichita Blue'. In *J. virginiana*, 'Burkii' makes a dense erect plant to 6m with the blue-grey foliage developing a purplish tinge overwinter.

Pines are excellent for shelter as the foliage approaches the ideal of 50% porosity. They also give good screening as, although the crowns are open, the foliage is carried in depth. They tend to develop rather broader crowns than the cypresses, but as young trees they are similarly narrow. They are also less amenable to clipping and pruning to control their spread.

P. contorta (lodgepole pine) makes an attractive tree with bright green leaves and massed yellow male cones in early summer. It is very tolerant of waterlogged soils and exposed windy situations and is an obvious choice for shelter planting in such locations.

P. nigra has dense dark green leaves in pairs and will make a good shelter or screening tree. The old foliage will appear dark in spring when deciduous trees are bursting into leaf but looks much lighter-coloured in late winter; the pine makes its new foliage in early summer at a time when the deciduous trees have settled down into their less flamboyant summer foliage. The closely related *P.*

leucodermis is similar but has more attractive cones. Both of these pines are suitable for soils over chalk and limestone.

P. pinaster has a rather open crown but is good for planting on sandy soils and has grey-green or glossy deep-green leaves and large bright-brown cones which are prominently displayed on the tree.

P. sylvestris (Scots Pine) has blue-green leaves and a two-tone bark which in the upper bole flakes in small papery orange scales. It makes a good screen when young, becoming a majestic tree with a rounded crown.

P. radiata is very good for shelter, especially in windswept coastal areas in southern and western Britain; it is not reliably hardy in most of Scotland. It is one of the fastest growing of all trees, soon averaging a metre per annum. The leaves are grassy green but in the distance appear almost black. The large cones remain unopened on the tree for twenty or more years, in nature only opening after a forest fire to release the seeds. *P. muricata* is similar but with bluish needles and grows very fast on barren sandy sites.

P. wallichiana makes an excellent screening or backcloth tree but is not suited to exposed positions. The leaves are bluish and hang in bundles of five. It will grow on limestone and chalk soils.

Specimen trees

The role of a specimen tree is to provide a focal point, such as at the end of a vista, to complement a lawn area or, eg in the front garden, to 'mark' the property in the street.

Ch. lawsoniana provides a wide range of specimen trees and most of the taller-growing named forms are good for this purpose. Narrow columnar growing forms include 'Allumii' and 'Columnaris' with blue foliage and 'Kilmacurragh' with dark green. These plants are appropriate where a pillar or exclamation mark is required, or to create a focal point in a small area. Broader-growing forms include 'Pembury Blue', one of the best of all blue-foliaged trees, and the several golden-foliaged trees mentioned above

under screening. 'Intertexta' has grey-green foliage which is in open, hanging sprays. Older trees develop a characteristic crown, with branches erratically arching out from the crown breaking the formality. 'Wissellii' has the blue-grey or dark blue-green foliage held in tight three-dimensional sprays which are carried on spaced branches and give a curiously effective tree. It is particularly striking in April when the massed pink male cones are prominently displayed against the leaves.

Ch. obtusa 'Crippsii' is the best gold-foliaged conifer; it slowly makes a broadly conical tree to 10–15m (33–50ft) at a medium growth rate of 20–30cm (8–12in) and has dense sprays of bright gold foliage.

Ch. nootkatensis, with its remarkably regular conical crown, makes a good formal specimen tree. Where informality is required, this species offers the Afghan hound tree or cultivar 'Pendula': it has an attractive gaunt open crown, the spreading branches arching up at the tips and curtained with hanging flat sprays.

J. chinensis 'Aurea' is one of the better golden-foliaged trees with a narrow ovoid-columnar or conic crown. It is slow-growing and young plants with mainly juvenile foliage are less strongly coloured than older ones. 'Kaizuka' makes a true character plant, with no two specimens looking identical. The habit is very irregular with bright green foliage and prominent blue cones carried on spaced and twisted branches. By comparison, 'Keteleeri', with its dense and very regular narrow conical habit and dark grey-green leaves, looks rather tame.

J. recurva var. *coxii* makes a small conical tree with spreading branches pendulous at the tips and with bright green foliage.

J. rigida makes a small tree to 8m (26ft) or a large sprawling shrub. The branches are nodding at the tips and carry pendulous foliage sprays. The leaves are bright green, except for a glaucous band on the inner surface, and very sharp.

J. scopulorum includes a number of good

FIG 99 Juniperus squamata *'Chinese Silver'*

small trees with blue or bluish foliage, such as 'Blue Heaven' and 'Moonlight' with conical habits as well as those mentioned above. It also includes the very narrow crowned and appropriately named 'Skyrocket', although this is sometimes listed as a form of *J. virginiana*. This makes a narrow upright plant which is approximately ten times as tall as wide. The foliage is blue-grey and it will grow to 8m (26ft) in 20 years. It can be very effective for creating an avenue in a small space, such as to join two parts of a garden, or to give continuity along a border.

J. squamata is a small to large shrub. 'Chinese Silver' makes an interesting large sprawling bush with its bright silver and blue foliage with pendulous tips. 'Meyeri' has steely blue foliage and makes a large shrub or small tree, although most attractive when young.

Pines

Pines usually carry the foliage in bundles of two, three or five leaves. As this affects their appearance and approximately equates to their affinities to each other, it is simpler to look at a range of the commercially available pines under these headings.

Five-needled and soft pines

P. aristata belongs to a group called 'foxtail pines' which are unusual for the needles being kept for many years, usually 15–20 and occasionally longer, against 2–3 or up to 5 in other species. This results in the crown being dense like a fox's brush due to the typically spaced pine branches being clothed with foliage along their length instead of only at the tips. It also has the attraction that it makes a small tree, only growing 8–10m (26–33ft) tall, and thus suitable for front gardens and other small spaces.

P. armandii makes a medium-sized tree with drooping bluish needles and large cones, green whilst developing in the summer of the second year (pine cones take two seasons to grow) before ripening brown. *P. wallichiana* is similar but with narrower cones. Another species is *P. ayacahuite* which has dense

foliage and much longer cones. *P. x ḫolford-iana* is the hybrid between the last two. These species, together with *P. monticola*, make very attractive leafy pine trees with relatively long soft foliage of a neat bluish-green colour but are scarce.

P. cembra has a dense and narrowly colum-nar crown with leaves dark shiny green on the outer face and bluish white on the inner surfaces. It makes a small slow-growing tree on a wide range of soils and situations. *P. koraiensis* is similar but with a more open crown and larger cones.

P. parviflora is a small tree with bluish foliage set on tiered branches, particularly in 'Glauca'. It is an interesting plant appropriate for sites where only a small tree or large shrub is needed.

P. peuce has a dense crown of greyish blue-green foliage. It is similar to *P. wallichiana* but much tougher, growing on a wide range of soils and withstanding exposure much better than any other soft pine.

The exquisite cones of Abies forestii *one of the many other garden-worthy conifers (not included in this profile)*

P. bungeana (lace-bark pine) is remarkable for the bark. This is grey-green and smooth but flakes in small round scales to reveal creamy-white or yellow which gradually darkens to green, olive-brown, red or purple. It is a soft pine but has the needles in threes and makes a small, rather slow-growing tree. *P. monophylla* is unusual in having single needles which are a good bluish-white colour and create a very open light crown. With lace-bark pine it has large edible seeds.

Three-needled pines

P. coulteri has stout greyish-blue needles which are held out pointing stiffly forwards and all around the shoot, up to 30cm (12in) long. The cones are bright brown with prominent hooked spines and enormous, weighing up to 2kg (4.4lb). *P. jeffreyi* is similar but with smaller cones and more bloomed shoots and a denser crown. *P. ponderosa* has greyer green and shorter leaves of only 10–25cm (4–10in) and a mature bark which has deep fissures between broad flat flaking plates which are yellow-brown, red-brown or pinky-grey. The cones can be an attractive purplish colour during the summer. All three species will make vigorous, bold large trees and thrive on a wide range of sites, including heavy clay soils.

P. radiata is discussed above as a screening plant but also makes a good and quick specimen tree for lowland and coastal sites.

P. patula is unfortunately less hardy than required and apart from the favoured western fringe of Britain it needs a sheltered and sunny spot. The bark is reddish to yellow-brown and scaly. The leaves are slender and droop down; they are light or yellow-green in colour and 15–30cm (6–12in) long. In the right place it is outstanding.

Two-needled pines

P. sylvestris is the native Scots pine. Old trees have a rounded billowing crown but in young trees it is narrowly conical. 'Aurea' is a delectable form in which the foliage is more or less the normal blue-green during the summer months; come the winter, however, it turns a bright gold, remaining so from December until April. 'Argentea' has bluer needles but makes a rather squat small tree. 'Fastigiata' forms an exclamation mark to 8m (26ft) tall with erect branches and can be used to accentuate a vista or mark a small space.

P. thunbergii has silky white buds and dark green needles. It is very tolerant of salt, making it suitable for coastal or roadside use. There is a selection called 'Oculis-draconis', in which the leaves have two yellow-white bands; these show up better in older trees in the autumn.

P. densiflora is similar to Scots pine in the reddish and flaky bark of the upper bole but has bright green and forward pointing leaves. 'Oculis-draconis' is a selection in which

each needle has two yellow bands, appearing like a dragon's eyes. The effect is stronger after good summers. 'Pendula' makes either a weeping small tree if trained onto a single stem or will cover the ground.

P. leucodermis has white shoots, an ash-coloured bark and rigid dark green needles. The cones are outstanding during July and August of their second season when they are a bright cobalt-blue.

P. pinea is the well known Umbrella pine from the Mediterranean region. In mature trees, the lower branches are lost and the crown is composed of a series of heavy, spreading branches, radiating out from the top of the bole like the spokes of an umbrella. Young plants retain the glaucous juvenile foliage for longer than in other pines.

P. montezumae is another most attractive species but only reliably hardy in mild areas. It has long pendulous needles in bundles of five but is not a soft pine (see above). A number of related species from Mexico are cultivated under this name, some of them being hardier than others.

Dwarf conifers

Dwarf conifers include both naturally small growing plants and genetic oddities which for some reason, perhaps due to an excess of growth restricting hormone, do not attain full stature. There is a full range of dwarf conifers available from plants growing 5cm (2in) in ten years to those making 10–15cm (4–6in) of growth annually. The most dwarf plants are not garden plants but need to be grown in the favourable conditions of an alpine house. At the larger end of the spectrum, dwarf conifers give way to slow-growing conifers; there is no absolute difference between the two and many of the slow-growing varieties are very attractive for a number of years if used as dwarf conifers.

Dwarf conifers can be valuable in several ways in the garden. Perhaps the current favourite application might be as ground-cover and there are several dwarf conifers capable of attractively suppressing weeds over a square metre or more of ground. They can be very useful for covering unsightly objects such as manhole covers; this is because (like groundcover roses) they root at a single point and grow outwards, whereas most low groundcover plants root as they grow over the surface and are therefore not able effectively to cover such barren objects. As with all groundcovers, the site does need to be free of perennial weeds before the conifers are planted. Another use is to provide an element of scale in an otherwise formless feature, such as a heather garden. Here the conifer can be used to punctuate the heathers whilst not growing too fast so as to dwarf them. Dwarf conifers can also be used effectively on a rockery, either as dwarf trees or for prostrate forms to clamber over rocks, etc. The larger forms can make isolated specimens in a lawn, as plant islands in a sea of green grass; obviously for this to be effective the plants need to be isolated and only in the very largest lawns is there room for two such dwarf conifers. Finally, they can make interesting collections in their own right, as apart from size, dwarf conifers provide the full range of textures, habits and colours of their larger progenitors, permitting a host of different features to be fitted into a limited space.

Ch. lawsoniana has given rise to over 200 different cultivars but only a few of these are good dwarf forms. 'Minima' has no stem but a series of upswept branches on which the erect sprays of green foliage are carried; it makes a globose plant. 'Minima Aurea' has a more ovoid habit and golden yellow foliage. 'Minima Glauca' has glaucous foliage. All three will very slowly make a plant up to a metre (3ft) high. 'Nana' is similar but has a single central stem and makes a more conical plant with glossier foliage. 'Lutea Nana' is similar to 'Minima Aurea' but has lighter-coloured foliage and is more reliably hardy in cold districts.

'Forsteckensis' has fern-like sprays of greyish blue foliage and makes a globose

bush to 60cm (2ft) eventually to 1–2m (3–6ft). 'Gimbornii' is globose or oval with a conical apex. The new foliage has a purplish tinge for the first year, thereafter glaucous blue-green.

'Green Globe' forms a bun with crowded rich-green foliage.

'Pygmaea Argentea' makes a globose bun. The shoots are creamy-white at the tips. It is best in light shade as full sun will scorch the foliage (see p290).

'Stardust' is a vigorous broadly conical dwarf which has fern-like foliage, coloured sulphur yellow.

'Tamariscifolia' makes a spreading plant in which the branches arch out from the centre of the bush, forming a nest-shaped depression. It will grow to make a plant eventually 3m (10ft) tall and 4m (13ft) in diameter, and has medium green or light bluish-green foliage.

Ch. obtusa has spawned a number of dwarf forms.

'Coralliformis' makes a dwarf plant to 50cm (20in) high and has thread-like twisted shoots, 'resembling coral in its contortions'.

'Nana' is a very slow-growing flat-topped bush, attaining perhaps 1m in a century. 'Nana Aurea' is faster and larger, to 2m (6ft) and has golden-yellow foliage. 'Nana Gracilis' forms a dense conical plant with a rugged shape and glossy foliage.

'Minima' is a very small slow-growing bun-shaped plant with light green foliage. It will make 10–15cm (4–6in) in diameter after 20 years. 'Caespitosa' and 'Juniperoides Compacta' are similar. All three are better treated as plants for the alpine house, as they are sensitive to sunscorch.

Ch. pisifera includes several slow growing cultivars. 'Filifera Nana' is a very dwarf form which will make 60cm (2ft) in 25 years. The foliage is in unbranched whip-like shoots which droop under their own weight.

'Nana' has bluish green foliage in fan-shaped sprays and makes a low dwarf bush.

J. chinensis has given a number of low growing forms which are sometimes listed under the name *J. x media*. 'Blaauw' has shortly

Dwarf conifers at the Hillier Arboretum, showing a great diversity of character and groundcover. The beds have a shingle mulch to maintain a cool root run (see p169)

ascending spreading branches with feathery sprays of bluish-green foliage. 'Plumosa' is similar but with drooping sprays of green foliage. Both will grow to a metre or so tall.

'Pfitzeriana' is a distinctive clone with branches which arch out and up at 45° to the horizontal, ultimately forming a flat-topped bush some 3m (10ft) tall with tiers of level foliage. It is useful for covering unsightly objects or as a tall form of groundcover. 'Pfitzeriana Aurea' has golden foliage sprays. 'Mint Julep' has bright green foliage and a more vase-shaped habit. 'Old Gold' is a more compact form with bronze-yellow foliage whose colour is retained overwinter.

J. communis is a variable shrub or occasionally a small tree. 'Compressa' is a dwarf exclamation mark, growing at the rate of 2–3cm (¾–1¼in) per annum to a maximum 80cm (2ft 8in). 'Hibernica' is big brother, with a similar exclamation mark habit, but making 3–5m (10–16ft) at annual rates of up to 20cm (8in).

'Depressa Aurea' is a spreading form in which the new growths are yellow, becoming bronze as they mature.

'Hornibrookii' is a ground-hugging form which slowly builds up a series of layers of foliage. 'Repanda' is similar but more vigorous, making mounds of spreading foliage to 30cm (1ft) thick. Both are good groundcover selections.

J. conferta is a prickly, prostrate species with glossy green leaves. 'Blue Pacific' is a form with blue-green foliage.

J. horizontalis is possibly the best groundcover conifer. It spreads over the soil surface and completely covers it, precluding weed growth. All the named forms are good plants. Foliage colour ranges from 'Bar Harbor' with steel-blue foliage, to 'Douglasii' in which the glaucous foliage turns plum purple in winter, to 'Wiltonii' whose leaves retain their bluish-grey colour overwinter.

J. procumbens makes a spreading plant 2m (6ft) across and up to 75cm (2½ft) high. 'Nana' is a smaller mat-forming clone.

J. sabina 'Tamariscifolia' is a spreading 'table-forming' bush which builds up a series of tiers of bright green or bluish-green foliage. It makes a good tall groundcover plant.

J. squamata 'Blue Carpet' and 'Blue Star' are two selections of 'Meyeri' which have steely-blue foliage. 'Blue Carpet' is vigorous and prostrate, growing no more than 30cm (1ft) high, whilst 'Blue Star' makes a dwarf rounded bush.

J. virginiana has produced several dwarf forms. 'Grey Owl' forms a spreading plant with slightly ascending branches and silvery grey foliage and makes a vigorous groundcover. 'Hetzii' has grey-green foliage which slowly builds up in tiers to 4m (16ft). 'Sulphur Spray' is a mutation with sulphur yellow foliage. All three cultivars are sometimes listed under *J. chinensis* or *J. x media*.

P. albicaulis 'Nobles Dwarf' ('Nana') makes a shrubby erect plant of compact habit, useful for giving scale.

P. koraiensis 'Compacta Glauca' forms a slow-growing plant with stout branches and blue-green foliage. 'Winton' has a wide spreading habit to 2m (6ft) and blue-green foliage.

P. leucodermis 'Compact Gem' has very dark green-black foliage and, growing at 2.5cm (1in) per annum, makes a rounded dwarf bush. 'Pygmy' is slower with a denser globose habit.

P. mugo is a dwarf mountain species which can grow to a maximum of 5–8m (16–26ft). 'Gnom' is a squat selection, gradually becoming a globose bush. 'Mops' is similar but sooner to make a rounded shape. 'Trompenburg' makes a very slow dwarf, growing no more than 5cm (2in) annually.

P. nigra 'Hornibrookiana' has stout, ascending branches which bear stiff glossy dark green leaves.

P. parviflora 'Adcock's Dwarf' is a dense slow-growing bush with short grey-green needles.

P. pumila makes an erect spreading shrub, rarely a small tree, to 6m with bright blue-green needles, 4–6cm (1½–2in) long.

P. strobus 'Prostrata' runs over the soil surface, making a low mound. It is too thin to make effective groundcover on its own but used with a gravel mulch it can be effective, especially if dwarf bulbs are planted to grow up through it in the spring.

P. sylvestris 'Beuvronensis' grows to 1m and develops as a low rounded bush; the annual growths are 6–7cm (2–3in) with bluish green leaves.

P. wallichiana 'Nana' a dense dome-shaped bush with drooping silvery blue needles.

CORNUS

Cornus (Dogwoods) is a truly noble genus of plants. In most other genera a horticulturalist selects out and propagates the best species and varieties for gardens. However, in the case of cornus nearly all of the species possess some good ornamental qualities in one form or another. The majority are small trees and shrubs of elegant habit. Botanically they have unusual features – the flowers of the showy species have conspicuous bracts, the petals being largely insignificant. They are starshaped, rather like a clematis in appearance. All the species have leaves arranged opposite each other on their stems, with the exception of *C. alternifolia* and *controversa.*

Cornus are easy to cultivate and generally grow in any good garden soil. The large-flowered varieties are not, however, successful on poor, shallow, chalk soils and the creeping *C. canadensis* requires an acid sandy/peat or leaf mould for success. This plant which is really a bit of an exception to the genus is a low-growing creeping plant, only 15cm (6in) high. It dies back to ground level annually. The plant has delightful small starry white flowers set amid a rosette of pale green leaves. In the right conditions it will form an attractive carpet of flower succeeded by vivid red fruits. A distinctive plant which makes an excellent and unusual ground cover.

Apart from the general elegance of the plants in this genus, there are those which are particularly spectacular in flower, leaf colour, beauty of their stem colour, and in the habit of their horizontal branches. Many possess all of these characteristics.

FIG 100 Cornus florida

Species particularly effective when in flower
C. nuttallii (Pacific dogwood). This medium-sized tree, of generally upright habit, can attain 15m (50ft). It has large floral bracts, at first cream coloured becoming white and then occasionally flushed pink; the foliage turns yellow, occasionally red in autumn. This plant is best planted in a rich soil that does not get too dry.

C. florida (flowering dogwood). As the English name suggests, this species and its varieties are grown specifically for their conspicuous flower-like bracts. Unfortunately, they are susceptible to spring frosts and indifferent ripening of the wood in much of Britain. It does, however, thrive in the south-east when well situated. The varieties 'Apple Blossom' is coloured as its name suggests; 'Cherokee Chief', a deep rose colour; and 'White Cloud' has brilliant white flowers and bronze foliage. These are the best of the selected varieties.

Cornus kousa var. chinensis. A mature specimen of this plant in full flower is a sight to be cherished. It is a large and truly elegant shrub, sometimes growing to small tree size. It flowers in great profusion along the gracefully arching horizontal branches in June, and remains in flower for several weeks. This is another great asset as few trees are in flower at this time. The flowers become cream coloured with age and are followed by unusual hanging strawberry-like fruit, with the leaves turning rich bronze and crimson in the autumn (see p55).

C. 'Norman Hadden' This small bushy, slightly tender, evergreen tree with pale sulphur-yellow floral bracts, also flowers in late June/July followed by large strawberry-like fruit in October.

C. mas (cornelian cherry) – The cornelian cherry, which has been cultivated in Britain for centuries, is very different in flower to the large bracts of the species described above. The yellow flowers are quite small individually but are produced in quantity on the leafless stems in February and March. It is, therefore, a most valuable shrub to the garden scene. This plant develops into a large shrub or small bushy tree, particularly worth considering to cheer up the wild garden still otherwise in the depths of winter. The autumn fruits occasionally produced are bright cherry-red and edible.

There is one notable cultivar of the cornelian cherry, 'Variegata'. This has prettily variegated leaves which have a white margin.

Coloured-barked dogwoods
Cornus alba (red barked dogwood) This is a well-known wide-spreading shrub that

Tiered branches of Cornus controversa *'Variegata'*

thrives in wet or dry situations. It is a vigorous plant, quickly forming a thicket of stems and requires plenty of space to avoid swamping other less vigorous plants. It is, however, ideal for mass planting and the red stems in the winter are particularly effective as a waterside planting. These coloured stems can be encouraged by hard pruning every other year in March. There are a number of cultivars that have been selected specifically for their coloured stems and also their variegated foliage, including

'Elegantissima'. This fine, adaptable plant has spectacular bright silvery variegation and can very effectively be used as a contrast to purple-foliaged plants. It is also ideal for brightening up dark corners. The variegation is white and mottled, the stems are red.

'Kesselringii'. Branches are dark brownish-purple, the unfolding leaves are reddish.

'Sibirica'. The shoots of this variety are a bright crimson colour. It is not a vigorous plant and should therefore be given a damp well-cultivated soil to maximise its growth.

'Spaethii'. The foliage of this plant is extremely bright. The leaves are yellow, variegated and considered by some to make this shrub one of the very best yellow-leaved plants. It has the advantage that the leaves do not get scorched by bright sun, neither do they lose the brightness of their colour during the season, as other yellow-foliaged plants tend to do.

C. stolonifera 'Flaviramea' is similar in growth to C. alba, but perhaps more rampant in wet conditions which it favours. The young stem colour is greenish-yellow and an excellent contrast to the red stemmed C. alba varieties.

All of these shrubs are effective for their winter stems and should be considered in conjunction with the willow species and varieties which include the yellow and orange shades. These and the white-stemmed brambles can make an extremely colourful winter garden display.

Finally there are two rather more distinct species of the cornus family which display a remarkable horizontal branching. These are C. controversa and C. alternifolia.

C. controversa is a small specimen tree and has slender and regularly forked branches which are clothed during June with broad clusters of cream-coloured flowers. In autumn small black fruits are produced and the foliage colour is often a rich purple-red. Even in winter the branches are a rich red colour.

The cultivar 'Variegata' is a particularly striking plant; it has irregular silvery variegation which draws even more attention to the horizontal branches. It is a slow-growing plant, best positioned as an isolated specimen to display its branching habit effectively and prevent its growing out of shape by competing with other adjacent shrubs.

C. alternifolia is a smaller plant of shrub rather than tree size. It displays similar characteristics to controversa. 'Argentea' makes a spreading flat-topped shrub 2.5–3m (8–10ft) high, the leaves have a creamy-white margin.

COTONEASTERS

There must be very few ornamental gardens that do not possess a cotoneaster of some description. They are truly the most indispensable hardy ornamental shrubs, ranging from prostrate creepers, mound-forming small bushes, to large shrubs, some even growing to small tree proportions. Their two greatest attributes are their ability to grow almost anywhere in any soil and the reliability and profusion of berries they produce in the autumn. In addition they all flower equally profusely, even if not spectacularly. Unfortunately, however, being spring-blossoming plants they have to compete with the cherries and rhododendrons and tend therefore to be rather overshadowed. They are nevertheless quite pretty in their own right, especially the smaller-growing varieties.

The deciduous species produce excellent autumn colour, along with their berries. Cotoneasters, like other genera containing evergreen and deciduous varieties, have a number of species that are neither truly evergreen nor truly deciduous, and vary with the severity of the winter and the local environment in which the planting is positioned. In a sheltered garden a specimen may be quite evergreen whilst the same plant in another garden in an exposed position may be leafless.

For the plantsman, the variety of different sizes and habits of the cotoneaster, coupled with the ability to grow in most situations, gives him the opportunity to plant this genera in almost any part of the garden. There is a cotoneaster to suit almost any space large or small – the garden designer's true friend. If you want to cover a manhole, clothe a steep bank, screen an unsightly object, cotoneaster can do the job, and being evergreen continue to do so all the year.

Large shrubs suitable for screening

The larger cotoneasters tend to be those which are variable in their evergreen hardiness. Possibly the finest of these is 'Cornubia' which will grow over 6m (20ft) high and, given the space, equally wide. By pruning to one stem it can be cultivated into a most attractive small tree. It is one of the semi-evergreen species and produces huge pendulous crops of brilliant red fruit which weigh down the branches in autumn. Closely related to this cotoneaster are four similarly tall plants: 'Rothschildianus', which has the distinction of being creamy-yellow fruited and is a wide spreading shrub when young; 'Exburiensis' is similar to 'Rothschildianus', but with apricot-yellow fruits, becoming pink tinged in winter; 'John Waterer' has red fruits and a wide spreading habit; and 'Pink Champagne', an equally large vigorous plant, with more slender arching branches and narrow leaves and smaller fruits, at first yellow, becoming pink tinged.

Medium to small shrubs

Cotoneaster franchetii var. *sternianus* is an extremely hardy medium-sized plant; rapidly reaching a height of 1.8m (6ft) or more with a graceful habit. The leaves are sage green above and silvery white beneath, the berries a bright orange red. This plant is evergreen or very nearly so.

C. lacteus is a fine evergreen shrub which grows to 3m (10ft). The young shoots are pleasantly covered with a dense white down. The flowers are more attractive than many cotoneasters and are a milky-white in colour.

C. glaucophyllus f. *serotinus*, another impressive cotoneaster, having the advantage of being late in flower and very late fruiting. The orange-red berries will persist throughout winter and on to April.

C. bullatus f. *floribundus* is one of the best deciduous large cotoneasters growing to 3m (10ft) and has handsome, conspicuously corrugated leaves. It has no great floral beauty but has a rich autumn leaf colour and has clusters of large red fruit early in the season.

Perhaps the most unusual cotoneaster is really a cultural form of curiosity rather than a species. *C.* 'Hybridus Pendulus'. Here the cotoneaster, which would normally be prostrate groundcover, is grafted onto a stem to make a small weeping tree. It is certainly a striking evergreen with its glossy leaves and pendulous branches, clothed with brilliant red berries in autumn and winter.

For flower and fruit *C. conspicuus* 'Highlight' is a spectacular shrub of medium size. The plant is spreading and mound-forming, gradually reaching its ultimate height of 2m (6ft). It produces a mass of flower, followed by large orange-red fruits. The berries are not attractive to birds and will usually persist throughout the winter. *C. distichus* var. *tongolensis* is a deciduous species which does, however, retain its leaves late into the winter. This plant is an extremely useful one, having a rather similar branching habit to *C. horizontalis*, but less flat and even more useful by virtue of its near evergreen polished green leaves. It is especially beautiful in fruit and has a rich autumn colour.

Cotoneasters generally cannot be considered the most beautiful in their shape and

FIG 101 Cotoneaster salicifolia

Groundcover

There are a variety of ground-smothering cotoneasters, the most well known of which being the deciduous **C. horizontalis**, with its herringbone-pattern branches. The autumn colour is undoubtedly very fine but the variety 'Variegatus', with its leaves edged with white, is one of the most charming variegated shrubs. In autumn the variegated cream leaves become suffused with red.

For the clothing of dry banks, even chalky ones, there is no better than **C. microphyllus**. A dwarf glossy-leaved evergreen, it is extremely hardy and tolerant of the most adverse conditions. It rarely grows more than 75cm (2ft 6in) high and forms a dense low thicket. The fruits are scarlet-red coloured. Its var. *cochleatus*, although slow growing, is more prostrate and the berries have particularly good colour.

Of the many other groundcovering cotoneasters *C.* 'Coral Beauty' and *salicifolius* 'Gnom' are good prostrate, branching varieties.

C. dammeri is one of the better-known evergreen groundcovering cotoneasters; it is prostrate in growth and has sealing-wax-red coloured fruit. One of the disadvantages of this plant as a weed suppressor is its low growth as weeds very easily grow through the thin foliage layer. The variety 'Skogholm', which grows to 45cm (18in) high, is rather better in this respect. It is particularly vigorous and wide-spreading. These are all extremely useful plants and may be grown in the open or as groundcover beneath other shrubs.

habit alone, they may have other attributes, but grace and elegance is not really one of them. There is however, one variety that is distinctly more elegant than the others, *C. salicifolius* var. *floccosus*. This one, of medium size, is the aristocrat among the cotoneasters. It is fully evergreen with narrow shiny dark green leaves, white woolly beneath, which are held on slender drooping fan-like stems. The bright red berries are smaller than most, but possibly more attractive. Unfortunately it may be subject to Fireblight, as is the species illustrated above. *C. splendens* 'Sabrina' is slightly unusual, having grey-green rounded leaves, it grows to 2m (6ft), with arching shoots and freely produces large orange-red fruit.

Daphne x burkwoodii – *deliciously fragrant and one of the most reliable of the genus*

DAPHNE

A fascinating and delightful genus of mainly dwarf and predominantly evergreen shrubs found in mountainous areas of Europe and Asia. Notable for the great diversity and beauty of their shape and form and, above all, for their deliciously scented flowers, produced from mid-winter to early summer.

Plantsmen, connoisseurs and particularly members of the Alpine Garden Society, prize daphnes very highly, growing the rarer dwarf or miniature kinds in pots and pans to a very high standard of perfection. Indeed, the rarer species of the genus have acquired the revered status of pampered primadonnas – this has perhaps been fostered by the scarcity of propagation material and the subsequent high price asked by nurserymen. Undeniably many daphnes are perverse and unpredictable in their performance and have a reputation for sudden inexplicable demise, or at least being short lived in cultivation. In spite of this, most of the hardy species can be grown in open positions in the garden in any well drained soil, whether acid or alkaline. Good drainage is very important, but equally there should be adequate water-retaining matter in the soil – peat, leaf mould, bark, etc to ensure that the plant does not dry out at the root. Placing stones over the root area if open to sunshine is a further method of ensuring a cool moist root run. In nature they are often found on the fringe of woods or on the north side of a rock or boulder and such a situation in the garden is likely to suit them better than an isolated sun-baked site. If these conditions can be found, the sceptical grower may be pleasantly surprised by the successful growth and comparative longevity of his daphnes. This said, daphnes do have their problems and can suffer decline, die-back of whole or part of the shrub, often resulting in a fairly rapid death. A number of causes can be responsible with the presence of virus disease heading the list. This may be spread by aphids or eelworm and will cause weakness and poor growth, with noticeable distortion, mottling, spotting or streaking of leaves.

It is best to destroy the affected plant and remove the soil from the area it has occupied. The use of poorly grown and often potbound and sometimes incompatible species of seedling daphne as rootstocks for grafted specimens of the more desirable species and cultivars is another source of deterioration and demise.

Daphnes for raised beds, rock garden or alpine house

There are a few choice daphnes which, by reason of considerable rarity, slowness of growth and resulting comparative high cost of purchase (or a combination of all three) seem to be grown largely by the connoisseur or alpine garden specialist. Most of these are not just botanical oddities but are very desirable, often spectacular, flowering plants. Until supplies become more readily available, perhaps with the increase of micropropagation facilities, fortunate would-be growers would be best advised to cosset them for safety's sake on a raised bed or well protected scree or rock garden reserved for similar aristocratic alpines. Several adapt well to pan culture and are often grown very skilfully by members of the Alpine Garden Society. Such gems include *Daphne arbuscula* from the Carpathian mountains which forms a dense narrow leaved evergreen hummock up to about 20cm (8in) high. It is closely related to *D. petraea* and is reported to be easier to cultivate. The fragrant, usually deep pink but variably coloured flowers, are produced in dense terminal clusters and can be effective up to six weeks in the spring. While it is much in demand for the alpine show bench as a pan plant, it is quite hardy and will make a fine small specimen shrublet for a well-chosen rock garden site. Essentially a collector's plant for alpine house culture, the slightly tender *D. jasminea* from Greece has incredibly brittle branches and is very subject to accidental damage. It is a variable species growing in nature as a gnarled crevice plant on limestone rock. The neat blue-green leaves are evergreen and a good foil for the beautiful and very fragrant flowers which are purple-pink with white centres. A relatively recent but exciting and hardy introduction from Northern Japan, D. jezoensis, seems to have a future outside for the specialist's rock garden. A small shrublet slowly reaching about 30cm (1ft), it produces fresh green leaves during autumn then remarkably frost resistant deep yellow flowers, sometimes lemon-scented, follow during the winter. The leaves fall in late spring. D. jezoensis appears to be happy on well-drained acid or slightly alkaline leafy soil which does not dry out, or equally as a pan plant for the alpine house. Finally, in this group we must not forget to include D. petraea, so much beloved and exhibited by Alpine Garden Society members and extolled by Farrer and other distinguished alpine authors for its spectacular display of deep pink flowers painting the crevices of limestone cliffs of Northern Italy. Given sunshine and moisture at the root at all times with impeccably good drainage, successful cultivation is not too difficult outside in raised bed or tufa boulder as well as alpine house pan, and is certainly a challenge worth rising to. D. petraea and its larger-flowered form 'Grandiflora' rarely exceed 15cm (6in) in cultivation, forming a dense evergreen shrublet covered for a long period between May and July with exquisite waxy fragrant rose-pink blooms.

Daphnes for general garden planting

Here is a selection from those usually available and more easily grown and established in the open garden. Without wishing to become tedious one should stress that ideally well-drained conditions and moisture at the root at all times is the best recipe for success with these beautiful shrubs. Among several newcomers to cultivation we have the very desirable winter-flowering D. bholua from the eastern Himalayas, making an upright shrub of 2–3m (6–10ft or more). In Nepal its pulverised bark is used for paper and rope making. The two hardy cultivars now in commerce are the deciduous 'Gurkha' with purple-rose fragrant and frost-resistant flowers and the evergreen 'Jacqueline Postill', with more compact habit and fragrant reddish-mauve flowers, which are white within and are produced from December to March. D. blagayana, with deliciously fragrant creamy-white blooms, is an evergreen of rather low and trailing habit found widely in light woodland over limestone throughout southeast Europe. It is recommended by Farrer among others that its stems are layered by placing stones or boulders on them.

Daphne cneorum, the garland flower, has justly earned the reputation for reliability amongst daphnes, and is one of the most spectacular in flower as well as one of the easiest to grow in sun or semi-shade on rock garden, raised bed or front of well-drained border, where it will quickly form a prostrate evergreen mat densely covered in spring with rose-pink fragrant flowers. 'Eximia', selected by A. T. Johnson, is considered the finest form with its larger deep rose-pink flowers, crimson in bud; 'Variegata', with golden margins to the leaves, is remarkably vigorous if shyer in flower. Daphne cneorum, crossed with D. caucasica, has produced the popular and reliable semi-evergreen garden hybrid x burkwoodii ('Somerset' is very similar); fragrant pale-pink flowers in May or June are well seen against the fresh green foliage on bushes up to 1m (3ft) high and as much through.

The evergreen D. collina from the hills near Naples in Italy is also reliable. It forms a dome-shaped bush about 60cm (2ft) with very fragrant purple-rose flowers in April and May. D. c. var. neapolitana (correctly x napolitana) is considered to be most probably a hybrid of collina with cneorum and in effect is an equally worthy narrow leaved collina with scented rose-pink flowers opening from April to June.

There are two well-known and frequently planted species producing very welcome scented flowers in winter and early spring – D. mesereum, the mesereon – a beautiful and

A new variegated daphne, Daphne longilobata *'Peter Moore'*

much loved deciduous species from woods in northern Europe and a rare British native. It will reach about 1m (3ft), the purple-red scented blooms covering bare branches in February and March, followed by attractive red fruits in summer. There are several variants, most notably 'Alba' ('Bowles White') of more upright taller habit and with white flowers and amber fruits. Alas, *D. mezereum* is very prone to virus; foliar feeding in early summer may help lightly affected plants.

The other winter-flowering species is the evergreen and slightly tender *D. odora* which is ideal as a patio plant near the house, where the heady scent of its purplish pink and white flowers can be enjoyed early in the year. Even when out of flower this is a handsome, mounded shrub with large lanceolate leaves up to 7.5cm (3in) long. It adapts well as a

conservatory plant in cold districts; the variegated form 'Aureomarginata' has a reputation for greater hardiness. *D. retusa* and the closely related species *tangutica* are both hardy and from China and are excellent small evergreen shrubs for patio or rock garden planting. *D. retusa* has a dense compact habit to 60cm (2ft) and a rose-purple flower, scented like lilac, in May or June and followed by red fruits, while *tangutica* is taller, more open in habit with larger leaves and white-purple tinted flowers in early spring and larger red fruits. An exciting new hybrid of *retusa* with x *burkwoodii* raised in western Canada is now becoming available. *D. x mantensiana* 'Manten' makes a dwarf compact evergreen shrub, combining the best of its two distinguished parents. The rose-purple scented flowers persist well into the summer. This is an excellent new daphne for patio or courtyard planting.

Finally, we are enthusiastic about a new Hillier introduction, *D. longilobata* 'Peter

Moore', a hardy semi-evergreen shrub reaching 1.5–2.5m (5–8ft) and effectively extending the range of variegated daphnes. It has narrow grey-green leaves, conspicuously margined creamy-white and white flowers in summer.

HARDY FERNS

Much loved by the Victorians for decoration of both garden and conservatory, ferns tended to go out of fashion during the middle of this century, indeed for some years after the Second World War it was difficult to obtain plants of any but the commonest native species. Happily today we have a resurgence of appreciation of these delightful shade-loving plants, and many of the most desirable species and forms are again being propagated.

Hardy ferns are good perennials and are not difficult to please in the garden; many are British native species, thriving in most fertile well-drained soils, particularly where there is a high humus content. Cool moist shady conditions are ideal, but several, such as *Blechnum* and *Asplenium*, will tolerate quite dry shady conditions and are found naturally inhabiting cracks and crevices of north-facing walls and mossy roofs. In the beauty they can inject into an otherwise dark, perhaps featureless area of the garden, ferns have much to commend them. The unfurling leaves in the spring of several species appear like exquisite felt-covered shepherd's crooks, or croziers; there is great diversity and delicacy of shape in their leaves, some having fronds of the finest filigree. Throughout summer and well into autumn they make a perfect foil for trees, shrubs and plants with which they may be safely associated. A clump of *Polystichum* (shield fern) or *Athyrium* (the lady fern) will often look 'just right' at the foot of a shady wall or by a stone seat. Some hardy ferns, such as *Phyllitis* (hart's tongue) and *Polypodium* (common polypody) are near evergreen in sheltered areas and several species will turn bronze, gold or russet in the autumn, others like *Blechnum* (hard fern) and *Osmunda* (royal fern) produce unusual erect spore-bearing fronds.

It seems useful to group a selection of the hardy ferns in the context of their best use in the garden scene, though these divisions should not be regarded as rigid.

Ferns for cool glades

Ferns can be used as groundcover or as specimens by tree boles or to blend with shade-tolerant shrubs and associate with other groundcovers like ivies and pachysandra and herbaceous plants such as hosta, brunnera, bergenia, dicentra, epimedium, pulmonaria and hardy geranium among many others. Most will blend well with early-flowering bulbs, such as winter-flowering aconite, snowdrop and crocus.

Adiantum pedatum is the hardiest of the maidenhair ferns, producing the typical dainty leaflets beautifully poised on 25–50cm (10–20in) slender wiry black stems. It needs a sheltered wind-free, shaded spot and will make an imposing clump when happily sited. Several very desirable dwarf compact geographic forms of this North American and Asiatic species are now becoming available.

In the lady fern (*Athyrium filix-femina*) we have one of our most delightful and elegant native species of our woods, the light green, much divided fronds show great variation and rise from shallow creeping stems to a height of about 30cm (1ft). For those who enjoy the unusual the Japanese painted fern, *Athyrium goeringianum* 'Pictum' (*A. nipponicum* 'Pictum') is unique and a delight – pale grey-green, broadly triangular fronds contrast superbly with dark red stems and leaf stalks and there is a subtle suffusion of this reddish hue into the bases of the leaflets. A compact grower for a sheltered position, spreading slowly to form a clump ultimately up to 50–60cm (1½–2ft) high.

The Buckler ferns (*Dryopteris*) are more robust British natives, *D. dilitata*, the broad Buckler attaining 60–100cm (2½–3ft) and forming mounds of broad delicately-divided fronds, seen well on a shady hedge bank, while *D. filix-mas* the male fern makes bold clumps of sturdy fronds like giant shuttlecocks, and grows well in most conditions in sun or shade – a useful filler in difficult corners.

One of the most handsome of European ferns, *Matteuccia struthiopteris*, the ostrich feather fern requires a sheltered, moist, but well drained site to display its magnificent fresh green 90cm (3ft) high shuttlecocks. It rambles gently by spreading underground rhizomes and looks well among taller shrubs, such as hydrangea or deciduous azalea. Less demanding and easily cultivated in semi-shaded woodland are the evergreen native shield ferns, particularly *Polystichium aculeatum*, the hard shield fern, with its dark green leathery fronds to 50–60cm (2–2½ft); *P. setiferum*, the soft shield fern has soft lacy fronds of more arching habit and a similar height. New unfurling fronds, their leaf stalks densely covered with pale brown scales, emerge delightfully in spring from a mound of old russet-brown leaves; a number of uncommon forms and cultivars are available, particularly 'Plumoso-divisilobum' with very finely divided feather-like fronds.

Ferns for waterside

Firstly we must include above all others the royal fern (*Osmunda regalis*) a truly regal species and a rare British native, worthy of a permanent position at the water's edge. Here it will slowly form mounds of brown osmunda fibre (once keenly sought by orchid growers) from which emerge, each spring, strong white silky unfurling fronds, which open to display blunt-ended leaflets and usually attain a height of 1.2–2m (4–6ft). Narrow brown spore-carrying leaflets appear at the apex of most fronds, one of the most stately of all ferns, the leaves turning warm golden brown in the autumn.

Matteuccia struthiopteris, the ostrich plume fern will also perform well in a shady waterside position, as long as sheltered and free drained, while *Onoclea sensibilis*, the sensitive fern, an American species, will colonise rapidly by underground stolons and is happier in boggy acid conditions. The fresh green fronds reach 30–60cm (1–2ft) with broad, coarsely scalloped or lobed leaflets. Forms with both red and green stems may be seen to good advantage at the Savill Garden, Windsor Great Park.

Ferns for shady paved areas, walls, mossy roofs, stumps and tree branches

The native hardy evergreen maidenhair spleenwort – *Asplenium trichomanes*, is a pleasing and familiar inhabitant of cracks and mortar crevices of shady walls; indeed it seems to enjoy well drained limy conditions, delightful rosettes crowd together usually 7.5–10cm (3–4in) high. The sterile evergreen fronds with thread-like black stalks and small green lobes are reminiscent of the maidenhair fern. It is often found in association with *Cetarach officinarum*, the rusty-back fern, which has larger, 10–15cm (4–6in) long leaves with conspicuous brown scales covering the undersides. The Hart's tongue fern (*Phyllitis scolopendrium*) (*Scolopendrium vulgare*) can often be found in similar situations, though it will grow much more luxuriant, up to 50cm (1ft 8in) in moist positions almost anywhere in sun or shade. The leathery, tongue-like fronds are undivided, pale green in colour and up to 45cm (1½ft) long – a distinct and conspicuous, if common, native making a pleasing contrast with other ferns in the garden.

Distinct again is the hard fern (*Blechnum spicant*), a native of acid soil and frequently seen slowly colonising shady dry banks. The sterile evergreen fronds are divided to the mid-rib and form rosettes from which emerge bright fertile fronds with narrower leaflets; very attractive and useful in the garden in dry shade. *B. penna-marina* from southern hemisphere temperate regions and Antarctica is not fully hardy with us, but is a delightful small and neat little plant for a sheltered shady banking or mossy wall top. The young fronds are attractively copper-tinted and grow to 7.5–10cm (3–4in) high, while *B. spicant* will reach 25–30cm (10–12in). All Blechnums require acid soil.

Finally, for a variety of similar situations, including mossy tree boughs, hedge bankings and wall tops our evergreen common polypody (*Polypodium vulgare*) is very adaptable. A ubiquitous fern with creeping roots found on mossy banks in chalk, limestone or gravelly areas. The lance-shaped fronds growing to 15–30cm (6–12in) high are deeply cut with widely spaced comb-like teeth.

HARDY ORNAMENTAL GRASSES AND BAMBOOS

Members of the Grass family familiar worldwide (*Gramineae*) are without doubt of the greatest economic importance, providing man with many of his most essential sources of food – wheat, rice, millet, sugar, pasture for livestock, and many other economically important foods and biproducts. For our gardens there are a number of highly ornamental hardy grasses and bamboos ranging from excellent groundcovering grasses a few inches high to bamboos towering to 4.5–5.5m (15–18ft) or more. Together they offer architectural grace and elegance, often combined with artistically satisfying and unusual floral effects – though perhaps without the flamboyance of other garden plants grown more particularly for their flower. Foliage of many species of both grass and bamboo can be attractively variegated; flower plumes or spikelets of pampas grass (*Cortaderia*), *Miscanthus* and *Stipa*, among others, provide welcome material for floral arranging and winter decoration. A number of dwarf grasses make excellent groundcover in both sun and shade, associating with and complementing such elegant shrubs as hydrangea, Japanese maple, azalea and rhododendron.

While most perennial species of grasses are herbaceous, growth being renewed annually from below ground, bamboos are strictly evergreen and perennial woody grasses. The taller species such as *Arundinaria simonii* and *A. murieliae* make good screens in sheltered areas, while dwarf sorts provide excellent evergreen and often variegated groundcover, particularly near waterside in sun or semi-shade. While many are clump forming, several species of both bamboos and ornamental grasses, once established, can be both vigorous and invasive, and need careful siting or they will engulf valued weaker plants. Such ornamental grasses as *Phalaris arundinacea* 'Picta' (gardeners' garters) or the dwarf bamboo *Arundinaria viridistriata* should not be planted in conventional herbaceous borders for this reason. Such beautiful, but vigorous species are best given a vacant corner or isolated area, perhaps surrounded by mown grass where their brightly variegated foliage can be highlighted and form a striking focal point of beauty and interest.

Both bamboos and ornamental grasses grow well in any well-drained, fertile soil, growing more rampantly in moist conditions. However, permanently wet land or an exposed situation should be avoided for bamboos. Most are now provided container grown by nurserymen for planting at most seasons; even so avoid planting bamboos in cold districts from December to March.

The occasional flowering of bamboos is a curious phenomenon not yet fully understood, in that all plants of one particular species tend to flower simultaneously over a wide area, including other parts of the world. Regrettably this often results in the death of the colony concerned. Some regeneration of growth has been achieved with certain species by cutting all canes down to ground level when flowering spikelets are first noted, followed by copious mulching with well-rotted farmyard manure and the addition of a good slow-release fertiliser. However, such action can be devastating, destroying any screening value the plant or colony may have had and if left one can be faced with a forest of unsightly dead canes. In these circumstances it is perhaps better to plant bamboos in small groups or as isolated specimens rather than to use one species as an important evergreen screen. Fortunately, groundcovering species seem less affected and less inclined to flower, while a group of single specimens of several choicer species can make an impressive planting and if they flower they will not all flower at once! Here are some of the best species and cultivars of both grasses and bamboos commercially available today with particular regard to their recommended use in the garden.

Matteuccia struthiopteris, *one of the most handsome of hardy European ferns with* Primula x pulverulenta

Grasses and bamboos for small gardens

These are suitable with trees, shrubs, ferns and herbaceous plants in sun or semi-shade.

With these requirements in mind there are two or three first-class low-growing perennial grasses and one sedge which should be included here. All have brightly variegated or golden leaves. *Hakonechloa macra* 'Aureola' ('Albo-aurea') is perhaps the most striking of hardy low-growing variegated grasses. It comes from Japan and has arching narrow leaves, conspicuously striped golden yellow and tinted with bronze. It has a neat tufted habit, slowly spreading and attaining a height of 30cm (1ft).

Milium effusum 'Aureum' – Bowles' golden grass. A delightful bright golden-leaved form of our native wood millet 45–60cm (1½–2ft). All parts of this elegant little plant are golden, it readily naturalises – not invasively – breeding true from seed.

The dwarf variegated sedge *Carex morrowii* 'Evergold' although slightly less hardy has the advantage of being evergreen. Small mounds of stiff narrow leaves are creamy-yellow variegated, 30cm (1ft).

These beauties look well in association with Japanese maples (*Acer palmatum* and *p.* 'Dissectum' cvs), mahonia, *Danae racemosa*, viburnum. Plant in groups of three or more grasses between the shrubs. Shade-tolerant herbaceous plants will live in well with both shrub and grass, including particularly *Ajuga reptans* 'Burgundy Glow', *Lysimachia nummularia* 'Aurea', *Gentiana asclepiadea*, bergenia, epimedium, hosta and helleborus and ferns.

Grasses and bamboos as specimen plants

Planted singly, or in groups of three or more of a kind, a number of grasses and bamboos can be very effective as focal or accent points in the garden. The familiar and stately tuffet-forming pampas grass *Cortaderia selloana* (*argentea*) makes a superb lawn specimen; sited well spaced from a dark background such as yew or cypress or evergreen hedge, its tall silvery-grey plumes reach 1.8–2.5m (6– 8ft) and are magnificent from late summer well into the autumn; healthy mature plants can produce fifty or more plumes at once. Where space is limited smaller, more compact 'Pumila' will do useful duty. There is also an interesting new cultivar from New Zealand, 'Gold Band' with narrow leaves golden variegated and plumes to 1.5m (5ft). The taller growing 'Sunningdale Silver' has looser more feathery plumes of great beauty. When tidying pampas grass plants in late autumn it is worth remembering to wear gloves, as the long arching evergreen leaves have razor sharp edges.

In favoured sheltered areas, particularly by waterside the Provence reed *Arundo donax* 'Macrophylla' makes an imposing specimen 2.5–3.5m (8–12ft) Broad arching blue-grey leaves are born on equally glaucous stout stems and there is a superb white variegated and rather more tender form 'Variegata' 3m (10ft). In cold districts this makes an exciting and different conservatory plant. In similar vein, we have the elegant, if somewhat invasive Miscanthus. Taller growing *M. sacchariflorus* with grey-green sugar-cane like growth will reach 1.8–2.5m (6–8ft) and make a good summer windbreak. The slender *M. sinensis* 'Gracillimus' is perhaps the doyenne of the genus with narrow greyish arching leaves with white central veins, 1.5–2m (5–6ft) with leaves marginally striped with cream and yellow, while 'Zebrinus' is slightly taller and distinct in its crosswise zebra stripes of golden yellow.

Among the many hardy bamboos, a few are particularly suitable as evergreen specimens for moist well-drained focal points in sun or shade, often combining beauty and elegance in a most subtle and satisfying manner. Bamboos will also adapt admirably to container and tub culture, making impressive and evergreen patio or terrace specimens. For either purpose, *Arundinaria murieliae* is considered to be one of the most beautiful species in cultivation, indeed it was thought worthy to name it after the daughter of the great plant hunter Ernest Wilson, who introduced it from China. Its graceful arching stems can reach 2.5–3.5m (8–11ft) but less if restricted in large tub or container. *A.* 'Gauntlettii', a clump-forming hybrid bamboo, has large handsome leaves and young canes which are bright green becoming purple-tinted with age; 1.5–2m (5–6ft). The generally taller-growing phyllostachys differ from arundinaria in their less invasive habit and zig-zag stems; notably the black bamboo *P. nigra* 'Boryana' produces quantities of graceful arching leafy stems up to 4m (13ft) high, at first green changing to yellow splashed with purple. This is a typical plant of Japan from which it originates. A rare and distinct species often difficult to obtain, the Chilean *Chusquea culeou* is unique among hardy bamboos in its solid stems (they do not flag if cut for floral arranging), and in its unusual bottle-brush-like leafy branchlets which are produced throughout the length of the tall olive green stems. A beautiful and desirable bamboo, particularly for those who collect the rare and uncommon.

Finally, another unique and contrasting bamboo for an especially prominent position in the garden can be found in *Sasa tessellata* (*Arundinaria ragamowskii*) whose shining green leaves up to 60cm (2ft) long are the largest of all hardy bamboos, and are borne impressively on arching canes, not usually above 2m (6ft) long. It is comforting to learn from Bean's *Trees and Shrubs Hardy in the British Isles* (8th Edition, 1976) that this elegant species has not been known to flower in cultivation.

GRASSES FOR PAVED AREAS AND PATIOS
There are several tufted or clump-forming grasses which make exciting specimens, effective in both foliage and flower when grown in small pockets in well drained sunny areas which are paved or gravelled. *Helictotrichon sempervirens* (*Avena candida*) has semi-evergreen blue-grey mounds of arching leaves from which erupt silvery oak-like inflorescences to a height of about 60cm (2ft). Much smaller, perhaps 15–20cm (6–

8in) and a popular paving or edging plant *Festuca glauca*, the blue fescue grass, forms delicate tufts of inrolled leaves. Spring division every other year and regular trimming ensures a good performance. *Molinia caerulea* 'Variegata' is another most desirable tufted small grass for a prominent position in paving; its creamy-white marginal variegation is effective throughout the growing season and in late summer and autumn purple-brown flower spikes are produced to contrast subtly with the foliage. *Stipa calamagrostis*, 60cm (2–2½ft) can be relied on for a long season of display, the arching green foliage and graceful glistening silvery plumes opening in July and deepening in colour as they fade in the autumn. *Stipa gigantea*, the largest of the genus, needs space to set it off and is too big for the small patio, but is very worthy of a prominent position elsewhere in the garden. A sunny, above all well-drained focal point is essential for this splendid grass. Semi-evergreen, tough pointed leaves form a basal mound from which arise tall stems 2m (6ft) of glistening golden spikelets. Divide clumps every other year in the spring.

Grasses and bamboos as groundcover
These are for banks, pond or stream side and under trees with light canopies.

There are several notable grasses and bamboos which are both good to look at and efficient and functional as labour-saving groundcover, albeit somewhat invasive. However, if correctly sited they are usually controllable, particularly if isolated in mown grass or confined to banks or areas where they cannot swamp weaker or immature plants or shrubs. Among the grasses are two strikingly variegated plants: *Glyceria maxima* 'Variegata' (*aquatica* 'Variegata') best grown as waterside plants where it will reach about 45–60cm (1½–2ft). Its strap-like leaves are conspicuously variegated with green, yellow and creamy-white and are tinted pink in both spring and autumn. *Phalaris arundinacea* 'Picta' – gardeners garters, is tolerant of a wide range of soil conditions, growing strongly to about 1m (3ft) whether dry or moist. The bold upright growth is brightly striped with white and can be most effective if well isolated and seen against a dark background.

Dwarf groundcovering bamboos, once established, are equally invasive, but have the advantage of evergreen foliage, sometimes variegated and effective all the year. Several species are now used increasingly as groundcover in town centres and other public places. As with taller varieties, these bamboos make excellent tub or container plants for paved areas. *Arundinaria pumila*, with purplish slender canes, and *A. vagans* and *A. pygmaea* all form green carpets, about 45–60cm (1½–2ft). Variegated, dwarf and groundcovering bamboos are a little taller. *A. viridistriata* (*auricoma*) is clump-forming and less invasive, usually maturing 1–1.5m (3–5ft) – it has predominantly golden yellow green-striped leaves, while *A. variegata* also has a tufted habit, attaining about 1m (3ft) with narrow, comparatively long leaves, striped creamy-white. One other lower growing bamboo *Sasa veitchii* (up to 1.5m or 5ft) creates an unusual effect of variegation by the natural withering of the margins of its large leaves. This produces the effect of parchment-white variegation and an isolated colony near waterside can be most effective at all seasons and particularly during autumn and winter. Finally, *Shibataea kumasasa* 45–60cm (1½–2ft), a rarely seen low-growing bamboo, is very worthy of a mention in that it is neat, compact and not invasive and is one of the most distinct of hardy bamboos, with robust zigzag stems and comparatively wide leaves in relation to their length.

HYDRANGEA

'How do I make my hydrangea as blue as Mrs Jones' plant?' This is the usual starting point when gardeners consider hydrangeas but is only really appropriate if a very limited view is taken of this valuable group of plants. Some of the Hortensia hydrangeas can look startling with vivid blue flowers but these are only a small part of the varied shrubs and climbers offered by this genus.

Although some hydrangeas offer features such as attractive barks, bold foliage and interesting fruit heads for use in flower arranging, the main element for the garden is their flowers. These are borne in large corymbs or panicles and are of two types. Most are rather insignificant fertile flowers or florets. These have small petals which are white, blue or pink; individually these flowers are nothing but make an impression in number, which is the way they grow, creating a haze of their principal colour. Outside of the fertile flowers, and in the wild flower occurring in much smaller numbers, are the sterile flowers which are normally called ray florets. These have three to five large sepals and are individually conspicuous. Their role is to attract insects to the flowers. Several species have thrown forms in which all or nearly all the flowers are of the flamboyant sterile form, especially the Hortensia group. At their best the Hortensias can look very attractive but may be said to lack the grace of the wild flower form. The ray florets do not fall when they have finished but persist to enhance the beauty of the fruiting heads.

Hydrangeas will grow on all soils, including chalk and limy ones. Most like a good quantity of moisture in the soil and should not be planted where it will dry out during the summer. On chalk and other soils which may dry out, organic matter should be worked into the soil and topped with a mulch to retain moisture. Also, avoid siting the plants where they will be exposed to the full effects of the sun.

In some species the pigment which colours the sterile flowers contains aluminium ions. The availability to the plant of

*The variegated Provence reed (*Arundo donax 'Variegata'*) with Chusa palm (*Trachycarpus fortunei*) and banana (*Musa*) at the Ventnor Botanic Garden, Isle of Wight*

aluminium depends to a very large extent upon the pH of the soil (see chapter 3); in acid soils aluminium is readily absorbed by the plant and this gives the bright blue colours. As the pH increases, aluminium becomes less available and the colour changes through purple to pink on alkaline soils. Plants which are naturally pink-flowered on neutral or alkaline soils will become purplish or bluish on acidic soils. Proprietary compounds are available to make aluminium ions available to the plant and these can be very effective where the soil is neutral but are less effective where the soil is veering towards being alkaline. Generally, either clear blue or clear pinks are attractive and the colours to avoid are the muddy purples. If your efforts to make them blue fail, try going the other way and having clearer pink flowers by applying lime (first check that no other plants in the area will suffer).

Hydrangeas are mainly shrubs but include a number of climbing species. Several make trees in the wild and there is no reason why they should not be grown as small trees in gardens. To do this will require an element of training by the removal of unwanted basal shoots but *H. aspera*, *H. heteromalla* and *H. paniculata* can all make unusual small flowering trees. The climbing species are useful for clothing the walls of houses or clinging to the trunks of trees. They have the considerable advantage of developing aerial roots which serve to attach the plant to the wall or trunk without the need for extensive artificial supports, although a little early guidance is useful. The shrubby species make good plants in the shrubaceous border, particularly in shaded sites, and as shrubs in woodland gardens.

Most hydrangeas require very little pruning. The flowers are produced from buds laid down in the previous summer and severe pruning will result in no flowers in the following summer. However, weaker and older stems should be thinned out. The exception to the above is *H. paniculata*.

Small shrub hydrangeas

H. macrophylla makes a small shrub of 1–2m (3–6ft) tall. It is excellent for coastal situations but needs some shelter in inland gardens if the flower buds are not to be killed over-winter. The species has given a multiplicity of different cultivars which are divided into two groups. The Hortensia cultivars, or mop-headed hydrangeas, have flowers composed exclusively or mainly of sterile ray florets. The flowerheads are generally large and rounded. The second group is known as the lacecap hydrangeas and these have normal flattened flowerheads but perhaps with more sterile florets than occurs in the wild species. With these forms, the beauty is partly from the sterile florets and partly from the haze of massed but minute fertile florets. The flowers normally open in July and last into August and September.

Mop-headed hydrangeas

'Altona' naturally has rose-coloured flowers but can be induced to turn blue. They are carried on strong stems and are long lasting, becoming green and in autumn turning red. It is hardier than most and less likely to be damaged by winter weather. It grows to around 1m (3ft). 'Europa' is similar, but less compact and will turn a deeper blue on acid soils.

'Ami Pasquier' has deep red or crimson flowers and is low growing, to 60cm or so.

'Ayesha' will attain a metre tall and has glossy green leaves. The flowers are in concave heads and are a greyish lilac-pink in colour.

'Deutschland' is deep pink and has the benefit of good autumn colour from the foliage; it makes a shrub up to 2–3m (6–10ft).

'Generale Vicomtesse de Vibraye' has good pink or blue flowers although the stems are rather weak. Along with 'Altona' it is one of the hardiest.

'Marechal Foch' has flowers from rosy-pink through purple to deep blue and is an early and free-flowering form growing up to 1.5m (5ft).

'Niedersachsen' is late-flowered and slightly tender. It has pale pink or pale blue flowers.

Lacecap hydrangeas

'Blue Wave' has blue fertile flowers and ray florets which may be pink or blue according to the soil pH; at their best they are gentian blue. It will make 2m (6ft) tall and is best in light shade.

'Lanarth White' and 'White Wave' have the ray florets pure white, although the fertile florets may be either blue or pink. Both are free flowering in open sunny positions and will grow 1–2m (3–6ft) tall.

'Mariesii' has almost invariably pink or mauve-pink ray florets but instead of being restricted to the periphery of the flowerhead, some are scattered throughout amongst the fertile flowers.

'Sea Foam' has blue sterile flowers and white ray florets. It is a small shrub whose leaves remain green until killed by frost in the autumn.

'Tricolor' has leaves which are variegated green, grey and pale yellow and pale pink to white flowers.

'Veitchii', with blue fertile flowers and white or pale pink ray florets, makes a lax growing shrub to 1.5m (5ft), best suited to light shade.

H. serrata makes a low shrub usually less than 1.5m (5ft) tall. It is related to *H. macrophylla* and flowering at the same time but generally hardier.

'Bluebird' has domed flowerheads composed of blue fertile flowers and large red-purple to sea-blue ray florets. It is drought tolerant and rather early flowering.

'Grayswood' is a selection with blue fertile florets and in which the ray florets begin white and age through pink and if grown in sunlight to bright red. 'Intermedia' is similar, except the fertile florets are pink. 'Rosalba' too is similar except the ray florets become blotched with pure crimson and the foliage is dull yellow-green.

'Preziosa' has the flowerheads composed

FIG 102 Hydrangea macrophylla *'Lanarth White'*

entirely of ray florets, although in smaller heads than in the Hortensia group. The flowers are rose-pink and very long lasting, eventually turning reddish-purple and remaining attractive in autumn. The coarsely toothed leaves are tinged purple when young and the shoots are purplish red. It is an excellent form, flowering very freely either in full sun or light shade.

The above four cultivars, but not 'Bluebird', do not develop blue ray florets on acidic soils or in response to the application of aluminium compounds.

H. arborescens can make a shrub to 3m (10ft) although it is usually much smaller. It is hardy and mainly represented by the following clones.

'Annabelle' has very large hemispherical heads of white flowers, nearly all of which are sterile. 'Grandiflora' has more globular heads of sterile white flowers. The stems are often too weak to support the flowerheads and they may need staking. 'Annabelle' and 'Grandiflora' flower from July into Sep-

321

tember. 'Sterilis' also has the flowerheads composed of white ray florets and flowers in June and July; it belongs to subspecies *discolor* (*H. cinerea*) which differs in the felt-like leaves.

H. quercifolia has remarkable leaves which are likened to those of the red oak and have five to seven scalloped lobes. The leaves may turn crimson, orange or purple in the autumn. This shrub to 2m needs a moist rich soil and a sheltered but not shaded position. The flowers are in erect panicles 10–25cm (4–10in) long and are white.

H. involucrata makes a small shrub to 50cm (1ft 8in) tall, although taller in mild areas. It is not reliably hardy but carries blue or rosy-lilac fertile florets surrounded by white or bluish-white ray florets from August into October. 'Hortensis' is a selection in which the more numerous ray florets are double and buff-pink in colour, although nearly white in shade. It needs a sheltered position.

Hydrangea paniculata *'Tardiva'*

Large shrubs and trees

These make large shrubs, naturally more than 3m (10ft) tall, or small trees up to 6–10m (20–33ft) tall.

H. aspera has the flowers in large corymbs up to 25cm (10in) across. The fertile florets are blue or purple and the ray florets white, pink or purple. The colour is unaffected by the soil pH, although some forms have much better flowers than others. The leaves are variable but often large, to 25cm (10in) and the stems have a buff-coloured peeling bark. It flowers in July and August, creating a bold display. It grows better on chalk than most other species and appears to need a rather dry soil for best development. The new growths can be susceptible to damage by spring frost. 'Villosa' is an excellent narrow-leafed form with large lilac-blue flowers.

H. sargentiana is a magnificent species which has stout bristly shoots and large corymbs of flowers in July and August. The ray florets are up to 3cm (1in) across and pinkish white. The fertile flowers are deep rosy-lilac. It needs a moist rich soil and a position which will give it plenty of sunlight but protection from the full force of the midday sun.

H. heteromalla makes a large shrub or small tree with large corymbs of white flowers. The ray florets can be up to 5cm (2in) across. The best form is 'Bretschneideri' which carries large flowerheads in late June and July; these are pure white at first, fading to light pink. The bark is chestnut-brown and peels. It is a very tough plant, tolerating drought, full sun and exposure. *H. xanthoneura* is a similar plant with creamy-white flowers carried in June.

H. paniculata is unusual in that it can be hard pruned in the spring and still give a good floral display, behaving more like *Buddleia davidii* than other hydrangeas. It can be grown either as a low shrub, a larger bush on a stem or leg or trained to make a tree. It does not need severe pruning to flower copiously, but pruning can be used to concentrate the growth into a small number of flowers, thus creating larger flowerheads. The wild species has mainly fertile flowers but the normal forms in cultivation mainly have ray florets. The flowers are white, fading to pink and carried in conical panicles which can be 50cm (1ft 8in) tall by 30cm (1ft) wide. 'Praecox' is the first to flower starting in mid July. Many of the florets are fertile. 'Grandiflora' develops the largest flowers and comes into bloom around the end of August. The flowers die off brown but are still attractive. 'Unique' is similar. 'Tardiva' is late-flowering, in September and October. A range of clones can thus be used to give a succession of large white flowers, either in the garden or for indoor decoration.

Climbing hydrangeas

H. petiolaris is the commonest climbing hydrangea and is very hardy. It will grow high up a wall or into the crown of a tree and along with the other species is self-clinging. It can also be very effective if used to grow over a mound. The stems have a peeling bark. The flowers are carried in June from short shoots which grow horizontally out from the wall or trunk and are white. Young plants may take a couple of seasons before they start to climb vigorously and a further two or three before flowering well.

H. serratifolia is an uncommon evergreen species with dark green leathery leaves. In late summer it bears the creamy-white flowers, composed of small fertile flowers and very few, if any, ray florets. It is hardy on a sheltered wall.

Decumaria is an uncommon genus of self-clinging climbers closely related to hydrangea but lacking ray florets. *D. barbata* is deciduous or semi-evergreen and makes a climber to 9m (30ft). The white flowers are produced in clusters 5–7cm (2–3in) across in June and July. It needs the protection of a wall except in the mild parts of the country. *D. sinensis* is an evergreen species climbing to 5m (16ft). It has fragrant yellowish-white flowers in terminal panicles in May.

Schizophragma is allied to hydrangea but

differs in the sterile florets being composed of a single sepal or bract, not three to five. The two species climb by aerial roots. They flower best in full sunlight but need a moist rich loamy soil.

S. hydrangeoides makes a deciduous climber capable of attaining 10m (33ft) or higher. The flowers are yellowish-white, sweetly scented and in corymbs 20–25cm (8–10in) across; they are carried in July. 'Roseum' has the sterile bracts tinged with rose.

S. integrifolium is also deciduous and differs in the larger flowerheads, to 30cm (1ft), and the larger sterile bracts which are up to 9cm long by 5cm wide (3½×2in).

ILEX (HOLLY)

This large genus of trees and shrubs contains a majority of evergreen species which are the most well known in our gardens; they are extremely hardy evergreens growing up to 21m (70ft) high. Holly occurs naturally throughout Britain, except in the extreme north-east. One of the greatest attributes is their ability to grow in sun or shade. *Ilex aquifolium* is common as an understorey plant in many of our beech and oak woods. The majority of the garden varieties originate from either *Ilex aquifolium* or the hybrid holly, *Ilex x altaclerensis* (Highclere holly). This holly originated from a cross between the common holly and the rather tender Azorean holly (*Ilex perado*). It is said that this greenhouse species was crossed in a nursery at Highclere, Berkshire, the resulting *Ilex altaclerensis* has the advantage of being more vigorous in growth, with rather larger handsome leaves which tend to have less spines. Both the common and the Highclere holly varieties make excellent hardy evergreen hedges, they are most useful in providing shelter in gardens, being dense-growing even down to ground level, the *aquifolium* varieties in particular. For preference, hollies like a moist loamy soil. Male and female flowers, which are relatively insignificant, are usually borne on separate plants, it is therefore important to ensure that both male and female plants are present in order that the impressive berries are to appear.

Hollies with good stem colour

Within the *I. x altaclerensis* group, due mainly to their extra vigour, there are a number of varieties whose stems are an interesting purplish colour. 'Hodginsii' has purplish young shoots and is more pyramidal in shape than most varieties; it is very hardy and has dark green rounded or oval leaves. In older specimens the leaves may have few or no spines. 'Purple Shaft', has been selected purely for its strong dark purple young shoots. 'Camelliifolia' is selected for the purplish shoots, the leaves are a dark shining green, reddish-purple when young. *Ilex aquifolium* does also have varieties with purplish stems but they are considered as a feature in conjunction with their variegated foliage.

Variegated foliage

Possibly one of the most satisfactory variegated hollies is *Ilex aquifolium* 'Handsworth New Silver', the leaf colour is especially good, being very dark green with a clear merging of white. This white variegation is most attractive with the purple stems. It is a female plant and therefore has the added berrying effect in the winter. 'Madame Briot' is another fine variety with purple young stems, and the leaves of this variety are strongly armed with thorns and green with a margin of gold and central mottling of gold and light green. *Ilex aquifolium* 'Ovata Aurea' is rather distinct from the other varieties as thick, shortly-spined leaves, margined gold, contrast beautifully with its deep purple twigs. It is a bright and neat variegated holly. The young shoots of 'Silver Queen' are purplish-black, the foliage dark green, faintly marbled grey, with a clear white marginal variegation, most effective when in active growth. There are numerous silver and gold variegated varieties and it is very much a matter of personal taste as to which are preferred.

Habit forms

In terms of overall shape there are a number of more upright-growing varieties, such as *I. aquifolium* 'Green Pillar' with its dark green shiny leaves, and *I. x altaclerensis* 'Camelliifolia', 'Purple Shaft' and 'Hodginsii', as previously described. *Ilex aquifolium* 'Pyramidalis' is conical as a young plant, broadening with maturity. It is excellent for its free fruiting and bright green leaves. There are two weeping holly varieties which, although of some interest, can hardly be described as the most elegant of weeping trees as they tend to form a dense mound of foliage. However, they can be trained on a single stem into a more attractive small tree. These are *Ilex aquifolium* 'Pendula' and 'Argenteomarginata Pendula'.

Coloured berries

For coloured berries, the hollies are of course famous and they are red, with the exception of a few varieties that have yellow berries, such as *Ilex aquifolium* 'Bacciflava' which has heavy crops of bright yellow fruits. *Ilex aquifolium* 'Pyramidalis Fructuluteo' has equally bright yellow fruit, and 'Amber' has bronze yellow fruits. The hedgehog holly, *Ilex aquifolium* 'Ferox' is a curious medium-sized shrub, possessing leaves which are puckered on their upper surface and furnished with short, sharp spines.

Dwarf hollies

There are silver and gold variegated varieties and small or dwarf species which are useful for the rock garden or scree. *Ilex crenata* is ideal as a dwarf clipped hedge. This species has tiny leaves very unlike the typical holly and has small shiny black fruit; its variety 'Convexa' is even smaller and particularly suitable for a dwarf hedge, the leaves are more convex and a glossy mid-green, its fruits reliable. *Ilex cornuta* rarely attains 2.5m (8ft) high and has leaves of a peculiar rectangular form, mainly five spined; the variety 'Burfordii' is very free fruiting with shiny green leathery leaves. *Ilex pernyi* is slow growing and usually only seen as a dwarf pyramidal specimen. However, given ideal conditions it may reach small tree size. It is unusual in having triangular spined leaves. 'Jermyns Dwarf' is a low-growing shrub with arching stems which forms a dense mound.

Of the deciduous holly varieties, *Ilex verticillata*, 'Christmas Cheer', a scarce variety, has particularly fine bright red fruits that persist throughout winter; the leaves are purple tinged in spring. It makes a shrub to 2m (6ft). Not suitable for chalky soils.

The blue-leaved hollies should not go unmentioned. Unfortunately, however, they do not seem to thrive in this country and therefore cannot be recommended when there are so many other desirable hollies available.

JAPANESE MAPLES

There are perhaps no other small trees or shrubs which, together with variation of shape and colour of foliage, are capable of adding such elegance and distinction to a garden.

As well as great beauty of grace and form, in the manner so typical of and appreciated by the Japanese, the many cultivars of *Acer palmatum* display much subtle diversity of leaf shape, from finely cut filigree to deeply-lobed large palmate leaves; in colour there is even more variation, fresh young spring growths appearing in many shades of green, pink and even crimson; one can enjoy summer leaves of bright yellow or cool green while other forms maintain crimson, red or purple foliage throughout the growing season. All tend to change as autumn comes, greens changing to gold or fiery orange and scarlet, while reds and purples will brighten to subtle tones of crimson and pink. There are an increasing number of variegated varieties now becoming available – finely cut leaves often combining fascinating blends of cream, pink, grey and green with patches of red. These again change as the season advances to autumn.

Although not confined to acid soils, Japanese maples blend superbly with rhododendrons, azaleas, camellias, heathers and their allies, enjoying the shelter and partial shade in which these shrubs thrive, equally they will grow on ideal rhododendron land – light sandy loam with plenty of organic matter present to improve water-holding capacity. On well cultivated alkaline soils, where plenty of humus is also present, they make good companions for hydrangea, particularly species like *aspera, villosa, paniculata* and *arborescens* and their varieties, with viburnum, euonymus, mahonia and many other shrubs which thrive in light shade. On any fertile soil shade-tolerant herbaceous groundcovers can be a perfect complement to Japanese maples, and in particular hosta, smilacina, bergenia, hardy geranium, helleborus, pulmonaria and tiarella and of course ferns and many of the dwarfer ornamental grasses.

Growing in containers

If your soil is really hopeless – solid chalk or undrainable pasty clay, or there is no suitable border position in your garden – do not despair; Japanese maples make excellent tub or container plants, particularly for a sheltered patio in light shade. The majority of the dwarf forms of *Acer palmatum* 'Dissectum' are excellent when grown in this manner or as bonsai specimens. John Innes Compost (JIP) with a generous amount of extra peat, leaf mould and perlite is an ideal compost. Sharp drainage is necessary, but equally the medium should have good water-retaining qualities and a container should certainly be shaded from hot sunshine. In winter, while Japanese maples will stand quite low temperatures in the open ground, remember to guard against soil freezing of container specimens – roots will be damaged or killed if frozen below minus 10°C (14°F) – when such severe weather is due, move your container specimens into the protection of cool greenhouse or garage or, if this is not possible, wrap the container in some insulating material such as polystyrene, held in place with hessian or burlap.

Siting is important

Like most aristocrats, Japanese maples are a little 'choosy' and careful siting is essential to obtain the best results. Allow adequate room for their ultimate growth, both in height and spread; they enjoy the association of ground-covering plants and shrubs which help to maintain a cool root-run and can usually be re-sited as the maple grows. In the British Isles light dappled tree shade is ideal, and freedom from draught and wind, particularly from the north or east, is essential. If a Japanese maple is unhappy in the site you have chosen, it will often show resentment by curling its leaves at the margins and there may be evidence of die-back of branchlets. If there is reasonable cover of taller trees, frost in the spring may not be a problem, but if your garden is low-lying, say in a river valley, a site should be chosen which does not catch early sun following frost.

Site preparation is especially important and the carefully chosen site should be equally well prepared, carefully removing roots of nearby trees which may be encountered, and incorporating a slow-release fertiliser, such as Vitax Q4, Chempak BTD, or one of the rose fertilisers, together with plenty of peat, pulverised bark or leaf mould, into an area well cultivated at least 1m (3ft) wide and 0.3–0.5m (1–1½ft) deep.

Commercially Japanese maple cultivars are usually bench-grafted under glass onto the roots of *Acer palmatum*, a variable species raised from seed. They are a crop needing great skill and specially sheltered circumstances to raise them to the standard required for sale, and to stand the best possible chance of establishment in your garden. They are inevitably more expensive than many other commonly grown shrubs and extra care by the gardener carrying out the installation is called for. When young Japanese maples in pots or containers are planted out into the open ground in the early spring, particularly

if they have over-wintered under glass, polythene or wooden slat-houses, they will
benefit from the shelter afforded by small
branches of evergreens, such as cypress or
laurel, cut from a hedge and stuck in closely
around the small young plant to protect
tender unfurling leaves from wind, sun or
frost, as the leaves open. In subsequent years,
if correctly sited, the developing shrub
should be acclimatised and its leaves will
unfurl as weather conditions allow. A 'wig-
wam' or tripod of bamboo canes is also an
excellent addition to safeguard the young
plant from accidental damage. Finally, do not
forget a mulch of coarse peat, bark or leaves,
applied to moist soil will further aid establishment by maintaining a cool root-run.
However, attention to watering will be vital in
all times of drought, and in the spring for two
or three years following planting, and should
not be neglected.

Pest and diseases
Fortunately, in the British Isles, Japanese
maples are not subject to serious insect
attack. Aphids may affect succulent young
growth in the spring, causing distortion of
shoots and leaves and when they infest
foliage in summer they will produce quantities of honey-dew, resulting in unsightly
stickiness upon leaves and shoots and the
growth of sooty mould. A regular spraying
with an aphicide such as Pyrethrin should
give adequate control.

Mercifully, Japanese maples are not widely
troubled with diseases in our islands –
however, the dreaded Verticillium Wilt is one
of the causes of die-back of twigs and
branches. This disease is regrettably not yet
fully understood and no cure is known. It is
often confused with a natural winter die-back
of unripened shoots or twigs. Verticillium
causes brown streaking under the bark of
shoots and twigs or branches of affected
shrubs. Rapid collapse and death of the tree
or shrub may occur. The body should be
removed and burnt and its site sterilised and
not re-planted. It is very important to sterilise

pruning tools as the disease can be spread by
the use of contaminated tools on healthy
plants.

Leaf scorching, shrivelling and twig die-
back may result from a number of causes
usually not associated with disease. As mentioned earlier, correct siting is of the greatest
importance to avoid damage of this nature,
resulting from exposure to wind, hot sunshine, salt-laden gales or spring frosts.
Equally short periods of drought can be
enough to cause severe burning, even de-
foliation, particularly with container-grown
shrubs which can be sensitive to irregular
watering – efforts should be made to keep
them consistently moist. Leaf burn can also
be caused by the excessive use of nitro-
genous fertilisers which produce soft, sappy
growth, very vulnerable to damage. Equally,
foliage which is wetted, even accidentally
during periods of hot sunshine can be quite
severely damaged and the shrub's appearance spoilt for that season. Fortunately, providing remedial action is taken, no permanent damage is done to established maples,
though very young plants may receive a
severe check, if not fatal damage.

The artistically satisfying form or shape of
Japanese maples, combined with their delicate often filigree foliage and remarkably
subtle variation in leaf colour, have been long
appreciated, indeed revered by the Japanese
for centuries. More than 250 cultivars of *Acer
palmatum* are now thought to be in cultivation. In recent years a considerable number
of new cultivars have arrived from Japan and
are being tried and tested in our nurseries
and arboreta. Some of those which have
proved most successful and rewarding are
now becoming commercially available and
we are struggling to remember a new batch
of Japanese names!

Here is a selection combining some of the
indispensable older varieties with several of
the best of the new, drawn up according to
predominant foliage colour throughout the
growing season – most will turn a varying

shade of yellow, orange, red or purple or a combination of these in the autumn before leaf fall.

Acer palmatum forms
Yellow and green leaves

The *Acer palmatum* cultivars are often divided into a number of groups according to dominant characteristics of the foliage – the 'Dissectum' group typically exhibits delicate, finely-cut leaves, with lobes pinnately or double pinnately dissected. Indeed, with its elegant filigree foliage 'Dissectum' has well earned the name of the lace-leaf maple. This is one of the indispensables; while the shape and colour of individual leaves may show some variation, the typical plant of commerce forms a mound of cascading branches up to 1.5–2m (5–6ft) high, rarely more, the shrub maturing broader than tall. Finely cut leaves usually open a delightful pale green, progressing to darker shades as the season advances and changing spectacularly to orange and scarlet before falling.

'Osakazuki' (Heptalobum group) is perhaps the most popular cultivar. Not without good reason, has it been offered by nurserymen since the middle of the last century. An excellent and vigorous variety, enjoying more sunshine than most other cultivars, ultimately it will make a small round-headed tree of 6m or more (about 20ft). The large seven-lobed rich green summer leaves are of lasting texture and turn the most brilliant and intense scarlet and crimson in the autumn. A carefully sited tree will perform spectacularly and reliably each year.

'Linearilobum' forms a small tree of upright, slightly arching habit ultimately perhaps 4m (12ft) or more; this seems to me just the right habit of growth to set off the bright green leaves with long narrow strap-like lobes which gives this cultivar a certain distinct elegance and charm.

Quite unique among Japanese maples is 'Ribesifolium' ('Shishigashira') – a small tree of unusual architectural form, slowly attaining 2m or even 3m (6–10ft). Its habit is upright, slightly spreading, but compact; the deep green seven-lobed leaves are curled and crimpled, each lobe elongated to a point. Autumn colour is usually a rich gold, some leaves suffused with crimson. Long cultivated, it makes an excellent specimen for the rock garden and adapts well to bonsai and container growing.

'Seiryu' is a delightful newcomer, in effect an upright growing form of 'Dissectum' the lace-leaf maple. Quite quickly attaining perhaps 4m (12ft) or more in ultimate height, 'Seiryu' makes a pleasing contrast to the more usually seen mound-forming cultivars of 'Dissectum'. Its spectacular autumn tints can vary from deep yellow to scarlet and crimson.

'Senkaki' ('Sango-kaku'). The coral bark maple has long been popular, especially for its delightful coral-red stems which are such a striking winter feature. It is very handsome too in its summer cloak of bright green leaves with five to seven lobes, which turn in the autumn to a pleasing blend of golden yellow with subtle overtones of apricot and orange. A vigorous, upright grower, spreading at its summit with age, it will, if well sited, often attain 6m or 7m (about 20ft) and has considerable potential as a focal point for garden or landscape.

Mottled or variegated leaves

Of elegant upright habit and dense twiggy growth 'Butterfly' is proving to be one of the most worthwhile of the variegated cultivars now becoming available. It is not slow in growth, makes a large-size shrub or small tree up to 3m or 4m (10–13ft). The pale or bluish-green summer foliage has five to seven irregularly shaped lobes and is generously variegated with creamy-white. In spring the newly unfurled leaves are marked with pink and in autumn the wide areas of the leaves assume vivid shades of crimson or magenta. All together this is a charming and dainty addition to our collection.

'Corallinum' is no newcomer, but has always been scarce, slow and difficult to propagate; nonetheless an absolute gem among Japanese maples. It makes a small compact slow-growing shrub, very suitable for foreground focal points in semi-shade. In spring and early summer the mainly five-lobed leaves and young stems are unique in their remarkable coloration which has been described as shrimp pink; this changes to a mottled or variegated green during the summer and often assumes crimson or scarlet tones in the autumn – in all, a magnificent small maple.

'Shishio Improved'. This elegant maple is often described as a more vigorous form of 'Corallinum', but the leaf colour is more crimson than pink. However, it is indeed an ideal maple for a sheltered patio, attaining ultimately 2–3m (6–10ft) when unrestricted at the root. It will also adapt well to container growing or bonsai culture.

Red, purple or bronze leaves

There are now several additions to the excellent range of red/purple maples which contrast so well with green forms in our gardens. Several of these are discussed below, but there will always be a place for the long-established stalwarts, such as 'Atropurpureum', although often showing variation in shape, size and colour of leaf when raised from seed, it remains a magnificent and reliable purple-leaved round-headed landscape tree up to 10m (30ft). The leaves are usually pale to crimson with the arrival of autumn.

Of the many selected cultivars within this colour range, the following are particularly noteworthy.

'Beni-maiko'. This is a fascinating dwarf bushy maple, ideal for a shady patio or for container growing. The spring and early summer foliage is a startling scarlet red, turning reddish-green as the season advances. There is an added interest in the small irregular leaves with strangely curving lobes.

Acer palmatum *'Dissectum'*

'Bloodgood'. A magnificent selection from 'Atropurpureum', now very popular, both in the USA and in Europe. Its large typically palmate leaves, up to 12cm wide (4½in), maintain a rich deep almost black-red hue well into late summer, paling to crimson before falling. The bright scarlet winged seeds make a striking contrast with the darker foliage. It forms a vigorous tree with broad crown, eventually 5m or 6m (15–20ft) high and through. However, we might wish that such a splendid maple had been given a more pleasing name!

'Crimson Queen' ('Dissectum' group). The persistence throughout the growing season of a good deep ox-blood-red leaf colour is also the main quality of this fine cultivar which is of American origin. This is a vigorous dissectum with large finely-divided notched leaves, the lobes up to 9cm (3½in) long. A change to scarlet heralds the arrival of autumn. 'Crimson Queen' may ultimately attain up to 3m (10ft) and forms a large mound of cascading branches.

'Nigrum' ('Dissectum' group). 'Ever Red' is of similar quality, again retaining the colour of its purple-red dissected leaves to the end of summer. An additional and very pleasing feature is apparent in the spring when the new unfolding growth is cloaked in silvery-grey hairs, an attractive and distinguishing feature of this older cultivar (see p146).

'Inaba-shidare' ('Dissectum' group). Although known in Japan for more than 100 years, this is a newcomer to western gardens. Again, its deep purple-red leaf colour is well maintained throughout summer, turning to crimson before falling. The seven-lobed well-divided leaves are exceptionally large, indeed up to 15cm (6in) long and wide, and the tree has more substance than most dissectums. It forms an erect, strong-growing tree with some cascading branches.

'Oshio-beni'. The young foliage of this cultivar in spring and early summer is bright orange-red, the typical palmate leaves changing to bronze or red-green as summer advances, and to scarlet with the arrival of autumn. This is also a vigorous upright grower with a spreading head, maturing to at least 5–6m (15–18ft). Some shade is desirable as there is a tendency for foliage to burn in full sun. Another newcomer to European gardens.

'Trompenburg'. Our review of the best Japanese maples commercially available today would not be complete without reference to this superb cultivar from the Trompenburg Arboretum, near Rotterdam. The leaves, with seven to nine lobes are distinct in their unusual and attractive lobe formation. The deep purple-red leaf colour is well maintained to the end of summer before turning bronze and then finally crimson before leaf fall. In all, this tree presents a unique and very pleasing aspect. With its vigorous upright, somewhat arching habit and an estimated ultimate height of 4m or 5m (13–16ft), 'Trompenburg' will make a magnificent specimen for garden or landscape.

Acer japonicum forms

The following two forms of *Acer japonicum*, plus the similar *A. shirawsanum* which are widely available remain among the most reliable and rewarding of Japanese maples.

'Aconitifolium' ('Filicifolium') makes a strongly-branched round-headed small tree up to 5m (15ft). Its dark green deeply-lobed leaves are of good substance and shaped like those of the herbaceous genus aconitum (monk's hood) – hence its cultivar name. Confusingly, its synonym Filicifolium refers to the fern-like appearance of its leaves and appears to provide its official common name of fern-leaved maple. Regardless of this confusion of names, its autumn colour is spectacular and persists longer than average, combining scarlet or crimson with touches of purple.

With 'Vitifolium' we have yet a further botanical reference in the large broad vine-like mid-green leaves of this cultivar. Forming a strongly branched tree ultimately up to 7m (22ft) or more in height, mature specimens are one of the autumn glories of

Westonbirt Arboretum in Gloucestershire when the colour of the falling leaves usually combines gold with scarlet, orange and crimson. This is perhaps the most robust and worthy of Japanese maples for general landscape planting.

A. *shirawsanum* 'Aureum', known (wrongly) as *A. japonicum* 'Aureum' although slow in growth, ultimately forms a large dense compact bush up to 5m (15ft) high and as much through. It is very rewarding and well earns its common name of golden full moon maple, displaying unfailingly, from early spring until autumn, its soft pale golden yellow leaves 6–8cm (2–3in) wide with sharply pointed lobes. In some areas the tips of the leaves are splashed with scarlet in the autumn.

LIGUSTRUM (PRIVET)
This genus has been neglected by gardeners and the horticultural trade. Surprisingly, there are some extremely interesting plants related to the well-known hedging privet (or oval-leaved privet) *Ligustrum ovalifolium*. This plant itself, if allowed to develop unclipped into a large shrub, will produce a mass of flowers in July in panicles 5–10cm (2–4in) high. The hedging privet is not in fact the common native privet (*Ligustrum vulgare*) which is an inferior plant generally and is less evergreen than *Ligustrum ovalifolium*, a plant that originated from Japan. Although one might say privet is rather dull as a hedge, it is undoubtedly a very amenable plant. It is after all one of our fastest evergreen hedges, it tolerates all soils, including chalk, and will grow in dry or wet shade. If nothing else will grow – try privet, it will inevitably succeed. It is a pity in some respects that it has become out of fashion and replaced by the ever increasing lines of Leyland cypress, a plant that is very much more difficult to cut and would far rather be a forest tree. As can so often be seen, Leyland cypress often does get out of hand and gets its own way. The golden privet, *Ligustrum ovalifolium* 'Aureum' is a reliably bright quick-growing hedge and it too is able to grow in the most hostile environments. It is slightly more graceful in habit than the green type.

Tree privets
There are few evergreen trees, excluding conifers that can survive our climate. Given reasonably sheltered positions, however, the privet family can offer some particularly handsome small trees. *Ligustrum lucidum* may grow to a height of 12m (40ft) or more, with a rounded crown and an attractive fluted trunk. For a non-coniferous plant this is certainly a very good sized evergreen tree. Only in severe winters it may lose its leaves, but can be regarded in general to be fully evergreen. It has large lustrous long pointed leaves and handsome panicles of white flowers in August and September. These panicles are up to 15–20cm (6–8in) in length. There are three desirable varieties of *L. lucidum*: 'Excelsum Superbum' is an excellent quick-growing variegated form, the leaves margined and mottled deep yellow and creamy white; 'Tricolor' has narrow leaves with an irregular border of white, tinged pink when young; 'Latifolium' has large camellia-like leaves and very attractive foliage.

Medium to large shrubs
The slightly smaller growing *L. sinense* will also grow to small tree proportions as a rounded tree to 10m (33ft) high. It is not, however, completely evergreen except in mild winters. For flower display it ranks as one of the best, having long dense sprays of white flowers in July. The dark purple fruits are equally produced in mass and will remain on the branches into January. The variety 'Pendulum' is smaller and has attractive hanging branches.

There are some privets with good foliage and flower, one of the best is *L. japonicum*, Japanese privet. This plant is ideal for screening or hedging attaining 2–3m (6–10ft). It has camellia-like leaves of a shiny olive green, 10cm (4in) long. It too carries quantities of white flowers in bloom from July to September. 'Rotundifolium' is more compact and rigid in growth with round leathery dark glossy green leaves. 'Macrophyllum' has larger, broad glossy black-green leaves and is more vigorous.

L. quihoui is undoubtedly the most elegant privet in bloom and is very much overlooked; the flowers are produced in August and September at a time when most trees and shrubs are well over and the flower panicles may be up to 50cm (20in) long. They are pleasantly fragrant, unlike most privet flowers which are rather unpleasant in odour. A warm, sheltered position for this plant is preferred for the purpose of ensuring that there is sufficient warmth at this late time of the year to open the flowers. Another rather ornamental privet is *L. chenaultii*, a semi-evergreen small shrub to large tree.

The evergreen shrub *L. delavayanum* grows 1.8–3m (6–10ft) and has a dense spreading habit. The leaves are small and thin textured. It flowers well, with dense panicles, white with violet anthers. The fruits are purplish-black.

MAGNOLIAS

Magnolias are planted for the beauty of their flowers and rarely for any other reason. Yet the fruits of some can be attractive, most make pleasant leafy plants and several have flowers which are deliciously fragrant.

The flowers are composed of two or more rings of sepals and petals but as it is impossible to determine which is which, they are collectively called tepals! These are thick and fleshy and easily bruised or damaged by frost. Inside the tepals is a mass of stamens and the carpels which enlarge into the fruit; both stamens and fruits can add to the display.

Magnolia x soulangiana is the hybrid much over-used in horticulture. This plant can look excellent and there are many different cultivars of it, ranging from those with large globular pure white flowers, such as 'Lennei Alba', to 'Lennei' which has goblet-shaped

Magnolia x loebneri *'Leonard Messel' bearing pink flowers in April*

rose-purple blooms. However, it is only one of several which have much to offer.

Magnolias range in size from shrubs growing a metre or so tall (*M. stellata*) to trees growing 15–20m (50–60ft) tall and needing up to 25 years before they flower. Flowering seasons range from those which bloom precociously early before the leaves emerge through plants which bear the last flowers late into the autumn. Most are deciduous but several of the best are evergreen.

The flowering season and the plant's habit greatly affects its use and positioning in the garden. Early flowerers are susceptible to damage by spring frost and therefore need protecting from this as far as is practical. Most frost damage occurs to plants exposed to the early morning sun, so a westerly aspect is likely to lead to less damage than an easterly one. Side and overhead shelter can be used to reduce the impact of sun and also to slow down the rate at which the air cools over night. However, if you garden in a frost pocket, it is probably better to forget about the early-flowering sorts except perhaps *M. cylindrica* and *M. salicifolia*, or accept that you will only get an adequate display every fourth or fifth season. Also, some of these varieties may come into leaf too early, so that the floral display is offset by the new foliage; this is especially so with forms of *M. x soulangiana* and *M. x veitchii* and a cold northern aspect which will delay leaf emergence may improve the display.

The flowers of *M. wilsonii* and its allies are carried in May or early June and hang down. To be seen effectively these need viewing from below, either by planting at the top of a bank or allowing them to grow over a path – they make much less of a display if sited in the distance in a shrub bed. Other early summer flowering ones, such as *M. officinalis*, tend to hide the fragrant flowers amidst the large bold foliage; these are better sited where the flowers can either be sniffed or seen from above. The evergreen species can be damaged by severe winters and are often planted against a wall for protection.

Magnolia will thrive on nearly all soils. A few do not like shallow chalky soils and they do not particularly like light sandy soils, but most will grow on these, albeit more slowly. They are excellent for heavy soils and prefer an adequate amount of moisture with satisfactory drainage.

They will not tolerate soil disturbance and will suffer if the roots are disturbed by digging or deep hoeing. They have thick and fleshy roots and if damaged these are inclined to rot. For this reason, they can be difficult to move and establish. They should be planted out when the roots are capable of making new growth – in early autumn or late spring so that any damage is repaired by the plant's own defence mechanism. Generally, container-grown plants are best, as these permit the new bush to be planted out without losing roots.

Precocious flowering magnolias – shrubs and small trees

These are the commonest magnolias in gardens and give very effective displays in April and May.

M. x soulangiana (saucer magnolia) is the ubiquitous one although not suited to shallow soils over chalk. The form offered as plain *M. x soulangiana*, particularly by cheaper outlets, has large tulip-shaped white flowers which are stained with a slightly muddy rose-purple. It forms a large spreading bush, ultimately making a small tree. The foliage is reasonable but the plants tend to look dull through the summer months. Growing summer-flowering climbers over them, such as *Clematis vernayi*, will add interest and as these can be cut back to near ground level in late winter, they will not interfere with the magnolia's display. In some seasons the flowers are not fully precocious and the new foliage detracts from the display.

A better result will be obtained by using either one of the following named cultivars or the species described below. 'Alba Superba' is a form with very fragrant flowers composed of nine tepals and forming a dense erect bush. 'Amabilis' has ivory-white flowers faintly flushed with purple at the base. 'Brozzonii' is another white-flowered form whose tepals are flushed purple at the base. The flowers, however, are very large, to 25cm (10in) across, and open in the second half of April, later than in most forms. 'Lennei' is probably the best form of this cross. It carries large richly coloured flowers in late April and into May, often with a small flush of flowers in the autumn. These are a beautiful rose-purple on the outside and white within. The tepals are obovate and 10cm (4in) long and broad, whilst it has leaves to 20×12cm (8×5in). 'Lennei Alba' is a form with ivory-white goblet-shaped flowers. 'Picture' has large reddish-purple flowers which are white within and fade to rosy-pink on the outside. It forms a vigorous erect shrub or small tree with rounded leaves and flowers from a very early age. 'Rustica Rubra' has faintly scented cup-shaped flowers which are rosy-red and up to 15cm (6in) across.

M. lilliiflora (also called *M. quinquepeta*) is one of the parents of *M. x soulangiana* and is mainly represented by the clone 'Nigra'. This has flowers which are very dark purple on the outside and paler or white within and near the tips outside, with the individual tepals 10–12cm (4–5in) long. They are carried late in May and early June, often with a late flush in the autumn. The flowers are quite striking in shape and colour, but some of the effect is lost as the leaves are partly, or with later blooms fully, formed when they are displayed. It makes a moderately compact bush.

M. denudata (Yulan, also named *M. hepta-peta*) is the other parent of *M. x soulangiana*. It has pure white cup-shaped flowers which are slightly fragrant. They are carried from March until May, depending upon the vagaries of the season but, if tempted into bloom too early, are often damaged by frosts. It makes a low wide-spreading tree, majestic when fully covered with flower. 'Purple Eye'

is a selection in which the flowers are suffused purple at the base of the tepals.

M. kobus has pure white flowers which are amongst the smallest in the genus at under 10cm (2in) across, yet are carried in such profusion on established plants to rival the effect of any other magnolia. They are also slightly fragrant and are the more effective for being carried on the totally leafless branches in April. This species makes a small conical tree, becoming rounded when older. It does not start to flower abundantly until some fifteen or so years old. It tolerates chalk and along with the following forms or hybrids, makes a more promising tree than *M. x soulangiana* for such sites.

M. stellata (star magnolia) makes a dwarf bush from 1–5m (3–16ft) tall. It is closely allied to *M. kobus* and better treated as a variety of it. The flowers have from 12–18 strap-like tepals which are spreading when the flowers open, then reflexed, giving the star outline. They are easily bruised or damaged by frost but as they open in succession in March and April they give an effective display for some weeks. 'Rosea' is a form with pink-flushed young flowers, fading to nearly white, and fewer tepals. 'Water Lily' has longer and narrower tepals and makes a taller shrub than the normally offered form of *M. stellata*.

Hybrids between *M. kobus* and *M. stellata* have been named *M. x loebneri*, although if the parents are treated as forms of the one species, the named clones will be referable to *M. kobus* as cultivars. They make excellent and very floriferous small trees or large shrubs worthy of space in any garden. 'Leonard Messel' has flowers with strap-like tepals which are lilac pink and deeper in bud. 'Merrill' carries masses of fragrant pure white flowers.

M. cylindrica is a delightful small tree or large shrub which deserves much wider planting. It flowers when less than 1m (3ft) tall and carries many white erect cylindrical flowers in April, followed by cylindrical fruits. The flowers are tolerant of some frost and the twigs when crushed smell of aniseed.

M. salicifolia (willow-leaf magnolia) makes an upright small tree which bears pure white flowers in April on the bare branches. The flowers are more tolerant of frost and thus this species is less affected than others. The twigs and leaves smell strongly of lemon-scented verbena when bruised. It is similar to *M. kobus* in flower but differs in the narrower leaves and being less tolerant of chalky soils. 'Jermyns' is a form with larger and more glaucous leaves and larger flowers with broader tepals. It flowers a fortnight or so later than the type and makes a more spreading bush. It is referable to var. *concolor* and was probably introduced by Veitch from Mt Hakkoda in northern Japan.

M. 'Kewensis' is a hybrid between *M. salicifolia* and *M. kobus*. It makes a narrow upright small tree loaded in April with masses of 6cm (2in) very fragrant flowers. It is suitable for chalky sites. 'Wada's Memory' is another form of this cross and equally delectable.

A large number of hybrids of mixed parentage have been raised from crossing between the above species or with other ones. They make excellent small trees or large shrubs. They include 'Heaven Scent' (with large goblet-like white flowers streaked with purple), 'Manchu Fan' (with more purple coloration), 'Peppermint Stick' (similar but more upright in growth habit), and 'Sayanora' (makes a large tree, bearing large white globular flowers). 'Jane' and 'Susan' (fragrant erect red-purple flowers) are more shrubby.

Precocious-flowering magnolias – large trees
These all make excellent large trees, majestic in late winter and early spring when carrying the flowers. They need woodland conditions and are, unfortunately, too large for most gardens. The flowers are hardy in bud but once they have started to open, they are susceptible to damage by spring frost and even in the favourable climate of Cornwall, good effective flowering is by no means an annual event.

M. campbellii (Campbell magnolia) makes a vigorous tree to 20m (66ft) with flowers 20–30cm (8–12in) across. Depending upon season, these are carried from February into April or even May. The bark is smooth and grey, finely roughened like an elephant's hide. The leaves are shiny greyish-green above and emerge with a reddish-purple tinge. In its native range in the eastern Himalayas the trees almost exclusively have white flowers (var. *alba* or 'Alba') but the pink-flowered plant is much commoner in cultivation. Seedlings take around 25 years to begin to flower, although grafted plants will flower in less than half this period. It does not like chalky or limy soils. 'Darjeeling' is a late-flowering selection from Sikkim with dark rose-coloured flowers. 'Ethel Hillier' is a white-flowered form with a pinkish tinge at the base of the tepals. Subspecies *mollicomata* differs in producing flowers on trees only 10 or so years old and in having flowers which are pink to rose-purple, although never with the purity of the best pinks of the type. 'Lanarth' is an outstanding form which has very large water-lily-like flowers which are cyclamen-purple or deep lilac-purple and large rounded leaves. In cold districts, it needs shelter on the wall of a house or in woodland.

The typical form and subspecies *mollicomata* have been crossed to raise a number of good and very vigorous hardy forms which flower at an early age, including 'Charles Raffill' with deep rose flowers which open rose-purple on the outside, paler on the margins and pinkish-purple within, and 'Wakehurst' which has flowers deeper in colour.

Hybrids have also been raised between this species and others in this affinity. 'Princess Margaret' and 'Michael Rosse' are both presumed to be *M. campbellii* crossed with *M. sargentiana* var. *robusta*. They make vigorous trees with large reddish-purple and soft purple flowers respectively.

M. dawsoniana makes a shrubby tree with large leathery leaves and bears attractive pale

rose flowers. It grows well on limestone (see the excellent tree at Bath Botanic Garden) but may be slow to flower.

M. sargentiana grows into a tall tree, magnificent in April or May when loaded with large purplish-pink flowers 20cm (8in) across. Var. *robusta* is an excellent shrubby tree which has clearer pink flowers, narrow leaves.

M. sprengeri occurs in cultivation in two forms. Var. *elongata* has pure white flowers with narrow petals. It makes an attractive hardy small tree but scarcely earth shattering in its beauty. Var. *diva*, however, has spectacular rosy-pink flowers, as well exhibited by the large tree near the entrance to Westonbirt arboretum. It is worth growing in any woodland garden and flowers in April, later than most forms of *M. campbellii*.

M. x veitchii is a hybrid between *M. campbellii* and *M. denudata* and the best form is 'Peter Veitch'. This makes a strong-growing tree with blush-pink flowers on the branches

Magnolia sprengeri var diva, bearing its large flowers before the leaves in April

in April. In most seasons it is glorious, although occasionally the new foliage may emerge with the flowers and detract from the display.

M. wilsonii and allies This group of four species contains probably the most exquisite of all magnolias. The flowers are carried with the mature new foliage in late May or June or intermittently until August and therefore are not likely to be damaged by spring frosts. They are creamy white and cup-shaped with a prominent boss of rich red, crimson or purple stamens. Unlike all other species, they are held hanging down (except in *M. sieboldii* where they face outwards), not carried above the branches. They thus need to be seen from below to be fully enjoyed, preferably at close quarters so that the delightful fragrance can be appreciated. The young flowers are pear-drop shaped, reminiscent of a spinning top or the weight on a plumbline. The fruits ripen in September and are pink or pinkish green. The carpels soon open to reveal the pairs of scarlet-coated seeds which are displayed hanging from silken threads.

M. wilsonii is the first to flower in May and June, bearing flowers 7–10cm (3–4in) across. It makes a large shrub or small tree to 8m (26ft) with erect and then arching branches. It will thrive on chalky and other soils.

M. sinensis flowers in June, producing 10–12cm (4–5in) diameter blooms with a scent of lemons. It has a spreading habit, more so than in *M. wilsonii*, with which it tolerates chalk soils.

M. sieboldii is unique in the flowers not being pendulous but held facing outwards; they therefore 'look you in the face' – better marks for presentation but without the pear-drop poise of the other species. They are not produced in a short flush but intermittently from May till August. It makes a spreading shrub, ultimately a small tree to 6m (20ft).

M. globosa has flowers which are globose and leaves, buds and shoots which are covered with rusty or tawny down when young. It flowers in June and makes a large shrub.

Large-leafed and summer-flowering magnolias

The following species produce their flowers at the ends of leafy branches during the summer. In some, they are rather lost amongst the foliage when seen from below, but this hardly matters as the foliage itself is large and bold, creating an impact in its own right. Several also have attractive fruits.

M. officinalis has leaves which are 30–50cm (1ft–1ft 8in) long and a third as wide and slightly glaucous beneath. The flowers are produced in early summer. They are yellowish-white with maroon stamens, strongly (and nicely) scented of certain proprietary antiseptic creams and 15–20cm (6–8in) across. The fruits are thick cylinders or egg-shaped, 10–12cm (4–5in) long by 6cm (2in) wide. Var. *biloba* is very similar, with the added characteristic that the leaves are deeply notched at the apex.

M. hypoleuca is very similar, differing in the slightly smaller leaves to 45cm (18in) which are wider, to half the length, and the larger brilliant red fruits which may be 20cm (8in) long.

M. macrophylla (big leaf magnolia) has the largest leaves of all. They are usually 37–62cm (15–25in) long by 18–30cm (7–12in) wide but can be up to 90cm (3ft) long. They are oblong ovoid, broadly heart-shaped at the base, bright green above and silvery grey with soft down beneath. The flowers are not exactly small, being 20–25cm (8–10in), up to 35cm (14in) in diameter, fragrant and are carried in early summer. This makes a magnificent foliage tree but should be planted in a sheltered position as the leaves are fragile and can be torn to shreds by strong winds and the new growths can be damaged by frosts.

M. acuminata (cucumber tree) makes a vigorous conic tree capable of attaining 15–20m (50–70ft) tall. The leaves are elliptic, to 23cm (9in) long and yellowish-green. The flowers are carried in June and are dull greenish-yellow and metallic blue, curious rather than flamboyant. They are followed by the immature fruits which are like small shocking red cucumbers and show up well against the foliage. The tree also develops an interesting grey or brown bark which fissures into short flaking ridges.

M. cordata is closely allied to cucumber tree but is smaller-growing with smaller leaves and has flowers which are a soft canary yellow. Occasionally it carries an autumn flush.

M. delavayi has one of the largest leaves of any hardy evergreen tree. They are sea green or bluish green and may be 35cm (14in) long. The highly fragrant flowers last for only a single day but an effective display is created as they are carried in succession from mid summer into September and may be 20cm

(8in) across. It makes a large shrub or small tree. Unfortunately, it is not reliably hardy and, apart from the mild western parts of the country, it needs the shelter of a wall. Even in Cornwall it is periodically cut back by hard winters but usually regrows. It is not fussy about soils and will thrive on chalky or limy ones.

M. grandiflora (bull bay or evergreen magnolia) is usually grown as a wall shrub, but in most of southern England is sufficiently hardy to stand as a free-growing tree with some shelter. The enormous flowers are up to 25cm (10in) across and have a spicy fragrance. They terminate the shoots and are produced in a succession from July until stopped by frosts in October or November. The leaves are glossy, yellowish-green and evergreen; they are clothed with rusty hairs on the lower surface. It will grow on all soils, including chalky ones. 'Exmouth' is an erect-growing selection with narrow leaves which flowers when young. 'Goliath' has flowers which may be 30cm (1ft) across when fully expanded and is probably the best form of the species.

M. virginiana (sweet bay) is a charming but surprisingly neglected species. It makes a small tree, unlikely to exceed 8–10m (26–33ft), and may be either deciduous or evergreen. The leaves are glaucous beneath. The flowers are very fragrant and at first creamy white, darkening with age. They are only 5–8cm (2–3in) across but are borne over a long period, from June until September and followed by attractive fruits which may colour a good red. It will thrive on all soils, including wet or rather water-logged sites, and tolerates chalky ones. For optimum development, it needs a sunny sheltered spot which does not dry out in summer.

RHODODENDRONS AND AZALEAS

Rhododendron is one of the greatest of all garden genera with an immense range of attractive plants. These include all the azaleas, a multiplicity of hybrids and named forms as well as several hundred hardy species; of the species alone, perhaps 400 in cultivation, most of them are available from a nursery-man somewhere. The plants range in size from carpeting alpines growing less than 30cm (1ft) tall to large forest trees, making 15m (50ft) in cultivation but up to 30m (100ft) in the wild. Despite, or perhaps because of, this amazing array, most gardeners grow the less desirable hardy hybrids which have floral attraction when in flower but are rather bleak evergreens thereafter.

The most important requirement of rhododendrons is that the soil does not contain more than a small quantity of free calcium ions. Rhododendrons need calcium just like other plants but where calcium is freely available it prevents them absorbing iron and other nutrients and poisons them. So if your soil is calcium-rich, such as those derived from chalk, most limestones and some clays in chalky or limestone areas, you are left with two options: either forget about growing rhododendrons and concentrate on other plants, or move. It is possible to ameliorate the soil so that you can grow them for a period or in large tubs, but the effect is far less satisfactory than can be gained from the same effort put into garden plants appropriate to your soil. Altering the soil to make it more acidic only really becomes realistic when it has a pH close to neutral.

In other respects rhododendrons are undemanding. They do not like very dry, heavy clay or waterlogged soils, although *Rh. thomsonii* grows in running water in Bhutan! If your soil is in these categories, it is possible to improve it by adding organic matter and draining away surplus water. Rhododendrons do not associate well with plants which dry out the soil and respond by becoming thin and lacking vigour. Grass is the worst offender and should be killed beneath the plants' rootspread but other greedy plants such as birches and larch can also be deleterious. Many of the early-flowering sorts need protecting from spring frosts, as does the new foliage of others whilst some plants also grow late into the autumn and can be damaged by early autumn frosts. These and others will thrive and flower better when grown under dappled shade, such as provided by oak trees. Finally, more than most plants, they do not like being buried. The depth of planting should be no deeper than the nursery soil level and the roots should then be covered by a generous mulch of organic matter.

Rhododendrons do not demand much cultural attention. The very floriferous ones benefit from the removal of the dead flowers (deadheading) so that the plant does not put energy into making unwanted seeds. All species grow better if they are given an annual mulch but will survive without it if given adequate water during the summer. Watering in early summer on dry sites is important but overwatering in late summer and early autumn should be avoided as this prevents flower set and may make the plant grow into the autumn with an increased risk of frost damage. Overgrown plants can be cut back and most will freely regrow from the base, although some of the larger-growing ones and those with smooth flaking barks may not. They benefit from a light application of fertiliser in the spring but not later in the year than June or early July. The nitrogen element should either be ammonium based or from an organic material, eg, hoof and horn.

Most rhododendrons are selected and planted on the basis of flowering time and flower colour. This is the wrong emphasis as flowers, even in the most abundant species with perfect trusses, are but a transient feature, rarely lasting much more than a fortnight or three weeks, and in the early flowering plants susceptible to damage by frost, snow or hail. The best use can be made of rhododendrons by considering the permanent features of foliage, bark and habit first and the flowers as a secondary bonus.

With such a bountiful group of plants it is impossible to give more than a brief outline of some of the range available. The approach used here is to discuss the species and primary hybrids under the headings of foliage, bark and habit, with reference being made to the flowers and flowering season and to treat hardy hybrids, azaleas and evergreen azaleas under their own headings.

Rhododendron cinnabarinum concatenans *has brilliantly blue new foliage*

Garden uses

Rhododendrons can be used in a variety of ways. The winter-flowering ones should be used to give that hint of spring but need positioning so that the flowers are protected from the early morning sun. The hardy hybrids will tolerate full sun and can be placed almost anywhere in the garden, forming evergreen flowering shrubs and sprawling trees. Many of the dwarf lepidote species and hybrids will also take some sun, including full sun if the soil is moist, and these can be very effective on a peat garden or in certain positions in association with heathers or dwarf conifers. The azaleas need either full sun or light shade to give their colourful displays, whilst the evergreen azaleas need some shelter from cold winds and light shade. Most of the species and their hybrids are best where they are protected from the full effects of the sun, at least for three or four hours each day; for these plants, light woodland makes the ideal setting.

Rhododendron species and their hybrids

The species have the benefit of generally more robust constitutions than many of the hybrids whilst making equally good garden plants.

Foliage

As all the rhododendrons in this group are evergreen, foliage is the most prominent aspect of the plant throughout the year. The foliage, however, comes in a range of features. The most striking foliage is exhibited by several of the large-leaved species.

Rh. sinogrande has the largest leaves of all, in young plants in moist western gardens they may be 80cm long, although 25–50cm (10–20in) by 15–30cm (6in–1ft) is more usual. The new growths are silvery and very attractive. It also flowers but only on older plants carrying fleshy creamy white or soft yellow blooms in April. It makes a small tree or large bush and needs a sheltered moist position; if you can give it this it is well worth growing.

Rh. falconeri has rugose leaves to 30cm× 15cm (1ft×6in). Underneath they are covered by a dense coat of hairs which are pale buff coloured in young leaves but darken to rufous brown by the time the leaves are two years old. The flowers in April are in large trusses of creamy white or pale yellow. The bark is red-brown and peeling or flaking. *Rh. arizelum* is similar but with smaller and more strongly coloured leaves and a less attractive bark. *Rh. rex* has longer leaves which are smooth above and have brown or chocolate downy covering. These all make large shrubs or small trees and whilst they are much more vigorous plants with woodland shelter, they will grow and produce good but smaller foliage in exposed positions.

Rh. macabeanum has leaves to 30cm (1ft), thick, leathery and dark glossy green above with white or greyish cream felt on the lower side. The new growths are very fine, silvery white contrasting with the erect red bud scales. It has yellow or yellowish-white flowers in April. It is one of the hardiest of the large-leafed species and makes a plant 3–9m (10–30ft) tall.

Rh. bureavii has leaves which are thickly coated with a bright rusty-red wool on the lower surface and dark green above. They are 7–13cm (3–5in) long and it makes a shrub 2m (6ft) tall. The flowers are white or rose but it should be planted purely for the foliage.

Rh. mallotum has leaves 8–17cm (3–7in) long and half as wide. They are dull dark green and wrinkled above but covered with a soft brownish-red woolly covering beneath. The flowers are carried in rounded trusses in March and April and are rosy-scarlet or deep crimson.

Rh. campanulatum subspecies *aeruginosum* has new foliage which is a rich verdigris-blue above, maturing to mid green. The underside is covered with cinnamon-brown felt. It makes a low shrub and the older stems have a peeling bark, brown with a coppery tinge.

Rh. cinnabarinum has beautiful glaucous blue new foliage for the summer months. The flowers in April to June are tubular-campanulate with an interesting waxy texture. The colour ranges from orange and apricot to cinnarbar-red and occasionally other colours. *Concatenens* is a particularly good form with very glaucous foliage and orange flowers. *Rh.* 'Lady Chamberlain' and 'Lady Roseberry' are two choice hybrids.

Rh. lepidostylum has glaucous blue foliage, particularly when new and during the first winter. It makes a dwarf rounded shrub to 1m. The flowers are pale yellow or greenish-yellow and carried in June.

Rh. leucapsis has foliage bristly and lustrous green above and glaucous bright blue beneath. The flowers, which open widely, are large, pure white with chocolate-coloured stamens, and are carried in February and March. It makes a small shrub 60–90cm (2–3ft) tall and needs a sheltered position if the flowers are to be enjoyed.

Rh. thomsonii has 5–10cm (2–4in) leaves which are roundish oval in outline and metallic blue when young. They become dark, slightly shiny green above and strongly bluish-white or glaucous green beneath. The bark is smooth and peeling, revealing a rich mixture of colours. In April and May it carries large fleshy blood-red or maroon flowers. It makes an excellent shrub, growing from 60cm–6m (2ft–20ft) tall. *Rh. wardii* has good yellow flowers in May or June but lacks the attractive bark.

Rh. calophytum has long rather narrow leaves which are medium green and 20–30cm (8–12in) long. The flowers are white to rose pink, carried early in the year in March or April. It makes a small tree from 5–10m (16–33ft) tall, distinctive in the very bold leaves in clusters at the tips of the shoots. It prefers a sheltered position but will grow reasonably in full sun.

Rh. argyrophyllum subspecies *nankingense* has leaves which are silvery beneath and a rich shiny green above and puckered with impressed veins. The best form is the attractive 'Chinese Silver' in which the new growths are silver and the flowers in May are a lovely clear pink.

Bark

Rh. barbatum has a bark which peels in thin sheets; the underbark is smooth and blue-grey whilst the peeling strips are plum coloured or deep purple. The bark is exhibited on branches a few summers old, so although this makes a large shrub or small tree 2–9m (6–30ft) tall, the effect is apparent even on fairly young plants. The flowers are bright scarlet to crimson scarlet and carried sometime from February to April, depending upon season. *Rh. argipeplum* (*R. smithii*) is similar in the bark with rose to deep scarlet flowers, broader leaves and coppery-plum coloured new growths.

Rh. hodgsonii has a bark which peels in sheets which are pink to cinnamon and reveal cream or mauvish green beneath. The leaves are large, 20–35cm (8–14in) long. Young foliage has an evanescent indumentum. The flowers are something of a letdown for such a fine bark and foliage plant but it can always be deadheaded before they open to their purplish-pink or magenta colours! It makes a tough large shrub or small tree.

Rh. triflorum has a peeling mahogany-red bark which looks very attractive with the sun shining through the bark flakes. It makes an upright shrub 2–3m (6–10ft) and has yellow flowers in May. The foliage is aromatic, with the pleasant scent of some floor polishes. *Rh. ambiguum* has leaves more strongly glaucous beneath and larger yellow flowers but lacks the beautiful bark. *Rh. lutescens* also lacks the attractive bark but has primrose-yellow flowers and bronzy-red new growths.

Habit

This section is used to 'correct' the imbalance above towards the taller growing species.

Rh. yakushimanum has been described as the most perfect rhododendron. It makes a rounded domed plant, slowly growing to 1.5–2m (5–6ft). The flowers are apple-blossom in bud, opening to pure white. The leaves are dark green above, convex and thickly covered with brown wool beneath. *Rh. yakushimanum* has been used in a

number of new crosses, collectively known as Yak hybrids.

Rh. williamsianum makes a spreading plant to 1m tall and 2–3m (6–10ft) across. The flowers are a good rosy red in April; leaves are heart-shaped and glaucous, to 5cm (2in).

Rh. forrestii makes a very prostrate plant with disproportionately large deep crimson flowers in April. Better flowering plants are its hybrids 'Elizabeth', 'Elizabeth Hobbie' and 'Scarlet Wonder', growing taller, up to 1m (3ft) or so.

Rh. racemosum makes a dwarf to medium shrub with masses of small pink flowers from most of the buds at the ends of the previous season's shoots. It flowers in March or April.

Rh. hanceanum 'Nanum' makes a hummock-forming shrub with creamy white or pale yellow flowers and bronze-coloured new growths.

Rh. fastigiatum is a dwarf compact shrub to 1m (3ft). It carries masses of purple or blue-purple flowers in April or May.

Rh. pemakoense makes a suckering shrub to 50cm (1ft 8in). The flowers are purplish-pink and 6cm (2in) across. It flowers profusely in March or April but needs protecting from frosts.

Rh. 'Bluebird' has a low, spreading habit and masses of rich violet-blue flowers in April. It is a hybrid of *Rh. augustinii*. Other similar hybrids are 'Blue Diamond' and 'Bluetit'.

Rh. 'Bowbells' forms a low, spreading plant richly covered with bright pink flowers in May and later with bronze new foliage.

Rh. 'Cowslip' is a compact and fairly dwarf plant which bears cup-shaped 7cm (3in) flowers in April or early May. They are pink in bud, opening to ivory white with a pinkish tinge.

Rh. 'Curlew' has a dwarf suckering habit to 30cm (1ft) tall and carries large pale yellow flowers in May.

Rh. 'Ptarmigan' has masses of white flowers in April and makes a dwarf spreading shrub.

Rhododendron *'Elizabeth Hobbie' – a first class dwarf*

Fragrance

Rh. decorum has large white or pale rose and fragrant flowers in late April to July. The leaves are medium green above and glaucous beneath. It slowly makes a large shrub and is more tolerant of lime in the soil than most species.

Closely related or possibly only a form of *Rh. decorum* is *Rh. serotinum*. This is a very late-flowering plant, blooming sometime during the period August to October. The scented flowers are white, flushed pink, with pink spots and a basal zone of yellow. It forms a medium to large shrub.

Rh. fortunei is similar to *Rh. decorum* but with lilac-pink flowers in May. *Rh. griffithianum* has fragrant white flowers also in May but with larger leaves and a peeling bark. It is only hardy in mild areas but has been crossed with *Rh. fortunei* to produce the Loderi group of hybrids. These make magnificent large shrubs or small trees for woodland conditions. The flowers vary in the different forms from pale pink to white but all in this group are April to May flowering and fragrant.

Rh. auriculatum has richly scented white flowers in July or August. The leaves are 10–32cm (4–13in) long and have ear-like lobes, at the base and need protecting from strong winds. It makes a large shrub or small tree. A hybrid of this species is *Rh.* 'Polar Bear'. This has trusses of 8–10cm (3–4in) fragrant pure white flowers, in late July, which individually may be 11cm across at the mouth. It is hardy but needs siting in open woodland. The leaves are light green and up to 30cm (1ft) long.

Rh. maddenii subspecies *crassum* has fragrant creamy-white or rosy-white flowers in June. It makes a small to medium shrub which should be planted in open woodland conditions.

Rh. ciliatum has a peeling bark and carries fragrant lilac-rose flowers in March or April. The leaves are bristly around the margins and it makes a shrub to 1m (3ft). It needs careful siting to protect it from spring frosts.

Early flowering rhododendrons

With emphasis on the 'all year round' characters, some of the plants, whose value is not that they have the best bark or flowers but simply that they flower in midwinter, have been missed and are discussed here.

Rh. dauricum flowers during January and February when it carries rosy-purple blooms. It needs some protection and makes a deciduous or semi-evergreen bush to 1.8m (6ft). Although compared to many later-flowering species the display is modest, it is very valuable for coming in midwinter and a plant or a small group is worth planting where they can be enjoyed at this season. *Rh. mucronulatum* is very similar but has larger leaves and flowers. It may open the blooms from late December until early spring, depending upon season and in a series of flushes.

Rh. 'Praecox' has flowers of a good rosy-purple and blooms during February or March. It makes a compact evergreen bush to 1.5m (5ft). The flowers are damaged by frost, so it needs siting away from frost-pockets or the early morning sun.

Rh. moupinense makes a shrub to 0.6–1.2m (2–4ft) high with a low rounded habit. The pink or white flowers are large and produced in February or March but need protecting from frost. It has an attractive flaking stem.

Hardy hybrids

These are a group of very tough old hybrids of mixed parentage which includes the common rhododendron, *Rh. ponticum*, and its allies. They will grow in full sun and on rather drier or less acidic soils than the species and their hybrids discussed above. They can be very useful for providing a bright splash of colour but are rather graceless after flowering is over for the year.

'Blue Peter' has in late May cobalt-violet flowers which fade to white at the centre.

'Britannia' has soft pinkish-scarlet flowers in late May or early June and leaves larger than average, to 22cm (9in) long.

'Cunningham's White' flowers open light

mauve in early May but soon fade to white with yellow speckles. It is more compact than other varieties.

'Cynthia' has deep rose-pink flowers in large trusses in May.

'Doncaster' has dark green leaves with a wrinkled margin. The flowers are dark red with a flare of black spots and carried in late May or early June. It has a bushy habit. 'Hugh Koster' is similar but the flowers are lighter in colour.

'Fastuosum Flore Pleno' has pale bluish-mauve flowers with a greenish or golden-brown flare.

'Gomer Waterer' has the flowers mauve in bud, opening nearly white with a mauvish-pink margin.

'Lady Clematine Mitford' has peach-pink flowers which fade to blush along the centre and makes a large dense shrub. It flowers in early June.

'Mrs G. W. Leak' flowers in mid May and has large light pink flowers which are deeper in colour on the three upper lobes. It has a fairly dense habit and makes a medium-sized erect bush.

'Nobleanum' is an old hybrid of *Rh. arboreum*. It flowers sometime from December to February or March, depending upon the weather and can be very attractive if the flowers are not damaged by frost. It is a slow-growing, erect shrub or tree with rose-coloured flowers.

'Pink Pearl' has flowers a good pink colour in bud and when newly opened, but they fade to a bluish colour and are almost white when they fall. In full sun it remains reasonably compact. 'Prof Hugo de Vries' has deeper flowers in bud which do not fade. Both flower in late May.

'Purple Splendour' has deep purple flowers with black flare markings. The leaves are blackish green. It makes a vigorous medium-size plant of dense growth and flowers in late May or early June.

'Sappho' has flowers mauve in bud but opening white with a heavy purple and black flare. The central lower lobe is often dupli-cated, giving two flares to guide bees. It is inclined to become leggy with time.

Azaleas were at one time put in a separate genus from *Rhododendron*. In horticulture they divide into two groups, the deciduous azaleas and the evergreen azaleas.

Deciduous azaleas add the dimension of autumn colour to their repertoire. Most are complex hybrids and bloom in late May and into June with large, flamboyant and fragrant flowers and need either light woodland or open situations.

Rh. luteum makes a shrub 2–3m (6–10ft) tall. The flowers are very fragrant and yellow. It is a tough plant and naturalised in parts of Britain.

The hybrid selections of this and other species are too numerous to mention more than a range to give an indication of the colour forms: 'Ballerina', white with orange flash; 'Cecile', salmon-pink with yellow flare, deeper in bud; 'Gibraltar', flame orange with yellow flare, deeper in bud; 'Homebush' rosemadder semi-double flowers in rounded trusses; 'Koster's Brilliant Red', glowing orange-red and 'Persil', white with an orange flare.

The following is a selection of azalea species which deserve wider planting, having much charm, and most flower at different times from the commonly cultivated hybrids.

Rh. amagianum makes a desirable large shrub for light woodland conditions. The soft scarlet flowers are carried after the leaves have fully expanded in July.

Rh. atlanticum makes a very hardy stoloni-ferous shrub to 1m (3ft) with fragrant white, flushed-pink, flowers in May. It needs a moist soil and can associate well with low-growing herbaceous plants.

Rh. calendulaceum has flowers of red, orange or yellow but they are scarcely fragrant. It makes a bush 2–3m (6–10ft) tall and flowers in May or early June.

Rh. canadense grows to 1m and carries the bright rose-purple flowers on the bare twigs in April. It is hardy and prefers a moist soil.

Rh. nakaharae is a very dwarf plant, growing no more than 30cm (1ft) high. The flowers are scarlet with a deeper flare and carried in late June or July. It makes a hardy little plant, growing well in full sun.

Rh. pentaphyllum gives good autumn colour and has bright rose-coloured flowers in April or May. It makes a bush 1–2m (3–6ft) tall and the leaves are in clusters of five at the ends of the shoots.

Rh. quinquefolium also has the leaves in whorls of five but has white flowers in April. The foliage is a bright pale green with a purple edge in spring, colouring well in autumn. It makes a low shrub.

Rh. schlippenbachii has new leaves which are suffused with purple and makes a rounded shrub 2–4m (6–13ft) tall. The saucer-shaped flowers are white or soft rose-pink and carried in April or May. It will grow well on drier sites than many other species and does not like strongly acidic soils.

Rh. viscosum is the swamp honeysuckle of the eastern United States. The flowers are viscous and produced in June or July. They are strongly fragrant and white or pink. It makes a bush to 2m (6ft) or so and will thrive on wet soils.

Evergreen azaleas
These are hybrids or forms of several mainly Japanese species and make low-spreading evergreen bushes from 0.6–1.5m (2–5ft) tall. They need some shade and shelter from the worst of winter weather. They flower in April or May and may be trimmed periodically to encourage flowering and prevent them growing too large. The following is a selection:

'Addy Wery', deep vermilion flowers in early May; 'Benigiri', bright crimson; 'Blaauw's Pink', salmon pink with pale shading, flowers early, hose-in-hose, ie with two complete sets of petals one inside the other; 'Bungo-nishiki', orange scarlet, semi-double, late; 'Hatsugiri', free flowering in late April or

A massed planting of Japanese evergreen azaleas

early May with magenta-purple blooms; 'Hinodegiri', bright red flowers contrasting with light glossy green foliage in late April or early May; 'Hinomayo', masses of phlox-pink flowers, dense habit; 'Kirin', silvery pink flowers but slightly tender and often used as a pot plant; 'Kure-no-yuki', very hardy and free-flowering dwarf compact plant with white blooms; 'Naomi' 5cm (2in) salmon-pink flowers in late May or early June; 'Palestrina', erect shrub, covered in May with 5cm (2in) white flowers; 'Vuyk's Rosy Red', deep rosy-red flowers around 7cm (3in) in diameter in late May or early June, compact spreading habit; 'Vuyk's Scarlet', low-growing with carmine red flowers in early May.

ROSES

As noted in the introduction to this chapter, one recent survey of garden plants found that hybrid tea and floribunda roses were grown in 96% of all gardens. This, perhaps, suggests there is not a need for a profile on roses. However, the genus *Rosa* contains far more than just hybrid teas! This profile will concentrate on the species and their hybrids, as well as the modern and old fashioned shrub roses, only mentioning hybrid teas and the like where they relate to these. Firstly, though, a brief review of these two groups may be appropriate.

Hybrid teas and floribunda roses

The characteristic which makes hybrid tea and floribunda roses so universally acclaimed is that they bear a large number of flowers as a series of flushes throughout the summer months. They are also amenable to growing on a wide range of soils and situations and will bloom freely despite a degree of benign neglect. Some have the added attraction of being strongly and pleasantly fragrant. However, it is fair to say that few have any beauty in foliage or fruit and the pruning regimes needed to give the best flowers result in the rose bed resembling a battlefield for all the interest it contains over winter. Also, many of them are susceptible to diseases such as

mildew and blackspot, and insect pests like aphids, requiring constant spraying or the acceptance of a less perfect result; in short, they have been described as a gift to the manufacturers of garden chemicals. The cultivars of hybrid tea and floribunda roses are constantly changing as new cultivars are selected and become the 'in' rose for that year. Of course, a few old favourites, such as 'Queen Elizabeth' and 'Peace' remain from year to year, but a profile of hybrid tea and floribunda roses in a book such as this will quickly become dated and irrelevant. The reader is therefore referred to the catalogues of rose nurseries for a review of what is currently 'in'.

What roses are profiled?

The groups of roses which are profiled are the species and their hybrids, modern shrubs, and some of the old fashioned varieties such as bourbons, and hybrid musks. These are all plants which require little pruning, have reasonable to good foliage, and most provide more than one season of display. They are all vigorous plants, little affected by diseases, such as mildew, and therefore do not need molly-coddling. The fact that largely they only flower once is scarcely to be held against them, after all, what other group of garden plants is required to flower throughout the year?

Garden uses

The roses profiled here range from dwarf shrubs to vigorous climbers. Their roles in gardens vary: they are used as climbing plants (for pergolas, fences and over trees and shrubs), in borders, for hedges, as ground-cover (especially for banks), and as specimen plants. Together they provide flowers from May through to autumn, attractive foliage for as long (a couple are reliably evergreen), fruits for both summer and autumn effect and one or two have unusual barks or other features.

As a group they are very tolerant of soil,

although not all will grow on all soils. There are, for example, species which are especially suitable for sandy barren soils, eg the *R. pimpinellifolia* and *R. rugosa* forms. Most will grow on clay and chalk soils, although waterlogged soils are best avoided or drained.

These roses vary in their pruning requirements. The species and shrub roses require very little. Mostly what is needed is to keep the plants within bounds and perhaps to remove older less vigorous shoots; fortunately the taller-growing climbers get on very well without any attention once they have been induced to grow into the right tree, which is just as well as they can grow 15m (50ft) up it! Some of the old fashioned varieties benefit from the removal of older wood and its replacement with young shoots from the base, but only a few will either tolerate or benefit from heavy pruning as given to their vulgar relatives. There are few horticultural sights more pathetic than to see, as one can occasionally on shrub areas on muncipal estates, attractive specie roses like *R. moyesii* hard pruned near to ground level in spring, thus ensuring copious foliage but no floral or fruiting beauty.

Species roses and their forms and primary hybrids
Early yellow-flowered shrub roses These make shrubs usually 2–3m (6–10ft) tall. The flowers are single and carried in May or early June. Were they never to flower they would still be worth growing for the dense feathery or fern-like foliage of a bright green or grey-green colour.
R. ecae makes a dainty bush 1.2m (4ft) tall with buttercup-yellow flowers. It should be planted in a sunny spot. 'Helen Knight' is often listed as a form of it but may be a hybrid with *R. pimpinellifolia*. It is stronger-growing with larger and faintly fragrant brilliant yellow flowers. *R. primula* is similar to *R. ecae* but the crushed or damp leaves are aromatic and the flowers are primrose-yellow and delicately fragrant.

R. hugonis is a neat shrub to 2–3m (6–10ft) which carries abundant soft yellow flowers on the graceful arching branches. The branches may bear large translucent thorns and the fruits are blackish red. 'Cantabrigiensis' and 'Headleyensis' are two early-summer flowering hybrids with good flowers and foliage.
R. xanthina is normally grown as 'Canary Bird' which makes a marvellous shrub with large 5cm (2in) canary-yellow flowers carried for four weeks or more from late May with an intermittent crop later. 'Golden Chersonese' is its hybrid with *R. ecae* and is spectacular in early summer.
R. sericea and *R. omeiensis* are unique in that the flowers have only four petals, although occasionally flowers with five are found. These two attractive species show considerable variation throughout their range in the Himalayas and China but always have interesting fern-like foliage with 9–13 leaflets. The flowers are pure white or pale yellow and can make an interesting if rather short-lived display in May. They are followed by the shiny bright red or orange heps which colour in July.

R. sericea 'Pteracantha' is the commonest form in cultivation. It is outstanding for the large flattened thorns or spines which give it its name (literally wingthorn). These may be 5cm (2in) long on the most vigorous shoots, although shorter on weaker twigs. They are bright red, crimson or purple depending upon whether seen in transmitted or reflected light. They can be particularly effective when the shrub is located where it can be viewed with the sun behind it. The thorns turn grey-brown in the second season, so for best thorn-effect, the older stems should be removed in early summer; however, the flowers are only carried on the previous year's shoots and most freely on the side branches which grew last year from the strongest shoots; for optimum flower and fruit, therefore, the strong shoots should be kept for three seasons.

Large-fruited roses (R. moyesii and allies)

R. moyesii is the commonest species of this group in gardens and very attractive both in June when carrying the 5cm (2in) single pink or blood-red flowers and in the autumn when ladened with the flagon-shaped heps, which are 4–5cm (1½–2in) long and covered with glandular bristles. The leaves are pale or glaucous green with 7–13 leaflets. It makes a desirable shrub capable of growing 3–4m (10–13ft) tall and as broad. 'Geranium' is a selection for the geranium-red flowers and also with larger smooth fruits. It makes a more compact plant with lighter green foliage.

R. macrophylla has even larger fruits and pink flowers on a large arching shrub to 3–5m (10–16ft). 'Master Hugh' was selected for the fruits which are 5cm (2in) or so long and turn through orange-red to bright red.

R. webbiana is a smaller shrub, no more than 3m (10ft), with pink flowers and shiny red bottle-shaped fruits.

R. davidii is similar to the above species but differs in the flowers and fruits being carried in small flower clusters, whereas in the above species they are borne singly or in pairs.

Three hybrids of *R. moyesii* are: 'Arthur Hillier' which makes a semi-erect large shrub with rose-crimson flowers, 'Highdownensis', which has cerise-crimson flowers over 5cm (2in) across and makes a vigorous shrub, and 'Hillieri' which develops an open, spreading habit and has maroon-red flowers, which are particularly striking when viewed with the sun shining through them.

Roses for sandy soils and ground cover

These species will all grow on 'normal' soils but are especially useful for dry sandy soils. They will also make effective groundcover, smothering weeds through their dense shrubby growth.

R. pimpinellifolia (Scotch or Burnet rose) is a

Rosa pimpinellifolia *growing on pure limestone in the Burren, Western Ireland*

small suckering shrub which in Britain occurs naturally on sand dunes near the sea, limestone heaths and other dry sites. It only grows to a maximum of a metre tall. It produces single white or pale pink flowers in May and these are followed by small dark brown or blackish heps. Var. *altaica* is a taller growing variety, to 2m (6ft). It has larger creamy-white flowers and makes an excellent hedge. 'Double White' is a selection which describes itself, although it will also grow to 2m (6ft). 'Glory of Edzell' is a low shrub with masses of pink flowers with yellow centres. 'Lutea' has buttercup yellow flowers.

R. nitida is a small suckering shrub which has rose-red flowers and shining green leaves which turn purplish red in autumn. *R. virginiana* is similar but has bright pink flowers from June to August and small rounded pink heps. *R. foliolosa* has fragrant and larger flowers, 5–6cm (2–2½in) across, produced from June onwards.

R. rugosa is noted for the glossy rich green leaves, strongly prickly stems and the large white or pink flowers with thin papery petals. The fruits are large and rich red or maroon; the flesh is tasty and rich in vitamin C. The flowers are carried from June onwards and the fruits colour from July till late autumn when the foliage turns yellow. It flowers on the current season's growths, so can be cut back hard unlike almost all other species. It will grow 3m (10ft) tall if left untrimmed but only 2m (6ft) if cut back to ground level in late winter. It is the hedging rose *par excellence*. 'Alba' is the white-flowered form and comes true from seed. 'Blanc Double de Coubert' is a white semi-double form. 'Fru Dagmar Hastrup' has rose-pink flowers and makes a smaller shrub, to 1.2m (4ft). 'Roseraie de l'Hay' has crimson-purple double flowers.

Other shrub roses

These are attractive shrubs, mainly flowering in midsummer and several have fragrant foliage.

R. x alba is the white rose of York and therefore of historical interest. It makes a shrub 2–2.5m (6–8ft) tall and has semi-double white flowers followed by oblong red heps.

R. bracteata is evergreen and will grow to 6m (20ft) against a wall or through a large shrub but is smaller if free-standing. It has large (10cm or 4in) white flowers which are lemon scented and have a boss of golden anthers. The fruits are orange-red, to 3cm (1in).

R. californica is a shrub 2m (6ft) tall with pink flowers. 'Plena' is the common form in cultivation and is very attractive in June/July when ladened with its semi-double flowers.

R. chinensis is of historical interest as the China or monthly roses were used to give recurrent flowering to the modern rose cultivars. 'Mutabilis' has strongly purplish new foliage and makes a small to medium slender shrub. The blooms are orange in bud, opening to buff shaded with carmine, before maturing through rose to crimson; they are also strongly tea-scented. 'Old Blush' has pink flowers produced in monthly flushes through the summer and scented of tea. 'Viridiflora' has double but greenish flowers!

R. damascena is noted for 'Trigintipetala' which is a small shrub with fragrant loosely double flowers of a soft pink colour. It is the rose whose petals are picked to make the perfume Attar of Roses. 'Versicolor' is another semi-double form, with the flowers white but blotched rose.

R. elegantula (*R. farreri*) is cultivated as the clone 'Persetosa'. This makes a rounded bush up to 2m (6ft) tall with fern-like leaves. The flowers are only 2cm (¾in) across, hence the common name threepenny-bit rose, but are very attractive when they are coral-red in bud and open to a warm soft pink. The coral-red fruits are small and accompanied by the autumn purple and crimson of the leaves.

R. eleganteria (*R. rubiginosa*) has pale pink flowers but is grown for the sweet fragrance of the foliage. This is particularly a feature when the air or leaves are damp. It can be hard pruned as a hedge, providing the aromatic leaves.

R. fedtschenkoana is a shrub to 2–2.5m (6–8ft) which has attractive pale glaucous foliage and white flowers which are carried over an extended season from midsummer. The heps are pear-shaped and red, 2cm (¾in).

R. foetida makes a small to medium suckering shrub with fresh green leaves and deep yellow 5–8cm (2–3in) flowers. 'Bicolor' has strikingly coppery-red petals on the inside and yellow on the back. 'Persiana' has double golden-yellow flowers.

R. gallica makes a suckering shrub to a metre tall. The flowers are rosy-pink or crimson and are aromatic, smelling of balsam. 'Officinalis' is the 'Red rose of Lancaster', with semi-double rose-crimson flowers. 'Versicolor' has semi-double flowers which are either white blotched with rose or rose blotched with white.

R. glauca (rubrifolia) has foliage which is glaucous with a coppery or purplish hue. It is very effective as a foliage plant amongst other shrubs, although the flowers are also attractive and clear pink.

R. multibracteata is a shrub capable of growing to 4m (13ft) and making a rounded bush. It has fragrant foliage and carries rose-lilac flowers followed by small globose orange-red heps.

R. roxburghii is quite unusual in the peeling, papery buff-coloured bark and the curious tomato-shaped fruits which are green, fragrant and spiny, hence the common name burr rose. Before the fruits can be formed, the fragrant rose-coloured flowers are carried. It makes a bush to 3m (10ft) and with time can develop a stout stem, almost a trunk.

R. soulieana has grey-green foliage on a dense rounded bush 3m (10ft) tall. The flowers in July are yellow in bud and open creamy white with golden-orange stamens; they are scented of cloves.

R. willmottiae has feathery leaves which are fragrant when bruised. It makes a rounded bush 1.5–3m (5–10ft) and has lilac-pink flowers followed by bright orange-red rounded fruits.

FIG 103 *Flowers of* Rosa filipes *'Toby Tristram'*

Tree-growing roses

The logical name for these would be climbers but this name would be confusing as it is used for taller-growing large-flowered derivatives of hybrid teas and floribunda roses whereas the plants discussed here are much healthier and more vigorous. They are capable of growing high into trees or over shrubs, less promising if kept restrained on a pergola or a fence.

R. filipes makes a most majestic climber, particularly in the form 'Kiftsgate' which is capable of reaching 15m (50ft). 'Toby Tristram' is smaller growing and more easily treated as a large shrub but will climb through trees. This species and its forms have the flowers carried on short lateral shoots in large clusters of 50–100 or more flowers. They are pinkish in bud, opening white, 4cm (1½in) in diameter and very fragrant. It creates a very strong impression in late June and July and again in autumn when the

masses of small heps ripen through orange to crimson scarlet. Young plants are slow to get going unless planted to full sun.

R. longicuspis makes a strong climber, growing 8m (26ft) or more into trees. It has very fragrant flowers in late June and early July. These are 5cm (2in) across with pure white petals and with a yolk-coloured boss of stamens. They are carried in clusters of 8–15 flowers. The leaves are glossy bright green, darkening with age but remaining shiny and are evergreen. It will quickly grow up through an old apple tree or over similar support and is more shade tolerant than *R. filipes*. It can be used very effectively to make an evergreen screen by growing it through deciduous trees and has the advantage over conifers in this situation in the fragrant massed flowers and orange-coloured fruits which remain on the tree over winter.

R. banksiae makes a strong growing climber in warm and sunny climes. In Britain, it needs the shelter of a sunny wall to flourish. The flowers are carried in large clusters and the leaves persist green into winter. The hardiest form is 'Lutea' which has double yellow and slightly fragrant flowers. 'Lutescens' has single yellow and more strongly-scented flowers. Var. *normalis* is the wild form and has very fragrant single creamy-white flowers.

R. brunonii is a rampant climbing species from the Himalayas. The pure white and very fragrant flowers are carried in large clusters above the foliage in June and are each 3–4cm (1–1½in) in size. 'La Mortola' is a good form of this species but not absolutely hardy. Recently seed has been introduced from Nepal and Bhutan by several collectors and these may give equally good but more reliably hardy forms of this species.

R. helenae is June-flowering and has fragrant creamy-white flowers in dense clusters and orange-red or scarlet fruits.

R. laevigata is evergreen but needs a warm

Rosa 'Scarlet Fire', a majestic modern shrub rose

sunny position to flourish and is best treated as a wall shrub. It has 10cm very fragrant pure white single flowers in late May or June.

R. 'Mermaid' is the result of crossing a Hybrid Tea rose and *R. bracteata*. It needs a sheltered position such as a sunny wall. The 10cm (4in) single yellow flowers are carried in succession from midsummer until the autumn and set off by the glossy foliage.

R. 'Wedding Day' is a strong-growing climbing cultivar capable of making 10m (33ft). It has rich lustrous green leaves and large clusters of very fragrant flowers in midsummer. These are yolk-coloured in bud, opening to creamy white.

Groundcover roses

These roses have low spreading habits and can be used to make groundcover. They are especially useful for covering banks where their long trailing stems can cover large areas, particularly if planted at the top. Initially the ground needs to be weedfree but once established they can effectively control weeds. Several other roses can be used for groundcover, such as the suckering species discussed above. The roses discussed here can be trained up pergolas or into trees and several were originally developed as rambler roses.

R. wichuriana makes a prostrate spreading shrub. The unbranched shoots snake across the ground, growing 2–4m (6–13ft) in a season. They branch in the second year and it is at this time that they start to smother weeds. The leaves are evergreen in mild districts. Flowers are carried on the lateral shoots from July into September and are pure white and 5cm (2in) across.

R. 'Max Graf' is a hybrid of *R. wichuriana* with *R. rugosa* and like the parents will control weeds once established. It makes a mound of spreading prickly stems growing to 1m (3ft) high. It has large clusters of small and fragrant pink flowers in midsummer. 'Red Max Graf' is a red-flowered sport (see p211).

The following four roses are ramblers which if unsupported will grow to make effective groundcover. 'Rosy Cushions' has

pink flowers with an ivory centre. 'Ferdy' has blooms salmon to fuchsia pink and is vigorous. In 'Swaney' the flowers are white and double whereas in 'Fiona' they are bright red and carried over a protracted period.

Modern shrub roses

These are colourful large shrubs. They can look very good in borders but do suffer from the problem of all prickly plants in such situations, such as access for maintenance; not that they particularly need maintaining, as they are a healthy bunch needing little formative pruning, but there is always the odd and very obvious weed which escapes all control measures as a small plant. Shrub roses make very good informal hedges but they are at their best when used, along with many specie roses, as specimen shrubs in grass areas or at focal points in the garden.

R. 'Fruhlingsgold' has semi-double flowers which are butter yellow when new and fade to creamy white. It makes an excellent plant to 2m (6ft) and carries the very fragrant flowers in early summer, with an occasional bloom later.

R. 'Fruhlingsmorgen' has a rather straggly habit but the strongly scented rose-pink flowers with a creamy centre and maroon stamens, followed by maroon heps, all set against the leaden green leaves make it an attractive garden plant. It flowers in May–June and September.

R. 'Nevada' makes a very attractive mound of light green foliage growing 2–2.5m (6–8ft) high and across. The flowers are semi-double, 7–10cm (3–4in) across, creamy white and carried in profusion along the branches in May–June with a smattering of blooms throughout the summer. 'Marguerite Hilling' is a sport of 'Nevada' with deep flesh-pink single and more fully recurrent flowers.

R. 'Scarlet Fire' has large single flowers 7–10cm (3–4in) across, carried in small clusters over several weeks in June and July. They have blazing scarlet petals with a velvety look, and yellow stamens. The heps ripen late, after other roses are leafless and turn bright red, lasting into late winter. It makes an effective shrub but can be trained against a wall.

R. 'Golden Wings' makes an upright bush to 2m (6ft) which has recurrent crops of 10cm (4in) clear yellow and strongly fragrant blooms.

R. 'Cerise Bouquet' has brilliant cerise-crimson double flowers set against a back-cloth of dull green leaves. It will make a large spreading bush, 4m (13ft) high and wider.

Bourbon roses

The Bourbon roses are a group developed in the nineteenth century. They make strong-growing shrubs with smooth pointed foliage and globular blooms. Several are recurrent flowerers, producing a succession of blooms. The old weak shoots should be culled in late winter.

R. 'Boule de Neige' has leathery leaves and pink flower buds which open to give pure white double flowers which are very fragrant and recurrent. It needs a good soil.

R. 'Honorine de Brabant' has sweetly scented pale pink flowers which are spotted or dashed with violet or purple. They are carried from midsummer on.

R. 'Madame Isaac Pereire' makes a large free-growing bush. The flowers are rose-carmine and richly scented. They are fully double and large.

R. 'Souvenir de la Maimaison' has produced a climbing sport which will reach 3m (10ft). The flowers are a soft creamy or blush-pink and carried in two flushes in midsummer and autumn.

R. 'Zepherine Drouhin' has thornless stems and coppery new foliage. It has cerise-pink, fragrant and semi-double flowers which are carried continuously from midsummer on into autumn. It can be trained as a shrub but is naturally a climber to 3m (10ft).

Old fashioned roses

These were the 'in' roses of yesteryear and have a certain charm of their own. They flower in June and July, when they are deliciously scented.

R. 'Belle de Crecy' makes a lax-growing bush to 1m (3ft). The flowers are carried erect, very double; they open cerise-pink, fading through soft violet to lavender-grey.

R. 'Blanche Moreau' makes an arching bush with sweetly scented small pure white flowers which are carried in midsummer and in a later flush.

R. 'Cardinal de Richlieu' has deep crimson, fading to maroon purple, flowers which are velvety in texture.

R. 'Comte de Chambord' has flat, fragrant clear pink flowers with a hint of lilac carried throughout the summer and autumn and set on a backdrop of light green foliage.

R. 'Fatin-Latour' has very double flowers which are pale pink. It makes a vigorous branching bush to 2m (6ft).

R. 'Henri Martin' has pure carmine flowers and mid-green leaves; it makes a shapely bush to 1.5m (4ft).

R. 'Koenigin von Danemark' has dark blue-green leaves which serve as a foil for the carmine flowers whose petals are edged pink.

R. 'Madame Hardy' has blooms which open creamy white, soon becoming pure white.

R. 'Maiden's Blush' has sweetly scented blush-pink flowers in dense clusters. The foliage is grey-green and it has very sweetly scented flowers.

R. 'Tour de Malakoff' is perhaps ungainly when grown as a shrub but makes a suitable climber to 3m (10ft) with the large blooms nodding down. The petals have an unusual mixture of tints, including magenta, violet, purple and carmine.

Hybrid musk roses

These make shrubs 1–2m (3–6ft) tall and have fragrant flowers carried in clusters from June into late autumn. Those formed in autumn on the strong growths of the current season contain many more flowers than the early clusters.

R. 'Buff Beauty' has apricot-yellow flowers scented of tea. The new foliage is coppery. It can be trained to climb into trees or over hedges and fences.

R. 'Cornelia' has a strong scent and lustrous dark green leaves. The flowers are coppery-pink with a hint of apricot.

R. 'Felicia' makes a well-rounded bush and is excellent for a hedge. The flowers are salmon or apricot pink, fading to silver pink.

R. 'Moonlight' makes a good climbing rose although it can be treated as a shrub. The milky-white flowers are rather small but carried in large clusters, especially in autumn, and set against the dark green foliage.

R. 'Penelope' makes a sturdy bush or hedge with broad dark glossy green leaves. The flowers are salmon-orange in bud, opening to creamy pink.

SALIX (WILLOW)

The willows are an extremely numerous and diverse genus, ranging from small creeping alpines to large stately trees. Surprisingly, in our gardens they are strangely under-used, with the exception of the large weeping willow which perhaps is to some the only known willow. It may well be that the success of the characteristically weeping habit of *Salix* 'Chrysocoma' (and *S. babylonica*) has in fact overshadowed the other species. It is a large tree and not suitable for the small garden.

Willows will grow in almost any garden soil and most flourish in damp situations. They do not do well on dry soil, particularly if very chalky. They do, however, thrive in ordinary soil providing it is sufficiently deep. They are useful in many difficult situations where the soil is in fact poor, but they are also useful as soil stabilisers, especially species such as *Salix daphnoides* and *S. purpurea*. There is a wide variety of shapes and sizes offered by the willow genus, from the large billowing upright status of the white willow (*Salix alba*), through to bushy species like the hoary willow (*Salix elaeagnos*), and on to the creeping stems of the prostrate *Salix repens* 'Argentea', the latter thriving in rather different situations, liking moist sandy soils by the sea. Many gardens are too small for the

Salix hastata *'Wehrhahnii', with delightful catkins*

362

weeping willow as unfortunately is all too often evident. There are in fact two small weeping willows, or at least shrubs that can be trained on standard stems, and these are much more suitable for all but the largest gardens: *Salix purpurea* 'Pendula' has long purplish shoots on which it carries leaves, glossy green above, vividly blue-white beneath; it grows in a weeping mound to 5m (16ft) in height. It has a dense head of stiffly pendulous branches and is most attractive with the bright yellow catkins in early spring. *S. caprea* 'Kilmarnock' only attains 3m (10ft).

One of the features of the willows, however, is their ability to grow at an alarmingly rapid speed. The contorted willow for example, (*Salix matsudana* 'Tortuosa') has been known to attain 17m (56ft) in ten years and this is only a medium-sized tree. The shrubby willows are particularly useful in this respect in attaining rapid, dense growth, ideal for summer screen planting, eg subjects such as *Salix gracilistyla, pentandra* (bay willow), *irrorata* and *humilis* to mention but a few.

They can be very usefully employed as short-term planting when mixed with other plants such as those that last for many years but are slower to get started.

There are larger willows too (like *Salix daphnoides*) which, although forming small tree size very rapidly, then slow down in growth and become much twiggier and do not become over large for the small garden, a very useful and comparatively rare attribute. Some of the large trees are faster growers in Britain, perhaps the fastest of all being *Salix alba* 'Caerulea', the cricket bat willow. Not, in fact, a commonly planted tree except in Suffolk and Essex where it is used for the production of cricket bats.

Willows with coloured stems

Although none of the willows are evergreen, many do provide us with the most beautiful coloured branches during the winter – red, orange, purple, and some with a white bloom reminiscent of the white-washed brambles (*Rubus cockburnianus*). Listed below are the principal stem-coloured species and the colours they produce:

S. acutifolia 'Blue Streak', a large graceful shrub, or often a small tree with polished blackish-purple stems covered with a vivid blue-white bloom.

S. alba 'Chermesina' (scarlet willow) brilliant orange-scarlet branches.

S. alba 'Vitellina' (golden willow), brilliant egg-yolk yellow shoots.

S. 'Basfordiana', a medium to large-sized tree with conspicuous orange-red twigs in winter.

S. daphnoides (violet willow), purplish-violet shoots, with attractive overlay of white bloom.

S. fargesii, polished reddish-brown shoots.

S. irrorata, purple shoots with a white bloom.

S. purpurea (purple osier), purplish shoots.

To encourage the production of the young vigorous shoots that display the most vivid colour, hard pruning each, or alternate years, in March is advantageous. However, even an upright plant, particularly a large mature specimen, such as *S. alba* 'Chermesina' or 'Vitellina', seen at a distance catching the winter sunlight can be a most charming sight.

All the above willows can be most effectively planted in arrangements with other stem-coloured trees and shrubs, such as silver birches, the white stemmed brambles (*Rubus cockburnianus*), stem-coloured dogwoods, snake bark maples and the polished bark cherry species, *Prunus serrula* and *P. maackii*. With these, along with other evergreen planting, it is possible to make a truly effective winter garden.

Catkins

Although willows are not the most ornamental of plants in flower, many do have fine catkins and these are more useful as they generally appear in late winter or early spring before or with the young leaves. Male and female catkins are produced on different plants and may both be attractive. However, the male catkins are generally the more ornamental. Our native goat willow or great sallow, (*Salix caprea*) illustrates well the difference between the two catkins. The male plant produces large yellow catkins known as palm, the female silver catkins are known as pussy willow. Of the various species the most impressive catkins can be seen on the small shrubby willows; *Salix lanata* (the woolly willow) has particularly attractive erect yellowish-grey catkins which look particularly fine with emerging silvery foliage. This plant is a rare native, but extremely useful and as effective as many of our foreign collected garden plants. *Salix hastata* Wehrhahnii, of similar habit, has delightful silvery-grey male catkins that turn yellowish with age. *Salix apoda* is a prostrate shrub ideal for the rock garden or scree, which also has silvery furry male catkins in the early spring before its leaves.

Salix bockii and *pentandra* are the odd ones out in terms of catkins in the willow family. *S. bockii* produces its grey catkins in late summer and autumn, whilst *pentandra* is covered with showy golden catkins set against the bright glossy leaves in June. It will make a tree to 10m (33ft). *Salix melanostachys* is also rather different and truly a most attractive plant. The catkins on this medium-sized shrub appear before the leaves and are a remarkable colour combination, being very dark with blackish scales and brick red anthers opening to yellow.

On *Salix triandra* (almond-leaved willow) the male plants have catkins that are almost mimosa-like and are fragrant.

Willow foliage

The majority of the willows have very pleasant foliage ranging from narrow lanceolate leaves to perhaps the less appeal-ing oval foliage of the common sallow. Perhaps the finest narrow foliage is that of the silver willow (*Salix alba* var *serica*). This is a less vigorous form of white willow to 10–15m (33–50ft) in which the leaves have an intense silver-white hue throughout the season – a great advantage over many other silver foliaged trees, such as the whitebeam which becomes greener as the leaves age. The tree

as a whole as seen from a distance is quite striking.

The shrubby *Salix elaeagnos* has leaves that are particularly narrow, like elongated leaves of a rosemary, and was formerly known as *S. rosmarinifolia*. The leaves are greyish, hoary at first, becoming green on the upper surface and white beneath. This plant is extremely effective in waterside planting schemes as it has a dense shrubby habit and grows rapidly but does not become over large in maturity.

The leaves of the contorted willow (*Salix matsudana* 'Tortuosa') are likewise narrow in shape but very distinctly crisped and curled, with a pale yellow-green colour, particularly in spring. The twisted and contorted branches and twigs gives this plant a unique appearance and, being rather upright in growth, it makes a useful contrasting shape and general effect when planted with horizontally branched subjects such as *Viburnum plicatum* 'Mariesii'. Although making a tree 15–20m (50–66ft) it can be coppiced or hard pruned in similar manner to those grown for winter twig colour.

The bay willow (*Salix pentandra*) has bolder foliage, oblong lanceolate in shape, of a dark glossy green on the upper surface and glaucous beneath; when crushed its leaves are aromatic.

Another very handsome shrubby willow, which also has deep glossy green leaves, is *Salix fargesii*. In this, the leaves are up to 18cm (7in) long, rather wrinkled, with veins that are deeply impressed in the upper surface. In addition to its attractive leaf, the shoots are stout and glabrous, of a polished reddish-brown in their second year. The winter buds are also attractive, being reddish, large and conspicuous. It has a pleasant wide-spreading habit and grows to 3m (10ft) high.

Salix magnifica has the largest and boldest leaves of all. These are 10–20cm (4–8in) long, usually likened to the magnolia foliage, but glaucous beneath and set on a stout purple petiole. It makes a large shrub 3–5m (10–16ft) tall and has purplish young twigs and foliage.

Finally, mention should again be made of *Salix lanata* (woolly willow) which as its English name implies has downy silver-grey leaves. These are of rounded shape and most attractive.

Some willows are particularly susceptible to pests and diseases. With the dwarf and small shrubby species, the foliage is likely to be 'burnt off' in mid-summer in hot dry southern gardens. This can be overcome simply by avoiding dry locations. Willow anthranose and scab may affect some species, weeping willow (*S.* 'Chrysocoma') being particularly susceptible. These diseases are most serious in a very wet spring and cause severe growth reduction of the willow's pendulous branches. Regretfully, there is little one can effectively do in terms of spraying a large tree but await its subsequent natural recovery.

SORBUS (ROWAN AND WHITEBEAM)

Sorbus is a very large genus, renowned for the rowans and whitebeams which make neat and colourful small to medium trees. Although primarily a genus of trees, there are several very useful shrubs, including one suitable for the peat garden, and another which associates well with heathers.

The species can conveniently be divided into the rowans (or mountain ashes) and the whitebeams, although there are a few species intermediate between these groups. The rowans have feathery leaves with many leaflets which in most develop brilliant autumn colours and white, red or amber-coloured berries. They thrive on acidic and neutral sites and will grow on chalk or limestone soils but are less reliable here. They prefer a rich moisture-retentive soil but tolerate poor sands and the like. The white-beams have simple leaves. In most the underside of the leaf blade is covered by a cobweb of fine hairs which give the leaf a

Rich glossy ladder-like foliage and berries of Sorbus scalaris

silver colour. In autumn, they often assume russet colours. The fruits are usually red, or greenish orange. Whitebeams are particularly useful for growing well on alkaline soils, such as over chalk, although they also thrive on acidic sands and normal soils. They are more drought tolerant than the rowans. In both groups, the flowers are in large clusters, usually in May or June, and in the occasional species they are pink, not white. As members of the apple family, they can be affected by the disease Fireblight which may kill or disfigure them. Otherwise they are largely disease-free.

They should be planted either in full sun or partial shade, such as in woodland conditions. They will not tolerate deep shade. The role of the taller sorts is to provide small trees giving the element of scale in the garden setting and also making possible sites for climbing plants such as roses. They are always changing with the seasons, from the new foliage, to the flowers in early summer, the mature foliage, the fruits and the autumn colour giving way to the winter silhouette. In the rowans with white or amber berries, these are often left untouched by the birds until well into the winter, although they and all the other species have berries valuable for the food they provide for birds. The shrubby species can be used in borders but are better placed within a sylvan setting.

They are easy to establish and most are available at sizes up to heavy standard trees 5m (16ft) tall. They are therefore a good choice for the impatient, or where an immediate tree is needed.

ROWANS

Trees with red and vermilion fruits

S. aucuparia (rowan) scarcely needs an introduction. It is a tough small to medium tree capable of growing in cold and exposed districts, yet attractive for the white flowers in May, the bright red berries which ripen around the beginning of August, and a reasonable display of autumn colour. Unfor-tunately, the birds often seem to discover the berries around the second week of August and in some years none last into September. 'Fructu Luteo' ('Xanthocarpa') has yellow fruits and these last much longer than the red-fruited berries; this therefore gives a better and more reliable fruit display. 'Asplenifolia' has the leaves fern-like and deeply cut and makes a good garden tree. 'Beissneri' has similar leaves but with a red stalk and turning a good yellow in autumn. The main feature is the coppery-brown bark which appears redder when wetted by rain. It is an interesting form, although the crown is rather open and too narrowly upright. 'Edulis' has larger berries and can be used to make jams and jellies. 'Fastigiata' has a narrow upright habit with rigid branches and dark dull green leaves which in autumn offset the large clusters of red berries.

S. commixta makes a narrow-crowned tree which assumes brilliant autumn colour, ranging from deep purple through to scarlet. The berries are bright red or vermilion. 'Embley' is an excellent selection of this species and has steeply ascending branches forming a narrow upright crown. The colour is scarlet then deep red in autumn.

S. esserteauana makes a small upright tree with several seasons of attraction. The new foliage is beautifully coloured pink and purple with impressed veins for a few days in spring. The summer foliage is a rich deep green, which acts as a fitting background for the big clusters of large white flowers in May or early June and the bright red berries in October; they turn red in autumn. 'Flava' has lemon-yellow berries which are less readily devoured by birds, therefore last longer.

S. sargentiana develops a rounded crown with rigid branches and large red rounded buds which are sticky like those of horse chestnut. The leaves are large and have large leaflets; they are rich green until turning brilliant red in autumn. The small scarlet berries are in enormous rounded clusters.

S. scalaris is an exquisite species. The new foliage is attractively coloured as it opens.

The leaves are frondlike with many glossy medium-sized leaflets closely set like the rungs of a ladder. These act as a foil for the white or creamy flowers and the bright red berries which are in clusters of up to 200. Finally, the leaves turn orange-yellow and scarlet in autumn. It grows to a small tree with a spreading and arching habit (see p151). *S. domestica* differs from the above rowans in having large edible fruits coloured green with a red flush. The bark is scaly and it makes a medium to large tree.

Trees with white, pink or amber fruits
S. hupehensis is an upright-growing small tree with sea-green kite-shaped leaves and berries which are small and pink. It is usually offered as var. *obtusa* or *S. oligodonta*. The tree often sold as *S. hupehensis* is *S. glabrescens* which has glistening white fruits on red stalks and parallel-sided leaves (see p54). A similar species is *S. forrestii* which has larger fruits, more than 8.5mm (⅓in) in diameter and makes a smaller tree, often only a large shrub. All three are excellent trees and colour well in late autumn, often not until early November. The berries colour in late October persisting well into the winter.
S. cashmiriana makes a large shrub or a small tree to 6m with a spreading habit. The flowers are pale pink, unusual in cultivated rowans but apparently frequent amongst the many shrubby species awaiting introduction from western Himalaya. The fruits are glistening white and 1–1.5cm (⅓–½in) in diameter. They persist long into the winter, hanging like marbles from the branches which are bent down under their weight. *S.* 'Harry Smith 12799' has smaller but purer white fruits and makes a shrub to 3m (10ft).
S. rehderiana is the species to which two good cultivars with feathery leaves belong. 'Joseph Rock' has a compact upright habit and berries which are creamy white, maturing to amber. They look very effective against the fiery autumn colours, red, orange, copper and purple, but last for several weeks after the leaves have fallen. 'Pearly King' has

similar foliage and autumn colour but berries which are rose pink, fading to white with a pink flush. It develops a rounded spreading habit and is similar to *S. vilmorinii* but a more robust plant.

Seedlings or hybrids of 'Joseph Rock' making erect-crowned small trees include 'Ethel's Gold' and 'Sunshine', both with golden-coloured fruits and 'Tundra' whose fruits ripen from green to pearly white.
S. vilmorinii only makes a spreading low tree, rarely taller than 6m (20ft). The leaves are fern-like, composed of nineteen to twenty-nine leaflets, and turn deep red in late autumn. The large 1cm (⅓in) juicy berries ripen deep maroon and gradually fade to almost white. It needs a moisture-retentive site really to flourish.
S. foliolosa (formerly called *S. ursina*) makes a small erect branched tree with fifteen to twenty-one leaflets. The fruits are carried in dense bunches which ripen pink then fade to almost white.
S. insignis makes a small to medium tree but needs a sheltered site. The leaves vary, in some forms (named *S. harroviana*) having only five or so very large leaflets individually to 15cm (6in) long. These forms are tender but the plant raised from Kingdon-Ward 7746 is hardy in woodland conditions and has leaves with 15–17 leaflets. The berries are very small, scarcely 5mm (¼in) in diameter but are carried in large clusters. They are late to ripen, turning pink only in the New Year. The buds are large and conspicuous overwinter; during the summer they are hidden in the clasping base of the petiole. 'Ghose' is close to the above, making a larger tree with crimson and glossy red berries. 'Leonard Messel' is a hybrid in this group, making a small upright tree with pink berries.

Shrubs
S. reducta is a suckering shrub to 1m (3ft). It grows well on a moist site sheltered from the midday sun. The leaves have nine to fifteen leaflets and turn bronze and purple in autumn. The flowers are carried in lax

clusters in May and followed by globose pink berries in early autumn. It associates well with heathers and dwarf conifers.

S. poteriifolia is a dwarf suckering shrub best suited to a moist position on the peat garden. It grows no taller than 30cm (1ft) and makes a neat little rowan but is rarely offered.

S. fruticosa is a dwarf shrub growing no more than 1.5m (5ft) tall. It was found by Joseph Rock and introduced under the name *S. koehneana*, which it is not, but as which it is sometimes offered. It makes a very useful shrubby rowan with glistening white berries carried on bushes 60cm (2ft) high. Coming from an arid part of western China, it will tolerate full sunlight on a hot dry site.

WHITEBEAMS

Trees

S. aria is the native whitebeam. It is characteristic of chalk and limestone downs in Britain but also found on sandy areas. The new foliage is vividly silvery due to the covering of hairs on both the upper and lower leaf surfaces, especially in 'Lutescens', and although the upper surface soon becomes glabrous, the hairs on the lower surface remain. It forms a dense-crowned upright tree with large clusters of creamy-white flowers in May, bright red fruits in September and October and russet autumn colour. 'Chrysophylla' has yellow foliage throughout the season, strongest so in spring, and turning butter yellow in autumn. It is an excellent form deserving wider planting.

S. vestita (formerly called *S. cuspidata*) is the Himalayan Whitebeam. It differs from *S. aria* in the longer more pointed leaves which may be 25cm (10in) long. They are dark greyish-green above and silvery beneath. The berries are green and russet and up to 1.5cm (½in) in size. It makes a medium-sized tree, whose foliage turns russet in autumn.

S. thibetica is usually offered as the clone 'John Mitchell' (formerly called 'Mitchellii'). This has very large leaves which are broad

Sorbus 'Leonard Messel' makes a small upright tree with an erect head of branches, its large leaves colouring well in autumn. It is a hybrid of S. insignis

elliptic or nearly rounded, to 12×10cm (5×4in). They are dark subshiny above and vividly silvered beneath. The autumn colour is the usual mixture of russets from this group of species but the leaves of this plant are slow to decompose; if left beneath the tree they can be very attractive in the February sun, when half will show the russet upper surface and the remainder the still silver lower face. The fruits are brown and 2cm (¾in) across. In time it makes a medium to tall tree, growing to 15–20m (50–70ft).

S. wardii has been confused with *S. thibetica* and is offered under this name with the Kingdon-Ward collection number 21127. It makes a narrow upright-growing tree with berries which ripen yellow or orange. The new leaves are silvery, becoming nearly glabrous and shiny medium green. They are strongly ribbed and 10cm (4in) or so in length. It is excellent where a narrow tree is needed, such as to punctuate a view within the garden, or to provide height without too much breadth.

S. megalocarpa is a remarkable whitebeam as unlike all the other species which flower after the leaves in May or June, this carries large clusters of creamy-white flowers on the bare branches or with the just expanding leaves in late March. The flowers are strongly fragrant and will scent the area around a tree but the temptation to cut them and bring them inside should be resisted – the odour is far too strong in a confined space indoors. The leaves are ribbed with 14–20 pairs of veins, dark green and up to 20cm (8in) long; they open bronze-coloured and may turn red in autumn. The fruits have been likened to partridge eggs and are up to 2.5cm (1in). Not quite in the class of the precocious magnolias (although less susceptible to spring frosts), it is an excellent small tree or large shrub for woodland conditions.

S. intermedia (Swedish whitebeam) is a very tough tree, tolerating coastal conditions, barren sites and atmospheric pollution. The leaves are strongly lobed and grey green. It is attractive in flower and when ladened with bright red fruits but as a garden tree is surpassed by other species.

S. alnifolia makes a tree with an upright habit and smooth beech-like bark. The foliage is dense and turns apricot-pink or orange-scarlet in autumn. The pure white flowers are followed by bright red or deep-pink fruits.

S. meliosmifolia makes a small tree or a spreading shrub. The bright green leaves are strongly ribbed with from 18–24 pairs of veins, and turn russet in autumn. The white flowers are hawthorn-scented and carried early, usually in April. They are followed by the bronze or dark green fruits which are covered in prominent pores and have a depression at the apex following the dropping of the calyx.

S. folgneri makes a most attractive small and rather narrow-crowned tree. The tapering leaves are medium green above and very silvery beneath. They are carried on slender shoots and the slightest breeze will display the undersides. In autumn, they turn golden-pink. The branches are slightly pendulous at the tips and the new shoots are covered with silvery-white hairs at first. The berries are usually red but are golden yellow in 'Lemon Drop'.

S. torminalis (Wild Service tree) is a medium-sized native tree which has a dark-brown bark which fissures into scaly plates. The leaves are shiny dark green and distinctly lobed, resembling a maple leaf. They turn crimson or yellow in autumn. The brownish fruits can be eaten after they have been bletted, ie exposed to frost which starts to decay them, but are rather too small. It will grow on most soils, except poor acidic ones but is best on heavy loams or clays.

Shrubs

S. x hostii makes a shrub to 4m (13ft) with a compact habit. The flowers have white petals which have a deep-pink margin giving a pinkish effect overall. The fruits are shiny-red and nearly 1.5cm (½in) across. It has elliptic leaves which are glossy dark green above and grey beneath. It should be given a sunny position and will thrive on most soils.

VIBURNUMS

The viburnums are a large genus consisting entirely of shrubby plants of small to large size, offering a quite remarkable variety of features.

There are flowers of different shapes and sizes, in shades of pink and white, many heavily scented, and the plants may be evergreen or deciduous. Many have fine berries and autumn colour on the deciduous varieties. Perhaps their greatest asset, however, is their tolerance of most growing conditions. They are extremely easy to grow and only unhappy in dry situations or poor soils. However, having said this, many grow well even on chalk, particularly those akin to the native wayfaring tree, *Viburnum lantana*, which grows naturally on the chalk downs in the south of England.

Apart from a very few species such as *Viburnum odoratissimum*, a large shrub coming from North-eastern India and having especially large evergreen leaves, all are extremely hardy, which for a genus containing so many evergreens is another great advantage to the plantsman. Even the severest of winters, which can brown the leaves, rarely does any irreparable damage. Certain species are especially useful in their ability to tolerate shady conditions, the deciduous guelder rose, *Viburnum opulus* and its varieties being particularly suited to wet or boggy conditions. The yellow leaved form Aureum actually requires some shade to avoid burning from the sun. Of the evergreens, *Viburnum davidii*, a low spreading shrub, with its large dark green leathery leaves will make excellent groundcover in the shade. The larger *Viburnum tinus* is also very tolerant of shady places.

Shape and form

In shape and form the viburnums offer mainly rounded shrubs with a few more upright in habit, such as *Viburnum x bodnantense* and its cultivars, 'Dawn' and 'Deben'

whereas *Viburnum plicatum* cultivars (Japanese snowball bush) gives us possibly the most effective horizontally-branched foliage shrubs, particularly the cultivar 'Mariesii'. This plant is a selected form with large lace-cap flowers which, when fully out, gives the effect of a snow-laden bush. It grows best in moist light soils, but this is not essential. It will grow to 3m (10ft) high and almost as much across.

Flower and fragrance

It is perhaps the attractive flowers of viburnum that have made them so popular in gardens. Most of them have white or pale pink flowers, of which some of the prettiest are those pink in bud, opening white. *Viburnum carlesii* 'Diana' being the best variety, having rounded clusters of flowers which are strongly and sweetly scented, very similar in fragrance to that of daphne. The most well-known flowering viburnum is *farreri*, popular for its late autumn pink flowers that continue into the winter; its hybrid *x bodnantense* has largely superseded *farreri*, although its foliage is less attractive. It flowers during March.

Another well-known variety for its pure volume of flowers is the snowball bush (*Viburnum opulus* 'Sterile') which produces large creamy white rounded heads of flower, though less delicate than most.

Some of the viburnums have flowers that at first glance resemble the lace-cap hydrangeas, this is an unusual feature where each head of flowers has two distinct types of flower. The showy parts advertise the flower to pollinating insects, these are the outside flowers which are sterile. The smaller insignificant mass of flowers in the centre are the fertile flowers. The flowers of *Viburnum plicatum*, which are held quite flat on horizontal branches in a double row, give the most pleasing effect and will last in flower for several weeks. In 'Pink Beauty' the white petals become pink with age. Of the lace-cap type all the guelder rose varieties, particularly 'Compactum', 'Notcutt's Variety', 'Xantho-

carpum', are very delicate in flower, but one species distinct from, but related to *Viburnum opulus*, is outstanding, that of *Viburnum sargentii* 'Onondaga', a small to medium-sized shrub, a real aristocrat of a plant, it has large maple-like leaves which in spring are a delightful reddish colour that complement the whitish outer lace-cap flowers and inner pink-budded flowers. It also continues its garden merits by providing fine autumn colour and red berries. It should however, be sited in a sheltered position to avoid leaf damage from early frosts.

Of the evergreens, *Viburnum x burkwoodii* produces a fine display of fragrant pink-budded white flowers from January to May, and develops quickly into a very useful medium-sized shrub.

Berrying species

The viburnum display some of the most spectacular berries of any of the shrubs. Regretfully, however, the majority of the most showy berrying plants will not set fruit unless pollinated by another seedling of a different clone. Usually it is necessary to have a number of such compatible shrubs to ensure

Viburnum carlesii 'Diana', with strongly scented white flowers, pink in bud

cross pollination. *Viburnum davidii*, the low-growing shrub with its dark glossy leaves, is one such plant, it has the most unusually bright turquoise-blue egg-shaped berries, particularly effective during the winter months. Another magnificent plant requiring grouped planting is the large shrub *Viburnum betulifolium*, the branches of which in autumn can be heavy with bunches of redcurrant-like fruits. There is one group of viburnums that will never let you down, *Viburnum opulus* and its related species; these are self-fertile and produce quantities of fruit. The species itself is a fine plant in berry, but there have been some named forms especially chosen. 'Xanthocarpum', the berries of this being a clear golden-yellow, becoming a little darker and almost translucent when ripe. 'Notcutt's Variety' has larger flowers and fruit with good autumn colour. In general all the deciduous varieties display autumn colour another reason why viburnums are exceedingly good value.

FURTHER READING

BEAN, W. J.
Trees and Shrubs Hardy in the British Isles
(vols 1–4) (J. Murray, London, 1970/80)

BRICKELL, C. D. and MATHEW, B.
Daphne – The Genus in the Wild and in Cultivation
(Alpine Garden Society, Woking, 1976)

BRIGEMAN, P.
Tree Surgery – A Complete Guide
(David & Charles, Newton Abbot, 1976)

BROOKS, JOHN
The Small Garden
(Marshall Cavendish Ltd, 1979)

BROWN GEORGE E.
The Pruning of Trees, Shrubs & Conifers
(Faber & Faber, 1972)

BUCZACKI, S. & HARRIS, K.
Collins Shorter Guide to the Pests, Diseases & Disorders of Garden Plants
(Collins, Edinburgh, 1983)

CHATTO, BETH
The Damp Garden
(Dent, 1982)
The Dry Garden
(Dent, 1978)

GRIFFITHS, A. N.
Collins Guide to Alpines
(Collins, 1987)

HAMWORTH-BOOTH, M.
The Hydrangeas (rev ed)
(Constable, 1986)

HILLIER BOOKS
The Hillier Colour Dictionary of Trees & Shrubs
(David & Charles, Newton Abbot, 1981)
The Hillier Manual of Trees & Shrubs
(David & Charles, Newton Abbot, 1984)

INGWERSEN, W.
Manual of Alpines
(W. Ingwersen & Dunns Print Ltd, 1978)

PEARSON, ROBERT (ed)
The Wisley Book of Gardening
(Collingridge, 1981)

PARRY, FRANCES
Water Gardening (Country Life Ltd, 1947)

RUSHFORTH, KEITH
Conifers (Christopher Helm, 1987)
The Hillier Book of Tree Planting & Management
(David & Charles, Newton Abbot, 1987)
Trees for Small Gardens
(Cassell/RHS, 1987)

RUSSELL, STANLEY
Stapeley Book of Water Gardens
(David & Charles, Newton Abbot, 1985)

STRONG, ROY
Creating Small Gardens
(Conran, Octopus Ltd, 1986)

THOMAS, GRAHAM S.
The Art of Planting (Dent, 1984)
Perennial Garden Plants for the Modern Florilegium
(rev ed) (Dent, 1986)
Plants for Ground Cover (rev ed) (Dent, 1986)
Climbing Roses Old & New (Dent, 1965)
The Old Shrub Roses (Dent, 1979)
Shrub Roses of Today (Dent, 1962)

TITCHMARSH, A.
Rock Gardener's Handbook
(Croom Helm, 1983)

UPWOOD, M.
An Illustrated Guide to Alpines
(Salamander, 1983)

VERTREES, J. D.
Japanese Maples
(Timber Press, Forest Grove, Oregon, USA)

Forestry Commission Leaflets
Young, C. W. T. *External Signs of Decay in Trees*
Pepper, H. W. and Tee, L. A. *Forest Fencing*
Pepper, H. W. *Chemical Repellents*

Forestry Commission Arboricultural Research Notes
Evans, J. & Shanks, C. W. *Tree Shelters*
Shanks, C. W. *Tree Shelters – A Guide to their use, and information on suppliers*
Patch, D. *Tree Staking*

Wisley Handbooks
Whole series, especially *Pruning Ornamental Shrubs*
(Cassells/RHS, 1986)

LIST OF SUPPLIERS AND USEFUL ADDRESSES

Suppliers of labels:

ANNAMARIE BERESFORD,
  Chantry Cottage,
  71 Arundel Road,
  High Salvington, Worthing,
  W. Sussex, BN13 3EN.
  Tel: (0903) 65353

DOLPHIN LABELS,
  25 Church Road,
  St Marks, Cheltenham,
  Glos., GL51 7AL

ANDREW CRACE DESIGNS,
  Bourne Lane,
  Much Haddam,
  Herts., SG10 6ER.

MacPENNY NURSERIES,
  Bransgore,
  Christchurch,
  Dorset.
  Tel: Bransgore 72348

Supplier of ceramic labels:

TOWY POTTERY,
  Rhandirmyn,
  Llandovery,
  Dyfed, SA20 0NR.
  Tel: (0550) 20192

Suppliers of trellis:

STUART GARDEN ARCHITECTURE,
  Barrington Court,
  Barrington, Ilminster,
  Somerset, TA19 0NQ.

THWAITES AND PITT (LANDSCAPE DESIGN LTD),
  Unit Eg/D,
  Dean Clough Industrial Park,
  Halifax, HX3 5AX.

MACHIN DESIGNS LTD,
  Ransome's Dock,
  London SW11 4NP.
  Tel: 01-223 4383
and in the USA at:
  652 Glenbrook Road,
  Stanford, CT 06906

CORREX TREE SHELTERS,
  Corruplast Ltd,
  Correx House,
  Moreland Trading Estate,
  Bristol Road,
  Gloucester, GL1 5RZ.
  Tel: (0452) 301893

PLASTIC NET TREE GUARDS,
  Netlon Ltd,
  Kelly Street,
  Blackburn, BB2 4PJ.

ALPINE GARDEN SOCIETY,
  Secretary, Michael Upwood,
  Lye End Link,
  St John's, Woking,
  Surrey, GU21 1SW.
  Tel: (04862) 69327

ARBORICULTURAL ADVISORY INFORMATION OFFICE,
  Forestry Commission,
  Forest Research Station,
  Alice Holt Lodge,
  Farnham,
  Surrey, GU10 4LH.
  Tel: (0420) 22255

ARBORICULTURAL ASSOCIATION,
  Ampfield House,
  Ampfield, Romsey,
  Hants, SO51 9PA
  Tel: 0794 68717

INSTITUTE OF CHARTERED FORESTERS,
  22 Walker Street,
  Edinburgh, EH3 7HR.
  Tel: 031 225 2705

ROYAL HORTICULTURAL SOCIETY
  80 Vincent Square
  London SW1P 2PE
  Tel: 01-834 4333

ROYAL NATIONAL ROSE SOCIETY
  Chiswell Green
  St Albans
  Herts, AL2 3NR
  Tel: (0727) 50461

SOCIETY OF LANDSCAPE AND GARDEN DESIGNERS
  23 Reigate Road,
  Ewell,
  Surrey, KT17 1PS.

GENERAL INDEX

Alder (*Alnus*), 254
Alpine Garden Society, 252, 308
Alpine house, 20
Altering the ph of the soil, 45
Amcide (Ammonium sulphamate), 167
Aphids, 57
Arboricultural Association, 177, 377
Artificial fertilisers, 173

Basic design work, 60
Beech (*Fagus*), 246
Birch (*Betula*), 274
Black polythene, 158, 170
Bonfires, 28, 195
Boundary problems, 129

Casaron G (Dichlobenil), 167
Cascades, 104
Choosing soft landscape materials, 105
Circulating pumps, 102
Climate, 46
    consideration of, 200
Climbers for pergola uprights, rustic tripods
        and arches, 251
    for shady walls, 250
Climbing frames, 16
Clout (Alloxydin sodium), 167, 190
Composting, 28, 195
Conservatories, 17
Contact herbicides, 165
Croquet lawn, 13
Cultivator, powered, 160

Dalapon, 167
Deer, 157, 175
Design treatments, formal and informal, 65
Dogwood (*Cornus*), 254, 301
Drainage, 44
Drainage inspection covers, 136
Drawing on planting details, 74
Dry gardening, 140
    conifers as upright shrubs or small trees, 242
    conifers of more spreading and rounded
        habit, 242
    low-growing sub-shrubs and herbaceous
        groundcover plants, 247
    ornamental bulbs and grasses, 243
    shrubs of mainly compact habit, 242
    small trees, 241
Dry shade, 243
    herbaceous plants, 244
    shrubby evergreen groundcover, 244
    shrubs, 243
Dwarf conifers, 297

Earthworms, 41
Eric Smith, the late, 221

Fences as boundaries and stockproofing, 93
Firethorn (*Pyracantha*), 246
Focal point plantings, 260
    Schemes A–D coloured foliage and floral
        effects, 260–3
    Schemes E–F plants with bold leaf effects
        and textures, 264–5
    Scheme G autumn colour, spring and
        summer flowers, 268

Scheme H winter bark effect, 269
Fountains, 104
Front garden, 74

Garden furniture, 100
Garden tool storage, 78
Garden waste, 28, 195
Glysophate, 28, 195
Grass areas – mowing, 188
    aeration and feeding, 189
    moss killing and weed control, 190
Grass seed, 105
Gravel, 96, 99
Greenhouses, 17
Groundcover, 192
Ground smothering plants, 111

Hardiness zones of the British Isles, 200
Hedges, 21, 186, 244
    clipping and pruning, 186
    formal and informal, 186
    preparation of ground and planting, 245
Herbaceous beds, 20
Herbaceous borders, 190
    plants, lifting and splitting, 192
Herbicides, residual or persistent, 165
Herbs, 21
Holly (*Ilex*), 325
Honey fungus (*Armillaria*), 57, 144
Hornbeam (*Carpinus*), 245

Improving soils, 44
Insect pests, 57
Inspection covers, 136
    plants for screening, 204
Irrigation, 28
Island beds, 212
Ivy (*Helix*), 231

Japanese evergreen Azaleas, 351
Juniper (*Juniperus*), 292, 293, 300

Keeping records, 159

Labels and labelling, 159
    ceramic and laminated plastic, 159, 160
    metal and permanent, 159
Lavender (*Lavandula*), 246
Lawn herbicides, 168
    Dicamba, 168
    Dichlorprop, 168
    MCPA, 168
    Mecoprop, 168
    2.4-D, 168
Lawn mowings, 195
Lime hating (calcifuge) and lime tolerant
        plants, 196
Loam, 41

Manures, 173
Maple, Japanese (*Acer palmatum*), 326
Micro climate, 48
Moss killers, 169, 190
Mulching, 157, 169
    black polythene, 170
    gravel, 169
    leafmould and peat, 169
    pulverised conifer bark, 169, 192
Mycorrhizae, 56

Nitrogen, 42
Nutrients – Nitrogen, Phosphorus, etc, 42

Potassium, 42, 54

Paraquat, 168
Parthogenic fungi, 57
Paths – slimy growth (algae), 194
    weed control, 194
Patios and courtyards, plants for, 229
    climbers for shady walls, 230
    climbers for sunny walls, 229
    hardy ornamental grasses & ferns, 237
    hardy perennials and groundcovering
        plants, 235
    roses and shrubs, 232
Paved sitting area, 12
Paving and paving patterns, 93
Perennials for groundcovering and shrub
        association, 216
Pest and disease control, 175
Peter Dummer, 233
ph and nutrient availability, 43
Photosynthesis, 52
Pine (*Pinus*), 289
Planning in three dimensions, 64
Plant grouping for effect, 257
Plant nutrition, 52
Planting, 145
    bare-root trees, shrubs and roses, 148
    container grown nursery stock, 152
    how to plant, 148
    root-balled trees, shrubs and conifers, 152
    trees, feathered and standard, 149
    when to plant, 145
Planting design by height, 110
Plants for
    compact medium height screening, 202
    courtyards, terraces and patios, 229
    difficult banks, 207
    inspection covers, screening, 204
    screening, 200
    selection, delivery or collection, 148
    solving problems, 201–11
Play and recreation areas, 13
Ponds, maintenance of, 193
Pool design, 102
Pools, ornamental, 16, 100
    liners, flexible, 101
    paddling and swimming, 16
Preparation of turf or rough grass area, 145
Privet (*Ligustrum*), 246, 333
Pruning clematis, 281
Pruning of newly planted woody subjects, 156
Pumps, circulating, 102
    for fountains and cascades, 104

Rabbits, 175
Rhododendron deadheading, 342
Rock gardens, 20, 252
    compact groundcovering and alpines, 253
    dwarf and slow growing conifers, 252
    dwarf shrubs, 252
Rocks and boulders, 97
Ronstar (Oxydiazon), 168
Rootout (Ammonium sulphamate), 167
Roots, functions of, 56
Round-up (Glysophate), 167
Rowan (*Sorbus*), 366

Sand-pit, 13
Shelterbelts, 50
Shrubaceous borders, 192, 212
Shrub borders, 13
Shrubs, 182

controlling or reshaping, 184
  how to prune, 185
  pruning to enhance attractiveness, 184
Simazine, 168, 194
Slow release fertilisers, 150, 327
Slugs and snails, 221
Sodium chlorate, 184
Soft fruit growing, 20
Soil, composition and texture, 40
Soil mounding, cut and fill, 105
Soil testing kit, 199
Soil type, ph, 196
Stakes and ties, removal of, 177
Steps, 93
Subsoiling, 44
Summerhouses, 17
Surveying the garden, 30

Tall screens and shelter, 24
Temporary storage – 'laying-in' or
  'heeling-in', 153
Tennis court, 13
'Theme Gardens', 268
The inherited garden, solving problems of, 124
The over-large garden, 132
The smaller garden, 137
The steep garden, 136
Timber retaining walls, 92, **94**

Tools and equipment, 160
  basic hand tools, 160
  clip-on tool heads, 160
  lawn mower and sprayers, 161
  powered cultivator and strimmer, 160
  T-handle system, 160
Transferring the design to the ground, 112
Tree guards and tree ties, 157
  plastic net, 158
Tree Preservation Orders, 182
Tree shelters, plastic, 158
Tree surgery, 177
Tumbleweed (Glysophate), 167
Tumbleweed gel (Glysophate), 192

Ultimate height and size of plants, 199

Vegetable gardening, 20

Wall shrubs and climbers, 230, 248, 250
  climbing and rambler roses, 249
  for lower walls, 250
  for north and east facing walls and
    fences, 249, 250
  for south and west facing walls and
    fences, 249, 250
Walls, 50, 76
Waste disposal, 194

Water gardens, 253
  marginal aquatic plants, 255
  planting pool plants, 255
  submerged oxygenating plants, 254
  waterlilies for large and small ponds, 253
  waterside herbaceous plants, 257
  waterside shrubs and bamboos, 255
  waterside trees for small ponds, 254
  waterside trees for large ponds and
    lakes, 255
Watering, 157, 174
Water points, 28
Water worn rocks, 102, 103
Weeds and weed control, 56, 158, 162, 190
  chemical, 165
  mechanical, 164
Weedol (Paraquat), 168
Weedout (Alloxydin sodium), 167
Weeping standard roses, 240
Weevils, 57
Whitebeam (*Sorbus*), 366
Willow (*Salix*), 255
Woodwork in the garden, 91

Yew (*Taxus*), 248
York stone paving, *11, 92, 98, 143*

INDEX OF PLANTS

(See under separate sections for Aquatic Plants, Bamboos, Conifers, Ferns, Grasses, Trees Shrubs & Climbers, and Perennials & Bulbs)

AQUATIC PLANTS

Acorus calamus 'Variegatus', 255
Alisma plantago-aquatica, 255
Butomus umbellatus, 255
Caltha palustris, 255
Glyceria maxima 'Variegata', 255
Iris kaempferi, 255
  laevigata, 256
Lysichiton americanum, 256
  camtschatense, 256
Mentha aquatica, 256
Nymphaea
  alba 'Escarboucle', 254
    'Froebelii', 253; 'Gonnere', 253;
    'Graziella', 253; 'James Brydon', 254
    odorata 'Alba', 253
    'Surlphurea', 254; 'Turicensis', 253
    'W. B. Shaw', 253
Pontaderia cerdata, 256
Ranunculus aquatilis, 254
  lingua 'Grandiflora', 256
Sagittaria sagittifolia, 256
Scirpus, 256
  tabernaemontani 'Albescens', 256;
  'Zebrinus', 256
Sparganium ramosum, 256
Stratiotes aloides, 254
Typha latifolia, 256
  minima, 256
Veronica beccabunga, 256
Zantedeschia aethiopica, 256

BAMBOOS

Arundianaria 'Gauntlettii', 317
  muriliae, 313, 316
  pumila, 318
  simonii, 313
  vagans, 318
  variegata, 318
  viridistriata, 313, 318
Chusquea culeou, 317
Phyllostachys nigra 'Boryana', 317
Sasa tesselata, 317
  veitchii, 318
Shibataea kumasasa, 318

CONIFERS

Abies forrestii – cones, **295**

Chamaecyparis
  lawsoniana, 245, 289, 292
    'Allumii', 245, 290, 292, 293;
    'Columnaris', 290, 293; 'Erecta', 292;
    'Fletcheri', 292; 'Forsteckensis', 297;
    'Gimbornii', 297; 'Green Globe', 297;
    'Green Hedger', 245, 289; 'Hillieri', 292;
    'Intertexta', 293; 'Kilmacurragh', 290, 293;
    'Lane', 292; 'Lutea', 290, 292;
    'Lutea Nana', 297; 'Minima', 297;
    'Minima Aurea', 297; 'Minima Glauca', 297;
    'Nana', 297; 'Pembury Blue', 292, 293;
    'Pottenii', 292; 'Pygmaea', **291**;
    'Pygmaea Argentea', 290, 297;
    'Stardust', 297; 'Stewartii', 292;

    'Tamariscifolia', 297;
    'Triomf van Boskoop', 292;
    'Winston Churchill', 292; 'Wisselii', 293
  nootkatensis, 292, 293
    'Pendula', 293
  obtusa 'Caespitosa', 297
    'Coralliformis', 297; 'Crippsii', 293;
    'Juniperoides Compacta', 297
    'Minima', 297; 'Nana', 252, 297;
    'Nana Aurea', 297; 'Nana Gracilis', 297
  pisifera, 292
    'Filifera Nana', 297; 'Nana', 297;
    'Plumosa', 292; 'Squarrosa', 292
X Cupressocyparis
  leylandii, 244, 246
    'Castlewellan', 246; 'Robinson's Gold', 246

Ginkgo biloba, 242
  'Tremonia', 242

Juniperus
  chinensis 'Aurea', 293
    'Blaauw', 242, 297; 'Kaizuka', 292, 293;
    'Keteleeri', 293; 'Mint Julep', 300;
    'Mordigan Gold', **207**, 242; 'Old Gold', 300
    'Pfitzeriana', 300; 'Pfitzeriana Aurea', 300
    'Plumosa', 300
  communis, 'Compressa', 252, 300
    'Depressa Aurea', 252, 300;
    'Hibernica', 300; 'Hornibrookii', 300
    'Repanda', 300
  conferta, 300
    'Blue Pacific', 352, 300
  horizontalis, 300
    'Bar Harbor', 300; 'Douglasii', 300;
    'Wiltonii', 300
  X media, 300
  procumbens, 300
    'Nana', 252, 300
  recurva var. *coxii*, 293
  rigida, 293
  sabina 'Tamariscifolia', 300
  scopulorum, 'Blue Heaven', 293
    'Moonlight', 293; 'Skyrocket', 294;
    'Springbank', 292; 'Wichita Blue', 292
  squamata 'Blue Carpet', 300
    'Blue Star', 252, 300; 'Chinese Silver', 294
    'Meyeri', 294, 300
  virginiana, 'Burkii', 292
    'Grey Owl', 300; 'Hetzii', 300;
    'Sulphur Spray', 300

Metasequoia, 289

Pinus aristata, 294
  armandii, 294
  ayacahuite, 294
  bungeana, 295
  cembra, 295
  contorta, 288, 292
  coulteri, 295
  densiflora, 296
    'Oculis-draconis', 296; 'Pendula', 296
  x holfordiana, 295
  jeffreyi, 295
  koraiensis, 295
    'Compacta Glauca', 300; 'Winton', 300

leucodermis, 292, 296
  'Compact Gem', 300; 'Pygmy', 300
monophylla, 295
montezumae, 296
monticola, 295
mugo, 300
  'Gnom', 300; 'Mops', 300;
  'Trompenburg', 252, 300
muricata, 293
nigra, 248, 292
  'Hornibrookiana', 300
parviflora, 295
  'Adcock's Dwarf', 300; 'Glauca', 295
patula, 296
peuce, 295
pinaster, 293
pinea, 296
ponderosa, 296
pumila, 300
radiata, 293, 296
strobus 'Prostrata', 300
sylvestris, 248, **291**, 293, 296
  'Argentea', 296; 'Aurea', 296;
  'Beuvronensis', 301; 'Fastigiata', 296
thunbergii, 296
  'Oculis-draconis', 296
wallichiana, 293, 294
  'Nana', 301

Taxodium, 289
Taxus baccata, 244, 248, 289
Thuja plicata, 248, 289
  'Fastigiata', 248
Tsuga dumosa, 179
  heterophylla, 289

FERNS

Adiantum pedatum, 237, 311
Asplenium scolopendrium, 312
  trichomanes, 312
Athyrium filix-femina, 311
  goeringianum (nipponicum) 'Pictum', 311
Blechnum penna-marina, 312
  spicant, 312
Ceterach officinarum, 312
Dryopteris dilatata, 311
  filix-mas, 312
Matteuccia struthiopteris, 312, **315**
Onoclea sensibilis, 311
Osmunda regalis, 312
Phyllitis scolopendrium, 312
Polypodium vulgare, 313
Polystichum aculeatum, 312
  setiferum, 312
    'Plumoso-divisilobum', 237; 312
Scolopendrium vulgare, 312

GRASSES

Arundo
  donax 'Macrophylla', 316
    'Variegata', 316; **319**
Carex morrowii, 'Evergold', 235, 316
Cortaderia
  selloana, 316
    'Gold Band', 316; 'Pumila', 316;

'Sunningdale Silver', 316
Glyceria maxima 'Variegata', 317
Hakenechloa macra 'Aureola', 237, 316
Helictotrichon sempervirens, 237, 316
Millium effusum 'Aureum', 237, 316
Miscanthus sacchariflorius, 316
  sinensis 'Gracillimus', 316
  'Zebrinus', 316
Molinia caerulea 'Variegata', 237, 317
Phalaris arundinacea 'Picta', 313, 317
Stipa calamogrostis, 237, 317
  gigantea, 237, 317

TREES, SHRUBS and CLIMBERS

Acer campestre, 245
  griseum, 51
  japonicum 'Aconitifolium', 332
    'Aureum' See shirasawanum 'Aureum'
    'Vitifolium', 332
  palmatum, 326
    'Atropurpureum', 330; 'Beni-maiko', 330;
    'Bloodgood', 330; 'Butterfly, 329;
    'Corallinum', 329; 'Dissectum', 329, **331**;
    'Dissectum Crimson Queen', 332;
    'Dissectum Nigrum', **147**; 332;
    'Heptalobum Osakazuki', 329;
    'Inaba-shidare', 332; 'Linearilobum', 329;
    'Oshio-beni', 332; 'Ribesifolium', 329;
    'Sango-kaku', 329; 'Seiryu', 329;
    'Senkaki', 329; 'Shishigashira', 329;
    'Shisio Improved', 330;
    'Trompenburg', 332
  shirasawanum 'Aureum', 333
Alnus glutinosa, 'Imperialis', 254

Berberis 'Bountiful', 273
  'Buccaneer', 273
  candidula, 272
  darwinii, 272
  francisci-ferdinandi, 273
  x frikartii 'Amstelveen', 272
  gagnepainii, 245
  'Georgei', 273
  hookeri, 273
  x interposita, 272
  julianae, 273
  linearifolia 'Jewel', 272
  panlanensis, 245, 273
  pruinosa, 273
  x rubrostilla, 274
  x stenophylla, 245, 272
    'Coccinea', 272; 'Corallina Compacta', 272
  temolaica, 273
  thunbergii, 245
    'Atropurpurea', 245, 273;
    'Atropurpurea Nana', 245, 273;
    'Aurea', 273; 'Dart's Red Lady', 245;
    'Red Chief', 273; 'Red Pillar', 273;
    'Rose Glow', 273
  valdiviana, 273
  verruculosa, 245, 272
Betula albosinensis, 278
  var. septentrionalis, 278
  alleghaniensis, 278
  ermanii, 277
  'Fetisowii', 277
  jacquemontii, 277
    'Inverleith', 277; 'Sauwala White', 277
  'Jermyns', **275**, 276, 277
  maximowicziana, 277
  medwediewii, 276

  nana, 276
  nigra, 278
  papyrifera, 277.
    var. kenaica, 277
  pendula, 274, 276
    'Fastigiata', 276, 277; 'Dalecarlica', 276;
    'Purpurea', 277; 'Tristis', 276;
    'Youngii', 277
  pubescens, 276
  szechuanica, 277
  utilis, 277
Buxus
  sempervirens, 50, 245
    'Handsworthensis', 245;
    'Suffruticosa', 245

Camellia
  japonica, 'Adolphe Audusson', 232
  x williamsii, 'Anticipation', 250
    'Donation', 250; 'E. T. R. Carlyon', 232;
    'Tiptoe', 232
Caragana
  arborescens 'Lorbergii', 240, 241
    'Pendula', 240; 'Walker', 240
Carpinus betulus 'Fastigiata', **178**
Ceanothus, 278
  arboreus, 'Trewithen Blue', 230, **279**, 281
    'A. T. Johnson', 280;
    'Autumnal Blue', 278, 280;
    'Blue Mound', 242, 280;
    'Burkwoodii', 278, 281; 'Cascade', 281;
    'Delight', 280, 286
  x delilianus
    'Gloire de Versailles', 242, 280;
    'Henri Desfosse', 280; 'Perle Rose', 280
  papillosus, 280
    var. roweanus, 280
  'Puget Blue', 280
  sorediatus, 280
  'Southmead', 280
  thyrsiflorus, 281
    var. repens, 250, 280
  x veitchianus, 280, 286
  'Yankee Point', 281
Clematis, 229, 281
  alpina, 285, 286
    'Frances Rivis', 229, 285; 'Ruby', 285;
    'White Moth', 285
  armandii, 281, 285
    'Apple Blossom', 285; 'Snowdrift', 285
  campaniflora, 285
  chrysocoma, 284
  cirrhosa, 284
    var. balearica, 284
  x eriostemon 'Hendersonii', 284
  flammula, 285
  florida, 'Sieboldii', 285
  x jouiniana 'Cote d'Azur', 284
  macropetala, 285
    'Maidwell Hall', 229, 285;
    'Markham's Pink', 285
  montana, 281, 284
    'Alexander', 284; 'Elizabeth', 284;
    'Grandiflora', 284; var. rubens, 284;
    'Tetrarose', 229, 284
  rehderiana, 229, 285
  tangutica, 286
  texensis, 285
  vernayi, 282, 286
  vitalba, 281, 286
  viticella, 285
    'Abundance', 285; 'Alba Luxurians', 285;

    'Kermesina', 285; 'Royal Velours', 285
    'Barbara Dibley', 282, 286;
    'Barbara Jackman', 286;
    'Beauty of Worcester', 286;
    'Bee's Jubilee', 286; 'Blue Gem', 286;
    'Comtesse de Bouchaud'; 'Dr Ruppel', 286;
    'Elsa Spaeth', 288; 'Gravetye Beauty', 285;
    'Hagley Hybrid', 288;
    'Heather Rushforth', **283**, 285; 'Henryi', 288
    'H. F. Young', 288; 'Huldine', 251, 288;
    'Jackmanii Superba', 282, 288;
    'Lady Betty Balfour', 288; 'Lasurstern', 288;
    'Marie Boisselot', 288;
    'Mrs Cholmodely', 288;
    'Mrs N. Thompson', 288;
    'Nelly Moser', 282, 288;
    'Perle d'Azur', 281, 288; 'The President', 288;
    'Ville de Lyon', **287**, 288;
    'Vyvyan Pennell', 288; 'W. E. Gladstone', 288;
    'Yellow Queen', 288
Colutea arborescens, 241
Convolvulus cneorum, 232
Cornus, 300
  alba, 302
    'Elegantissima', 304; 'Kesselringii', 304;
    'Sibirica', 304; 'Spaethii', 304
  alternifolia, 304
    'Argentea', 304
  canadensis, 301
  controversa, 304
    'Variegata', **302**, 304
  florida, **301**
    'Apple Blossom', 302;
    'Cherokee Chief', 302; 'White Cloud', 302
  kousa var. chinensis, **55, 302**
  mas, 302
    'Variegata', 302
  'Norman Hadden', 302
  nuttallii, 301
  stolonifera 'Flaviramea', 304
Cotoneaster, **203**
  bullatus 'Floribundus', 305
  conspicuus 'Highlight', 305
  'Coral Beauty', 306
  'Cornubia', 305
  dammeri, 306
    'Skogholm', 306
  distichus var. tongolensis, 305
  'Exburiensis', 305
  franchetii var. sternianus, 245, 345
  glaucophyllus f. serotinus, 305
    var. vestitus, 245
  horizontalis 306
    'Variegatus', 306
  'Hybridus Pendulus', 305
  'John Waterer', 305
  lacteus, 245, 305
  microphyllus, 306
    var. cochleatus, 306
  'Pink Champagne', 305
  'Rothschildianus', 305
  'Sabrina', 306
  salicifolius 'Gnom', 306
    'Repens', **78**
    var. floccosus, 306
Crataegus monogyna, 245
Cytisus
  battandieri, 230
  'Yellow Tail', 230

Daphne, 308
  arbuscula, 253, 308

bholua, 309
  'Gurkha', 309; 'Jacqueline Postill', 309
blagayana, 309
x burkwoodi, **307**, 309
  'Somerset', 309
cneorum, 253, 309
  'Eximia', 309; 'Variegata', 309
collina, 309
  var. neapoltiana, 309
jasminea, 308
jezoensis, 309
longilobata 'Peter Moore', **310**
x mantensiana 'Manten', 242, 253, 310
mezereum, 309, 310
  'Alba', 310; 'Autumnalis', 310
x napolitana (neapolitana), 309
odora, 310
  'Aureomarginatum', 310
petraea, 309
  'Grandiflora', 309
retusa, 310
tangutica, 310
Decumaria barbata, 324
  sinensis, 324
Disanthus cercidifolius, **267**, 268

Elaeagnus
  x ebbingei, **206**, 247
    'Gilt Edge', **258**; 'Limelight', 247
Escallonia, **246**
  macrantha, 246, **247**
Eucryphia glutinosa, **223**
Euonymus fortunei, 'Emerald Gaiety', **206**

Fagus sylvatica, 246
Fremontodendron 'California Glory', 249
Fuchsia 'Madame Cornelissen', **239**

Genista lydia, **210**

Hebe x franciscana 'Blue Gem', 246
Hedera
  canariensis, 'Gloire de Marengo', 230
  colchica, 'Dentata Variegata', 230, 244
  helix 'Glacier', 230
    'Goldchild'; 'Hibernica', 244
Hydrangea, 319
  arborescens, 321
    'Annabelle', 321; 'Grandiflora', 321
    ssp. discolor 'Sterilis', 323
  aspera, 324
  heteromalla, 324
    'Bretscheideri', 324
  involucrata, 323
    'Hortensis', 323
  macrophylla 'Altona', 320
    'Ami Pasquier', 320; 'Ayesha', 320;
    'Blue Wave', 320; 'Deutschland', 320;
    'Générale Viscomtesse de Vibraye', 320;
    'Geoffrey Chadbund', 232; 'Lanarth', **321**;
    'Lanarth White', **321**; 'Maréchal Foch', 320;
    'Mariesii', 321; 'Niedersachsen', 321;
    'Sea Foam', 232, 321; 'Tricolor', 232, 321;
    'Veitchii', 321; 'White Wave', 321
  paniculata, 324
    'Grandiflora', 324; 'Praecox', 324;
    'Tardiva', **323**; 324; 'Unique', 324
  petiolaris, 324
  quercifolia, 323
  sargentiana, 232, 324
  serrata, 321
    'Bluebird', 321; 'Grayswood', 321;

'Intermedia', 321; 'Preziosa', 321;
  'Rosalba', 321
serratifolia, 324
villosa, 324
xanthoneura, 324
Hypericum beanii 'Gold Cup', 213
  calycinum, **193**
  kouytchense, 237

Ilex x altaclerensis, 247, 325
  'Camelliifolia', 325; 'Hodginsii', 325;
  'Purple Shaft', 325
  aquifolium, 247
    'Amber', 326;
    'Argenteomarginata Pendula', 326;
    'Bacciflava', 326; 'Ferox' and cultivars, 326;
    'Green Pillar', 326;
    'Handsworth New Silver', 325;
    'Madame Briot', 325; 'Ovata Aurea', 325;
    'Pendula', 326; 'Pyramidalis', 326;
    'Pyramidalis Fructuluteo', 326;
    'Silver Queen', 325
  cornuta, 326
    'Burfordii', 326
  crenata, 326
    'Convexa', 326
  x meserveae, 326
  pernyi 'Jermyns Dwarf', 326
  verticillata 'Christmas Cheer', 326

Ligustrum chenaultii, 334
  delavayanum, 334
  japonicum, 333
    'Macrophyllum', 334; 'Rotundifolium', 334
  lucidum 'Excelsum Superbum', 333
    'Latifolium', 333; 'Tricolor', 333
  ovalifolium, 243, 333
    'Aureum', 246, 333
  quihouii, 334
  sinense, 333
    'Pendulum', 333
  vulgare 'Aureum', 333
Lonicera x americana, 230
  nitida 'Ernest Wilson', 246
  periclymenum, 'Graham Thomas', 230

Magnolia, 334
  acuminata, 340
  campbellii, 338
    var. alba, 338; 'Darjeeling', 338;
    'Ethel Hillier', 338; 'Lanarth', 338;
    ssp. mollicomata, 338
  'Charles Raffill', 338
  cordata, 340
  cylindrica, 336, 337
  dawsoniana, 338
  delavayi, 340
  denudata, 337
    'Purple Eye', 337
  globosa, 340
  grandiflora, 249, 341
    'Exmouth', 249, 341; 'Goliath', 249, 341
  'Heaven Scent', 338
  heptapeta, 337
  hypoleuca, 340
  'Jane', 338; 'Kewensis', 338
  kobus, 337
  liliiflora, 337
  x loebneri, 337
    'Leonard Messel', 240, **335**; 'Merrill', 337
  macrophylla, 340
    'Manchu Fan', 338; 'Michael Rosse', 338

officinalis, 336, 340
  var. biloba, 340
  'Peppermint Stick', 338
  'Princess Margaret', 338
  quinquepeta, 337
  salicifolia, 336, 337, 338
    'Jermyns', 338
  sargentiana, 339
    var. robusta, 339
  'Sayonara', 338
  sieboldii, 241, 339, 340
  sinensis, 340
  x soulangiana, 334, 336
    'Alba Superba', 336; 'Amabilis', 337;
    'Brozzonii', 337; 'Lennei', 334, 337;
    'Lennei Alba', 334, 337; 'Picture', 337;
    'Rustica Rubra', 337
  sprengeri var. diva, **339**
    var. elongata, 339
  stellata, 337
    'Rosea', 337; 'Water Lily', 337
  'Susan', 338
  x veitchii, 339
    'Peter Veitch', 339
  virginiana, 341
  'Wada's Memory', 338; 'Wakehurst', 338
  wilsonii, 237, 336, 339, 340
Mahonia, 272
  aquifolium, 273
    'Apollo', 272
  'Buckland', 273; 'Charity', 273
  japonica, **206**, 272
    'Lionel Fortescue', 273
  nervosa, 272
  repens, 'Rotundifolia', 272

Olearia, 246
  avicenniifolia, 246
  macrodonta 'Major', 246

Pachysandra terminalis, 225
  'Variegata', 225
Parthenocissus quinquefolia, 250
Phormium and cultivars, 233
Pieris, 233
  japonica 'Little Heath', 233
Pittosporum, 246
  tenuifolium, 246
Potentilla, 246
  'Elizabeth', 246; 'Goldfinger', 246;
  'Primrose Beauty', 246
Prunus, 246
  x cistena, 248
  laurocerasus, 248
    'Otto Luyken', **211**
  lusitanica, 248
    ssp. azorica, 248; 'Variegata', 248
  spinosa, 248
Pyracantha, 246
  coccinea, 'Sparkler', 230
  'Orange Glow', 246
  rogersiana 'Flava', 246
  'Soleil d'Or', 230; 'Teton', 246

Quercus ilex, 248
  suber, 242

Rhamnus
  alaterna 'Argenteovariegata', **47**, 242
Rhododendron, 341
  amagianum, 349
  ambiguum, 345

argyrophyllum ssp. nankingense, 345
   'Chinese Silver', 345
argipeplum, 345
arizelum, **187**, 344
atlanticum, 349
auriculatum, 348
barbatum, 345
bureavii, 344
calendulaceum, 349
calophytum, 345
campanulatum ssp. aeruginosum, 344
canadense, 349
cinnabarinum, 344
   'Concatenans', **342**
ciliatum, 348
dauricum, 348
decorum, 348
falconeri, 344
fastigiatum, 347
forrestii, 347
fortunei, 348
griffithianum, 348
hanceanum 'Nanum', 347
hodgsonii, 345
lepidostylum, 345
leucaspis, 345
lutescens, 345
luteum, 349
macabeanum, 344
maddenii, 348
mallotum, 344
moupinense, 348
mucronulatum, 348
nakaharae, 233, 351
pemakoense, 347
pentaphyllum, 351
ponticum, 248
quinquefollum, 351
racemosum, 347
rex, 344
sinogrande, 344
schlippenbachii, 351
serotinum, 348
sinogrande, 344
thomsonii, 345
triflorum, 345
viscosum, 351
williamsianum, 347
yakushimanum, 345
   ssp. makinoi, 345
'Bluebird', 347; 'Blue Peter',
'Bowbells'; 'Britannia', 348;
'Cowslip', 347; 'Cunningham's White', 348;
'Curlew', 347; 'Cynthia', 349
   'Doncaster', 349;
   'Elisabeth Hobbie', 253, **347**;
   'Fastuosum Flore Pleno', 349;
   'Gomer Waterer', 349; 'Hugh Koster', 349;
   'Lady Clementine Mitford', 349;
   'Lady Elisabeth', **163**; 'Mrs G. W. Leak', 349;
   'Nobleanum', 349; 'Pink Pearl', 349;
   'Praecox', 348; 'Prof Hugo de Vries', 349;
   'Ptarmigan', 347; 'Purple Splendour', 349;
   'Sappho', 349
Azalea – deciduous
   'Ballerina', 349; 'Cecile', 349;
   'Gibraltar', 349; 'Homebush', 349;
   'Koster's Brilliant Red', 349;
   'Persil', 349
Azalea – evergreen
   'Addy Wery', 351; 'Benegiri', 351;
   'Blaauw's Pink, 351; 'Bungo-nishiki', 351;

'Hatsugiri', 351; 'Hinodegiri', 352;
   'Hinomayo', 352; 'Kirin', 352;
   'Kure-no-yuki', 352; 'Naomi', 352;
   'Palestrina', 352; 'Vuyk's Rosy Red', 352;
   'Vuyk's Scarlet', 352
Robinia 'Hillieri', 242
   hispida 'Macrophylla', 230
Rosa 233–5, 240, 248, 249, 353–63
   x alba, 356
   banksiae, 359
      'Lutea', 359; 'Lutescens', 359
      var. normalis, 359
   bracteata, 356
   brunonii, 259
      'La Mortola', 359
   californica, 356
      'Plena', 356
   chinensis, 356
      'Mutabilis', 356; 'Old Blush', 356;
      'Viridiflora', 356
   damascena 'Trigintipetala', 356
      'Versicolor', 356
   davidii, 354
   ecae, 353
   eleganteria, 356
   elegantula (farreri) 'Persetosa', 356
   fedtschenkoana, 357
   filipes, 'Kiftsgate', 357
      'Toby Tristram', **357**
   foetida, 356
      'Persiana', 357
   foliolosa, 356
   gallica, 357
      'Officinalis', 357; 'Versicolor', 357
   glauca, 357
   helenae, 359
   hugonis, 353
   laevigata, 359
   longicuspis, 359
   macrophylla, 354
      'Master Hugh', 354
   moyesii, 354
      'Geranium', 354
   multibracteata, 357
   nitida, 356
   omeiensis, 353
   pimpinellifolia, 354, **355**
      var. altaica, 356
      'Double White', 356; 'Glory of Edzell', 356
   primula, 353
   roxburghii, 357
   rubigonosa, 248
   rugosa, 356
      'Alba', 356;
      'Blanc Double de Coubert', 356
      'Fru Dagmar Hastrup', 248, 356
      'Roseraie de la Hay', 248, 356
   sericea, 353
      'Pteracantha', 353
   soulieana, 357
   virginiana, 356
   webbiana, 354
   wichuraiana, 360
   willmottiae, 357
   xanthina, 353
   'Aloha', 229; 'Arthur Hillier', 354;
   'Belle de Crecy', 361; 'Blanche Moreau', 361;
   'Bonica', 235, 240; 'Boule de Neige', 361;
   'Buff Beauty', 361; 'Canary Bird', 240;
   'Cardinal de Richelieu', 361;
   'Cerise Bouquet', 361;
   'Comte de Chambord', 361;

'Cornelia', 248, 361; 'Crimson Showers', 240
'Dublin Bay', 229; 'Elegant Pearl', 234
'Emily Gray', 240; 'Fairy', 235;
'Fantin-Latour', 361; 'Felicia', 248, 361;
'Ferdy', 360; 'Fiona', 240, 360;
'Fruhlingsgold', 360; 'Fruhlingsmorgen', 360;
'Gentle Touch', 235; 'Golden Wings', 361;
'Graham Thomas', 234; 'Helen Knight', 353;
'Henri Martin', 361; 'Highdownensis', 354;
'Hillieri', 354; 'Honorine de Brabant', 361
'Iceberg', 229;
'Koenigin von Danemarck', 361;
'Madame Alfred Carriere', 249;
'Madame Gregoire Staechelin', 249;
'Madame Hardy', 361;
'Madame Isaac Pereire', 361;
'Maiden's Blush', 361; 'Maigold', 229;
'Marguerite Hilling', 360; 'Marjorie Fair', 234;
'Max Graf', 360; 'Mermaid', 360;
'Moonlight', 361; 'Nevada', 360;
'Nozomi', 235; 'Penelope', 361;
'Raubritter', **78**, 235;
'Red Max Graf', *171, 211*;
'Robin Redbreast', 235;
'Rosy Cushion', 235, 360;
'Sanders' White Rambler', 240;
'Scarlet Fire', **359**, 360; 'Schneezwerg', 361;
'Souvenir de Claudius Denoyel', 249
'Souvenir de la Malmaison', 361;
'Stanwell Perpetual', 248; 'Swaney', 360;
'Sweet Magic', 235; 'Tour de Malakoff', 361;
'Wedding Day', 360;
'Zéphirine Drouhin', 361
Rosmarinus, 248
   officinalis 'Fastigiatus', 248
      'Severn Sea', 248
Ruscus aculeatus, 243

Salix, 363
   acutifolia 'Blue Streak', 364
   alba, 'Caerulea', 364
      'Chermesina', 255, 364, 365; 'Sericea', 365;
      'Vitellina', 255, 364
   apoda, 365
   'Basfordiana', 364
   bockii, 365
   caprea, 365
      'Kilmarnock', 364
   'Chrysocoma', 366
   daphnoides, 364
   elaeagnos, 365
   x erythroflexuosa, 253
   fargesii, 364, 365
   hastata 'Wehrhahnii', **363**, 365
   irrorata, 364
   lanata, 365, 566
   magnifica, 365
   matsudana 'Tortuosa', 364, 365
   melanostachys, 365
   pentandra, 365
   purpurea, 364
      'Pendula', 364
   rosmarinifolia, 365
   triandra, 365
Sambucus racemosa 'Plumosa Aurea', 223
Schizophragma
   hydrangeoides, 325
      'Roseum', 325
   integrifolium, 325
Skimmia laureola, **155**
Solanum crispum 'Glasnevin', 230
Sophora tetraptera, 'Grandiflora', 242, 249

Sorbus, 366
  alnifolia, 372
  aria, 370
    'Chrysophylla', 370; 'Lutescens', 370
  aucuparia, 368
    'Asplenifolia', 368; 'Beissneri', 368;
    'Edulis', 368; 'Fastigiata', 240, 368;
    'Fructu Luteo', 368
  cashmiriana, 369
  commixta, 368
  cuspidata, 370
  domestica, 369
  'Embley', 368
  'Ethel's Gold', 369
  essertauana, 368
    'Flava', 368
  folgneri, 372
    'Lemon Drop', 372
  foliolosa, 369
  forrestii, 369
  fruticosa, 370
  'Ghose', 369
  glabrescens, **54**, 369
  harroviana, 369
  'Harry Smith 12799', 369
  x hostii, 372
  hupehensis, 369
  insignis, 369
  intermedia, 372
    'Joseph Rock', 369; 'Leonard Messel', **371**
  megalocarpa, 372
  meliosmifolia, 372
  'Pearly King', 369
  poteriifolia, 370
  reducta, 369
  rehderiana, 369
  sargentiana, 368
  scalaris, **151, 367**, 368
  'Sunshine', 369
  thibetica 'John Mitchell', 370
  torminalis, 372
  'Tundra', 369
  vestita, 370
  vilmorinii, 369
  wardii, 372

Viburnum, 373
  betulifolium, 374
  x bodnantense, 373
    'Dawn', 373; 'Deben', 373
  x burkwoodii, 374
  carlesii, 'Diana', 373, **374**
  davidii, 373, 374
  farreri, 373
  lantana, 373
  odoratissimum, 373
  opulus, 373, 374
    'Sterile', 373; 'Xanthocarpum', 374
  plicatum, 373
    'Compactum', 374; 'Mariesii', 373;
    'Notcutt's Variety', 374; 'Pink Beauty', 373;
    'Xanthocarpum', 374
  sargentii 'Onondaga', 374
  tinus, 248, 373
    'Eve Price', 248

Zenobia pulverulenta, 233

PERENNIALS and BULBS

Acaena buchananii, 235
  microphylla, 235

Acanthus mollis var. latifolius, 235
Achillea 'Coronation Gold', **223**
  mollis, **191**
  'Moonshine', 216
Aconitum, 216
  x biocolor 'Bressingham Spire', 216
  septentrionale 'Ivorine', 216
Agapanthus, **266**
  campanulatus 'Albus', 216
  Headbourne Hybrids, 216, 233, 243
Ajuga
  reptans 'Atropurpurea', 216
    'Burgundy Glow', 216
Alchemilla mollis, 191, 216, **227**
Anaphalis triplinervis, **223**
Anemone blanda, **139**
  x hybrida 'Bressingham Glow', 216
    'Queen Charlotte', 216, **222**;
    'White Queen', 216
Artemisia
  absinthium 'Lambrook Silver', 235, 243
  maritima f. canescens, 216
Aster, 216
  amellus 'King George', 217
  novae-angliae 'Alma Potschke', 217
  novi-belgii 'Audrey', 217
    'Little Pink Beauty, 217
Astilbe, 217
    'Bressingham Beauty', 217; 'Fire', 217;
    'Irrlicht', 217
Astrantia, 217
  major 'Sunningdale Variegated', 217

Bergenia, 217
    'Ballawley', 217; 'Evening Glow', 217;
    'Silverlight', 217
Brunnera
  macrophylla, 217
    'Variegata', 217

Campanula, 217
  alliarifolia 'Ivory Bells', 217, 235
  lactiflora, 217
    'Loddon Anna', 217;
    'Prichard's Variety', 217
  latifolia 'Alba', **271**
    'Brantwood', 217
  persicifolia 'Telham Beauty', 235
Clematis x durandii, 284
  heracleifolia, 284
    var. davidiana, 284
    'Wyevale', 284
  integrifolia, 284
Crambe cordifolia, 235
Crinum x powellii, 235
Crocosmia, 235
    'Citronella', 217, 235; 'Emily McKenzie', 217
    'Lucifer', 217, 235
Delphinium, 219
  belladonna 'Lamartine', 219
    'Cliveden Beauty', 219; 'Summer Skies', 219
Dianthus x allwoodii 'Doris', 235
    'Excelsior', 235
    gratianopolitanus, 235
    'Mrs Sinkins', 235
Diascia, 235, **238**, 243
  cordifolia 'Ruby Field', 235
  rigescens, 235
Dicentra, 219, 236
  eximia 'Alba', 219
    'Luxurians', 219
  spectabilis, 219

Dictamnus albus, 236
  purpureus, 236
Dierama pulcherrima, 236

Echium, **127**
Epimedium, 219
  perraldianum, 219
  x rubrum, 219
  x warleyense, 219
  x youngianum 'Niveum', 219
Euphorbia, 220, 236
  griffithii 'Fireglow', 220
  polychroma, 236, 243
  robbiae, 220 244
  wulfenii, 236

Filipendula 'Gold Plate', 216

Galtonia candicans, 243
Gentiana, 220
  asclepiadea, 220
    'Alba', 220
Geranium, 236
    'Ann Folkard', 220
  endressii 'A. T. Johnson', 220, 236, **227**
    'Wargrave Pink', 220
    'Johnson's Blue', 220, 236
  macrorrhizum 'Album', 236
    'Ingwersen's Variety', 220, 236
  sanguineum var. lancastriense, **107**
  wallichianum 'Buxton's Variety', 220, 236
Gypsophila paniculata 'Rosy Veil', 220

Helianthemum, 220
  nummularium 'Amy Baring', 220
    'Firedragon', 220; 'Jubilee', 220;
    'Mrs C. W. Earle', 220;
    'Rhodanthe Carneum', 220;
    'Wisley Pink', 220; 'Wisley Primrose', 220
Helleborus, 220
  foetidus, 220
    lividus var. corsicus, 221, **230**
  niger, 220
  orientalis, 220
Hemerocallis, 221
    'Golden Chimes', 221; 'Pink Damask', 221;
    'Stafford', 221
Heracleum mantegazzianum, **126**
Hosta, **219**
    'August Moon', 221
  crispula, 221, **231**
  fortunei, 'Albopicta', 221, **234**
    'Aureomarginata', **147**
    'Halcyon', 221
  lancifolia, 221
    'Royal Standard', 221
  sieboldiana 'Elegans', 221, **227**
    'Frances Williams', 221
    'Thomas Hogg', 221
  undulata, 221
  ventricosa 'Variegata', 221

Iris, 222
  foetidissima, 222, 244
    'Variegata', 222, 244
    'Mary Barnard', 222
  pallida dalmatica 'Aurea', 222
    dalmatica 'Aureovariegata', 222
    'Variegata', 222
  unguicularis, 222
    'Mary Barnard', 222

Kirengeshoma palmata, 222, 236
Kniphofia, 222
   caulescens, 222
   galpinii, 222
   'C. M. Prichard', 222; 'Little Maid', 222;
   Shining Sceptre', 222

Lamium, 224
   maculatum, 224
     'Beacon Silver', 224, 236
Lavandula, 224, 246
   angustifolia, 224
     'Alba', 224; 'Hidcote', 191, **224**;
     'Munstead', 224; 'Rosea', 224
   vera, 224
Lavatera olbia 'Rosea', 236, 243
Liriope muscari, 224 236
Lysimachia, 224
   nummularia 'Aurea', 224
     'Creeping Jenny'
   punctata, 224
Lythrum, 224
   salicaria 'Firecandle', 224
   virgatum 'Rose Queen', 224

Narcissus pseudonarcissus, **139**
Nepeta x faassenii, 224
   'Six Hills Giant', 224
Nerine bowdenii 'Fenwick's Variety', 236, 243

Oenothera missoriensis, 236
Ophiopogon planiscapus
   'Nigrescens', 225, 236
Origanum vulgare 'Aureum', 236
Osteospermum, 236, 243
   barbarieae, 236
   'Buttermilk', 236
   ecklonis 236

Pachysandra
   terminalis, 223
     'Variegata', 223
Paeonia, 225
   'Bowl of Beauty', 225;

'Duchesse de Nemours', 225
'Karl Rosenfield', 225
officinalis, 225
   'Alba Plena', 225; 'Rosea Plena', 225;
   'Rubra Plena', 225; 'Sunshine', 225
   'Sarah Bernhardt', 225
Penstemon, 236
   'Evelyn', 236, 243; 'Garnet', 236, 243
Phlox, 225
   maculata 'Alpha', 225
   paniculata 'Dodo Hanbury Forbes', 225
     'Harlequin', 225; 'Marlborough', 225;
     'Prince of Orange', 225;
     'Sandringham', 225; 'Starfire', 225;
     'White Admiral', 225
Phygelius, 233
   aequalis 'Yellow Trumpet', 233
   'Devil's Tears', 233; 'Moonraker', 233;
   'Winchester Fanfare', 233
Polygonatum x hybridum, 225
Polygonum, 225
   campanulatum, 225
   vacciniifolium, 225
Potentilla, 225
   'Gibson's Scarlet', 227
   nepalensis 'Miss Willmott', 225
   x tonguei, 223
Primula pulverulenta, 315
Pulmonaria, 227
   angustifolia 'Azurea', 227
   saccharata, 227, 237
     'Argentea', 227; 'Bowles' Red', 227;
     'Pink Dawn', 227

Rodgersia, 227
   aesculifolia, 227
   pinnata 'Superba', 227
   tabularis, 227
Rudbeckia, 227
   fulgida 'Goldsturm', 237
Ruta graveolens 'Jackman's Blue', 227

Salvia, 228
   nemorosa 'Lubecca', 228

officinalis, 228
   'Icterina', 228; 'Tricolor', 228
Santolina, 228
   chamaecyparissus, 228
     var. *nana* (var. *corsica*), 228
   pinnata 'Edward Bowles', 228
   virens, 228
Scabiosa, 237
   caucasica 'Clive Greaves', 237
     'Miss Willmott', 237
   rumelica, 237
Schizostylis
   coccinea, 237
     'Gigantea', 237; 'Mrs Hegarty', 237
Sedum, 228
   'Autumn Joy', 228; 'Ruby Glow', 228
Smilacina racemosa, 228
Stachys, 228
   macrantha, 228
   olympica, 228
     'Silver Carpet', 228, 237

Thymus, **237**
   serpyllum 'Albus', 237
     'Coccineus', 237; 'Pink Chintz', 237;
     'Porlock', 237
   vulgaris 'Aureus', 237
     'Silver Queen', 237
Tiarella cordifolia, 228

Verbascum, 237
   bombyciferum, 237
   'Gainsborough', 237; 'Mont Blanc', 237;
   'Pink Domino', 237
Veronica, 237
   austriaca 'Crater Lake Blue', 237
Vinca, 228
   major, 228
     'Variegata', 228
   minor, 228
     'Bowles' Variety', 228;
     'Gertrude Jekyll', 228; 'Variegata', 228

Waldsteinia ternata, 228, 237